STANDING
to Experts and Auth

Sharon Presley is the co-editor of

Exquisite Rebel: The Essays of Voltairine de Cleyre

SUNY Press, 2005

STANDING UP

To Experts and Authorities

How to Avoid Being Intimidated, Manipulated, and Abused

Sharon Presley, Ph.D.

The Solomon Press, New York
Raymond S. Solomon Psychology Series, Book One

COPYRIGHT © 2010 BY SHARON PRESLEY

All Rights Reserved

No Part of this book may be reproduced or transmitted in any form or by any means, now in existence or yet to be devised, including electronic, retrieval, photocopying, digital, or tape recording, without the written permission of the Publisher, except for brief passages or quotations to appear in book reviews or critical articles. The author's and publisher's rights will be strictly enforced. Requests for permissions should be submitted to:

THE SOLOMON PRESS
98-12 66th Avenue; suite two
Rego Park, NY 11374 [USA]

Email: solomonpress@solomonpress.com

Phone: 718-830-9112
Fax: 718-830-0351

Every effort has been made to give proper acknowledgment and fair compensation for quoted material. Any omission of credit or non-compensation will be corrected at the earliest opportunity.

In preparing this book for publication, the author and the publisher present its contents solely as educational and informational material, and do not endorse any product, procedure or therapy described herein. Accordingly, the author and publisher assume no responsibility and disclaim all liability of any kind, however arising, as a result of using the subject matter of this book.

This is the First Book in the RAYMOND S. SOLOMON PSYCHOLOGY SERIES.
A SOLOMON PRESS BOOK

COVER DESIGN AND COVER ART BY DUNCAN LONG

Hard cover ISBN: 978-0-934623-88-0
Soft cover ISBN: 978-0-934623-87-2

The SOLOMON PRESS is a division and imprint of PUBLISHERS CREATIVE SERVICES INC.

Dedication

To the memories of

my mentor and professor, Dr. Stanley Milgram,
who taught me so much about obedience to authority

my friend, Robert Anton Wilson, who lived and
breathed resistance to authority every day of his life

and

my friend and colleague Vince Miller
who fought unjust authority with every fiber of his being

Contents

ACKNOWLEDGMENTS   ix
ACKNOWLEDGMENTS AND PERMISSIONS   x
INTRODUCTION   xi

PART I: THE BASICS: HOW TO STAND UP
WITHOUT FALLING DOWN   1

Chapter One: Seduction of the Situation: Why People Obey   3

Chapter Two: Psychological Kung Fu: How to Question Experts
and Stand Up to Authorities   27

PART II: WRESTLING WITH PROFESSIONALS WITHOUT
GETTING BRUISED   53

Chapter Three: Don't Trust Me: I'm A Doctor:
Questioning Physicians, Psychologists and Psychiatrists   55

Chapter Four: Don't Take This Job and Shove It:
Dealing with Bosses without Getting Fired   93

Chapter Five: Services from Hell: Surviving Lawyers,
Contractors and Other Professionals without Getting Ripped Off   129

Chapter Six: All the News That's Not Fit to Print: Thinking
Critically about the Printed Word   169

PART III: I AM NOT A NUMBER: QUESTIONING
BUREAUCRACIES AND INSTITUTIONS   203

Chapter Seven: Not Just Another Brick in the Wall:
Graduating Intact from Educational Institutions   213

Chapter Eight: Your Call Is Not Important to Us:
Getting What You Deserve From Consumer Services   243

Chapter Nine: You *Can* Fight City Hall: Tackling Government
Bureaucracies and Dealing Effectively with the Police   283

PART IV: WHAT'S NEXT?   313

Chapter Ten: Won't Get Fooled Again: Wrapping It Up and
Taking It with You   315

NOTES   339
INDEX   359

Acknowledgments

MANY PEOPLE HAVE MADE contributions to this book in one way or another. Some need to remain anonymous—all the people who provided me with stories (not always intentionally . . .) for this book. This includes some of my ex-students as well as colleagues, friends, and acquaintances. Their stories liven up the text as well as illustrate the ideas.

Others I can acknowledgment more openly. First of all, I'm grateful to the late Sidney Solomon, father of Raymond Solomon, publisher of Solomon Press, who believed in this book and encouraged it. I'm grateful also to Ray, who liked the book so much he made it the first book in his new psychology line.

The person who most influenced the structure of this book was Dr. Paula Caplan, who wrote *You're Smarter Than They Make You Feel*. Her now (unfortunately) out-of-print book provided many valuable ideas about how to stand up to experts that I've used in this book.

Thanks to the knowledgeable people who agreed to give me their thoughts, either in interview or by email: Georg Bueschi, ArLyne Diamond, William Gore, Dick and Irene Riemann, Natasha Shebeko, Art Smith, Beka Wildman, and Shannon Wirchniansky.

Others who gave me helpful feedback and information include Nancy Dale, Felix Herndon, Carolyn Imhoff, Gretchen Reevy, Adriene Sere, Melanie Swan and Ofer Zur.

I also appreciate the helpfulness of the staff of the Martinez branch of the Contra Costa County Public Library. They cheerfully renewed many of my reference books over and over again. Thanks to Patrick for that missing page number.

But most of all, I want to thank my partner Art Smith, who was the best editor anyone could have, faithfully going over every chapter and making many insightful suggestions, as well as proof reading. He also put up with all the *stürm und drang* of finishing the manuscript and cooked breakfast every morning. What more could I ask?

SHARON PRESLEY
July 28, 2009

Acknowledgments and Permissions

Grateful acknowledgment is made to the following publishers and persons for permission to quote excerpts from previously published material:

From *Beating the System: Using Creativity to Outsmart Bureaucrats*, copyright© 2005 by Russell L. Ackoff and Sheldon Rovin, Berrett-Koehler Publishers, Inc., San Francisco, CA. All rights reserved. www.bkconnection.com Reprinted with permission of the publisher.; the American Civil Liberties Union online at http://www.aclu.com, with permission of the ACLU; American Civil Liberties Union of Northern California online at www.aclunc.org, with permission of the ACLUNC; Ann Bauer, "Psych Meds Drove My Son Crazy" online at http://www.psychrights.org, with permission of Law Project for Psychiatric Rights; Howard Bloom, "The Puppets of Pandemonium" in ed. Russell Kick, *You Are Being Lied To: The Disinformation Guide to Media Distortion, Historical Whitewashes and Cultural Lies*, copyright© 2001 by the Disinformation Company, New York, and online at http://www.disinfo.com. Reprinted with permission of the Disinformation Company Ltd; *Talking Back to Ritalin*, copyright© 1998 by Peter Breggin, Common Courage Press, Monroe, ME, with permission of the author; *Dancing with Lawyers*, copyright© 1992 by Nicholas Carroll, Royce Baker, Lafayette, CA. Reprinted with permission of the author and Hastings Research, Inc.; Contractors from Hell online at http://www.contractorsfromhell.com, with permission of Jody Costello, founder; Christopher Elliott online at http://www.elliott.org, with permission of the author; Don Feder and Accuracy in Media online at http://aim.org and http://www.boycottnyt.com, with permission of AIM; *Bullies, Targets & Witnesses*, copyright © 2003 by Suellen Fried and Paula Fried, M. Evans and Company, New York. Reprinted with permission of the publisher; *Never Work for a Jerk*, copyright © 1987 by Patricia King, Barnes and Noble Books, New York., with permission of the author; *Unreliable Sources: A Guide to Detecting Bias in the Media*, copyright© 1991 by Martin A. Lee and Norman Solomon, Lyle Stuart, New York. Reprinted with permission of Norman Solomon; *Examining Your Doctor: A Patient's Guide to Avoiding Harmful Medical Care*, copyright © 1995 by Timothy B. McCall, M.D.: Citadel Press, Secaucus, NJ. Reprinted with permission of the publisher; *Teaching the Restless* by Chris Mercogliano, Copyright © 2003 by Chris Mercogliano. Reprinted with permission of Beacon Press, Boston; *The Bully at Work: What You Can Do to Stop the Hurt and Reclaim Your Dignity on the Job*, copyright© 2000 by Gary Namie and Ruth Namie, Ph.D. Sourcebooks, Inc., Napierville, IL, and online at http://www.workplacebullying.org. Reprinted with permission of the authors and Workplace Bullying; From *Sexual Harassment on the Job*, copyright© 1999 by William Petrocelli and Barbara Kate Repa, Nolo Press, Berkeley, CA. Reprinted with permission of Barbara Kate Repa; Project Censored online at http://www.projectcensored.org/, with permission of Project Censored; Dan Rather's article in Kristina Borjesson, ed., *Into the Buzzsaw*, Prometheus Press, Amherst, NY, 2004, original interview copyright 2002 by the BBC and Dan Rather. Reprinted with permission of the BBC and Dan Rather; Raymond Lloyd Richman, Ph.D. online at http://www.guidetopsychology.com, with permission of the author; Ripoff Report® online at www.ripoffreport.com, with permission of Ed Magedson, founder and editor; *Bullying*, copyright © 2005 by Kathleen Winkler, Enslow Publishers, Inc, Berkeley Heights, NJ. Reprinted with permission of the publisher; Ofer Zur's recommendations online at http://www.zurinstitute.com/choosing.html, with permission of the author.

Introduction: Take Back Your Power

EXPERTS AND AUTHORITIES can take your power away by intimidating, manipulating, abusing and bamboozling you. Examples are everywhere: Physicians tell you to leave your treatment to them because *they* are the experts. Bureaucrats give you the run-around. Clerks and customer service reps say it can't be done. Bosses bully you or expect you to help them cheat. A professor gives you an unfair grade. The examples are nearly endless. If you don't recognize what they are doing or know how to stand up to them, they've got you.

Anyone can be intimidated. It's easy to uncritically go along with authority and experts. All kinds of people do it, including smart people. This book can change that. You can learn to be more mindful of what experts and authorities say. You can learn techniques for spotting and avoiding manipulation by experts, for avoiding the "seduction of the situation," and for standing up to unjust authority. You'll get guidelines on how to spot situational factors that affect you when you don't even know it. You'll learn how to avoid playing the passive role in a power relationship. You'll learn the best way to convince companies to be fair to you. You'll read about positive strategies for making yourself less vulnerable to the pressures of authority and persuasion and learn techniques for dealing effectively with all kinds of experts—doctors, lawyers, contractors, city bureaucrats, and other professionals. Every individual has the power to stand up to experts and authorities. That's what you'll learn to do—take back your power.

Becoming aware of how social and personal factors influence you to go along with alleged experts or self-styled authorities is the first step to standing up to them. Some of the factors in the situation that can affect your attitudes without you being aware of it include titles (e.g., Dr. or Professor), clothes (e.g., uniforms or lab coats), or appearance (e.g., attractive people). Unquestioned, unacknowledged scripts that you unconsciously play out in relationships such as doctor-patient or employer-employee may make you more vulnerable to being manipulated. Personal factors such as lack of self-confidence, childhood parental messages telling you not to question, or feelings of helplessness can erode your ability to stand up for yourself. Because this awareness is so important, I start off in Chapter One with a look at the research on what I call "the seduction of the situation"—how the social situation influences you to give in to authority.

Unlike some "pop psych" books that spin fluffy advice based on the author's pet ideas or on a handful of clinical case studies, the suggestions in this book are all based on sound scientific research as well as practical experiences that have worked. I've included the footnotes and references so, you can, if you wish, check them out yourself rather than merely trusting the "expert" in this case, namely me. I have also included additional sources of information, including books and Web sites. No single book can say everything there is to say on a topic this broad. On complex issues, you can and probably should look further. Part of the *raison d'etre* for this book is to provide resources for further investigation. Even in our current Internet world, it isn't always easy to find what you need or even to know what you need to find. So the resources are there to help you dig deeper. If you don't know how to use the Internet or do not have access to it, go to a public library. Librarians are taught how to do research and they love to be asked to help. They are a wonderful resource; don't hesitate to ask them to help you.

In this book, we'll look at specific settings in which authorities or experts can intimidate or abuse you, including institutions (e.g., schools and universities, bureaucracies), the workplace (e.g., unethical bosses or bullying colleagues, asking for a raise), media (e.g., news programs, magazines), and professional services (e.g., medical care, tech support, lawyers, contractors). We'll also explore standing up for your rights when dealing with the police and other government agencies. Real-life examples will show you how people have been intimidated and how some of them have successfully avoided being taken in by experts or have been effective in standing up to authorities. You'll read about practical, concrete steps for interacting with experts and for standing up to unjust authorities. In real life we don't always succeed, so there'll also be examples of efforts that have failed and even a few that deservedly failed because the person was wrong. In real life, we aren't always right or deserving of what we ask for and we need to recognize that too.

Introduction

WHAT THIS BOOK IS NOT

Let me say a few words about what this book is *not*. It is *not* a book about how to manipulate others. It is *not* intended for those who feel they are entitled to anything they want just because they want it. It is not intended for bullies, whiners, narcissists, and chronic complainers who just want to get whatever they can get and to hell with what's right. This book is intended for those who have legitimate gripes, reasonable questions, and sensible issues. It's for those who have been treated unfairly because they don't know how to deal effectively with authority. I've always had a soft spot for the underdog.

Unfortunately, there are no easy guidelines to separate the legitimate wheat from the merely demanding chaff. I do know that being fair and observing the rights of others makes for a better world. I also think being fair is ultimately more practical and effective in the long run and often in the short run. I hope that my readers will agree that being fair—standing up to authorities and questioning experts only when your issues are reasonable and justifiable—is a desirable and morally appropriate course.

A CRITICAL TOOL: CRITICAL THINKING

The most important tool to help you deal effectively with experts and authorities is critical thinking. "Critical thinking," say Brooke Noel Moore and Richard Parker, authors of the textbook, *Critical Thinking*, "is the careful, deliberate determination of whether we should accept, reject, or suspend judgment about a claim —and of the degree of confidence with which we accept or reject it."[1] Regardless of the situation, applying the principles of critical thinking can help you sort out the real from the false, manipulation from mere differences, inappropriate pressure from simply good advice. You won't always be right. You'll sometimes make mistakes. But making your own decisions based on critical thinking, even if you're wrong, strengthens you psychologically and makes you better able to withstand pressures from authorities and sharper at spotting expert manipulation.

A WORD ON DEFINITIONS

Many people use the terms "expert" and "authority" interchangeably but, while the terms overlap, they don't actually mean the same thing. Sociologist Robert Bierstedt makes an important distinction that I think is useful.[2] Experts, he says, use persuasion. He points out that expertise—skill and knowledge in a particular area—is something we are free to accept or not. Authority, however, uses coercion. Authorities are those who have power over us whether we agree to it or not, for example, government bureaucrats or police officers. So, we may say, for example, that Omar Sharif is an authority on the game of bridge but what we really mean is that he is an expert. A person can have authority without being an expert—need I say, for example, that government bureaucrats often fall into this category? On the other hand, experts may not have authority in the sense of power. Therefore, I have continued to use the phrase "expert and authorities" rather than just collapsing them into one and have, in some cases, treated them differently. The techniques we may wish to use in dealing with experts, though overlapping, are not necessarily always the same ones we may want to use with authorities in the sense I've defined.

WHO SHOULD READ THIS BOOK

I've tried to write a book that has something for nearly everyone. If you're young, there's a lot you don't know about the world yet. You may not yet have enough experience to deal effectively with authorities. You may be naïve or easily intimidated. For you, I have new, eye-opening information. If you're a woman who has undergone the typical gender-stereotypical upbringing, you might sometimes be too timid to question authorities. For you, I offer encouragement and suggestions for being more assertive. If you think of yourself as fairly experienced in the ways of the world, I have something for you too—specific techniques for dealing with authorities and experts that you may not have thought of yet. I've been questioning experts and authorities for a long time but, in doing the research for this book, I found many ideas that were new to *me* and they may be new to you too. It's a challenge writing a book for every level of experience but I hope that I have succeeded in writing a book that everyone can put to good use.

THE ANECDOTES IN THIS BOOK

All the examples in this book are real. I didn't make anything up. Some stories come from books or articles I've read but most have been gathered over the years from my experiences as well as from people I know—e.g., friends, family, and my students. In order to protect privacy and confidentiality, the names have, of course, been changed, and occasionally some minor detail that could breach confidentiality.

I invite readers to send me real-life experiences that illustrate the principles and suggestions in the book. If my advice works for you, I'd like to hear about it. If it doesn't work for you, I'd like to hear about that too. There's always something to be learned from every experience. As they say in science, the only bad experiment is one that you don't learn from. You can contact me through the web site for this book: www.standuptoauthorities.com. There'll be a blog where you can share your experiences or ask advice about a particular issue. If you are female, I may even use your example (with your permission, of course) in my follow-up book, which will be specifically addressed to women's special concerns to a greater extent than is possible in this book.

TAKE BACK YOUR POWER

Armed with new awareness as well as practical techniques and useful resources, you'll have the tools you need to avoid being the victim of "expert" advice that isn't right for you and to stand up to unjust or unhelpful authorities. You have the power to take control of your life, to just say no to bad advice, pressures to conform, scam artists, or demands for inappropriate obedience. When they tell you that you have to do it their way, you can seize your power, stand up, and say "sez who?" and be successful. Every individual, including you, has the power to stand up to experts and authorities. You just have to make the choice to do it.

SHARON PRESLEY

STANDING UP

to Experts and Authorities

PART

I

The Basics: How to Stand Up without Falling Down

CHAPTER

1

The Seduction of the Situation: Why People Obey Authority

HOW TO THINK CRITICALLY ABOUT AUTHORITY

Imagine that you've volunteered to be in a psychology experiment at a famous university. You're told to flip a toggle switch on a shock generator every time the other subject makes a mistake in recalling a series of word pairs. Each time you flip the switch, the poor guy gets a jolt of an additional 15 volts of electric shock. At the end of the shock generator board, the label reads: "Danger: Severe Shock. 450 volts." After the shocks reach 150 volts, the guy starts screaming, "Let me out of here. I've got a heart condition. My heart is bothering me." Meanwhile the experimenter in a white lab coat, ignoring this man's plaintive cries, tells you: "The experiment must continue." What would you do?

Most of you are probably thinking some equivalent of this: "Are you kidding? I'd quit. No way would I continue to shock a guy who's complaining about a heart condition!" You probably imagine that most people would react as you have. And you would be dead wrong.

If you've ever taken an Introductory Psychology class, you recognize the famous Milgram experiment on obedience to authority. No experiment in social science has had more impact. How many subjects broke off when the subject complained about a heart condition? How many continued to obey the experimenter until the very end—till 450 volts? The results, totally unexpected and in fact . . . shocking . . . made Dr. Stanley Milgram the most famous social psychologist in the world. Fully 65% of the subjects continued to obey the experimenter until the very end, until the 450-volt switch.

Why? Were the subjects lusting to witness pain? Thirsting to see others hurt? Lacking in moral conscience? Not at all. They were ordi-

nary people, swept up in a situation for which they were not psychologically prepared. They were concerned about the man with the heart condition. They complained to the experimenter. Yet under the pressure of the experimenter's unrelenting demands, they obeyed and went on shocking the subject. In spite of their consciences and their concerns, they failed to see the big picture. They lost sight of the (moral) forest for the (situational) trees. They concentrated on their duty to the authority in charge rather than their moral duty to their fellow human being.

Why? If not desire to hurt ... then what? Something few people ever consider. Unrecognized pressure from the situation around them, plus unquestioned and unconscious social conditioning, lulled them into an unwittingly immoral choice. They had been seduced by the situation and they didn't even know it.[1]

NONE OF US WANT to be taken in or pressured by experts or intimidated by authorities. Most of us have sometimes had doubts about an expert's advice or disagreed with an authority's directive. Few of us relish the idea of obeying unjust or cruel authority. Yet nearly all of us, at one time or another, have had trouble voicing our concerns. Sometimes we didn't even recognize that we were bamboozled or pressured. Sometimes we've gone along without questioning because we didn't even realize we should or could disagree. Why are we so easily seduced? Why do we have so much trouble confronting authority? Why do we have so much trouble even realizing that we *have* been bamboozled and seduced by the situation? It's a question that intrigues social scientists and lay people alike.

WHY WE DEFER TO EXPERTS AND AUTHORITIES

The reasons that people are so easily intimidated by experts, so deferent to authority, so unwilling to stand up and question, are complex and multi-layered. There are no simple, quick answers. To answer the questions thoroughly would take a whole book in itself. We might, for example, first look at the background role of culture, of upbringing, of personal and emotional factors that influence individuals, the role of institutions such as school, state, and, of course, the media.

We might start with what we learn as children. From parents who tell us to obey—"Why? Because we said so"—to schools that encourage children to be "good little boys and girls," not to question but to be docile, not to think for themselves but to memorize. Being critical of authority is not a lesson that the average student learns. Cultural institutions encourage obedience and deference, not resistance and questioning. TV teaches us to value social approval and care more about things and appearance than self-worth and independence. Our peers don't want us to be different from them; conformity to peer pressure is a virtue. But these general factors, as influential as they are, merely provide a background milieu in which deference to authority can occur. They are not enough by themselves to explain our reluctance to stand up to authorities and experts.

MOTIVATIONAL FACTORS

One way to approach the question of why our relationship with authority is so difficult is to look through the lens of motivation. In examining behavior, psychologists often ask, "What purpose does it serve for the individual? What motivates the individual to act in certain ways?" In their discussion of the motivations behind social influence, psychologists Kenrick, Neuberg, and Cialdini suggest that people are motivated by three goals in their social interactions—to choose correctly, to gain social approval, and to enhance self-image.[2] Research suggests that people have a fundamental motivation to be competent, to master their environment and to gain rewards and resources. "To do well," point out Kenrick et al., "we must choose well."[3] Since we can't be competent in every area, following the advice of experts helps us choose rapidly and correctly most of the time. Because we also tend to assume that authorities are experts, we often use authority as a shortcut to correct choice. It's all a matter of trust. In many cases this is a sensible way to proceed. The catch—experts and authorities are not always correct or reasonable.

Another shortcut used to make good decisions, according to Kenrick et al., is following the actions of peers.[4] We frequently decide what to do by looking at what others, particularly similar others, are doing and then follow their lead. Psychologists call this social validation. Following the lead of others not only gives us cognitive shortcuts, it also elicits approval from them. This is what drives teenagers to demand the latest overpriced sneakers. This is why your neighbor just bought a gas-guzzling SUV like the one on the next block.

Seeking social approval is an important human motivation. We are all social animals, after all. Because it can be emotionally painful to be an outcast, most of us seek some degree of social acceptance and avoid social rejection. We learn the norms and expectations of our culture, our family, and our peers, and are motivated to go along with the norms in order to gain social approval. If we don't go along with the opinions of our family or peers, we fear they may reject us. If we reject the advice of experts, we may look foolish. If we disobey authority, we may be reprimanded or worse. These are all painful outcomes that can hurt our self-esteem and our self-image.

Individuals are also motivated to have a good image of themselves. People can enhance and validate their self-image by making good choices. Because we want to look competent, we like to maximize our strategies for making what appear to be good choices. Unfortunately this does not always result in using rational strategies or making choices that are, in fact, good.

It's generally accepted by psychologists that there are individual differences in motivation that lead some people to seek social validation and even social approval more than others. Personal factors, such as childhood experiences that undermined one's self-esteem, feelings of helplessness and powerlessness, and other fears, make some people more vulnerable to seeking the approval of others. For similar reasons, some people learn to fear or be deferent to authority more than others.

SITUATIONAL PRESSURE

We live in a culture that encourages deference to authority and discourages critical and independent thinking. We are motivated to be seen as competent and we seek social approval. All this sets the stage for understanding how vulnerable we are to outside pressures and influences. But it's not just overt pressures from the experts and authorities or our peers that make us succumb. What happens is subtler than that. It's not necessarily even the person who seduces us into acquiescence, deference, or obedience, it may merely be the situation.

SO EASY TO BE SEDUCED BY THE SITUATION

Many people don't realize just how easy it is to be bamboozled and seduced. They may not understand how much our behavior is unconsciously influenced by situational factors—subtle aspects of the situation or characteristics of other people that have an effect on how we act. In Western cultures, people often tend to assume that they freely choose their behavior with little outside influence. We may have free will, but we don't act in a vacuum. We are influenced by many factors, both internal (e.g., our values, moods, internalized rules we've learned from our parents, schools, and churches) and external (e.g., actions of other people, presence of authority figures). Social science research shows over and over again the powerful impact of situational factors. Subtle things—what the authority is wearing, how the furniture is arranged, what titles the authority has, the use of body language—are examples of factors that can have an effect on how willing we are to go along with authorities or experts without even realizing it.[5] I call the influence of these factors the "seduction of the situation." Most of the time, we don't succumb to them consciously or intentionally. Nor is it the case that the experts necessarily manipulate the situation intentionally, although that can certainly happen. Much of the time, the process is more covert. That's why we need to become aware of how it works if we are to avoid its influence.

OUR CHOICE

As seductive as these influences can be, we do have a choice. Once we recognize that these factors have the potential to affect us, we have the power to resist their lure. But we need guidelines. What do we look for? What are the hidden factors? What does social science research tell us that can help us stand up to experts and authority? Here are some suggestions that can help you spot the unseen factors that influence you to go along, even when it is unreasonable and against your best interest to do so.

How to Recognize When You Are Being Seduced by the Situation

Many factors, from titles to credentials, from physical appearance to clothing, from reputation to symbols, can work their subtle influence on us, soothing us, beguiling us. Knowledge and awareness are the best weapons against the insidious seductive powers of the situation around us.

BE SMART: DON'T BE HOODWINKED BY CREDENTIALS

Authorities have a way of defining the situation for us, presenting themselves as experts through the use of titles (e.g., Dr. or Professor), credentials (e.g., Ph.D. or M.D.), or positions (e.g., CEO or Director). Most of the time, this is useful and relevant information. We want to know that the experts have a background in the topic they are talking about and appropriate credentials or experience to support their expertise. Checking for a relevant background is important. If experts offer no relevant experience or background, be cautious about their advice. But here's the catch—the fact that someone has a degree or title doesn't necessarily mean that they know what they are talking about. We need to look more closely.

It's easy to be swayed by fancy titles or impressive-sounding credentials. But credentials are not enough. Look to see if the credentials are relevant to the area in which the authority is claiming expertise. A Ph.D. in one area doesn't necessarily mean that the person is an expert in another area. A well-known talk show host—let's call her "Dr. L"—has been giving psychologically-oriented advice for many years. Many people in her audience, however, are unaware that her Ph.D. is in physiology, not psychology.[6] We can accept or reject her advice on other grounds, but we should not accept her advice simply because she calls herself "Dr."

A trickier version of the credential problem—because it's hard for us to spot it—is the meaningless credential. If a person is going to present himself as an expert because of a degree, make sure it's from a reputable university. There are ways to get Ph.D.s without attending a recognized school with an accredited curriculum. John Gray, author of the mega-best-selling book, *Men are from Mars, Women are from Venus,* and the ensuing series on "Martian" men and "Venusian" women, for example, does have a Ph.D. in psychology. Few people know, however, that it's from a "diploma mill" closed down several years ago by the State of California for giving out dubious credentials not backed up by accreditation from legitimate sources.[7] Since Gray's degree lacks credibility, his claims need to be examined on other merits.

On the other hand, don't dismiss an expert's advice simply because he or she doesn't have a fancy degree. There's lots of ways to gain expertise, including years of experience in the relevant field. If someone has been working in an area many years and has a widespread reputation for competence and a track record of success, that goes a long way toward establishing her "credentials." The late Ann Landers, the advice columnist, for example, didn't have a Ph.D. but her many years of experience and her common sense made her advice sensible more times than not. And, unlike certain other media advice-givers, few people have challenged the overall appropriateness of Landers's advice.

Look up credentials on the Internet or in reference books at the library. Look for criticisms of the person. If the expert has questionable advice, someone will almost certainly have noted it on the Internet. Librarians can help you if you're not sure how to search.

SEPARATE THE MESSAGE FROM THE MESSENGER

When looking for advice, it's important to evaluate the *content* of the message, regardless of who is saying it. Even experts can be wrong. Even people whose opinions we respect can sometimes be wrong. Sometimes people we dislike may be right. It's foolish to either accept or reject a piece of advice or opinion merely because of who says it. Look for the evidence. Look for the logic. Think about how the advice or opinion squares with your own knowledge. Don't be taken in and seduced by irrelevant characteristics of the person.

ASK YOURSELF: AM I DAZZLED BY THE EXPERT'S APPEARANCE?

- Beauty

We all know that ad agencies think beautiful, sexy women help sell cars and beer. Few of us, however, realize how pervasive and insidious the impact of attractiveness is on our evaluations in general. The title of a landmark research study, "What is Beautiful Is Good," tells it all.[8] Study after study show that we judge beautiful people—however unconsciously—more favorably than their less attractive peers. Good-looking people, for example, tend to be seen as smarter, more moral, more accomplished and happier. Psychologists call this tendency to evaluate people in an overall positive light once a positive impression (in this case based on looks) has been formed the "halo effect."[9] But—you guessed it—good looks don't actually make your smarter or more moral. Beautiful people have, for the most part, the same problems and abilities as everybody else. Don't be seduced by an expert's attractive appearance.

What makes us fall for the superficial lure of beauty? What makes us unconsciously react so positively toward attractive people? No one does it intentionally. No one consciously assumes that beautiful people are wiser or know more. Most of us would laugh at the suggestion. But beauty can seduce us nonetheless. In the USA, we live in a society obsessed with beauty, thinness and youth; we're constantly bombarded with images in magazines, ads, TV, and movies of glamorous, computer-enhanced and retouched faces and bodies of beautiful, impossible people. It's hard not to be affected.

- Gender

Beauty isn't the only way appearance can lull us into uncritical acceptance. Even in these more enlightened times, gender is often unconsciously used as a standard for evaluation without regard to the person's actual qualifications. Without realizing that they are doing it, many people give more credence to a male expert than a female expert, particularly if the area is stereotypically associated with men. In another landmark study, psychologist Philip Goldberg asked college women to rate an article.[10] One group was told that the author was "John McKay" and the other matched group was told that the author was "Joan McKay." Even though the two articles were identical, the one identified as written by a male was rated more highly than the same article when it was allegedly written by a female. Other more recent research indicates that men with traditional gender attitudes are still likely to devalue women's work.[11]

Gender and area of expertise can interact to affect our evaluations. If a topic is stereotypically viewed as "masculine," (e.g., politics), many people tend to assume a man is more competent than a woman. If the topic is stereotypically "feminine," (e.g., psychology of women) a woman will tend to be viewed as more competent.[12] If we look at it objectively, it's clear that these assumptions are sheer prejudice, not good sense. The particular person's expertise and credentials are what is important, not his or her gender. Don't be seduced by unquestioned gender stereotypes.

- Clothing

What authorities are wearing can also have a big impact on our willingness to go along with them. People are often dazzled by uniforms, snappy clothes, or expensive suits. Uniforms are particularly seductive. A study by psychologist Leonard Bickman demonstrates the "power of a uniform."[13] He found that people were more likely to comply with a stranger's request to put money in an expired parking meter when the stranger was wearing a security guard's uniform or even a milkman's white coverall uniform (it used to be possible to get milk home-delivered!) than when he was wearing ordinary street clothes. The milkman's uniform couldn't be more irrelevant but it had an effect on people's responses, nonetheless. Social psychologist Brad Bushman replicated this study with a male stranger wearing scruffy clothes, a business suit, and a firefighter's uniform at different times.[14] Sure enough, the same effect. People were more likely to comply when the stranger was wearing either a business suit or a firefighter's uniform. Firefighters deserve our respect for other reasons, but in this case, the uniform was totally irrelevant to the merits of the situation. The fireman, the businessman, and the poorly dressed man were all supposedly trying to be helpful to an unknown third party. The actual merit of the request should have been independent of what the requester was wearing.

Uniforms can dazzle us, regardless of gender. In another study replicating Bickman's field experiment, Bushman tested willingness to obey a woman wearing a uniform, a business suit, or scruffy clothes.[15] Though the business suit did not make a difference in the rate of compliance, wearing a uniform did. People were significantly more likely to comply when the woman was wearing a uniform. Uniforms do indeed have the power to unconsciously seduce us.

Many anecdotes also support what research confirms. A friend of mine tells a humorous but instructive story about the time his brother went on to an army base wearing navy blue mechanic's coveralls. When Joe started dismantling an old disarmed missile that was on display outside, the MP's came by and asked him what he was doing. "Dismantling the missile," he nonchalantly said. "Oh, OK," they said, satisfied, and went on their way. Apparently his uniform plus the air of confidence he displayed added up to the "right script." In today's climate, the military might be less likely to be so careless but ordinary people can still be fooled. Scam artists know that many people, especially the elderly, will not question a uniformed man at the door, claiming, for example, to be from the local utility company.

A dramatic example of the power of a "uniform" in a nonmilitary setting is provided by the famous Milgram experiment on obedience to authority cited at the beginning of this chapter.[16] The researcher, in his white lab coat, keeps insisting that the experiment must continue. Ignoring the other participant's screams—who, unknown to the actual subject, was an actor faking his responses—65% of the subjects continued obeying the white-coated man until the end of the experiment, when the shock generator registered "Danger, Severe Shock, 450 volts." Though there were many other factors contributing to this willingness to obey authority, the scientific aura created by the lab coat was one important ingredient. In another experimental variation in the Milgram series, an ordinary man not wearing a white lab coat gave the same instructions to a new set of participants.

The rate of obedience dropped to 20%. Ad agencies understand this principle very well. If the product being advertised is a pharmaceutical drug or a science-related product, it's common for the actor in the commercial to be wearing a white lab coat to establish a "scientific" aura.

AM I BEGUILED (OR TURNED OFF) BY THE PERSON'S REPUTATION OR IDEOLOGY?

- People We Like

When listening to the advice or opinion of authorities and experts we like—either because we agree with their political or social point of view or because they have a famous reputation—there's a common tendency to just go along with whatever they say and not question. We trust their opinion either because we have agreed with it in the past or because the person is billed as an expert and so we assume he must know what he is talking about. Many times this works out OK but not always. No matter how much we agree with experts—famous or not—it's important to think about what they are saying and whether it makes good sense. Let me say it again—experts aren't always right. People we disagree with most of the time are not always wrong. We need to judge for ourselves and not just accept or reject opinions at face value based on our feelings about the person.

Look past reputation to the content. Look at whether it makes sense or raises unanswered questions. Director Michael Cimino scored a big hit with the film, "The Deer Hunter." On the strength of this, Hollywood bankrollers gave him mega-bucks to do "Heaven's Gates." If they had looked at the early rushes, they would have withdrawn their money in a flash. The movie was so unwatchable that it became one of the biggest financial debacles of the decade.[17] They should have looked at the content of the movie, not just at Cimino's reputation.

You can compare what the expert is saying with your previous experience to see if it makes sense. Let's say, for example, that you really like talk show host Dr. Laura Schlessinger's stance on taking individual responsibility for one's actions. "Society made me do it" just doesn't cut it with you. That's certainly a reasonable position. But when she makes a flat claim that mothers who work outside the home harm their children, you might ask yourself—"Is it really that simple?"[18] What if your mother worked outside the home—were you scarred for life? Chances are, many of your friends' mothers worked outside the home too. Did they turn out so bad? Anecdotes, even when they're your own, don't prove or disprove anything by themselves; instead we have to look to scientific research for evidence. But our own experiences and observations *can* stimulate us to think about issues and help us raise questions. In this example, it pays to be skeptical because most social science research suggests that what Schlessinger is saying is not, in fact, true. What most research actually shows is that the quality of the mother's relationship with the child may be more important than whether she does or does not work outside the home, an answer that seems intuitively obvious once you stop and think about it.[19] That's the key—stop and give some thought to what the expert is saying before you accept or reject it.

- People We Don't Like

Automatically rejecting the opinions of people we disagree with or dislike without listening to what they have to say is also commonplace. Just as it's normal to assume that people who have good reputations or points of view we like are likely to have information that we will agree with, it's normal to assume that people whose views we dislike have nothing to offer. A common example of failure to separate the message from the messenger is assuming that those whose political or social beliefs are different from ours have nothing worthwhile to say. Many people only listen to or read the commentators that they agree with. From conservative Rush Limbaugh "ditto-heads" to "knee-jerk liberals," the political landscape is littered with people often reduced to unthinking ideologues because they don't listen to any point of view besides their own. It's an easy way to get fooled and it's certainly not critical thinking.

Let's say, hypothetically, for example, that Joe Tootshishorn, a local political columnist you despise, has written a column proclaiming that the DARE ("Dare to keep kids off drugs") program doesn't work. The local state assemblywoman you voted for is beating the drums for DARE. You could just ignore that jerk Tootshishorn. Or you could read his column to see if there is any substance to his claims. What if he cites several studies done by reputable social scientists at accredited universities that show the

DARE program doesn't have any significant effect in reducing drug use in teenagers?[20] What then? Do you say "Stick it in your ear, Joe, I don't care" or do you say, "H-m-m, I need to look into this more. Maybe, there are more effective ways to deal with the teen drug problem." It seems to me that the latter response is more reasonable. So what if Tootshishorn is a fathead? If the information he is touting is correct, the content of the message is more important than the messenger.

AM I UNCONSCIOUSLY RESPONDING TO THE BODY LANGUAGE OF AUTHORITY?

Nancy Henley and other social scientists have extensively studied the subtle characteristics of nonverbal communication. Henley, who calls it the "politics of touch," has closely examined how body language communicates power.[21] More powerful individuals, for example, are more likely to touch the less powerful than vice versa. Thus the boss touches the secretary, the physician the patient, the teacher the student, and so on. Other examples of cues used by those in power include using direct eye contact with you when they speak but not when you speak, interrupting others, and sitting in a relaxed position while the less powerful sit up straight. All of these cues unconsciously communicate the seductive aura of power, a message whispering that you should listen carefully to this powerful person. Don't be taken in. Listen to the message, not the messenger.

On the other hand, nonverbal language can sometimes be your friend. Eyes that shift around a lot, too much fidgeting, a strained voice, a mouth that smiles when the eyes don't, are all signs that the person may be lying, according to psychologist Paul Ekman.[22] Unless you are an expert yourself in reading body language, you might misinterpret the signs, but nonverbal signs such as these examples should at least put you on your guard.

SEPARATE THE SITUATION FROM THE MESSAGE

It's easy to be dazzled and bewitched by the surroundings and trappings of the environment around us—plush settings, intimidating surroundings, emotionally charged symbols. Unless we make a conscious effort to think about how they are affecting us, we may be lured in. Ask yourself the following questions:

AM I UNCONSCIOUSLY RESPONDING TO THE SUBTLE ENVIRONMENT OF AUTHORITY?

It may surprise you that even the arrangement of furniture can make a difference in our response to authority. Research shows, for example, that having a desk between the expert and the client creates more of a feeling of status than if the desk is against the wall.[23] When the desk is against the wall, the expert and the client face each other directly. This arrangement suggests a peer relationship; in contrast, the desk in between the two people distances the expert and allows him to control the use of space more, thus giving him more of an air of authority. Don't be intimidated by furniture!

AM I LETTING MYSELF BE SWAYED BY THE SYMBOLS OF POWER AND AUTHORITY?

The Nazis brought the use of symbols of power to new heights (or perhaps "depths" is a better word!). From symbols of German unity (the German imperial eagle) to unique symbols creating a special identity (the Nazi swastika); from crisply tailored uniforms and big hats (nearly every totalitarian regime uses big hats, as watching the History Channel will show you) to emotionally charged propaganda, the Nazis swept up ordinary Germans into going along with ideas that went against the norms of every civilized society and religion. If you think people are immune to all that now or that Americans wouldn't fall for such obvious tactics, you couldn't be more wrong. Not too many years ago, Ron Jones, a high school teacher in an affluent Northern California city, decided to try an impromptu experiment in his history class.[24] He started explaining Nazi Germany to his students. He talked to them about the concept of "strength through discipline." But somehow things got sidetracked. The discipline, consisting of actions such as sitting up straight in their chairs and having a special identifying "wave," took on a life of its own.

Jones told them that the wave was a symbol of a nationwide group interested in political change. Within a few days, students from other classes wanted to join in. Students who were not part of the group were treated as outsiders. Students within the group became compulsive about the discipline. Very creepy—but not as creepy as the ending of this naturalistic observational study. Jones told the students to attend a rally in the auditorium in which the national leader of the organization would appear via film to talk to them about the organization. Expectantly they waited—but then what came on the screen was not a national leader; it was a film of the infamous Nazi Nuremberg Rally and other hideous actions of the Third Reich! These students received a starkly dramatic lesson about how ordinary people can be taken in by the emotional symbols of authority.

Flag-waving and patriotic symbols are often misused around the world, as well as in the USA, to appeal to people's emotions rather than their reason. For many people, emotions are more powerful motivators than appeals to reason. Emotions have the power to short-circuit our thinking processes and lead us astray when they are manipulated by authorities with hidden agendas. If you feel a wave of emotion washing over you as a result of what the authority is saying, stop and think. Are you being a critical thinker or are you being caught up in the moment? Are there other ways to think about the issue? Don't be lured by cheap emotional gimmicks.

THINK THINGS THROUGH: DON'T JUST PASSIVELY REACT

Because we find cognitive shortcuts so useful, it's easy to just passively accept the norms of authority or the advice of experts without questioning them. Actively examining our attitudes and assumptions can help us be less passive reactors, less likely to be seduced by old habits and lured by the easy path of least resistance.

ASK YOURSELF: AM I JUST RESPONDING THE WAY I WAS TAUGHT TO REACT TO AUTHORITY BY MY PARENTS OR SCHOOL?

When in the presence of experts who claim special knowledge or authorities who exude power and well—"authority," it's easy to just passively go along. In spite of the much-vaunted individualism of American culture, most Americans, and, for that matter, most people around the world, have been trained to obey authority since they were children. It starts in the family—"Do what I say. Why? Because I said so." It continues in school, where teaching children to be "good little boys and girls" who obey the rules and will grow up to be "good citizens" is often more important than reading, writing, and arithmetic. The natural rebellion of the teen years, though often merely consisting of conforming to peers instead of parents, usually withers completely on the vine of "responsible" adulthood. By then, we have been thoroughly trained to "do what we're told," but now, instead of parents and teachers, it's experts and authorities who tell us what to do.

DO I FIND MYSELF SAYING YES TO AN AUTHORITY THAT I HAVE DOUBTS ABOUT BUT I KEEP ON GOING ANYWAY?

Many people have been taught not to be "quitters." They go along with requests of authorities because they think they should follow through on the commitments they've made previously. Psychologists call this "entrapment."[25] Many of the people in the Milgram experiment, for example, thought they had to continue because they had agreed to participate. They lost sight of the fact that the experimenter told them at the beginning of the study that they could stop at any point if they wanted to. Instead of pausing to think about what was going on in the experiment and whether they really wanted or needed to continue, they passively fell into the old familiar habitual attitude of "not being a quitter." If they had been less passive, they could have asked themselves, "Am I obligated to continue this experiment even if the guy in the other room is being harmed? This is nuts. I didn't agree to something like that!"

Or maybe people don't want to lose the "investment" of time or resources they've made in a situation. Perhaps, for example, someone is in a job she doesn't care for, with a boss who is asking her to carry out tasks she resents; but she says to herself, "I've already invested three years in this job, I don't want to throw that down the drain." Does the old adage "throwing good money after bad" come to mind? It should. In every situation, there are pros and cons to consider, of course. If you're two years away from retirement, the "investment" is real and worth a great deal. But if you could eventually be in a better and more satisfying job if you have the courage to try, then the current investment may not be such a sound one. Sometimes it *is* best to cut your losses.

AM I JUST GOING ALONG WITH THE AUTHORITY BECAUSE IT WOULD BE RUDE TO BREAK OFF?

Many people have been trained to be polite and nonconfrontational at any cost. They unconsciously react as if being polite is the most important value in the situation, without considering whether there might be more important values. Milgram called this reaction "situational etiquette."[27] People in his experiment, wanting to be "good subjects," had trouble breaking off and saying no to the experimenter even when the participant supposedly being shocked in the other room was yelling that he had a heart condition. But what is more important—being polite or being humane? Sometimes we lose sight of the big picture because we are too concerned with obeying well-engrained norms such as being polite. But who says we have to be polite to someone asking us to do something harmful or stupid? Look at the big picture rather than automatically responding based on old habits. Don't be seduced by unquestioned norms.

AM I LETTING MYSELF GET SUCKED INTO A COMMITMENT I DIDN'T REALLY INTEND?

Be sensitive to initially small, trivial steps that can escalate into big commitments. Psychologists call this the "foot-in-door" technique."[27] For example, a person makes a small request that seems innocuous, perhaps merely signing a political petition, then a few weeks later asks you to put a sign in your window advocating a stand on that issue. Research shows that more people say yes to the window sign if it has been preceded by the smaller request. Religious and self-help cults know this technique very well. First they ask you to just come by their meeting.

Then they ask you to come to several more meetings, then they ask you for money, then they ask you for involvement . . . and soon you're sucked in. You may scoff but many people have fallen for this ruse. For most of us, it takes on a more subtle form, perhaps, for example, a request from the boss to do a minor task that is outside our job description. But watch out if he then demands more and more irrelevant tasks; he may be using the foot-in-the door technique. Or perhaps a director for a charity we like asks us to just give two hours to a fund-raising committee. That doesn't sound like too much, we think, so we say yes, even though our schedule is busy. Then pretty soon we are being asked for more and more hours . . . and then, it's a lot harder to say no.

Be Alert: Don't Be Fooled, Fleeced, or Flummoxed

The warnings or caveats above are far from an exhaustive list of how we can be seduced by the situation. Throughout this book, I'll describe other red flags. But these examples do show us that if we want to stand up for ourselves and avoid being fooled or misled by experts and authorities, our first lines of defense are alertness, knowledge, critical thinking, and careful evaluation.

RESOURCES

BOOKS

[also see references in Chapter Two]

These books explore the social science research on persuasion, social influence, and obedience to authority.

Thomas Blass, Ph.D. (Ed.) *Obedience to Authority: Current Perspectives on the Milgram Paradigm*. Mahwah, NJ: Lawrence Erlbaum, 2000. Not for the casual reader but it is an excellent collection of academic articles discussing and updating the Milgram research.

Robert Cialdini, Ph.D. *Influence: The Psychology of Persuasion*. New York: Collins Business, 2006 [available in many editions]. Con games, advertising, and deference to authority are some of the areas covered in this highly informative, entertaining exploration of influence techniques and how they can induce automatic, mindless compliance. It's solidly based on participant observation and other psychological research, with a humorous and engaging style that makes it popular with students (and everyone else!).

Paul Ekman, Ph.D. *Emotions Revealed, Second Edition: Recognizing Faces and Feelings to Improve Communication and Emotional Life*. New York: Holt, 2007. A leading expert on the psychology of reading faces discusses his research. The new TV show "Lie to Me" is based on Ekman's research. His (slightly) more technical book is titled *Telling Lies*.

Nancy Henley, Ph.D. *Body Politics: Power, Sex and Nonverbal Communication*. New York: Simon & Schuster, 1986. A classic study of how nonverbal body language communicates power and how this affects gender relationships.

Joel Kramer and Diana Alstad. *The Guru Papers: Masks of Authoritarian Power*. Berkeley, CA: North Atlantic Books, 1993. A philosophical call to take back the authority that people have unknowingly invested in others, this book examines the techniques used to covertly control others in the guise of imparting knowledge or "doing what's best for you." Asserting that the doctrine of self-sacrifice is used as a tool of control, it unmasks authoritarianism in the areas of addiction, intimate relations, cults, and Eastern and Western religions.

Stanley Milgram, Ph.D. *Obedience to Authority: An Experimental View*. New York: HarperCollins, 1974. No study in social psychology is more famous than the Yale "shock experiment" that demonstrated how easily ordinary people obey the demands of authority. In clear terms, Milgram details a series of experiments that explore the situational factors (e.g., proximity of the victim, diffusion of responsibility) that affect obedience to authority. The powerful effect of these factors—something the average person usually underestimates—is one of the most important lessons of this classic study.

Anthony Pratkanis, Ph.D. and Elliot Aronson, Ph.D. *Age of Propaganda: The Everyday Use and Abuse of Persuasion*. New York: Holt, 2001. A highly readable analysis of the patterns, motives and effects of mass persuasion efforts to influence how we think, how we vote, and what we value. Drawing on the history of propaganda and research in social psychology, it shows us not only what the tactics are but why they work and how we can protect ourselves from manipulation.

Philip Zimbardo, Ph.D. *The Lucifer Effect: Understanding How Good People Turn Evil*. New York: Random House, 2007. A thorough and recent examination of the ways people are seduced by the situation by one of psychology's leading researchers. He discusses in detail the famous Stanford prison simulation experiment that he conducted back in the 70s, another landmark study as important as the Milgram experiment.

Philip Zimbardo, Ph.D. and Michael Leippe, Ph.D. *The Psychology of Attitude Change and Social Influence*. New York: McGraw Hill, 1991. A highly readable but thorough exploration of the social psychological research on these topics. Zimbardo is one of the leading experts in this area.

WEB SITES

Critical Thinking about Social Influence and Conformity

[also see references in Chapter Two for practical applications]

The Seduction of the Situation

Influence by Robert Cialdini
www.rickross.com/reference/brainwashing/brainwashing20.html
A summary of Cialdini's ideas and research.

"The Wave" by Ron Jones
www.ronjoneswriter.com/wave.html
A gripping account, based on an actual event, of how ordinary high school students became entrapped in mindless conformity and unthinking obedience to authority through clever manipulation.

"The Perils of Obedience" by Stanley Milgram
home.swbell.net/revscat/perilsOfObedience.html
Adapted from an article that Milgram wrote for *Harper's* magazine.

The Stanley Milgram Web Site
www.stanleymilgram.com
An overview of Milgram and his work by his biographer, Dr. Thomas Blass.

Links on Attitudes, Persuasion and Influence
www.geocities.com/l_zinkiewicz/socialpsych.html
Home page with many links to articles and materials about social influence.

"What is Beautiful is Good: Physical Attractiveness Bias in Hiring"
www.hofstra.edu/pdf/ORSP_Shahani-Denning_Spring03.pdf
An overview of the research on the effect of physical attractiveness.

"The Sexual Politics of Interpersonal Behavior" by Nancy Henley and Jo Freeman
www.jofreeman.com/womensociety/personal.htm
Article on body politics, nonverbal behavior and gender.

Web Sites for Critical and Independent Thinking

Resources for Independent Thinking
www.rit.org

Articles, reviews and links to resources for independent and critical thinking.

The Skeptic Society
www.skeptic.com
Dr. Michael Shermer, the director, and author of *Why People Believe Weird Things,* has one of the best organizations in the "skeptic" business—debunking silly ideas that people believe without good evidence. A great resource for critical thinking. Check out Dr. Shermer's many fine books.

The Critical Thinking Community
www.criticalthinking.org
The Foundation and Center for Critical Thinking work to improve instruction in primary and secondary schools, colleges and universities. They offer many resources for critical thinking, including books, tapes, seminars and conferences.

Articles about Critical Thinking

The next best thing to reading a critical thinking textbook is checking out the following articles about faulty reasoning.

"Tricks of Persuasion: Fallacies of Argument: The Top Hits Of Bad Reasoning"
peernet.lbpc.ca/edombrowski/media_criticism/02gfallacies.html

Logical Fallacies
www.logicalfallacies.info
Many of the most common reasoning mistakes are discussed.

Critical Thinking Web
philosophy.hku.hk/think
This educational web site provides over 100 free online tutorials on critical thinking, logic, scientific reasoning, creativity, and other aspects of thinking skills.

"Critical Thinking: What Is It Good for? (In Fact, What Is It?)"

www.csicop.org/si/2006-02/thinking.html
CSICOP is part of the skeptic community and offers many resources for critical and skeptical thinking.

UPDATES

For updates on books, web sites, web site URLs and links (they sometimes change), articles and other relevant information, check the web site for my book: www.standuptoauthorities.com

CHAPTER
2

Psychological Kung Fu: How to Question Experts and Stand Up to Authorities

One Christmas Eve afternoon, Adela was driving a car borrowed from a friend. A cop pulled her over and gave her a present she didn't need—a ticket for driving a car with expired plates. After handing the ticket over to the friend, she thought no more about it. But the friend flaked on her and the letters from the Department of Motor Vehicles started coming. Then three months later, a much more serious one arrived—a warrant demanding that she pay a large sum of money or else face arrest. She had to act.

Standing in line behind others at the ticket payment window downtown, she saw that the clerk was being ruthless, brooking no excuses. Adela knew she had a good defense so she demanded a hearing before a judge. The clerk scowled, insisting that the judge would be angry if Adela pursued the matter. Adela did not give in; she knew she had the right to a hearing.

At the hearing, Adela, presented her case. She had ignored the letters from the DMV, not only because her friend kept telling her that he would take of the problem, but also because she was distraught and worried about an important project she was working on. She produced a letter from her physician, stating that she was being treated for a stress-related condition.

Adela could have let herself be intimidated by the clerk's haughty air and nasty insistence. She could have just meekly given in and paid the large sum even though she did not think that she had done anything wrong. But she knew that judges have more leeway to interpret rules than clerks do. She knew the power of paper, of documentation. She got that letter from her doctor. She stood up to authority and won—case and fine dismissed!

As children, we learned to defer to those who have power over us; we may have even learned to think of ourselves as powerless. Social science research tells us that as adults, many of us unconsciously adopt, often without questioning, social roles that play out these power scripts—parent-child, teacher-student, physician-patient, boss-employee.[1] We automatically and unconsciously put ourselves into the roles of either the more or the less powerful. If we think of ourselves as the less powerful in these scenarios, we may imagine that we have no choice but to accept the advice of experts and the power of authority.

Power is a frequently misunderstood word. There are two kinds of power—power over oneself and power over others.[2] What you need to stand up to authorities and experts is not power over *them*, but power over your own attitudes and behavior. You don't have to accept the powerless role you may have learned or adopted. You don't have to be a victim.

The key is to understand how your power gets taken away from you—not necessarily through deliberate intent on the part of experts and authorities, though that can happen—but through the seduction of the situation and the unquestioned, unconscious power of scripts being played out.

Experts and Authorities Intimidate Us

Experts and authorities, whether intentionally or not, often intimidate us by virtue of their very expertise or status. They want us to believe them and do what they say. This doesn't mean they are intentionally trying to scam us or scare us. Obviously the advice of experts is often reasonable, but even when we are not certain about how good their advice is, it can be hard to resist their influence. Usually, authority figures aren't *consciously* trying to create fear or intimidation. But it's a fact that they often do, and they exploit this fear (consciously or not) to get what they want, often to our detriment. When you have good grounds for questioning, you don't have to cower before authorities or experts.

I've adapted many of the points below from Paula Caplan's book, *You're Smarter Than They Make You Feel: How the Experts Intimidate Us and What We Can Do about It*. It's an excellent book on critical thinking about experts that is now out of print but well worth the effort to track down a used copy.

RIGHT TO QUESTION

The first step is to realize that you have the *right* to challenge authorities. You have the right to question experts. In a very real sense, *the experts are working for you.* That means you're the boss, not them. Even if the authority is a government official, remember that you, as a taxpayer, are ultimately footing part of the bill. Government is, after all, supposed to be your servant, not your master, so don't be intimidated. In real life situations, we still sometimes lose sight of the fact that we do have the right to question what authorities and experts say.

Some people feel almost like children in the presence of authorities, but authorities are not our parents; we are not their children. As adults, we now have a responsibility to think for ourselves; we have the right to question things that don't make sense to us. Lack of knowledge doesn't mean that you should give authorities *carte blanche* to compel you to accept their advice without question.

Is it morally right to grant experts the power to make decisions for you, for them to make you feel that you have no right to complain or ask questions? What if a physician told your mother not to ask questions about her medications, even if she was having some troublesome side effects? Would that be acceptable? Of course not. If it's not acceptable for the experts to treat your mother that way, why would it be OK for them to treat you that way? Bringing your fears out into the open and identifying exactly why you are afraid to speak up helps put things into perspective. Even if you find out that the experts are right, speaking up and finding out their reasons may give you peace of mind and make you feel less powerless.

BE PREPARED

The next step, in many cases, is to search out some facts or information about the issue or problem that you want to bring up with the expert. Where you look depends on the topic of your concern. The library, the Internet and even friends, are possible sources of information. After an operation for removal of a pituitary tumor, for example, Joyce felt weak and had trouble walking without a cane. When she looked up her medication on Internet medical sites, she learned that lower body weakness was a common side effect. This information allowed her to ask sensible questions of her physician and request a lower dosage of the drug and, eventually, a change in the medication. The doctor was not the problem; Joyce just needed to know the right questions to ask. By actively participating in her treatment, she felt more like an equal partner than merely a passive patient.

No matter what kind of expert you deal with, there's a way to find information that will make you savvy and well-informed. If your plumbing needs fixing and you don't know an ell-joint from a plunger, ask a friend who is a fix-it whiz what questions to ask. Or check out the web sites of the TV home improvement shows or the home improvement stores; they have lots of tips and information. If you want to make a request of a government official, look up the relevant rules and regulations. Many city and state codes are posted on the Internet. If you want to ask for a raise, look up the average salary for your job. That may be on the Internet too. Be creative and give some thought about where to find the information you need. If you're not good with searches on the Internet, ask a computer-savvy friend or even the librarian at your public library to help you. Some articles that may help you search are listed in the Resources section.

Knowledge is power. Armed with relevant information, you'll be able to ask better and more well-informed questions. By presenting yourself as a knowledgeable person who is actively participating in the process, you are less likely to be seen as a supplicant and more likely to gain respect from the authority.

LIST OF QUESTIONS

Before your appointment, arm yourself with a list of questions that you'd like to have answered. You might ask about, for example, what the different approaches or alternatives are, what the pros and cons for each alternative are, how long will it take to implement the advice, how long will it take for the approach to be effective, and what the long-term implications or consequences of each approach are likely to be. If the expert favors a particular approach, ask him to explain his reasons.

Writing out questions will help your mind from going blank when you confront the power of the authority or the jargon of the expert. If the experts know that you have this list, they will also be more likely to assume you've thought about the issue and have some knowledge. This may make them more cooperative and less likely to try to fool you or gloss over your concerns. A list can help you gauge time and distribute it sensibly. If the discussion veers off, you can, for example, remind the expert that you still have additional questions.

Paulina, a former student of mine, is a shy person who often gets flustered when confronted with authority. When she felt that her boss was upset with her because of an incident that occurred when she was invited to dinner at his house, she came to me for advice. I suggested she organize her thoughts on paper. Here's what she said about my advice: "The first thing I did was write down everything I felt was important to mention to my boss. At times I can get really nervous. I often forget what I want to say and of the things I do say, it usually doesn't make sense or I forget important details. Writing everything down was very helpful in this situation. By doing so, I did not leave out any important information and the discussion matter was in a thoughtful and organized manner. On my sheet of paper, I also wrote down the times I wanted to show my boss the Internet articles. This way I could remember to show him the articles that corresponded with what I was explaining." Her discussion with the boss went well and, she reported, the work atmosphere is much less tense. Paulina added, "Your advice has given me the confidence to handle a stressful situation. I feel like I was able to stand up for myself and my values, as well as call attention to and end being treated rudely."

A list is like having an ally with you. It supports you and backs you up, just as an ally would. It gives you a powerful tool that allows you to have control of the situation and direct the flow of information, thus maintaining a balance between you and the expert.

PUT IT IN WRITING

If you have a complaint or a conflict that needs to be resolved, prepare as much documentation as you can. A written document is far more powerful than verbal descriptions. For one thing, it suggests that a copy exists elsewhere as a record that cannot be brushed aside or ignored by the authority as verbal comments could be. For example, if you are being harassed at work, keep track of the particulars with a notebook. Jot down the details of each encounter with the person harassing you—exactly what happened, what time and date, who the witnesses were, if any, and any other relevant information. If the street you live on desperately needs a stop sign, document the accidents and near misses. Canvass your neighbors for their observations; gather signatures on a petition.

Be creative about what documentation might support your case, as Adela did in the case cited at the beginning of this chapter. Sometimes, we can anticipate how documentation might save the day. Consuela, a high school teacher, occasionally ran into the problem of parents who lied to the administration. Even though she had met with these parents about their child's poor grades, they insisted to the principal that they had never talked to her. The principal was reluctant to contradict the parents. After several similar incidents, Consuela learned to document everything and record all conferences.

Having documentation makes your request look more legitimate and your excuses less lame. Examples of documentation may include photos, videos, signed affidavits, witness statements, police or medical reports, or relevant expert literature. As a college professor, I am in a position of authority over my students. Around exam time, I hear a lot of excuses about why they are missing the test. Auto accidents, dying grandmothers, and flu epidemics seem to "somehow" dramatically increase right before a crucial exam. If a student brings me actual written proof of illness, accident or funeral, I'm much more likely to allow them a makeup exam.

Be prepared with documentation before your meeting. Don't wait for the authority to ask. Having intelligent questions or written documentation will also make you feel more self-confident and more powerful. That feeling of self-confidence is an important aspect of your next step—mental preparation or psyching yourself up.

MENTAL PREPARATION: PSYCH YOURSELF UP

Your mental attitude will have a big impact on how well you deal with the expert or authority. Your mental status is important; the person you are facing may pick up on your fear and uncertainty. If you go in with mental hat in hand, with an air of timidity or abject deference, you've already defeated yourself. You have allowed yourself to be in a power down position. Mentally preparing or psyching yourself up will help you come to the situation with the right mental set. Assume that your cause is just and your questions reasonable. That's what Adela did. She was polite but confident before the judge. Be on the offensive, not the defensive.

Even if you don't feel totally self-confident, behave as if you did. "Fake it till you make it" is sound psychological advice in this context.[3] Not only will you make a stronger impression on the expert, the mere act of behaving as if you are self-confident can create a self-fulfilling prophecy. An air of confidence will make a difference in the way experts interact with you and make you feel more powerful.

DRESS FOR YOUR SUCCESS

A confident demeanor isn't the only way to have an impact on the expert. How you dress can make a difference too. The research that I discussed in Chapter One shows that appearance and dress can make a big difference in how you perceive authority.[4] It can make a difference in how they perceive you too. Use this information to your advantage.

Most of us are familiar with the concept of "dress for success." Though you and I may disagree with some of the specifics suggested by the book of that name (e.g., wear navy blue business suits), there's no question that your appearance has a major impact on how others perceive you. Dress in a way that makes you feel good about yourself and makes you feel powerful. There are no fixed rules—what makes us feel powerful won't be the same for everybody. However, it's often a good idea to dress in a way that puts you on the same level with the expert, a peer rather than a supplicant. If you have an appointment with your lawyer or with a government official, for example, dress in a professional way—either a business suit or dressy casual, depending on which makes you feel most comfortable. In any meeting with a professional or bureaucrat, you need to appear serious but also need to feel at ease. Even if you are taking your car to a mechanic, a professional appearance can put you in a position of greater credibility than T-shirts and ragged jeans, particularly if you are a woman.

One of my favorite stories about the power of dress comes from a former student of mine. Krystal, a 30-ish black woman, took her young daughter in to see her physician at the HMO. Because of time constraints, she had to go to the appointment right after work and so was wearing a business suit instead of the jeans and sweatshirt she would have normally worn. Usually in this HMO, patients get whisked through as fast as possible. Instead, Krystal was amazed at how much time the physician took and how thorough his exams and questions were. Because she had already learned about the power of appearance in my social psychology class, she (correctly, I suspect) attributed the change in the way she and her daughter were treated to the fact that she was dressed in the business suit.

It isn't fair, but research shows that women are more likely to be judged by their appearance than men so having a smart, tailored appearance can be even more important for a woman than a man.[5] Find the right balance—not too frilly and "feminine," not too "masculine," and not too provocative either. Appearing too glamorous or seductive will backfire. You want to be taken seriously, not auditioned for the casting couch.

FINE TUNE YOUR APPROACH

Sometimes, it can be helpful to think about the right approach and the most effective communication style before a meeting. Though you should be prepared to be firm but nonthreatening, regardless of the situation, different situations may call for different approaches. If your meeting is with a professional (e.g., lawyer, accountant, financial adviser), for example, ask questions without seeming to question his authority. Don't put him on the defensive by asking hostile questions. Be prepared to speak calmly in a quietly assertive manner. Don't be rude or pushy. If you are meeting with your boss, approach her as a team player. Be mentally prepared to be helpful and cooperative while making your request. It may be appropriate, for example, to point out some of the ways that you are an asset to the team.

ESTABLISH RAPPORT

When you first meet with an expert or authority, it's important to set the right tone. Start out the meeting in a pleasant manner. Be prepared with a disarming question or a statement that will establish rapport or put you on equal grounds with the other person. You might begin, for example, by asking a question that you know the authority may be willing to answer and may feel good about. For example, "What do you think is the problem here?" or "Is this a common problem?" A comment that establishes common ground can also help set the pleasant tone you seek, as long as it doesn't sound phony. For example, "I know you are as concerned as I am about the issue of urban pollution . . ." or "I really like the tropical fish in your office. I used to raise them" may help establish rapport. This can decrease the likelihood of the expert being defensive. If you hate the idea of stroking the expert's ego, suggests psychologist Paula Caplan, don't think of it as an "ego stroke"—think of it as setting a pleasant, cooperative tone.[6] There *is* a difference.

Even if the purpose of your meeting is to present a complaint, resist the temptation to be confrontational or belligerent. Being rude will put the expert on the defensive and make her less likely to grant your request or come up with a suitable solution. I understand how tempting it is to be hostile when you are angry about a problem or issue, but remember to ask yourself what are your goals—to be righteous or to get information and results? The end result of establishing rapport, rather than being rude, is an open channel of communication, where the authority or expert will be more likely to actually *hear* what you say.

QUESTIONS TO BE ANSWERED

At the beginning of your conversation, tell the authority or expert how many questions you'd like to have answered. Ask how much time can be set aside. If it's not enough, ask for more time or another appointment. Confirming these details at the beginning is "setting the agenda." By taking the initiative to set the agenda, you have control and have created a better balance of power. This gives you an advantage. You may want to give the expert a written list of your questions. When you have a list of five clearly important questions, the authorities who really want to help may be less likely to say "Well, our time is up." It can also jolt them into realizing that their time constraints are unreasonable. If the experts are truly professional and reasonable, they will be happy to answer questions. If they are unwilling, you may want to seek advice elsewhere.

By being assertive, you are more likely to get your important questions answered. On the other, be aware of the practical limitations of a long list of questions. Be selective about the questions to be asked. Rank them in order of importance or priority. In any given visit, you may not have time to ask every question that occurs to you. Don't expect the expert to answer too many questions at one time. Suddenly adding more questions toward the end of the meeting is likely to annoy the expert. When I discussed my book idea with one of my physicians, he agreed that a written list of questions or symptoms was very helpful but mentioned that questions thrown at him at the last minute were disruptive to the schedule and put him in an awkward spot. If you have too many questions, you may have to schedule a longer visit or come back another time. Remember that annoying the expert unnecessarily will not help you get want you want.

TAKE NOTES

Bring a notebook with you. As your authority or expert speaks, take careful notes. This may increase your critical thinking as well as theirs. Taking notes forces you to focus on the essence of what's being said and helps you spot inconsistencies. The authority will almost certainly be more careful and responsible about what he is saying if the words will be written down. *Be careful, this can also backfire if he gets defensive.* If the authority reacts defensively, make mental notes instead and write your thoughts down immediately after the meeting. Taking notes that you can refer to later or jotting down notes after the conversation can help you spot lapses in logic or a failure to answer your questions.

The persuasive strategies that authorities use to mold your thinking will have less power over you when you are taking notes. Not only will you be less attentive to such cues while you are taking notes, the act of writing puts you in a more equal give-and-take situation. You are no longer merely a passive supplicant, you are an active participant. This subtle change in the balance of power can have a positive effect on your self-confidence as well as changing the authority's perception of you. Unless the authority becomes defensive, your active participation is likely to enhance your credibility and increase his estimation of your intelligence and seriousness.

ASK TO EXPLAIN JARGON

When experts use highly technical specialized language or say something you don't understand, ask the expert, "Would you please explain that in words I can understand?" Don't be shy about this. Sometimes jargon is used to fool you, sometimes it's just because the experts forget that they're using jargon. Either way, they have an obligation to make things clear to you. Remember that whether you are paying for their services or not, they are, in a psychological sense, in your employ. That means that their job is to provide you with information you can use, not just show off how much they know.

SPOT NONVERBAL CUES

Watch out for the symbols of authority I discussed in Chapter One. This includes dress, arrangement of furniture, and body language. Being aware of them can neutralize any potential negative effect on you. Is there a desk between you and the expert? Push your chair to the side if possible. If that isn't practical, rest your hands or notebook on the desk. Claiming part of the space subtly shifts the power to a more balanced situation. If even that is not practical, mentally remove the desk. If the expert is being particularly pompous or intimidating, imagine him with a silly hat on or use some other mental technique to remove the sting of his manner.

Be aware of your nonverbal body language.[7] Are you slumping over? Sit up straight. Watch out for clues that you are tense or nervous. Don't draw your body in, with arms crossed, shoulders forward. Be expansive. Perhaps put your arms on the arm of the chair instead of meekly in your lap. Make steady eye contact; don't keep looking down. Eye contact, good posture, and expansive gestures, as research shows, are all associated with being perceived as powerful.

WATCH YOUR LANGUAGE

Be alert to your use of language. Language can communicate either power or weakness.[8] Speak carefully and clearly—don't mumble. Put energy into your voice without overdramatizing your concerns. Don't speak too softly. A soft or flat tone makes you sound weak. Avoid sounding whiny or begging. This will turn people off and annoy them or make them take you less seriously. Be crisp, positive and mildly assertive in your tone. Rehearse with friends or family until you feel confident, if necessary. If this seems like "putting on an act," than so be it. Remember the adage "fake it till you make it."

Watch out for other uses of language that can make you appear weak. Tag lines that turn statements into questions (e.g., "This is a good plan, isn't it?") and rising inflections at the end of sentences that, in effect, turn them into questions may be perceived, particularly by men, as indicating uncertainty or lack of confidence.[9] Such language will put you in a power down position. Avoid meaningless words such as "um" or "like" when used as an interjection (e.g., "Like, you know what I mean?"). If you find yourself using language this way, train yourself not to do it, at least in the presence of authorities.

Sometimes a question may contain its own answer. Consider the following scenario and three different ways of stating the same question: a timid student knocks at your door and asks "You don't want to buy a box of band candy, do you?" This sets up the student for defeat. A more neutral way of asking the question is "I'm selling candy to raise money for our school band. Would you like to buy some?" Obviously a better approach. But there's a third way that may be appropriate in some contexts: "Wouldn't you like to buy some band candy?" This assumes already that the customer would like to buy the candy. Same content in all three questions, but the form of the question is likely to affect the outcome. Think about how you state your questions. Don't set yourself up for defeat.

A behavior that puts you in a power down position is letting others interrupt what you are saying. Research shows that men are more likely to interrupt women than vice versa, so if you are female, be especially on your guard.[10] Don't let experts (or your colleagues) interrupt you. Be polite but firm. You might say something like "I know that you have some important points to make, but I also need to state my case. Please let me finish what I'm saying." Or "I think the conversation will go more smoothly if we take turns speaking." It's important to maintain a balance of power in meetings with authorities even if you have to actively challenge them on a behavior that disempowers you.

Another subtle way language can be used by authorities, however unintentionally, to put you in a power down position is through the use of nonparallel uses of names (e.g., the boss is called by her last name, the clerk by his first name). Psychologist Nancy Henley's research, for example, shows the more powerful are likely to be called by their last name and the less powerful by their first name (e.g., boss-secretary, teacher-student, lawyer-client).[11] Unless the custom is so strongly established that questioning it could backfire (e.g., physicians or professors—unless they say otherwise), insist on being addressed as an equal. If your attorney introduces himself as Mr. Jones, ask him to address you as Mr. or Ms. (or Dr., if appropriate!) Smith. If the expert uses her own first name in introducing herself, then by all means, use her first name and allow her to use your first name. Parallel usage is especially important for women because lack of it adds to the subtle power differential that continues to exist between women and men, even in modern society. If the introduction doesn't include exchange of names, you have to make a judgment call about whether it is more appropriate to call the expert by first or last name.

If you have a title (e.g., Ph.D.), use it when appropriate. Occasionally some people are shy about using their Ph.D. because they don't want to appear pompous. False or excessive modesty is a disempowering liability. You probably don't want to use the title with your neighbors, but in encounters with experts and authorities, it will bump up your status considerably, thereby putting you in a more powerful position. Kendra was in a minor arbitration dispute with a university. The arbitrator, being polite, asked her if she preferred to be called "Miss" or "Ms." Recognizing that this was as situation where she needed to appear firm and not weak, Kendra responded brightly, "Actually, it's Dr." Just for the record, she won the arbitration.

DON'T BE INDISCRIMINATELY POLITE

Being polite is the civil thing to do and it's good for establishing rapport too, but don't overdo it. Being excessively polite when it isn't called for puts you in a power down position. Many people have been taught that it's rude to be assertive or that it's not nice to talk back to authority figures. But stop and think about it—is asking questions or standing up for yourself rude? If someone is rude to you or trying to harm you, are you obligated to be polite? Why should you? Don't get stuck in the trap of inappropriate politeness. Don't worry about whether the authorities think you are too pushy or impolite or simply not very nice for asking questions. If they are treating you badly, why should you care what they think of you? Remember the point is not to convince them that you are nice but to get the information you need!

One common example of overpoliteness is apologizing when it is neither necessary nor appropriate. If you are paying the expert, you have nothing to apologize for. Even if you are not paying them, they are presenting themselves as experts who can provide advice—that's their job. You are not imposing on them; don't act like you are. Here's a typical example. I had a student once—a 50-ish woman, intelligent but oversocialized to be polite. Nina kept apologizing for asking questions and even for coming to my office hours. I gently told her that my office hours were for her benefit, not mine, so she didn't need to apologize. I did not interpret her behavior as weak, but it's likely that she was overly apologetic in other contexts where her deferent attitude would be interpreted negatively.

Apparently being overly apologetic is a common problem that many women recognize in themselves. Whenever I talk about it in class, I always see heads nodding. Depending on your culture or your gender, some of you may have been conditioned to be polite in every encounter and to avoid being confrontational at all costs. My advice is—get over it! If someone is acting boorish, being condescending, or worse yet, trying to pull a fast one because you are a woman or from a non-American culture, *they* are the rude ones, not you. Once they step over the line of civil behavior, they are no longer automatically entitled to polite treatment. Don't let yourself be intimidated by their boorishness.

TAKE TIME TO THINK

Experts, for example, salespeople, often use high-pressure techniques to get you to go along with them. "This special offer ends soon, act now . . ." or "We need your decision right now . . ." are examples of common ploys. If you are being pressured to make a decision or agree to something in a voluntary situation (this suggestion won't work if you are stopped by the police!), ask for time to think about it. Sometimes just taking a few minutes to think outside the expert's presence and power can give you the mental and emotional space you need to think clearly. Have a set of standard phrases prepared that you can use when necessary, for example, "Your suggestion is very interesting. Let me think it over and get back to you" or "My policy is to always think about any important decision for a few days." Get things in writing. If the expert still pressures you, just leave and don't come back.

LOOK FOR BIAS

Think about whether vested interests, close-minded points of view, stereotyping, or prejudice are present in your encounter with the authority or expert. When you recount your interactions with authorities to your friends and family, ask them if they hear signs that the authorities are biased. For example, is the plumber pushing you to OK an expensive redo of all the plumbing in the house without convincing you of the need? Maybe he just wants to inflate his bill. Does your therapist seem intent on getting you to blame your family even if you had a good relationship with them? Ask yourself whether you feel uncomfortable about pressure from the expert. If you do, then it's a smart idea to examine what he or she is saying more closely.

Be aware of how aspects of your appearance can potentially have an impact on how you are perceived. Be alert for the possibility of bias based on stereotyping—on the basis of age (too young or too old), ethnicity, occupation or other factors about you. Take our earlier example of Krystal, the black woman who wore a suit to see her daughter's physician. Every black person is aware that subtle, unrecognized stereotypes may be operating against them when they are dealing with white people. Because the business suit made her look like the professional she is, wearing it helped offset some of that potential stereotyping.

Age is another potential basis for stereotyping that can interfere with effective interactions with authorities and experts. Donna took her aging mother, Beatrice, to the doctor's office. Beatrice had a double strike against her—she was in her 70's and was hearing-impaired. The hearing problem made her seem less alert than she actually was. Even though she was intelligent and not the least bit senile, the physician was condescending in his tone and spoke more to Donna than to Beatrice. What Donna should have done was politely but firmly say to the doctor that her mother was hard of hear, then ask him to speak up a little more loudly and talk directly to Beatrice. Ageism is a kind of prejudice. Don't let experts treat you or your loved ones differently simply because you (or they) are older.

At the opposite end of the age spectrum, young people often have trouble being treated appropriately. If you think you look too young to be taken seriously, take steps to give yourself more credibility and bridge the generation/culture gap. Wear professional-looking or dressy casual clothes to your appointment. Don't wear the latest fads or your old comfy jeans. Save that for your friends. Be careful of your language and tone. Don't use slang that makes you look flip or that might not be understood by an older generation. Be professional in your demeanor. However, in my experience, many young people today are just as likely to be snippy and rude as deferent and unsure of themselves. Being snippy and flip with authorities may be emotionally satisfying, but it won't get you what you want. It won't make you look more powerful, it will just make you look too immature to be taken seriously.

If you run the risk of being stereotyped in other ways, whatever it may be, offset its possible effect by dressing smartly, being courteous, speaking clearly and calmly, being well-prepared, and asking intelligent questions.

BRING BACKUP

Emotions or overinvolvement in an issue can make it hard for you to be composed or objective. If you are seeking advice about a complicated or emotionally charged issue, bringing a friend or relative along as backup can be very beneficial. The police do it when responding to a dangerous or suspicious call; you should too. Another person can be a more objective observer than you and provide you with moral support to boot. If, for example, you are seeing a medical doctor about a life-threatening disease, a trusted friend can calmly ask the questions you are too upset to think of at the time. If you need to talk to a lawyer about a complicated legal issue that is upsetting to you, someone less emotionally entangled in the issue may be able to help you get through the meeting better than you could on your own. Having a friend along will also make the situation seem less intimidating.

If you need to buy a product or obtain technical services that you know nothing about, having a more knowledgeable person along may save you from spending unnecessary money or getting something you don't need. If, for example, you want to buy a new computer but don't know a floppy drive from a motherboard, having a computer whiz along to ask about all the right features will increase your chances of getting what you really need and nothing more. Businesses make frequent use of consultants; you can too.

Gender stereotypes can have a big impact here. Women especially have to watch out for shady dealings when it comes to products and services traditionally associated with males. A sly kind of sexism sometimes occurs when a woman is buying, for example, a computer or a car or, most classic of all, taking her car to a new mechanic. The mere presence of a male, even if he wouldn't know a carburetor if it came up and tipped its hat, will discourage most shyster attempts. If this seems too old-fashioned and even a little sexist, ask yourself what's more important—

making an ideological statement or getting what you want without getting ripped off?

ASK: ARE YOU BEING TREATED FAIRLY?

Consider whether the suggestion by the expert seems unfair or inconsistent. If you yourself are the one who needs help from the system, always ask yourself, "If my parent or child or best friend were being dealt with in this way, would I consider it unfair, biased, or cavalier? In what way? Is the authority simply too rushed to give me a full explanation of what is happening? Would I be furious if he treated someone I care about in that way?" It's often easier to see unfairness when we imagine others in the situation rather than ourselves.

When Chuck was in junior high school, he took French and English classes during the summer. Even though he got 100% on the final exams, the high school he transferred to refused to give him credit. Insisting that the rule was hard and fast, the person he spoke to in the administrative office claimed that they did not give credit for work done at other schools. Though reluctant to speak up, he realized that if this had happened to his sister, he would have been furious. He also realized that no one was likely to pay attention to a 13-year-old so he told his father, Sam, about it. The father made an appointment with the principal the next day. At first the principal quoted the rules, as expected. But Sam, insisting that the rules were unfair, kept pointing out that Chuck had spent the whole hot summer studying instead of playing like the other kids. The principal was so impressed with Sam's appeal that Chuck was granted credit for both classes.

Let me be clear on one thing. My advice is not intended for people who want to con the system themselves. Be honest with yourself about whether you are actually being treated unfairly. Chuck had a legitimate gripe. He has taken the classes in good faith, done well in them, and has a perfectly reasonable expectation that the credits would be transferable. That isn't always the case. Linda, an 8th-grade teacher, had a student who was warned time and time again, along with her parents, that failing grades would keep her from graduating. When it came time for graduation and it was clear that Dana, the student, was not going to getting the diploma, her parents accused Linda of having it in for Dana. They were unwilling or unable to see that Dana was the problem, not the teacher.

If your gripe is unfair, take responsibility for it and accept the negative consequences. Being honorable is more important than winning at all costs. Just on a practical level, asking for what you don't deserve can easily backfire and make the authority resentful and even less likely to help you.

WATCH FOR LIES

Watch for blatantly false or highly suspicious statements. Psychologist Paula Caplan gives the example of an "expert" who claimed that the (alleged) fact that there are no women chess masters suggested to him that women's spatial abilities are inferior.[12] This outrageous statement so startled her that she questioned his other, more complex claims too. (There *are* women chess masters, by the way).[13] The claims of salespeople are especially suspect. While at a beauty supply house to buy shampoo, Betty was told by the clerk that using the shampoo available at drug stores was like washing with Ajax cleanser. Betty was willing to believe that some of the more expensive shampoos were better in quality, but this statement was just too much. She left without buying anything. If an expert makes a statement that you find questionable or offensive, don't just ignore it. It's a red flag telling you to be alert and summon your critical thinking skills.

ASK FOR WRITTEN INFORMATION

Information gathering doesn't just occur before your meeting with experts. Always ask for written information when it's appropriate. Ask for brochures or articles that you can take away with you, so that you can think critically about the issues when you are on your own or with friends or family. If no written material is available from the expert, ask for lay references you can look up for yourself online or in a library. Not only do you want all the information that you can comfortably digest to help you make decisions, asking for more information will give you more credibility with the expert. She will see that you are serious and willing to be an active, intelligent participant in dealing with the problem.

Look for relevant material on the Internet. Learn to use search engines effectively. Here are a few suggestions for those unfamiliar with searches (yes, such people exist, and include some of my friends). Start with the major directory/search sites, such as Google or Yahoo. If you get too many hits to look through, narrow the search by including additional terms. For example, "plumbers" is too general; you will get thousands of hits. "Plumbers complaints" still gets too many. "Plumbers complaints California" gets the California State Contractors Licensing Board, complete with instructions on filing a complaint.

Watch for synonyms and equivalent terms. For example, what we call an "intercom", the Navy calls "Interior Communications"; the Air Force and Naval Aviation like to use the acronym "ICS." If you were looking for industrial strength intercoms for a business, you would never find the vendors who sell mostly to the Military without including their jargon. You may have to poke around a bit till you see what terms are going to work for you.

Most search/directory sites have a "help" button to assist with search tips; most of them also have an "advanced" button, allowing more complex searches. For example, searching on "interior communications" gets lots of resumes where people have had this type of training in the Military. The advanced search allows you to search on "interior communications" and filter out any hits with the word "resume" in them. Play around for a while till you get the hang of it. Also try more than one search engine. Though Google is the biggie, others may be useful too and less full of annoying commercial sites that may not be what you are looking for.

Check out different web sites, shop around for different sources. But watch out for flaky answers. There's a lot of space cadet stuff on the Internet. Apply your critical thinking skills to find sensible information and consensus from experts with appropriate credentials. See the Resources section below for some materials that can help you be a critical consumer of online resources.

CHECK FOR OPTIONS

The advice, program, or solution the expert offers may not be your only choice. Be aware of your range of options. If the problem is serious or expensive, you may want to ask for advice from another expert. The "second opinion" is a standard feature of modern medical practice; why not extend it to other kinds of expert advice? In other kinds of situations, check with your friends or other people who have been through the same system about the full range of options for dealing with the problem or topic. Let them act as your "consultants."

Look for alternative sources of information. If you have physical symptoms that physicians can't alleviate, for example, explore the nonmedical alternatives. Certain nontraditional practices may have value in the right circumstances. If you have gotten poor results from high-priced lawyers or therapists, consider other lower-priced options such as paralegal clinics or sliding-scale therapy clinics. The Internet is often the most effective way to shop for options but don't overlook librarians. They are trained to search for information and they love to be asked to help. If your local library is limited, try the nearest college library. There's usually a way for local residents to get a library card or access to a college library.

CONSULT WITH OTHERS

Getting feedback from trusted others is a good way to get an objective perspective. Tell friends and family members what the authorities are saying to you and have a brainstorming session with them aimed at identifying which questions you need to ask and which ones you have asked, but remain unanswered. It's easier to apply critical thinking when you're not in the immediate presence of intimidating authority.

ASK WHO ELSE CAN HELP

Don't assume that the expert you are dealing with is the only one who can solve the problem. If the authority with whom you are currently dealing is not helping you or is seriously upsetting you, think about who else might be more willing to help. Don't just passively accept the unsatisfactory answer you've been given. Frequently, going up the chain of command can bring satisfaction. If a clerk or low-level bureaucrat, for example, is telling you he can't help you, ask for his supervisor. The further up, the more likely the authority is to be cooperative. Because they have more decision-making power than low-level clerks, managers and supervisors are much more likely to be willing to help you. Here's a typical scenario: Martin had forgotten to make a credit card payment and discovered that the deadline was that day so he called to make a by-phone payment. The call representative pointed out that Martin had missed the company's deadline by several hours (even through it was still the same day). When the call rep said she couldn't help him, Martin insisted on talking to the supervisor. The supervisor was willing to waive the late fee. Don't assume, however, that asking for the supervisor will always get you what you want. If you are asking for something unfair or clearly beyond the rules, don't expect to win just because you complain. The authorities are going to be more cooperative if they see that your issue has reasonable grounds.

MODEL SOMEONE ELSE

> *"What would Xena do?"*
> —1990s bumper sticker

Here's a method that can help you if dealing with authorities is difficult for you. Think of someone you see as a calm person who handles him/herself well. It can be someone you know personally or even be a character from a book, movie, or TV. Think about his or her behavior and attitude and use it as a model. Ask yourself how that person would act in such a situation. When you are feeling too intimidated to ask questions or push for answers, pretend (in your own mind) that you are this model person who is calm, unintimidated and powerful in every situation. A clever bumper sticker manufacturer has apparently caught on to this idea and issued a "What would Xena do?" sticker. For those of you who missed the TV series, Xena, the "warrior princess," was not only calm and unruffled by even the most calamitous situations, she kicked serious derriere too. Xena may not be your cup of mocha latte, but you can pick someone who is meaningful to you.

PRACTICE, PRACTICE, PRACTICE

If some of the techniques that I've suggested in this chapter seem foreign to you, you can learn to feel more at ease with them. The key is practice. Try a little role-playing with a friend. Keeping your chosen role model's example in mind, pretend that your friend is the expert you need to consult and act out a possible scenario. It may sound like a strange thing to do, but practicing ahead of time will make the actual encounter seem more familiar and less overwhelming. Even reading the list of questions you have prepared aloud will make you less likely to stumble and stutter when you are in the real-life situation. Remember that new skills always take time to learn. You wobbled when you got on a bicycle for the first time but after a little practice, it was a snap. Standing up to intimidating authorities may never become a "snap" but you *can* learn to do it with enough ease to get you through. It's up to you.

RESOURCES

BOOKS

Patti Breitman and Connie Hatch. *How to Say No Without Feeling Guilty*. New York: Broadway Books, 2001. Lots of practical tips on how to say no in nice ways to family, friends, dates, and high maintenance people. Friends and family may not be "experts and authorities" but the suggestions in this book can help you with other kinds of people too.

M. Neil G. Browne and Stuart M. Keeley. *Evaluating Online Resources*. Upper Saddle, NJ: Prentice Hall, 2002.

Guidelines by two professors on how to think critically about web sites.

Paula J. Caplan. *You're Smarter Than They Make You Feel: How the Experts Intimidate Us and What We Can Do About It.* New York: Free Press, 1994. This unfortunately out-of-print book has many excellent suggestions for standing up to experts.

Robert Cialdini. *Influence.* Boston: Allyn & Bacon, 2000. (available in many editions; I have another edition and publisher listed in a different chapter!) Cialdini's book is both substantive and engaging, with both research and suggestions.

Nancy Henley. *Body Politics: Power, Sex, and Nonverbal Communication.* Englewood Cliffs, NJ: Prentice-Hall, 1977. The psychology of gender, nonverbal behavior and power.

Anne P. Mintz. (Ed.) *Web of Deception: Misinformation on the Internet.* Medford, NJ: CyberAge Books, 2002. This book is a gold mine of in-depth information about the scams and misinformation on the Internet.

WEB SITES

Critical Thinking about Authority and Influence

[also see references in Chapter One]

Resources for Independent Thinking
www.rit.org
A nonprofit educational organization with articles, tapes, and other materials that encourage critical thinking about authority. Some of these articles formed the basis for the book you are now reading.

Lucifer Effect
www.lucifereffect.com
The web site for Dr. Zimbardo's book (see Chapter One) has many resources and articles dealing with critical thinking about influence and unjust authority and how to resist. The articles include:

- "A Ten-Step Program to Build Resistance and Resilience"
- "Reversing the Process of Good People Turning Evil: Positive Social Influence and Civic Virtue"
- "Dr. Z's 20 Hints about Resisting Unwanted Influences on You"
- "Why We Conform: The Power of Groups"
- "Resisting Influence"
- "Celebrating Heroism"

Stanley Milgram
www.stanleymilgram.com
Biographer Thomas Blass's web site for Dr. Stanley Milgram. There are untold thousands of references on the Internet to the Milgram experiment and his conclusions about how easily people obey unjust authority. This is a place to start.

"Resisting the Temptation of Authority"
www.pickthebrain.com/blog/resist-the-temptation-to-submit-to-authority

"Questioning Authority—Excerpts from the book *Trust Us, We're Experts*"
www.thirdworldtraveler.com/Public_Relations/Question_Authority_TUWE.html

"Normative Social Influence"
www.changingminds.org/explanations/theories/normative_social_influence.htm
Suggestions for resisting the effects of social influence.

Social Influence
www.rickross.com/reference/brainwashing/brainwashing20.html
A summary of Robert Cialdini's ideas on social influence.

"The Sexual Politics of Interpersonal Behavior" by Nancy Henley and Jo Freeman
www.jofreeman.com/womensociety/personal.htm
Article on body politics, nonverbal behavior and gender.

Critical Thinking about Web Sites on the Internet

"A Guide to Critical Thinking about What You See On the World Wide Web."
www.ithaca.edu/library/training/think.html

"Thinking Critically about World Wide Web Resources"
http://www.mscare.org/cmsc/Articles-Thinking-Critically-about-World-Wide-Web-Resources.html

"Evaluating Web Pages: Techniques to Apply & Questions to Ask"
www.lib.berkeley.edu/TeachingLib/Guides/Internet/Evaluate.html

"How to Evaluate A Web Site"
www.llrx.com/features/webeval.htm

Snopes
www.snopes.com
With the tag line "Rumor has it," Snopes is *the* place to find out if the stories you read on the Internet or in your email are true or "urban legends." Lots of info about many kinds of scams and frauds.

HOW TO DO WEB SEARCHES

Pandia.com
www.pandia.com/goalgetter/
Billed as a "short and easy search engine tutorial."

Media Awareness Network
www.media-awareness.ca/english/resources/special_initiatives/wa_resources/wa_teachers/tipsheets/search_internet_effectively.cfm
An article on "How to search the Internet effectively."

UPDATES

For updates on books, web sites, web site URLs and links (they sometimes change), articles and other relevant information, check the web site for my book: www.standuptoauthorities.com.

PART
II

Wrestling with Professionals without Getting Bruised

CHAPTER
3

Don't Trust Me, I'm a Doctor: Questioning Physicians, Psychologists and Psychiatrists

Rosa's grandmother had a foot problem which her physician diagnosed as athlete's foot, but the ointment and medicine prescribed did little good. Not only did the condition not go away, her hands and feet became extremely cold. She finally had to be taken to the emergency room when a cut on her toe became swollen and discolored. A foot specialist there told her that she never had athlete's foot, she had diabetes. She had been misdiagnosed all the time! The woman's toe had to be amputated right away because of infection and blood clotting. Too bad she didn't question her physician sooner.

GOING TO A PHYSICIAN, even for a routine visit, can be a bit disconcerting. Visiting one when you're really worried about some strange symptom can be totally unnerving. Physicians can be intimidating so it's easy to just go along with what they say without questioning. But medical mistakes happen all the time. Godlike as some physicians want us to believe they are, they are human beings like the rest of us. Critical thinking and willingness to challenge an expert, as the above scenario shows, is as necessary with medical professionals as with any other kind of expert.

Other experts in the medical and mental health fields with degrees after their names can be just as intimidating. There's a mystique surrounding psychologists and psychiatrists as well, but, contrary to this mystique, they don't, in fact, have x-ray vision into your psyche. They can make mistakes or give bad advice just as physicians can, so your dealings with them also require critical thinking and assertiveness.

In this chapter, my advice is intended for dealing with individual doctors and hospital staff. Chapter 8, which deals with consumer complaints, addresses the problem of dealing with medical insurance companies, a whole issue in itself!

PHYSICIANS

There are a number of excellent books on critical thinking about physicians. I'd like to share some of their advice with you and apply the methods I detailed in Chapter 2 to that advice.

Preparing ahead of time to deal with experts begins with picking a good doctor. Just as in any profession, there *are* bad doctors, points out Timothy McCall, M.D., author of *Examining Your Doctor*.[1] According to McCall, a UCLA/Rand Corporation study found that 27% of all deaths overall in hospitals are caused by poor quality medical care.[2] Most problems don't stem from the kind of sensational malpractice cases played up by newspapers. Most come from careless examinations, too many tests, unnecessary surgery, risky drugs—all problems that critical thinking and asking questions could help prevent.

LOOK AT CREDENTIALS

Don't just pick a physician out of the phone book—or out of your health insurance company's list of approved physicians! And just because your Uncle Jim likes Dr. Brown doesn't necessarily mean she's the right doctor for you. Friends and family may respond on the basis of whether they like the physician personally, not necessarily on the doctor's competence. Here's what

> **Key Concepts**
>
> - Look up credentials
> - Be prepared
> - Have questions in writing
> - Question procedures
> - Seek second opinions
> - Seek alternative information

else McCall and others suggest *not* to use as guides: Forget physician referral services; they're just glorified ads. Don't necessarily use other physicians' recommendations either. "Doctors," says McCall, "commonly refer patients to doctors they wouldn't choose for themselves."[3] And you thought that a physician referral would be a good idea! No doubt many referrals are good; but be careful. There may be better ways to pick a doctor, particularly if what you need is a specialist.

What several of the books critiquing physicians recommend is to ask insiders. Residents and hospital nurses who work with physicians will be more objective—if you ask them off the record. They can be an especially valuable resource for seeking a specialist. You might have to drop by your local hospital to get their names and contact numbers, but it'll be worth the effort if you get good advice.

You also want to look carefully at the physician's credentials. Did he or she attend a US medical school (all US schools are accredited). Schools outside the US may be more variable in quality. Where did he train after medical school? What kind of rating does the hospital where he served their internship and residence have? University hospitals have the most prestige but may also turn out "super specialists" who may be too narrowly focused for your problem.

If you need a specialist, you should check to make sure she is Board Certified in her specialty. This certification requires a complete training program and a rigorous exam. Not all physicians who call themselves "specialists" are board certified. One study found that 67% of allergists and 43% of plastic surgeons have not met this requirement.[4] Do you want someone who hasn't had the right training and proved she understands her specialty messing with your face? Of course not. But how do you find that information? The American Board of Medical Specialties will send you a free directory by calling 1-800-776-CERT or you can go online to its web site at www.abms.org.

Another wise precaution is to make sure that the physician you have in mind has no black marks against his or her record. The American Medical Association won't tell you but the National Practitioner Data Bank will. It collects information on disciplinary actions and malpractice payments. The best source on disciplinary actions by state medical boards is the Public Citizen Health Research Group (www.citizen.org).

RIGHT TO QUESTION

Once you've picked a physician, you need to look at how you are treated. Does he take enough time with you? Does she allow you to ask questions without brushing them aside? Does he really listen to what you have to say and ask careful questions about your symptoms? Does she treat you in a patronizing way or does she treat you like an equal? You want a doctor who will work with you, not dictate to you from "on high."

Isadore Rosenfeld, M.D., author of *Power to the Patient*, points out that you have the right to be fully informed about your health status and your physician's qualifications.[5] If you need surgery, you have the right to know your surgeon's and hospital's track records for the procedure you need. How many operations of this kind has the surgeon done? What is the success rate? How does this compare to other hospitals? How many year of experience does the surgeon have? The best source of this information, suggests Rosenfeld, is the hospital administration.

Make sure your physician is up-to-date on the latest research and standards. Ask about what he or she does to keep up with new developments in the field. Younger physicians may be more hip. A Harvard Medical School study found that doctors who graduated from medical school 20 years ago were 38 to 48% less likely to follow current standards. Death rates from heart attacks increased as length of time in practice increased. Older doctors were more likely to under-treat depression, breast cancer and high blood pressure. On the other hand, older doctors, because they have more experience, were better at diagnosing complex medical problems.[6]

BE PREPARED: GETTING READY FOR THE VISIT TO THE PHYSICIAN

If this is your first visit to a new physician, think about what kind of information would be helpful: medical records such as X-rays from a previous physician, names and dosages of drugs you are currently taking, any drugs you are allergic to, family medical history, personal health logs, and so on. Request previous medical records and write down pertinent information. Organize and make notes on your health situation in a concise way. What are your symptoms? Be as specific as possible, noting physical effects, frequency of occurrence, time of day the symptoms occur and other possibly useful information.

Do your homework. Look up your symptoms on the Internet at a site such as webmd.com or from a good reference book, such as *Taking Care: Self-Care for 100 Common Symptoms and 20 Long-Term Ailments* by Michael B. Jacobs M.D. and colleagues or *Power to the Patient* by Isadore Rosenfeld. Rosenfeld's book, for example, offers recent information on diagnosis and treatment of most common ailments. He spells out what medicine and tests to insist on. Do some research on the prescription drugs that may be relevant to your condition. Note the side-effects of the drugs so you can discuss them with your physician.

When going into the hospital, bringing a record of your medical history is a good idea. Include your primary physician's name and number, your allergies, a list of all your medications, and the name and number of the person to contact in an emergency. Lots of mistakes occur in hospitals, so having your medical record may cut down on the chance of the staff screwing up.

PUT IT IN WRITING

From this information, prepare a list of questions that you want to ask the physician. Include not only obvious questions such as "What do the symptoms mean?" but also the following: "What are the possible treatments?" "What are the risks associated with the treatment?" "What are the potential side-effects of the treatment?" "How likely are the side-effects of the medicines?" Here's where your prior research allows you to ask the right questions. If relevant, ask about the course of the disease: "Is it progressive?" "Are there possible complications?" "Does the family need to be alerted to any issues?" "Are there organizations or support groups that can provide help?"

PSYCHING YOURSELF UP

Go in to the visit with the attitude that you want to be an active patient, not just a passive recipient of pronouncements from the doctor. A study reported by Carol Svec, author of *After Any Diagnosis*, found that passive, uninformed patients were more depressed, functioned less well and recovered less quickly than more active patients.[7] Mind and body do work together, as any health psychologist can tell you.

QUESTIONING PROCEDURE

Don't hesitate to question medical procedures that don't make sense to you. Ask for an explanation from your physician. Before actually talking to your doctor, for example, a nurse or physician's assistant typically takes your blood pressure and your weight. This is normal, but occasionally she may go beyond this routine. Once in a while she may ask you to do something that the physician hasn't ordered. Don't be afraid to question why. Dan, for example, was in for second visit to a podiatrist for a possible broken toe. The assistant got out a TENS unit, a nerve stimulation device that can reduce pain, and was going to hook it up to Dan's toe. The doctor had not discussed this with Dan, so he protested. The doctor never mentioned it when he came in, so Dan concluded that the assistant had gotten confused about his condition and that it was appropriate to speak up.

Physicians themselves make mistakes. Medication errors are widespread, according to a recent report by the Institute of Medicine.[8] Such errors harm 1.5 million people per year and kill several thousand. One tragic example is the case of Betsy Lehman, who died after her doctor mistakenly gave her four times the appropriate dose of a toxic drug for her breast cancer. Be informed about dosages by talking to your pharmacist or researching the drug on the Internet. Be sure to inform your doctor or the hospital of other drugs you are taking.

Questioning procedure is even more important in a hospital setting. The horror stories abound as in the case of Rhode Island Hospital, which had *three* cases of wrong-side brain surgery in *one* year.[9] Two of the patients recovered but one died. However, the worst problems, as I noted previously, are not the high-profile cases that lead to malpractice suits. According to an article in the *AARP Bulletin*, hospital-acquired (nosocomial) infections are the eighth-leading cause of death in the US.[10] Katharine Greider, the author of this chilling article and a specialist in medical issues, provides a number of horror stories about people who died, not from their illnesses per se, but from infections they caught in the hospital. Many hospitals, she reports, are not as careful about controlling infections as they should be. Procedures that are not conducive to safety should be questioned. If nurses or other staff members, for example, do not wash their hands before touching the patient, they can spread staph or other infections. Be alert to careless practices and don't put up with them.

Sometimes the policies and procedures in hospitals are arbitrary rules that don't always make sense. Deanne was in a semi-private room in the hospital, but she was the only patient in the room at the time. Several friends wanted to see her but, because of their busy schedules, they were limited in the times they could visit. When one of the visits extended past regular visiting hours, the nurse came in and demanded that the visitor leave. Deanne tried to explain that her visitors had difficult schedules and that there was no other patient for the noise to bother. The nurse didn't care. Deanne refused to make the visitor leave. Another nurse came in and gave the same canned speech about visiting hours. Deanne demanded to talk to a hospital administrator. When an administrator who had been leaving the building finally showed up with her ID badge ostentatiously (and inappropriately) displayed on her raincoat, Deanne knew she had won. Once again, she explained the situation to the administrator. Because Deanne, though polite, was very firm and assertive, the administrator, sensing defeat, backed down.

Hospital staff can sometimes make mistakes. You should be alert for such possibilities. Here's a mild example but there are many stories with far more drastic consequences. Monica was a diabetic who was in the hospital for an unrelated matter. She overheard a nurse outside her room explaining to a student nurse how to do an insulin injection. Monica had two problems with this scenario—she wasn't about to let this inexperienced nurse use her as a guinea pig nor did she use insulin injections to control her diabetes! She adamantly refused to let the nurse give her the injection. If you think a procedure is wrong, don't hesitate to speak up and say no. You have the right to refuse any procedure you want! Let me repeat; you can refuse any procedure you want. Look at that set of papers they give you when you check into the hospital—the one that spells out your rights as a patient.

Sometimes, in spite of the fact that you have the right to refuse medication, the staff may ignore you if they think you are, for example, too sedated to know what you are saying. You may have to resort to extreme measures, if the consequences could be drastic. Here's a horror story that I decided to quote in full because readers need to know that this can happen. Forewarned is forearmed, as they say. It would have had a tragic ending if Cheryl, the patient, had not been both quick-witted and adamant.

> "I was in the hospital being prepped to receive chemotherapy. I had been through many cycles of treatment already, and pretty much knew what to expect. I would be in the hospital for five days, receiving several large infusions of Adriamycin and a smaller infusion of Cisplatin, which is the more toxic of the two chemicals.
>
> A doctor I had never met before came into the room with several underlings. He took a cursory look at my chart and then "gave the orders" for the doses to be administered. I was listening to him, and noticed he had reversed the doses by mistake. The doc had ordered a large amount of Cisplatin, and a small amount of Adriamycin, then breezed out of the room before I could point this out to him.
>
> I told the underlings that a mistake had been made. They didn't take me seriously. I asked them to go find the doctor and bring him back. They refused. I told them if they gave me the doses he ordered, it would kill me. They told me I was under the influence of sedatives and that everything was fine. I began to panic. I knew they would soon be giving me a lethal dose unless I could convince them to listen. To my horror, no matter what I said, they wouldn't go check it out for me.
>
> When I started threatening to pull out the needles and leave, they decided I needed more sedatives. Realizing I only had a few moments before they would knock me out completely, I did the only thing left I could think of: I picked up the phone from my hospital bed and dialed 911 to report that the hospital was about to murder me. I told the operator that a mistake in doses had been made, that nobody would

listen to me, and that when I ended up dead, I'd like this recorded call for help to be broadcast on the news. When the hospital staff realized who I was talking to, they were horrified. As an effort to shut me up, one of the nurses FINALLY went to double check the orders. Thankfully after that, the doses were straightened out. Those assholes never did apologize to me though.

Not all of the stories like this have happy endings. Always be alert if you are in a hospital. Do not *ever* hesitate to protest something that doesn't make sense or that troubles you. As Cheryl's case shows, your life may depend on it.

TALKING WITH YOUR PHYSICIAN

Tell your physician that you want to be an active participant in your health care. If the doctor seems put off by that approach, consider getting another doctor. You want your physician to be your ally, not an antagonist. Show him your list of questions and ask if there will be enough time to go over the list. If you confidently ask for quality time and show you are a thoughtful person who has carefully prepared for the visit, you have a better chance of getting the kind of health care you want.

Go over the information you have prepared with your physician, Be entirely open about all your symptoms but describe them objectively, not in an overly emotional way. Be sure to tell your physician what drugs you are currently taking and ask about possible interactions with any new drug prescribed. If there isn't enough time to discuss every question on the list, ask the physician for a return visit.

Here are the questions about prescriptions that the American Pharmacists Association suggests that you ask your physician or pharmacist: [11]

- What is the medication's name? What is it supposed to do?
- How and when do I take my medication?
- How long should I take it?
- What about taking other medications or drinking alcohol at the same time?

- Should I change my activities?
- Could this medication give me an allergic reaction?
- Should I expect any side effects?
- What if I'm pregnant or breastfeeding?
- How should I store my medication?

If your physician is unwilling or unable to answer these questions, your pharmacist will be more than willing to do so. The American Pharmacists Association provides a useful and informative web site for consumers at http://www.pharmacyandyou.org. To its list, I would add: What about interactions with diet or vitamin or other supplements? Asking these questions will help you avoid medication errors, which as I noted above, is appallingly common.

TAKE NOTES

Carefully write down your physician's answers to the questions you ask about treatment options, medicines, side-effects, and the like. You can use these notes later to assess whether you are satisfied with the visit, to devise a list of questions for the next visit, or to investigate further on the Internet. Also remember that taking notes tells the physician that you are serious about being an active participant.

CLEAR UP JARGON

If the physician uses medical jargon you don't understand, ask for an explanation in plain language. Don't be afraid to say "I don't understand. Would you please explain?" Remember that the doctor is working for *you*. You not only need to understand your medical situation, you have a right to ask so that you *can* understand.

On the other hand, if the physician talks to you in a condescending, simplistic manner, don't let him get away with it. Ask for further in-depth explanations. Tell him that you would prefer a more specific explanation, even if it means he has to use medical terms.

BRING BACKUP

If you have or suspect a serious or life-threatening illness, bring a friend or family member with you. You may, understandably, be too emotionally wrapped up in your problem to ask objective questions. Let your personal ally ask the questions that you may be too upset to ask. If the diagnosis is life-threatening, have your ally ask whether the diagnosis is certain, what the risks associated with the treatment options are, if the treatments are controversial, risky or experimental, whether there other approaches or treatments, and if a second opinion is advisable.

Bringing a family member along may have another benefit. According to a study reported in Svec's book, doctors spend more time with a patient if the family is present.[12] It's one more way to be taken seriously.

SECOND OPINIONS

With some diagnoses, you may want to ask for a second opinion just as a matter of course; for example, if the diagnosis is life-threatening or uncertain. If the treatments or drugs are experimental, controversial or risky, a second opinion is likely to be in order.

If you are unsatisfied with the results of your visit or your treatment, don't hesitate to ask for a second opinion or seek another physician. Physicians don't always get it right, especially if they are not specialists. Georgina, for example, had a serious rash on her hand that was itchy, red and weepy. The medication that her internist gave her seemed to do no good at all. Finally, she wised up and went to a dermatologist, who diagnosed the exact condition and gave her a different prescription. The rash cleared up almost immediately.

Rosa, whose grandmother lost her toe, was one of my students. If she had taken one of my classes sooner, I would have told her that the grandmother should immediately go to a podiatrist or other specialist for a second opinion. Athlete's foot is not hard to treat; something else was clearly wrong. Even an Internet search on the symptoms could have told them that diabetes was a better bet as a diagnosis than athlete's foot. I can't know what was going on in the physician's mind who gave her such bad advice but one thought that occurs to me is that the elderly are not always taken as seriously as they should. Or perhaps she was unable to communicate her symptoms effectively. Here's where an ally accompanying the grandmother might have helped.

SEEK ALTERNATIVE INFORMATION

Don't simply passively depend on what the physician tells you or the treatment prescribed. Look up the latest information about your problem. "Most doctors are practicing 10 to 20 years behind the available medical literature and continue to practice what they learned in medical school," says William Shankle, M.D., Professor, University of California, Irvine. "Doctors do not seek to implement new treatments that are supported in the literature or change treatments that are not."[13]

Several books and web sites offer information about symptoms. Sometimes matching up symptoms with diagnosis can help you figure out whether a second opinion is a good idea. Try to find a book that is less than four years old and is written by a physician or someone with reasonable credentials and endorsements from medical doctors. A few suggestions are in the Resources section at the end of this chapter.

A good source of online information if you have questions about the safety or efficacy of the treatments being suggested is the Public Citizen Health Research Group website (www.citizen.org). This independently funded organization gives useful warnings about medications, medical equipment, over-the-counter remedies and other health treatments that are known to have adverse side effects. It also offers a monthly newsletter to help you keep up with the latest health issues.

Look up information about the drugs you are prescribed. Physicians are not always as well-informed as they should be and some blindly prescribe whatever the pharmaceutical reps are pushing. This is old news but well worth keeping in mind. Newer is not necessarily better; safety and efficacy are more important than free samples. Some states have even started "unsales" programs to train reps to give nonbiased information to physicians.[14] You can read some unbiased information about drugs for yourself in *Powerful Medicines: The Benefits, Risks and Costs of Prescription Drugs* by Jerry Avorn, M.D.

ALTERNATIVE OPTIONS

Sometimes, it may pay to investigate alternative options outside the conventional treatments. This doesn't mean taking weird concoctions suggested by your Aunt Marcia or some dubious treatment by well-meaning but air-headed New Agers (there's lots of nutty stuff out there) or other nonprofessionals. It means finding and looking critically and thoughtfully at alternatives that have a track record of success and have been examined by medical practitioners. There are many stories of people who have been unsatisfied with the advice of their physician. When the treatments didn't work, they looked elsewhere, often with success. Two useful books that explore reasonable alternative options are *Own Your Health* by Roanne Weisman with Brian Berman, M.D., and *The Best of Alternative Medicine: What Works? What Does Not Work?* by Kenneth Pelletier, M.D. Conventional physicians and skeptics scoff at many alternative treatments, but the number of success stories suggests that you may want to read and then decide for yourself. Even skeptics can sometimes be dogmatically wrong.

A typical story is the case of Jacqueline Miller, which is described in Weisman's book.[15] In 1997, Miller fell from a ladder, resulting in a serious spinal cord injury. Her physicians told her she might never walk again and advised her to accept her situation and just learn to live with it. Miller refused to accept this prognosis. Through a series of treatments, both conventional and unconventional, including acupressure, acupuncture, massage and physical therapy, as well as sheer determination (never underestimate the power of the human mind), she gradually proved her physicians wrong. Five years after the injury, she cooks, drives, types (with two fingers), and walks with a walker. She even learned SCUBA diving. Her original doctors had told her the best she could hope for was a limit of a ten-foot "walker shuffle"; but, as of the writing of Weisman's book, Miller was up to a quarter of a mile and expecting to increase her range.

Sometimes it takes persistence to find the right diagnosis. In her book, *What Doctors Don't Tell You*, Lynne McTaggart discusses her own long odyssey toward better health.[16] In the early '80s, Lynne developed some strange symptoms including eczema, irritable bowel syndrome, and allergies. For 3 years, she made the rounds of medical circles and even tried New Age therapies. Nothing helped. Finally she read an article about Candida albans (also known as Candida albicans) or thrush of the body, a rare form of this fungal disease. The symptoms matched her own. She sought a specialist, who confirmed her self-diagnosis. Candida albans, as it turns out, depresses the body's immune system. The treatment that worked was a combination of drugs and supplements, along with a diet of fresh, unrefined foods.

CONSULT WITH OTHERS

If you have a serious or chronic condition, it can often be helpful to seek a support group, either locally or online. These groups can provide useful practical information as well as moral support. This may not lengthen your life but it can improve the quality of your life. One health researcher found, for example, that women with advanced breast cancer in a support group had less pain and better moods than similar others who did not attend support groups.[17] Though other research about the efficacy of support groups is mixed, the evidence suggests that they can at least be helpful emotionally, especially if you lack emotional support from your family or friends. Ask your physician or local hospital about local support groups for your condition. Larger metropolitan newspapers usually have such listings also. Many reputable support groups can be found online and offer easy access to a community of people willing to share their experiences. Look for ones that are connected with a hospital or other medical group. Online sites will often list local groups that meet in person as well.

WRITTEN INFORMATION

After your diagnosis, read up on the treatments, prognoses, and drug side-effects associated with your disease. Isadore

Rosenfeld's book, *Power to the Patient,* is one source but there are many others. Look up your medical condition on the Internet to see what reputable sites associated with hospitals and medical associations have to say about it. If you have a science background, go to Google Scholar and find some of the original medical research on your condition if it's available. Researching the disease will not only help you understand your problem but will help you formulate questions to ask the physician on your next visit. It can also help you to cope more effectively with serious or chronic conditions. Studies by health psychologists show that "proactive coping," or upfront efforts to ward off or modify stressful events, is beneficial.[18]

Psychologists and Psychiatrists

Everyone has emotional problems at one time or another. Usually we can cope, but sometimes we need professional help. However, many people refuse to consider professional help in this area even when they are clearly suffering and not in control of their problem. "I'm not crazy," they say, "I don't need a shrink." This is not critical thinking about authority; it's denial. As I tell my students, a psychotherapist is a specialist just like any other. If you have a physical ailment, you go to a physician. If your car isn't working, you go to an auto mechanic. Emotional and psychological problems are not shameful, they're human. And I can assure you that mental health professionals did not spend years in graduate school learning what ordinary folks already know! They are specialists in that most complex of areas, the human mind. It's a tougher subject than auto mechanics by a long shot (no offense to mechanics).

But let's say that you don't have that unwarranted prejudice and are willing to seek professional help. What then? Picking a competent mental health professional can be even harder than picking a good physician. While the stereotypes about therapists, like most stereotypes, are overexaggerated, it *is* true that there are bad therapists out there who frankly need help themselves.

PSYCHOLOGIST OR PSYCHIATRIST?

First of all you have to decide whether you want to choose a psychologist or a psychiatrist. A psychologist is someone with a graduate degree in psychology, usually a Ph.D or a Psy.D. This includes clinical psychologists who are trained to treat a wide variety of mental problems, or counseling psychologists who deal primarily with ordinary garden-variety problems such as marital conflicts or test anxiety at school. For further information about the different kinds of psychologists and therapists, a brief discussion can be found at http://www.guidetopsychology.com or you can do an online search. You can also consult a recent textbook on abnormal psychology. Your local college library will have such texts.

A psychiatrist is a medical doctor with an M.D. who specializes in mental problems. If you automatically assume an M.D. is better, you just flunked the therapy critical thinking test. It depends on the problem. For many emotional and behavioral problems, you're better off with a psychologist. They are trained in many different kinds of treatments that seek actual behavioral or attitudinal change, not just "coping" with symptoms. Psychiatrists, who receive less graduate training in actual therapy techniques, let alone psychology classes, than psychologists, tend to be trained to see mental problems as diseases to be "cured" with psychiatric drugs. While there are many competent psychiatrists who do use what is sometimes called the "talking cure" (i.e., talking out the problem with a client), too many think the first line of treatment are drugs that may help some but also may mask the symptoms and do not "cure" the problem.[18] More on that later.

However, psychiatrists have their place. If you seek help for a problem that is clearly physical in origin, such as amnesia as a result of an accident or a drug-related psychosis, or if you are schizophrenic, then a psychiatrist is the right choice. If an antidepressant might help, then a psychiatrist may be the best choice. But, just for the record, don't assume depression is physical in origin and that the "cure" is Prozac or some other psychoactive drug. More on that later, too.

PSYCHOLOGISTS

Picking a Psychologist or Psychotherapist

Psychologists who treat people's emotional and behavioral problems are called psychotherapists, but be careful. In some states, anyone can call herself a psychotherapist, even without appropriate credentials. Some of the same guidelines as for picking a physician apply here. Don't just pick one from phonebook and sign up. Unfortunately there aren't as many informational resources as for physicians so, unless you have a referral from someone whose judgment you trust, you may have to resort to the phonebook. But if you do, then use the guidelines below. However, you might also call up the counseling center of your local college or university and ask for several referrals. It's better than blindly using the phone book.

What those who have written on the subject of picking a therapist will tell you right away is to interview several prospects until you find one that fits the criteria below and that strikes a resonant chord with you. Don't just start seeing the first one you talk to. Call up several prospects and request an interview. Tell them that you are "shopping around." If they're unwilling to be interviewed, cross them off your list. You can ask some questions over the phone at no cost but for a thorough interview, you should expect to pay for the visit. Don't be miserly about this; it's your psyche at stake here.

Raymond Lloyd Richmond, Ph.D., a psychologist and author of the "Guide to Psychology" web site I cited above, offers some useful advice about the initial interview: "Don't jump to any conclusions. Someone might seem like the best psychotherapist in the world, but someone else further down your list of candidates might be even better. You never know, so see everyone on the list. And remember that this interview process, however long it takes, is really part of the process of getting help. You will learn many things about *yourself* just in this initial selection process."[19] He also goes on to say that if you feel uncomfortable with the therapist or you don't think he or she meets your criteria, politely terminate the interview. If the therapist has a problem with that, asserts Richmond, you have learned something important—the therapist is not competent and is not right for you. Remember not only do you have the right to question, you have the right to make the choice that you feel is best for you. That's more important than being so "polite" that you are cowed by a disapproving therapist.

"But what questions do I ask?" you might say. "I don't have a clue." First of all, asking the right questions is only part of the interview. As you'll see from the criteria below, paying attention to nonverbal cues is also part of the process. If the therapist seems arrogant or distant, it's not a good sign. If the office seems "show-offy" or ostentatious, that's not a good sign either. But you may be surprised to learn that in the case of psychotherapists, credentials, licensing, and experience are not necessarily as important as you might imagine. In his book, *House of Cards: Psychology and Psychotherapy Built on Myth*, research psychologist Robin Dawes, Ph.D. presents evidence that licensed professional psychologists are not necessarily any more effective as psychologists than others of comparable intelligence who are minimally trained.[20] Contrary to the common wisdom, in several studies, the credentials and experience of the psychotherapist were unrelated to the outcome. Neither was length or type of therapy, with the possible exception of behavioral techniques for certain well-defined problems such as depression (cognitive therapy works the best) or phobias (behavior modification therapy works the best). One of the few relationships suggested by the research is the presence of "accurate empathy."[21] The criteria suggested by Dr. Ofer Zur below, as you will see, rely heavily on signs of empathy and friendliness.

However, many psychologists do recommend asking about training and credentials so it's probably a good idea to include that as part of your initial interview. Checking out the therapist's school on the Internet might be of some value. If the degree is from a college or university that you can't find much information about, isn't accredited by some reasonable accrediting organization or it sounds like "Space Cadet U," I'd be nervous about it, research or no research. John Gray, one famous psychologist who admittedly is more well-known for writing books than for conducting therapy, got his Ph.D. from a school that was closed down by the State of California for offering fraudulent degrees.[22] You might not want to go that route! On the other hand, another psychologist I know obtained his Ph.D. degree from a diploma mill (though not his other credentials and training!) and is a fine therapist who has helped many people. Sorry but there are no easy answers. You have to use multiple criteria and a bit of common sense.

Here is a list of criteria that will not only help you pick a therapist but serve as a guide about whether to continue seeing that therapist. It is reprinted with permission from the web site of Ofer Zur, Ph.D., a practicing and licensed clinical psychologist (www.zurinstitute.com).[23]

CHECKLIST FOR CHOOSING A THERAPIST

1. Seems warm and accepting. Has a sense of humor, however willing to challenge you when necessary.
2. Is emotionally healthy. Seems to feel at ease with himself/herself. Does not seem anxious, arrogant or depressed.
3. Does not suffer from a God complex. Decent, respectful, not condescending. Neither shows off, belittles nor demeans. Check walls for over-abundance of certificates, awards or prizes. Check for excess of jewelry, silver, or gold.
4. Is trained in talk therapy, not just in "pill therapy." Watch out for someone who offers medication (e.g., Prozac) as the solution to your problems.
5. Accepts and encourages the idea that clients are entitled to shop around for a therapist before they commit. Is willing to talk to you on the phone for at least 10 minutes so you can interview him/her thoroughly.
6. Accepts the idea that consultation or second opinions may be helpful in the course of therapy.
7. Lets you explain your problems, doesn't tell you what they are prematurely or try to fit you into a standardized box (e.g., co-dependent, you have been molested, etc).
8. Is active and engaged. Quit right away if the therapist avoids discussions, does not answer most questions, or pretends to be a "blank wall." Successful therapy needs ongoing dialogue and authentic relationships.
9. Has more than one clinical orientation and promises to fit his/her approach to your specific problems and not impose his/her pet approach on all patients.
10. Is flexible in terms of what is appropriate and helpful. Contrary to common practice, some clients can benefit from a walk in the park or a home visit; and a touch still has more healing power than volumes of words.

11. Is not rigid or paranoid about seeing you or engaging with you in the community. Accepts that you may bump into each other during religious services, your children's school or on the basketball court. Does not hide behind the professional persona.
12. Presents you with clear office policies, including limits of confidentiality, clients' rights, etc. Read the contract carefully before you sign.
13. Talks to you on the phone in between sessions if necessary.
14. While flexible in many ways, still maintains clear and healthy boundaries. No hugging unless you initiate it, no sexual innuendo, no business offers.
15. Seems professional, knowledgeable, and an expert (writer, teacher, supervisor) and above all competent, human and experienced.
16. Communicates well with parents when treating children and adolescents. A delicate balance must be reached between respecting adolescents' privacy and not keeping parents in the dark.
17. Does not focus exclusively on your childhood or inner life. Make sure that the effects of real-life pressures, such as long commute, children or harassing boss, are dealt with.
18. Shares your basic moral and political values but does not work hard to prove to you how much they are like you (e.g., "I was molested too "). It's okay to ask about the therapist's values.
19. Is flexible about who can be part of therapy. At times, it is helpful to bring your friend/lover, child, or parent with you to therapy.
20. Conducts regular evaluations of progress in therapy, including discussion of treatment plans. Listens to your assessment of what is helpful and what is not during the course of therapy.
21. Takes responsibility for not being effective when therapy does not progress over time. When therapy has not yielded any significant results for a long time, neither blames you nor continues to take your money.
22. Is willing to go over this list with you without being offended or defensive.

RIGHT TO QUESTION BUT . . .

Once you've found a psychotherapist who seems to fit these criteria, you need to be prepared to be honest and open with the therapist but not a doormat. You have the right to ask questions and discuss your issues with the therapist. As with seeking medical help, you should be prepared to be an active participant in your recovery. However, in therapy, there's an issue called transference that may become a problem. "If for any reason you do not feel comfortable with the psychotherapy," says Dr. Richmond, "be sure to tell the psychologist *exactly* what you are experiencing. Quite often, psychotherapy provokes uncomfortable feelings, known as a transference reaction, and the whole point of treatment is to deal with these feelings *in the treatment*, not to run away from them."[24] If you are suddenly feeling uncomfortable because of the issues raised, consider the possibility that it's just transference and discuss your feelings with the therapist before you chuck him or her out the metaphorical window.

YOUR RIGHT TO PROTEST

However, sometimes it's obvious that the problem is not you but the therapist. If the therapist's behavior clearly violates one of the criteria about or makes you uncomfortable through his actions, rather than the issues being raised, you have the right to leave. Sophia, for example, had debilitating agoraphobia (irrational fear of being away from the safety of home) that gave her panic attacks. She tells of her first experience visiting a therapist. He asked her to sit down at a desk across from him. He stared at her wordlessly and she stared back apprehensively, mentally imagining dollars going down the drain as the minutes ticked away. Finally she said to him, "Aren't you going to ask me anything?" His response was "I was waiting for you to free associate [say the thoughts that randomly come into your head—a technique sometimes used by therapists but not at this stage!]." No questions, no "why are you here?" Nothing. She knew this was not the way therapy normally works, so she got up and walked out, finding the help she needed elsewhere.

ASK FOR FEEDBACK

As Dr. Zur suggests above, expect the therapist to conduct regular evaluations of your progress in therapy, including discussion of treatment plans. If he or she doesn't do this, ask for a progress report on how well you are doing. Make sure that you give the therapist feedback about what is helpful to you and what is not and then discuss it with her or him.

ASK FOR MORE INFORMATION

Ask about reading material, books or Internet sites that might be helpful to you. Many good popular books have been written on psychological issues (see below for some guidelines to picking a good self-help book). There are many good psychology self-help books, for example, that discuss the techniques of cognitive behavioral therapy, which deals with the underlying irrational and exaggerated beliefs that typically accompany depression (e.g., "I'm worthless," "I never do anything right," Nothing I do will help"). One of the most highly regarded books in this area is *Feeling Good: The New Mood Therapy* by David Burns, M.D.[25] His accompanying book, *The Feeling Good Handbook*, goes into more detail on techniques that you can use on your own. If you have some bad habits you would like to break or you engage in "negative self-talk" (beating yourself up verbally), this book can be a useful adjunct to therapy. If you aren't quite prepared to see a therapist, this book can also help you if you conscientiously apply the techniques.

CONSIDER ALTERNATIVE OPTIONS OR A DIFFERENT OPINION

Maybe you think the therapist is OK, but you don't seem to be making any progress. You might consider another therapist or another therapeutic approach. Cynthia, a student of mine, confessed to me that she was suffering from depression. She had been seeing a therapist that she thought was very nice, but she didn't feel that she was getting much out of the sessions. When I asked her about the therapist, Cynthia said the woman was a relationship therapist and mainly asked about Cynthia's boy friend and issues concerning their relationship (they were having some problems but, based on what she said to me, this seemed to a result of Cynthia's depression, not the cause). I suggested to her that this might not be the most useful approach. Her description of the therapist sounded too much like what I call the "touchy-feely" approach; it makes you feel good but doesn't necessarily solve your problems. I recommended that she try a cognitive therapist and see if that helped. She followed my suggestion and later reported back to me that the cognitive therapist was much more helpful to her. The moral of the story: don't be afraid to switch therapists if you are not satisfied with your progress.

Psychiatrists

BE PREPARED

If you or a family member decides to see a psychiatrist, there are a number of additional considerations to think about. Since psychiatrists are medical doctors, you may want to come to his or her office prepared with your medical history. For one thing, there's a good chance that the psychiatrist will want to prescribe a psychoactive drug. If you are depressed, for example, drugs such as Prozac, Zoloft, or Paxil may be prescribed. Unfortunately many psychiatrists today are more likely to give you a prescription for one of these drugs than do actual psychotherapy. But all drugs have side effects, and psychoactive ones are no exception. You may also want to ask about the interaction of these drugs with other drugs you may be taking, thus the necessity of bringing your medical history.

You might want to look up information about some of the

common drugs that might be prescribed for your problem and learn about the side effects, so you can decide whether this is the route you want to take. Many people have been helped by these drugs but many people have not. Read both sides before you make up your mind. The potential dangers of psychiatric drugs are spelled out (and backed up with research evidence) in *Your Drug May Be Your Problem* by Peter Breggin, M.D. and David Cohen, Ph.D. Dr. Breggin, who has been a gadfly in the psychiatric community for many years, has been called the "Ralph Nader" of psychiatry. The organization he founded, the International Society for the Study of Psychiatry and Psychology (www.icspp.org), is dedicated to critical thinking about what he considers the treatment excesses of the psychiatric establishment, including drugs and electroshock. However, because of his severe criticism of psychiatric drugs, Dr. Breggin is controversial, as any such establishment gadfly inevitably is. Read both sides and decide for yourself.

You should also be aware that research shows that the single best treatment for depression is not drugs but cognitive therapy.[26] In many cases, psychiatric drugs may be helpful for controlling symptoms so that the person can cope with his or her psychological issues in a more effective way. However, the drugs per se don't "cure" depression, they merely treat the symptoms. Cognitive behavioral therapy, which I describe above, is the treatment of choice for effective recovery. If you are depressed, the expert you choose, whether a psychiatrist or a psychologist, should be well-versed in this treatment method.

CHOOSING A PSYCHIATRIST

Apply the same criteria for choosing and staying with a psychiatrist as for a psychologist or physician. You want one who is going to be empathetic, nonautocratic, willing to spend time with you instead of shuffling you out the door as quickly as possible with a prescription in your hand, and is willing to treat you with respect. Ask what therapeutic techniques he uses in addition to drugs. Ask if he uses cognitive therapy. If he is vague or evasive, look for another psychiatrist more amenable to actual therapy rather than mere medication.

ASK FOR MORE INFORMATION

If the psychiatrist prescribes drugs, ask for information, including potential side effects and interactions. If she can't or won't give your information, or tells you not to worry, then ask a pharmacist about the effects. Be especially cautious about taking too many different kinds of drugs at the same time. A chemical cocktail of uppers, downers, pain pills and sleep aids, for example, is asking for trouble. The story of poor Anna Nicole Smith, who died of an accidental drug overdose, is a case in point. All the drugs were legal and prescribed by her physicians. Investigators said she had been taking chloral hydrate and methadone (both are sedatives), several anti-depressants and anti-anxiety drugs (also downers), and an anti-flu remedy, among other drugs.[27] Enough to depress practically any nervous system to a complete halt! Was she fully informed of the potential interactions of this psychiatric soup? I doubt it, and so do many commentators. If you think this is just a bizarre fluke, think again. Basically the same thing happened more recently to actor Heath Ledger. In 2008, Ledger died from an accidental overdose of six types of prescribed painkillers and sedatives. Ellen Borakove, spokesperson for the New York Medical Examiner's office, said the cause of death was "acute intoxication by the combined effects of oxycodone, hydrocodone, diazepam [Valium], temazepam [Restoril], alprazolam [Xanax] . . ."[28] These are only two of many such stories I've heard over the years. Be informed; it may save your life.

YOUR RIGHT TO QUESTION AND PROTEST

If you or someone you care about is under the care of a psychiatrist who wants to prescribe drugs, it's a good idea not only to read books on both sides of the drug debate but to do some online searching about the possible dangers. Armed with good information can keep you from being the victim of psychiatric misdiagnosis.

The Law Project for Psychiatric Rights is a website that provides many horror stories about abuse and misdiagnosis in the mental health system. One of the stories, for example, involves a teenage boy who was autistic. His mother tells the story of how "psych meds drove my son crazy."[29] Ann Bauer describes her son as "unique and funny and odd. He was difficult in some ways but incredibly easy in others." When he became depressed about a romance that didn't work out, his parents took him to a psychiatrist. The psychiatrist prescribed Abilify, a new antidepressant. Bauer then recites a shocking horror story of how the son's behavior deteriorated and spiraled out of control, becoming crazy and gross. He began eating like a pig, gained a huge amount of weight, and neglected his hygiene. That drug was abandoned and another, an anti-psychotic called Geodon, was prescribed.

Then as Bauer puts it, "things really got bad," and her son's behavior went from "unpredictable to entirely random." He exhibited signs of autistic catatonia, standing frozen without moving for long periods of time. Fortunately at that point, Bauer decided to do her Internet homework. She found that all the medical research articles said the drugs her son had been prescribed were *contraindicated* for autistic catatonia. They never should have been prescribed for an autistic person in the first place. She was able to get a referral to the Mayo Clinic, where her son started recovering and slowly getting back to his normal self. Unfortunately, not all such stories have happy endings.

The morale of this tale: do not assume that psychiatrists necessarily know what they are doing. Do research on the drugs you are being prescribed and question. Find out what the possible side effects of suggested drugs are. Look to see if there are horror stories about the side effects. And if what you find worries you, stand your ground. Find another psychiatrist or therapist who will consider alternatives. It's your psyche (or your loved one's psyche) and you have the right to choose.

How to Think Critically about Psychological Self-Help Books

If you don't feel that you need to go to a professional, here's some suggestions for choosing a psychological self-help book that are based on my article on the web site of Resources for Independent Thinking (www.rit.org). Pop psych books are a thriving business. Some are good; some are bad. They can be very helpful if you pick the right ones, but knowing what to look for and what to avoid is the key. The guide below was adapted from *The Authoritative Guide to Self-Help Books* by John Santrock, Ann Minnett, and Barbara Campbell.[30] I have added some of my own examples and suggestions to theirs.

- Don't select a self-help book because of its cover, its title, its flashy advertising campaign, or because it is this year's "fad" book.

Self-help is big business. Big-budget advertising doesn't mean the book is bad but doesn't mean that it's good either. Don't be lured by flashy advertising, the author's claims on a TV talk show, or testimonials by celebrities. Instead, look beyond the cover and take into account the next eight strategies.

My favorite example of this is *Men Are from Mars, Women Are from Venus* by John Gray. Glitzy title, big advertising campaign, fad book and absolutely no references to back up his claims. Right. But more on Gray and his book later. Other suspect sample titles include *Secrets About Men That Every Woman Should Know* by Barbara De Angelis and *Looking Out for Number One* by Robert Ringer. Both of these titles bombed in the ratings by professionals in *The Authoritative Guide to Self-Help Books*.[31]

Many self-help books are based on anecdotes, dubious testimonials, and a few case histories. But a few examples prove nothing. Anecdotes are not science. If you want to know what behavior can really be changed and what can't, based on reputable scientific research, an excellent book by a highly respected research psychologist is *What You Can Change . . . And What You Can't* by Martin Seligman, Ph.D. He objectively presents what research evidence suggests about a wide variety of behaviors and how amenable to change they are. He examines emotional issues, such as anxiety, depression, and anger, as well as changing habits. Checklists and self-analysis questionnaires are also included.

A book that can help your through the mine fields of self-help (with some caveats) is *The Authoritative Guide to Self-Help Books* by John Santrock, Ann Minnett and Barbara Campbell. However, in my review of this book, which you can find online at www.rit.org, I point out, for example, that Carol Tavris, Ph.D., a respected social psychologist and writer, notes that the samples used for the ratings are drawn only from clinical psychologists, not from other academic or research-oriented psychologists.[32] She, as well as Dr. Zur, is also troubled by the endorsement of some books that have no empirical merit, such as *The Courage to Heal.* But given these caveats, the *Authoritative Guide* can be very helpful. Many of the books that get high ratings deserve them, especially the ones the authors say are based on empirical research, and many of the books that get low ratings also deserve them, especially the ones that are labeled as "fluffy."

- Examine the author's professional credentials.

Just about anybody can get a self-help book into print if the publisher thinks it will sell. Most good self-help books are written by people who have gone through rigorous training at respected universities and who are mental health professionals. Many cognitive therapy books are of this kind.

But you still have to judge the book by all of the criteria listed here because there are a few good books by nonprofessionals and some bad books by professionals. Simply because someone has a Ph.D. or an M.D. doesn't necessarily mean the book is any good. For starters, some degrees mean little. John Gray's Ph.D., for example, is from a correspondence school that was forcibly closed by the California Department of Consumer Affairs in 2001 after a judgment that found that the school "awarded excessive credit . . . to many students" and "failed to meet various requirements for issuing Ph.D. degrees."[33] Dr. Laura's (Schlessinger) Ph.D. is not even in psychology, it's in physiology.[34] But even reputable degrees are no guarantee that the book is a good one. Many mental health professionals, for example, don't like Joyce Brothers, Ruth Westheimer, or Wayne Dyer, all of whom have reputable doctoral degrees, because the professionals believe their advice is simplistic and glitzy.[35]

Do an Internet search on the author's name and see if the writer is controversial or subject to criticism. Read both sides before you decide. Merely being controversial isn't a bad thing per se; it depends on *why* an author is controversial. John Gray is controversial because many social scientists think his advice is simplistic, sexist, and not backed up by evidence. Peter Breggin is controversial because he challenges the widely-held notion that drugs like Prozac and Zoloft are safe and highly effective, a view that makes many psychiatrists really unhappy and threatens the psychiatric establishment. The difference is that Breggin backs his controversial claims up with scientific evidence and Gray does not.

- Select a book that makes realistic rather than grandiose claims.

Most problems don't arise overnight and most can't be solved overnight. Be skeptical of anything that sounds easy, magical, and wondrous. Coping effectively with virtually all of life's problems—motivation, stress, exercise, parenting, divorce, addiction—is not easy; it's often a lifelong project.

The authors of *The Authoritative Guide to Self-Help Books* use the examples of *The Beverly Hills Diet* and *Dr. Atkins' Diet Revolution*.[36] Both books, they write, make extravagant claims, taking a narrow approach to weight loss that fails to emphasize the importance of a balanced diet and exercise.

A recent example of a popular self-help book that makes grandiose claims that defy common sense as well as psychological research is *The Secret* by Rhonda Byrne. Her "amazing" principle is the "Law of Attraction." Funny, I never heard of this one in all my years of reading about and teaching psychology. How did I miss it? Oh, that's right, it's a "secret!"

It's one thing to say that positive thinking is a good idea (psychologists would agree).[37] It's quite another to claim that if you want something bad enough, you *will* get it. Yes, if you take the appropriate actions, you *may* get what you want, but thinking per se is not enough. Anyone who accepts this idea is engaging in the silliest sort of wishful thinking. I also have to agree with one Amazon.com reviewer who wrote: "By far the most offensive part of the message is the suggestion that people who have pain in their lives are somehow attracting it with their thoughts. Darfur rape victims did not ask for it. Children who are molested did not ask for it . . . To suggest that their 'incorrect thinking' is the cause of this is sickening."[38] Sickening and utterly without any rationality or scientific evidence whatsoever.

- Examine the evidence presented in the book.

Many self-help books are not based on reliable scientific evidence but rather on the author's biased anecdotal experiences. Watch out for a book based mainly on testimonials, a small number of interviews, or a few clients seen in therapy. Most authors of good self-help books will describe the research evidence and provide a bibliography and citations in the appendix. Be cautious if this information is not provided.

A comparison of two books on gender communication illustrates the importance of looking for evidence. John Gray, in his best seller *Men Are from Mars and Women Are from Venus,* discusses the differences in communication styles that he believes exists between women and men. But all his evidence is anecdotal; none of his suggested solutions are backed up with anything other than his claim that they work. He has no references, no bibliography. Why should we trust him? Because he is making lots of money? I don't think so.

Contrast Dr. Gray's book with another on the same topic: Deborah Tannen's best selling book, *You Just Don't Understand.* Dr. Tannen's book has an extensive bibliography and annotations so you know what research she is basing her conclusions on and could look up the citations for yourself. If you did, you would find that most of the references are scientific research reported in peer-reviewed journals that are highly reputable. Furthermore, her Ph.D. is from the University of California, Berkeley and she teaches at Georgetown University[39] Her credentials are eminently respectable, unlike Gray's. Whose conclusions do you think are more reasonable and reliable? I'll vote for Tannen.

- Select a self-help book that doesn't oversimplify. Look for one that recognizes problems may have multiple causes and that suggests alternative solutions.

People love easy answers but the truth is that we are complex beings living in a complex world. Watch out for simplistic solutions to complex problems. Most problems are affected by a multitude of factors, including present circumstances, personal attitudes and belief systems, health status, personality, and upbringing. Among the worst offenders: some of the books on diet, relationships, codependency, and the "inner child."

One example in *The Authoritative Guide to Self-Help Books* is Leo Buscaglia's book, *Loving Each Other.*[40] Buscaglia was a popular fad in the '70s and '80s, promising that what the world needed was more hugs. But, said the critics, the book was "insubstantial fluff" that offered no solutions about how to get there. Maybe the Beatles can get away with saying "all you need is love" but they were musicians, not therapists. Psychologists need to do better than this.

Another example given in *The Authoritative Guide to Self-Help Books* is Susan Forward's book, *Toxic Parents*.[41] Forward, write the authors, asserts that if you were ever frightened by your parents as a child, then they were "toxic" parents. But, as the authors point out (and many developmental psychologists would also), every parent has at one time or another frightened their child because the parents have the power to mete out discipline as part of the socialization process. That doesn't mean that the parents are "toxic." It takes more than one behavior, especially one taken out of context, to consider a parent dysfunctional.

- A self-help book that focuses on one specific problem is better than one that offers a general approach to solving *all* your problems.

Books that try to solve *all* of life's problems are usually shallow and lack the precise, detailed recommendations that are needed to solve a particular problem. Watch out for books that generalize too much. A book that tries to tell you, for example, that codependency is *anything*, and *everything* is codependence is suspect.

The authors of *The Authoritative Guide to Self-Help Books* single out codependency guru Melodie Beattie as an example of this approach.[42] She offers much too sweeping a generalization. Instead they point to books such as *Feeling Good* by David Burns, M.D., which I have mentioned previously, as an example of a book that pinpoints one area—cognitive therapy—and discusses its appropriate applications.

- Don't be bamboozled by psychobabble and slick writing.

Watch out for "hip" and vague language that says such things as "You've got to get in touch with your feelings," or "You've got to get it." Don't be taken in by overly "friendly" writing that pulls you in or books that only have one or two ideas that could be summed up in to two or three pages. Psychobabble books often degenerate into motivational and inspirational sermons or cheerleading that lacks precise strategies and detailed recommendations for change.

Gray's book, *Men Are from Mars, Women Are from Venus*, is one example of this kind of writing. His overly cutesy, overly familiar style and simplistic analogies (e.g., "the caveman") should be a red flag. Another red flag is his easy, unquestioning acceptance of tired gender-role stereotypes and his subtle insinuation that it is the women who must compromise more than the men. Excuse me, why is that? In contrast, Tannen's *You Just Don't Understand* is straightforward and engaging without being smarmy or sexist. She doesn't give an easy "10-point plan" for success. Instead, she suggests that good communication is an ongoing process that requires discussion, give and take, and willingness to see each other's perspective, and take them seriously. Any communication expert will tell you that this suggestion makes good sense.

Another example of a slick writer who leans heavily on gender stereotypes is Joyce Brothers, a media personality and psychologist who has pumped out a long string of self-help books. In my opinion, she is one of the worst offenders in the genre I derisively call "pop psych," as opposed to "popular psychology." Glib, not well-researched but, unfortunately, very popular books are her forte. The authors of *The Authoritative Guide to Self-Help Books* are no fans of hers either. They list her book *What Every Woman Should Know about Men* as "strongly not recommended" because it relies heavily on tired gender stereotypes.[43] In the words of the authors, her book should have been titled *"How to Placate, Coddle and Reassure Men in Today's Society."*

I have seen such examples in other books Brothers has written and, as someone who has taught Psychology of Women for more than 25 years, I am profoundly annoyed by her cavalier attitude toward women and her *lack of research evidence* to substantiate her ideas. A far better book, solidly based on actual research evidence about gender, is *The Mismeasure of Woman* by Carol Tavris, Ph.D. Though its main thrust is not "what you should know about men," it does deal with relationships between women and men in a balanced, reasonable way that does not cater to stereotypes on either side.

- Be leery of authors who complain about or reject the standard knowledge of mental health professionals.

Look at what the complaints are based on. If the basis of the attack is that professionals are overly concerned with scientific evidence, consider this a red flag. Many New Age authors fall into this category, claiming that they are years ahead of their time yet offering nothing but psychobabble to back up their assertions. The authors of *The Authoritative Guide to Self-Help Books* put L. Ron Hubbard, the founder of scientology, into this category and I would agree.[44] Hubbard was a science fiction writer, not a psychologist. Funny thing, his "nonfiction" books read like science fiction. In contrast, there are anti-psychiatric establishment writers such as Dr. Breggin, who do provide scientific research evidence to back up their complaints about the mental health establishment.[45]

CONCLUSION

Your health, both physical and mental, is in your hands. Take responsibility for both. Yes, use the experts, but use them wisely. Be prepared to think carefully about their recommendations, question when you are not sure, seek out additional information, and examine different views and options. Don't be passive. Take an active part in your recovery. You will be the healthier for it.

RESOURCES

BOOKS

Medical Issues

Jerry Avorn, M.D. *Powerful Medicines: The Benefits, Risks and Costs of Prescription Drugs.* New York: Vintage, 2005.

Michael B. Jacobs, M.D. and Select Faculty of Stanford University School of Medicine. *Taking Care: Self-Care for 100 Common Symptoms and 20 Long-Term Ailments.* New York: Random House, 1997.

Barbara M. Korsch, M.D. and Caroline Harding. *The Intelligent Patient's Guide to the Doctor Patient Relationship: Learning How to Talk So Your Doctor Will Listen.* New York: Oxford University Press, 1997.

Janet R. Maurer, M.D. *How to Talk to Your Doctor: The Questions to Ask.* New York: Fireside Books, 1986.

Timothy B. McCall, M.D. *Examining Your Doctor: A Patient's Guide to Avoiding Harmful Medical Care.* Secaucus, NJ: Citadel Press, 1995.

Lynne McTaggert. *What Doctors Don't Tell You: The Truth about the Dangers of Modern Medicine.* New York: Avon, 1998.

Kenneth Pelletier, M.D. *The Best of Alternative Medicine: What Works? What Does Not Work?* New York: Simon & Schuster, 2000.

Alan J. Steinberg, M.D. *The Insider's Guide to HMOs: How to Navigate the Managed-Care System and Get What You Want.* New York: Penguin Books, 1997.

Carol Svec. *After Any Diagnosis: How to Take Action Against Your Illness Using the Best and Most Current Medical Information Available.* New York: Three Rivers Press. 2001.

Roanne Weisman with Brian Berman, M.D. *Own Your Own Health: Choosing the Best from Alternative and Conventional Medicine: Experts to Guide You, Research to Inform You, Stories to Inspire You.* Deerfield, FL: Health Communications Inc., 2003.

Psychological Issues

Peter R. Breggin, M.D. *The Anti-Depressant Fact Book: What Your Doctor Won't Tell You About Prozac, Zoloft, Paxil, Celexa, and Luvox.* Cambridge, MA: Da Capo Books, 2005.

Peter Breggin, M.D. *Medication Madness: A Psychiatrist Exposes the Danger of Mood-Altering Medications.* New York: St. Martin's Press, 2008.

Peter Breggin, M.D. and David Cohen, Ph.D. *Your Drug May Be Your Problem: How and Why to Stop Taking Psychiatric Medications.* New York: HarperCollins, 2000.

David Burns, M.D. *Feeling Good: The New Mood Therapy Revised and Updated.* New York: Avon, 1999.

David D. Burns, M.D. *The Feeling Good Handbook.* New York: Plume, 1999.

Robin Dawes, Ph.D. *House of Cards: Psychology and Psychotherapy Built on Myth.* New York: Free Press, 1996.

Grace E. Jackson, M.D. *Rethinking Psychiatric Drugs: A Guide for Informed Consent.* Bloomington, IN: Authorhouse, 2005.

John W. Santrock, Ph.D., Ann M. Minnett, Ph.D., and Barbara D. Campbell. *The Authoritative Guide to Self-Help Books.* New York: Guilford Press, 1994.

Martin E. Seligman, Ph.D. *What You Can Change . . . And What You Can't: The Complete Guide to Successful Self-Improvement.* New York: Fawcett, 1994.

WEB SITES

Medical Issues

The American Board of Medical Specialties
www.abms.org
Maintains a list of all Board-certified physicians and their specialties.

The American Pharmacists Association
www.pharmacyandyou.org
Provides consumer information about drugs, including breaking news about problems with drugs and supplements.

Public Citizen Health Research Group
www.citizen.org
Gives useful warnings about medications, medical equipment, over-the-counter remedies and other health treatments that are known to have adverse side effects. It is independently funded and has no ties to pharmaceutical companies.

Patients are Powerful
www.patientsarepowerful.org/index.cfm
A not-for-profit group that provides many useful tips, including forms to request information from physicians. It's also good for patient complaints.

Pharmed Out
www.pharmedout.org
Another source of information about prescription drug issues; it's publicly funded so has no ties to drug companies.

WebMD
www.webmd.org
Provides a vast array of information about diseases and diagnoses, treatment and care, as well as the latest research on medicine and medical issues.

Independent Drug Information Service
www.rxfacts.org
Affilated with Harvard Medical School and the PACE Program of the Pennsylvania Department of Aging, it has unbiased information for both physicians and patients.

American Association of Retired People (AARP)
www.aarp.com/health/
Learn about medical options and compare brand name and generic drugs here. AARP also have good articles on health issues in its newsletter and magazine.

Psychology and Psychiatry

Critical Thinking about Psychology:

Resources for Independent Thinking
www.rit.org
See my essays on psychological issues such as self-help books, the article on why people believe in ESP for the wrong reasons, and others.

Zur Institute
www.zurinstiture.com
The web site of Ofer Zur, Ph.D. offers suggestions on

how to pick a good therapist as well as mini-courses for practicing clinicians.

A Guide to Psychology and Its Practice
www.guidetopsychology.com
The web site of Raymond Lloyd Richmond, Ph.D. offers information about the practice of clinical psychology. It gives suggestions on how to evaluate psychotherapists.

Critical Thinking about Psychiatric Drugs:

International Center for the Study of Psychiatry and Psychology
www.icspp.org
This is the web site of the organization that Peter Breggin, M.D. founded. It has a list of all of Dr. Breggin's books, as well as articles and links to related sites.

Psychiatric Drug Facts with Dr. Peter Breggin
www.breggin.com
Articles written by Dr. Breggin on the subject of psychiatric drugs and their harmful effects. Click on the button that says "Dr. Breggin's professional website."

Law Project for Psychiatric Rights
www.psychrights.org
The purpose of the Law Project for Psychiatric Rights is to promote and implement a strategic legal campaign for psychiatric rights and against unwarranted court-ordered psychiatric medication. Includes a long list of horror stories about abuse by the mental health system.

UPDATES

For updates on books, web sites, web site URLs and links (they sometimes change), articles and other relevant information, check the web site for my book: www.standuptoauthorities.com

CHAPTER

4

Don't Take This Job and Shove It: Surviving Bosses and the Workplace

Marcela had been working as an assistant to two lawyers. When she had a chance to be the full-time assistant to a senior partner, she was delighted. She was not so delighted when she only got a $1000 a year raise. Her husband Ken, noticing that she was upset, asked her what was wrong but had to drag it out her. She had waited 18 months for a raise and thought she deserved more. Ken suggested that she tell her boss but she resisted. When finally she did speak up to her boss, he responded that he didn't know she hadn't gotten a raise last year. The boss doubled her raise. But Patricia King, author of Never Work for a Jerk, *the book from which this anecdote was drawn, points out that Marcela should have asked for a raise six months before. Her reticence to speak up cost her six months worth of extra salary. "Some people still think that all they have to do is work hard and wait for someone to notice," writes King. "You'll be a wallflower for a long time if you wait for someone to ask you to do the salary waltz."[1] If you don't stand up and ask for what you want, how do you think you will get it?*

No one's job goes smoothly all the time. Many of us have had hassles at work, or troublesome bosses or managers. We may have wanted to question a boss's decision on a new directive. Perhaps we disagreed with a performance appraisal or wanted to ask for a raise. Maybe we have been the victim of bullying or harassment. It isn't always easy to just quietly do your job. Too much pressure, too many deadlines, too few benefits, cranky co-workers, lazy managers—few of us have escaped the stresses of the workplace.

Though there are many kinds of issues that arise in the workplace, I'll deal here with the most common problems and issues: difficult bosses, asking for a raise, questioning policies or performance appraisals, sexual or racial harassment, and bullying.

Key Tools

YOUR RIGHT TO QUESTION

Remember that you have a right to question or to protest. You have a right to ask for a raise or object to bad behavior. You have a right to see performance appraisals or other documents in your personnel file. No one has a right to bully or harass you no matter who they are. Isn't this the advice you would give someone else who was being mistreated? Then apply it to yourself. The meek may inherit the earth but meanwhile they still have to go to work everyday.

PREPARE YOUR CASE

No matter why you need to talk to or confront your boss, you need to carefully prepare your case ahead of time. In Chapter Two, I talk about some ideas for looking up information and writing out questions and concerns. Here, the first step is to identify the issue or problem you want to discuss. Be clear, specific and concise. Think out the questions you want to ask, detail the alternatives that you want to suggest, consider the pros and cons of the issue you raise. Show the benefits to the organization. When you put it in writing, remember the style of your boss. Does she or he like a lot of detail, or just the facts? Take this into consideration when you put it in writing in a succinct and logical way.

If you are asking for a raise, you should state why you deserve a raise—detail what you have achieved for the company and how you have benefited the company in some specific ways. If questioning company policy or your performance appraisal, be prepared with specific questions and alternatives. Detail in specific ways in writing why you think the appraisal or policy is inappropriate.

In *What Do I Say When . . . A Guidebook for Getting Your Way with People on the Job*, author Muriel Solomon gives the example of Ava, an executive assistant who had been at the same job for nine years with excellent ratings.[2] When she discovered others at similar jobs were getting paid more, she took action. She obtained figures for the going pay range for her kind of job from her professional organization and from her company's personnel department. Then she combed the want ads and called a few employment agencies. Ava also listed the additional duties she has assumed without pay during the last year.

SEEK ALLIES

Ask around look for allies in the company. Does anyone else agree with you about the problems in the policy? Consult with other co-workers. What do they think of the policy? Find out if they have suffered the same harassment or bullying. See if they are willing to be quoted.

PUT IT IN WRITING

Have a list of questions to be answered, if appropriate. Detail the problems with the policy, as you see it. List the reasons why you think you deserve a raise. Have a detailed day-by-day chronicle of the harassment or bullying. Something on paper has a force that merely verbal protestations do not have. Having it on paper has a psychological effect of its own.

Here's a gratifying story about the power of the written response (and research). Paulina, a student of mine, came to me with an unusual problem that was solved by putting the right information in writing. She had been invited to her boss's house for dinner and informed him ahead of time that she was a vegetarian. But unfortunately the boss was unclear on the concept, to say the least, and every dish served had meat in it. The boss apparently assumed it was merely a preference of hers and that she could and would eat meat under the right circumstances. Being a shy person, Paulina merely politely declined the dishes without arguing her case. She later learned that the boss thought she was rude and things became strained at work.

I suggested first of all that Paulina put her point of view in writing. Since she was shy, she had a hard time standing up to authority figures and having "cue cards" would help her present her case without faltering. Secondly I suggested that she point out to him that assuming that vegetarians could eat meat if necessary is like asking an orthodox Jew or Muslim to eat pork; it is a violation of personal and religious principle. But most importantly, I suggested that she find some information on the Internet that pointed out that eating meat would make vegetarians sick. Paulina followed my advice. Her boss (who she suspected didn't really believe her before) actually read the information she had printed out and apologized for the misunderstanding. Things are fine at work now, she told me. She feels that the Internet printout was what really did the trick.

PSYCH YOURSELF UP

Mentally prepare for the meeting. Psych yourself up to be positive and agreeable rather than confrontational or contentious. Being argumentative or hostile is not the approach most likely to succeed. Being reasonable and open will get you much further. Remember that being assertive is not the same as being aggressive. You are not trying to force your boss to agree with you, you are just trying to stand up for yourself. If the boss thinks you are being aggressive, it will just create unnecessary resistance.

If you are a woman, be careful. Women have a tougher time when it comes to being assertive. Some men find assertive women threatening, seeing them instead as "aggressive." It's an inappropriate double standard but my women students who work in business situations assure me it still happens. So being positive and pleasant while you are being assertive is even more important for you than for a man. It's unfair but we have to deal with it.

In every encounter with a boss, manager, or executive, keep in mind that it is a power situation but that doesn't mean you are a servant or a slave. Always present yourself as a person with power. Be assertive without being overbearing or arrogant. You may not be as powerful as the boss but you are not powerless, so don't act like a supplicant. Timidity will not impress your boss, it will only weaken your position. If acting assertively is a problem for you, read *Your Perfect Right* by Robert Alberti and Michael Emmons. It's considered by many psychologists to be the single best book on learning how to be assertive.[3]

Fine tune your approach. Is the boss a straightforward, no-nonsense person? Make your presentation short and to the point. Provide any further detail needed with paper documents. Be mentally prepared to be assertive and succinct. Is the boss empathetic and warm? You can give more details about your issue and perhaps more openly express your concerns. But remember that whatever your boss's style, you need to communicate your concern in a way that shows how it benefits the company, not just you.

DRESS FOR SUCCESS

You probably already dress appropriately for work. But a meeting with the boss or manager is a day to pay special attention to how you look. Wear a smart outfit, one that makes you feel both comfortable and professional. Today is not the day for the blouse that's just a bit too snug or the denim jeans that are just a little faded. Dress professionally. If you are a woman, an attractive tailored pant suit or dress might just be the right outfit. If you are a man, a nice sports jacket with coordinated pants could be an asset. You want to project both confidence and professionalism so summon up every device that will help you feel that way.

The Specifics

ASKING FOR A RAISE

Let's say that you've been working of the company or office several years, with increasing responsibilities. You haven't had a raise in a year and you think you deserve one. But be honest with yourself; raises aren't always automatic so have legitimate reasons, not simply your desire to make more money.

Prepare your case and put it in writing

First of all, you need to prepare your case. Why do you think you deserve a raise? Do some relevant background research. Find out what you can about salaries in your area for comparable work. Look on the Internet. Do research to find out what people in comparable jobs earn. Examine written company policy in regard to raises. Discuss the issue with the personnel department. Find out what criteria are used for determining raises and then detail how you meet the criteria. Have it all in writing when you meet with the boss. Cynthia, a student who asked me for advice about how to get a raise for her job as a dental assistant, was pleasantly surprised to find out that this technique worked. Unlike her previous attempts at getting a pay raise, the one in writing was successful. Kevin, a restaurateur, says he rarely gets pay raise requests in writing but when he does, he gives more consideration to the request.

Psych yourself up to deal with objections

Be prepared for any objections your boss might have. Money's tight? How have you been good for the company's profits? Does she claim that you don't have enough experience or time with the company? Your investigations into written company policy on raises or comparable policies elsewhere will provide you with ammunition for your response. Keep a folder or portfolio of your accomplishments (notes you have been taking on tasks completed—see below) that will help you organize your thoughts.

Ava, the executive assistant mentioned previously, rehearsed her talk with a colleague, trying to think of and counter the objections her boss might raise. "He'll say, it's company policy to give raise only when . . . and I'll say "But isn't it also company policy to acknowledge . . ." Or the boss might say "If I give you a raise, it'll have a domino effect we can't afford." Ava then could respond "I know you can't afford across-the-board raises, but don't you want to motivate the special people like me who get you the results you want?"[4]

Based on your research on comparable pay rates in other companies, be prepared to ask for a specific amount and to justify it by pointing to your research. Don't be shy or modest. This advice is especially important for women. Research shows that women typically ask for less pay than men do.[5] Don't be sexist to yourself! Find out what your job and level of experience are worth in the market and don't be afraid to ask for the same rate as men. If you are vague about how much of a raise you want, your boss might give you a raise all right—a mere pittance or token—and then what can you say? "You got your raise, didn't you?" he'll say, and you'll be in a weak position to complain.

Don't be afraid to argue for the rate you think is appropriate. Ava prepared herself in her rehearsal. If the boss were to say, for example, "I agree your job is worth another $5000, however $2000 is the absolute limit . . ." Ava was prepared to say "Since we agree that my work is worth another $5000, surely you understand that a $2000 increase is not sufficient. Why don't we split the difference at $3,500?"[6]

RESPONDING TO A PERFORMANCE APPRAISAL

Prepare your case

Prepare mentally to take an active role in the meeting with your boss, suggests Patricia King, author of *Never Work for a Jerk!*[7] Get a copy of the form that the boss will use to evaluate you so you'll know what to expect. Then do your own self-appraisal ahead of time. Being ready to give a balanced appraisal will not only help keep you from being defensive about the boss's criticisms, it will help you to be calmer in the face of any criticisms because you will have an appropriate response ready.

King also suggests keeping a folder in your desk throughout the year in which you drop notes about your work—efforts on special projects, extenuating circumstances for things that go wrong, etc. If you have gone above and beyond the requirements on a project, make a note of how much extra effort you put into it. If others have praised your work, note the comments and the name of the person who said it. If you have anything in writing from others, make sure you keep a copy. At my university, all faculty have Personnel Action Files in which our evaluations are placed. I always make sure that any positive letter or email a student writes to me or to the Chair of my Department goes into that file. Try to be creative about what is possible in your work situation.

Psych yourself up

When you talk to your boss, remember to psych yourself up to play an active part with confidence but not arrogance or conceit. Don't be on the defensive and don't play the supplicant. Look for an opportunity to give your own appraisal of your performance but be honest and succinct. Leave your boss something to say! Remember to adopt a tone of voice and posture that exudes confidence without either false cheeriness or hangdog surrender. A demeanor that is relaxed but firm, assertive but peaceful, is the right balance.

If the boss criticizes you, be calm and don't get emotional or upset. Ask her to give specific examples of behavior or performance issues, particularly if the comments she makes start veering off into personal remarks. The appraisal isn't or shouldn't be about your personality (unless team playing is the issue) so don't let it go there. If getting along with others is one of the issues, ask the boss for specific examples of where you were less than effective, and how you could improve your communication style. Otherwise gently steer it back to performance. Ask her what she likes about the way you do your job. As King notes, some bosses think their job is to concentrate on the negative and not note the positive. I've certainly seen this in academia. One professor told me that his department chair always made a big deal of the 20% of negative student comments that he usually gets and glosses over the 80% of positive ones. His response is to write an analysis, citing the percentages and noting the imbalanced perspective, then putting this into his Personnel Action File. You can respond by pointing out the positive aspects of your performance that you have already made a mental list of in your pre-meeting preparation. Be sure to give specific examples—always more convincing than vague generalities.

If your boss makes valid criticisms, agree with him and indicate your willingness to improve. You might ask for suggestions on how to improve. This shows that you have a professional attitude. Remember not to be defensive, just speak in a calm matter-of-fact way, no matter how much the criticisms sting. Be willing to honestly face your weaknesses in the same tone that you assert your strengths. Solomon suggests trying to extract valuable lessons from the boss's comments.[8] Pay attention to the criticisms so that you can concentrate on improving your performance and making a better impression next time.

Put it in writing

If there is an appraisal form or written evaluation, it usually goes into a personnel file. You have a right to see this file; do make use of this right. If the form allows comments, make them. If you are allowed to place materials or comments, do so, especially if you have been criticized. If you think you have been criticized unfairly, write a dispassionate defense that is specific and detailed about why you think it is inappropriate. Sometimes such diligence really pays off. One professor at my university found out that not only had an inappropriately negative evaluation been placed in his Personnel Action File (PAF), so had a negative student letter that he was never notified about. This was a breach of the union contract; nothing can legally go into a PAF without notifying the person. So he wrote a detailed analysis of why he thought the evaluation was unbalanced, also noting the breach of contract. Then he sent a copy to the Dean of the School that oversaw his department. After that, he always received notices of everything going into his file. He also made sure that positive student letters did go into his PAF and regularly checks it just in case!

In most corporations you have the right to place a response in the file. You might do this if the issue is not so severe as to require a grievance procedure or if you have no union. You can also ask to be evaluated by someone higher in the chain. If your evaluation is so negative and so unfair that it might harm you, you should consider filing a grievance. Talk to someone in the personnel department, your boss's boss, higher level manager or your union about what your options are. Make sure you write something for your personnel file that counterbalances the evaluation and put in it what you want them to know about your performance.

Consider alternative interpretations

However, suggests psychologist ArLyne Diamond, Ph.D, a consultant for professional and management development, before taking the drastic step of filing a grievance, talk to the other side.[9] Sometimes people get negative evaluations because of simple misunderstandings. Dr. Diamond gives the example of Maria, a young assembly-line worker who got written up for leaving her shift before her replacement showed up. Maria had waited till her shift was officially over but the replacement was late. Because she had bad hemorrhoids, Maria was in great distress but was too embarrassed to tell the supervisor at the time she left. She had previously informed the supervisor that she had a medical problem but the supervisor had not really listened to her. When Maria questioned the negative report and carefully explained the problem to her boss, the report was removed from her record.

QUESTIONING POLICY

Prepare your case

First be clear on what your objections or concerns. Lay them out logically. Then do some research and ask yourself questions. How does the new policy fit in with company guidelines? Is it consistent with previous policy? Does it violate the union contract or ethical guidelines? Do other companies have comparable policies? How will the policy affect employee morale?

Put it in writing

After you have identified the issue and done some research, boil your objections or concerns down to a few succinct points. Write down each point, attaching any relevant documents. This is especially important if you are easily tongue-tied or shy. Be prepared with workable alternative suggestions. Spell them out in writing. Written comments have more power than merely spoken ones and you can leave them with your boss to think about!

When you talk to the boss about your concerns, be sure to listen carefully to her replies and make it clear that you understand her side as well as your own. If you want to make a difference, you have to use good communication skills. That means listening, being fair-minded, acknowledging the boss's point of view and being reasonable about possible solutions. Be prepared for a tradeoff or compromise you can live with.

Pay attention to body language

Pay attention to how you are presenting yourself. Appear confident and calm, not too timid, not too aggressive. Use a confident, non-deferent tone of voice with no whining, no inappropriate apologizing. Speak clearly and look the boss in the eye. Don't slump in your seat or fidget. All the positive behaviors will make a good impression; the negative will pull you down.

Watch the boss's body language too. King gives the example of a woman who gradually learned to interpret her boss's nonverbal behaviors.[10] After repeated suggestions Jackie made seemed to fall on deaf ears, she figured out when to change *her* behavior. When he started fiddling with his tie, she changed her approach. When he swiveled around in his seat, Jackie asked him what he thought of her idea. When he looked out the window and fiddled with his tie, she beat a swift but graceful retreat. Pay attention to the cues that tell you that you are using the wrong (or right!) approach.

Consider alternative points of view

When you are questioning policy, it's important to recognize that there are two sides to the issue. If you have a problem with a policy that makes no sense to you, Dr. Diamond suggests that you start out assuming good will. Consider the possibility that there may be a good reason that you are unaware of that could change the unfavorable picture you have constructed. That's why talking (rather than ranting) to the boss or supervisor is a good idea. Diamond, for example, was a consultant for a company that manufactured micro-processing equipment. A group of assembly-line workers were upset because they were suddenly asked to change the format of the run while in the middle of creating a set of wafers. To go back and forth from one process to another took over an hour and clearly was less efficient. However, when they learned the reason, they were willing to accept the change. It turned out that the customer wanted 100 discs upfront before committing to the pending order of 10,000. The change in procedure was necessary in order to produce the required "probationary" discs in order to confirm the sale.

Seek allies

When questioning policy, it's also especially important to seek allies. Do others in the company have a problem with the policy? Are they willing to be quoted? Are they willing to go with you to the meeting? The old saying that there is strength in numbers is true here and backed up by social psychology research.[12] Several people who object to a policy will have more impact than merely one person objecting.

Unions can be your ally too. If you are a member of a union, talk to your union rep and see what he or she suggests. Unions are (usually) there to help you so don't overlook this valuable resource. As with the breach of contract above, there may be a violation that can be turned to your advantage or used as leverage to get you what you want. At one university, Daniel, a part-time lecturer, was told that he was only going to get two courses for the next semester though his contract called for three. The Chair claimed that another person who did not have a contract was more qualified for the third class than Daniel was. Daniel knew that there were classes that he had taught before that he could have been assigned. He immediately contacted the California Faculty Association representative. The rep agreed that the Chair's action was grounds for a grievance. After hearing from the union, the Dean apparently agreed; a class appropriate to Daniel's experience was added to the department schedule the next week. No surprise. The added class was much cheaper for the university than a protracted grievance procedure would have been, especially one that the university would certainly lose.

RESPONDING TO AN ORDER FOR UNETHICAL BEHAVIOR

What if your boss asks you to do something you consider immoral or unethical? Some requests from bosses may be difficult or a real pain; that's not unusual. But occasionally the request steps over a line. Fudging data, padding expense accounts, even lying to clients—all happen. Understandably, this is a dilemma for employees who fear for their jobs. I can't tell you what to do in such a situation—that's something you have to decide for yourself. However, here's what some work experts from a *San Francisco Chronicle* panel suggest.[13]

Clarify the situation

Make sure you understand what the boss is trying to accomplish. Maybe there is another, less morally ambiguous way to reach the same goal, says Dave Murphy. Susan Urquhart-Brown once had a boss who asked her to get new business cards and change her work title because it would sound better to an important client. She reluctantly agreed but later wished she had refused. She realized that she could have accomplished the same, more ethical end by emphasizing her "experience with similar clients to assure the new client that we could effectively handle its business." Eleanor Jacobs concurs. If you think the boss has just had a momentary lapse of judgment, try to talk him out of it and point our other possible solutions, she suggests. Be creative and think about alternatives.

Decide what your values are

If you still are uncomfortable with what the boss is requesting, think about what is important to you. Of course your job is important; losing it can be costly and make your life difficult. But there may be more at stake than just your job.

You have to live with yourself the rest of your life, not your boss. If once you step over the line, what might the boss ask you to do next? Do you want to go down that path? What if the boss's ideas backfire? Maybe you'll be the one in the crossfire. Maybe you'll be the scapegoat. If that happens, your reputation is shot.

Your reputation and integrity plus your experience may be all you have to sell, writes Evelyn Dilsaver. She suggests that you ask yourself "Would I do this if I knew it would appear on page one of the newspaper?" No? Then maybe you don't want to do it. It may not be worth it five years from now when you still hate yourself for doing it.

Voice your concerns

If you are uncomfortable, say so, suggests Odette Pollar. "Refuse by saying, 'I am uncomfortable in this situation, and would prefer not to,'" she writes. Sometimes, continues Pollar, the person requesting may not realize you think it is unethical. "Discuss your concerns openly and you may come to an understanding." She also suggests checking with the human resources department for clarification of company policy. It's a polite and straightforward way of putting the brakes on a questionable behavior without being too confrontational.

Be creative about ways to say no in a polite, nonconfrontional manner. One way to handle the situation, suggests Anne Sparks, is to challenge the boss by asking if he would ever be able to fully trust your honesty in the future if you went along with such a policy now. This not only protects your reputation, it gives the boss a new perspective on his request that may give him something to think about. If the request is for illegal behavior, Pierre Mornelle suggests saying "I'll do anything for you, except go to jail."

If all else fails

If the boss still insists and you do not want to comply, get out, suggest several of the experts on this panel. The consequences to your reputation and self-esteem are too great. Do you really want to work in such a morally tainted atmosphere? And, as I suggested above, you don't know what the consequences for you will be if you do comply. What could happen may be a lot worse than simply getting a new job.

BULLYING

Bullying at work is a big problem in America. According to a study reported at bullybusters.org, one person in six has experienced bullying at work. Another study had even more alarming statistics—nearly 45% of all U.S. workers say they have worked for an abusive boss. More than half of all targets of bullies are women (57%) and the majority of targets of women bullies are other women (71%).[14]

If the preponderance of women both as perpetrators and victims surprises you, think of it as a power issue. Women have traditionally had less power than men. Now that women working outside the home are commonplace, women have a venue for exercising power they didn't have before. Some women abuse their power, perhaps because they want to be "as good as men," i.e., tough and macho. Or perhaps they are taking out their own feelings of powerlessness by trying to control others. These women may even fail to see that other women are more vulnerable than they are, and thus not recognize that what they are doing is bullying. But at the same time, women are still perceived as less powerful and assertive than men, so they are also more vulnerable and "safer" targets for bullying than men.[15]

Although "we've come a long way, baby," says Diamond, "There are still many women who are very vulnerable and desperate to keep their jobs." There are always bullies sexually preying on these types of women. Those of us who are stronger need to recognize this tendency and help protect women who are more vulnerable.

Many women, suggests Diamond, have not learned to be assertive in appropriate ways. They either fall into the traditionally passive or manipulative modes that women have been taught or else they become aggressive because they mistake such behavior for assertiveness. Men know how to "arm-wrestle" each other in more friendly, nonverbal ways, says Diamond. "Women" she advises, "need to learn to come into their own power without being aggressive." If you are a woman being bullied or are the bully yourself, two books that could help you act in more effective ways are *Your Perfect Right* by Alberti and Emmons and, if you are the really timid type, *The Assertive Woman* by Phelps and Austin. Both books faired well in a survey rated by clinical psychologists.[16]

The Bully at Work by Gary Namie, Ph.D. and Ruth Namie, Ph.D. defines bullying as the "the repeated, malicious verbal mistreatment of a Target (the recipient) by a harassing bully (the perpetrator) that is driven by the bully's desire to control the Target."[17] If you are being bullied at work, the solution may not be easy. Bullies are people with feelings of inadequacy and powerlessness. Bullies feel inadequate so they attempt to compensate by lording it over others and acting as if they are superior. They try to feel better about themselves by controlling others and displacing their bad feelings on others. Perhaps you've heard the term "inferiority complex." It means compensating for some real or imagined deficit by acting like you are in fact superior instead. Well, that's what's going on here. It's helpful to recognize that bullying is pathological behavior and to understand that resolution of this problem is not likely to be simple.

Who gets bullied?

Some people are more likely to be the victim of bullying than others. Bullies look for easy targets. They like to target "nice," cooperative people. "Bullies eat 'nice' people alive," say Namie and Namie.[18] The nice guys, the skilled ones, the ones other people like and go to for help. Though cooperativeness is not a weakness, bullies see it that way; they imagine that nice, cooperative people will not oppose them. Bullies look for victims who put up no resistance. Many people hate conflict and try to avoid it; bullies exploit this.

Consider alternative explanations

Sometimes, however, what may at first glance seem like bullying is merely a matter of style. Diamond gives the example of Dwayne, a senior vice-president of a small company, with a booming voice and little patience. In actuality he was a kind and gentle man when you got to know him but his bombastic style was misinterpreted by one of his employees. Donald thought he was being bullied and went to an attorney. When both sides were brought together to discuss the problem, at Dr. Diamond's suggestion, it became clear that behavioral style was the issue, not bullying. The employee agreed to come back to work and the VP agreed to pay attention to how he behaved when rushed. The moral of this story—talk to the alleged bully before you take the problem up the line. Tell him how you are feeling and try to clear the air. If the person is cooperative and willing to discuss the situation with you, you may be able to resolve the matter without resorting to stronger tactics. If the person continues to be unpleasant and uncooperative, then you know you have a true bully on your hands and need to move on to the next tactic.

Psych yourself up

You can head bullying off at the pass by not letting yourself be a target in the first place. Psyche yourself up to be firm and assertive. Act like you are not afraid even if you are. If a bully pushes you, push back. Being "nice" won't work with a bully. No matter how much you hate confrontation, you must stand up for yourself when dealing with the bully. "Bullies," say Namie and Namie, "scan the groups for the weakest."[19] They are lazy and want easy pickings. If you resist and don't give in to their unreasonable requests, they are likely to find another target.

There are many individuals who hate confrontation and they shy away from it, hoping it will go away. If you are one of them and you are being bullied or harassed, get over it! Ignoring bullying won't make it go away; it will only encourage the bully. Read *Your Perfect Right* for tips on how to be more assertive. If you are being bullied, prepare your retort ahead of time. Then you are ready for the bully next time.

Watch your language, both verbal and nonverbal

Bullies are especially sensitive to weakness displayed through timid behavior and language. Hesitant walking pace, shoulders pulled inward, head down, few hand gestures and other behavioral signs of shyness or fear of intimidation and aggression are flashing neon lights saying "bully me, bully me." Turn the lights off. Pull those shoulders back, look straight into the bully's eyes, don't be self-effacing and deferent. If this is hard for you to do because you are shy or easily intimidated, take an assertiveness course or read *Your Perfect Right*.

Be aware of the language you use. Don't be unnecessarily apologetic or timid in your tone of voice. Don't let yourself be interrupted. Don't be polite for the sake of politeness when it's not appropriate, i.e., when you are being intimidated or bullied. Don't make self-defeating, self-denigrating statements such as "I'm sorry but I was never good at this," or "I guess I'm just not cut out to do this job. I'm such a screw-up." Don't give the bully ammunition to cut you down. Do speak in a strong, confident voice, firmly and with no apologies.

People with indirect styles of communication, especially those from cultures demanding that women be submissive and tentative, says Diamond, might have to stretch their comfort zone and become more direct. The boss may interpret indirectness as a sign of weakness or uncertainty. If you have learned to be indirect because you think it is more polite or less confrontational, get over it. You can be polite and direct at the same time. Inappropriate politeness will not get you what you want.

Consider alternative actions

If you have a boss or co-worker who is clearly a bully and is not willing to discuss your concerns with you, you should take these concerns to your Human Resources Department, other supervisor or higher-level manager, and discuss the possible solutions. In a big company, for example, you may have the option of transferring to another department. Glenda was in a department where she was under pressure to work much more than the standard 40-hour week. Her manager demanded that the entire group work every evening until 9 or 10 at night, as well as at least one weekend day. At first, she was OK with this because she was single and had no children. But then she met a man with whom she was beginning to develop a serious relationship and wanted to spend more time with him. She told her supervisor that she wanted to work fewer hours and suggested that she work 10–12-hour shifts three days a week instead of the usual five days. The response of the woman boss was to scream, "You are betraying me!" Instead of surrendering to this over-the-top behavior, Glenda went to Human Resources and requested and got a transfer.

Seek allies

A united front is a strong front and bullies don't like that. They want a weak target. If several people confront the bully, he may back down. This may be especially true if the bully is a needler rather than a brash bully. Needlers tease and provoke to intimidate their peers. Solomon suggests needling the needlers till they get the point.[20] Encourage others to gang up on the needler. In Solomon's example, Cliff got his colleagues to gang up on Don when he made a cutting remark. Taking turns, they asked him to make his criticism clear, then explain his explanation, then clarify his clarifications . . . you get the picture.

Seek alternatives

Stanford professor Robert Sutton, author of the provocatively titled book, *The No Asshole Rule*, suggests if you have less power than the person who is bullying, the best choice may be to leave the organization. If that isn't feasible, then avoid contact with this person or just don't care as much. Check out emotionally. "Passion is an overrated virtue in organizational life and indifference is an underrated virtue," he writes.[21] For those who want a more active (or maybe passive-aggressive) approach, he suggests finding subtle ways to gain more control. One woman whose boss kept stealing her candy fashioned Ex-Lax to look like the candy. When her boss would yell and rant on the phone, she would put him on speakerphone and do her nails. After he finished screaming, she could then reason with him.

More ways to cope with bullying

If you are the victim of a bully, recognize that you have a right to stand up for yourself and protest. You shouldn't have to put up with it so don't. Here is a summary of additional suggestions based on tips from the Workplace Bullying Institute (WBI) and the book *The Bully At Work* by Gary and Ruth Namie:[22]

1. Name it. Legitimize It.

Whether you call it bullying, psychological harassment, emotional abuse, give it a name. Recognize that what the bully is doing to you is not right and you did not ask for it. Naming the problem is healing and gives you permission to protest.

2. Take Time Off to Bullyproof Yourself

If you are feeling overwhelmed and emotionally harassed by the bully, take a short sick leave and regroup yourself. Here are some tasks that the WBI suggests you could accomplish during this time:

    a. Check your mental health with a professional outside the workplace. Decide whether you are emotionally stable

enough to fight back or need to quit for your health's sake.
b. Check your physical health. Emotional trauma is stressful and can lead to physical disease, e.g., hypertension.
c. Look for internal policy violations that can be reported. Be prepared to cite them. Research federal and state options. Many cases of bullying are discriminatory and therefore illegal.
d. Gather information about the economic impact bullying has on productivity. If there is a high turnover rate at your workplace, it costs your employer money in recruitment and interviewing costs.
e. Start looking for a new job in case none of the suggestions below are enough.

3. Expose the Bully.

According to the Workplace Bullying Institute (WBI), you have little to lose by exposing the bully since 7 out of 10 bullying victims either get fired or leave voluntarily for health reasons. If the bully retaliates and the company doesn't stop it, it's time to move on. Your mental and physical well-being are more important than any job.

a. Make the business case that the bully is costing the company too much money by citing the statistics that you have gathered about the economic impact of bullying. Put it in writing and give it to your boss or the boss's boss.
b. Give the employer one chance. If the employer sides with the bully, quit and find a job where you will be respected. But sometimes, says the WBI, the employer is looking for an excuse to get rid of the troublesome bully. Give them the ammunition they need.
c. If you do leave the job, the WBI suggests that you do not go quietly. Tell others why you are leaving. It will be emotionally healing for you and perhaps encourage others who are also being bullied to do the same.

However this last suggestion from the WBI needs to be carefully weighed and considered. Going out in dramatic style may be emotionally healing but it may also prevent you from getting a good reference from your employer. Take this possibility into account and then decide what the best exit strategy for you is.

HARASSMENT

Sexual harassment, which is a kind of bullying, is also common in the workplace, though greatly underreported. Nearly one-third of women workers have reported sexual harassment but only 5–15% report it to their employers.[23] Ethnic and racial harassment, though less common, still occur also. You don't have to put up with it and your company shouldn't allow it. If obnoxious behavior directed toward you is making you uncomfortable, you have a right to protest.

First, let's be clear on what is meant by sexual harassment.

Here's how the Equal Employment Opportunity Commission (EEOC) defines sexual harassment:

> "Unwelcome sexual advances, requests for sexual favors, and other verbal or physical conduct of a sexual nature constitutes sexual harassment when submission to or rejection of this conduct explicitly or implicitly affects an individual's employment, unreasonably interferes with an individual's work performance or creates an intimidating, hostile or offensive work environment."[24]

So sexual harassment isn't just the *quid pro quo* of "sleep with me or you lose your job.' One of the most common kinds of sexual harassment is what is legally termed the "hostile work environment." If someone is making unwanted sexual remarks to you or engages in other behavior that make you uncomfortable and refuses to stop, that's sexual harassment. Graphic sexual pictures publicly and prominently displayed, uninvited and unwanted attention, vulgar language, inappropriate staring at or making fun of your sexual anatomy, all constitute sexual harassment. Today, says Diamond, a hostile work environment can also include just being around others who use foul language, sexual innuendo, or tease. The theory is that by being exposed to this (like second hand smoke), even indirectly, constitutes an environment that is emotionally or psychologically anxiety-provoking. Sometimes decisions are made that an environment is hostile when only one or two mild events cause someone to complain. Other times, the "hostile environment" is real and palpable.

At a university I once taught at, for example, one of the professors constantly stared at the breasts of women in his class. It was so noticeable that not only were the women students extremely reluctant to come to his office hours alone, the men in the class were uncomfortable too. The professor had created a hostile environment in the classroom.

One of the most common such workplace complaints is about pinups. OK, so it may be fun for some men to look at pictures of half-naked or even naked women. But hey, guys, it's time to grow up. This doesn't belong in a professional workplace. That's the first thing I would say. Another way to deal with adult men who act thirteen is by using humor. In the documentary video, "Dangerous Propositions," written by journalist Linda Ellerbee, which I have often used in my classes, a woman truck driver faced such a situation.[25] When she came to deliver the bill of lading, she saw particularly sexually graphic pictures under the glass on the counter. She smiled sweetly and said, "Oh, is this your family? You must be very proud of them." The guy behind the counter turned bright red with embarrassment.

But a hostile work environment isn't necessarily just men ogling women. Harassers come in both genders and all permutations. Men harassing men, women harassing men, and women harassing women count too. It doesn't have to be your boss or your professor; it can be a co-worker or even a nonemployee. At one university, April, a female professor, was the subject of inappropriate sexual remarks by one of her male colleagues with whom she shared an office. Because it was a colleague and the remarks were just borderline enough to be ambiguous (at least at first) she was reluctant to speak up. But when colleague made comments about her breasts and made references to "servicing" her, she finally had enough so she reported it to her Chair. The offender was reprimanded and moved to a different office. Less than what he deserved but at least he left her alone after that.

Harassment doesn't have to be just sexual in nature. Harassment and/or discrimination of any nature are prohibited by law. When Dr. Diamond teaches courses in sexual harassment, she always tells her workplace students that sexual harassment is the model for all forms of harassment and discrimination. There is a whole list of "protected groups," but all groups should be protected from teasing, bullying, harassment, or discrimination. People can be harassed on the basis of race, ethnicity, political views, or even country of origin.

One of my former students, Helga, a young woman from Germany, told me about one of her first jobs after immigrating here. The boss, no less, would greet her every morning with a mocking Nazi salute and *"seig heil."* Since she was not at all sympathetic to the Nazis, this made her very uncomfortable. When he refused to stop, she finally quit and found another job. She didn't know it at the time but what he was doing was illegal in the State of California where she worked and she could have brought legal action against him.[26] The labor laws in California and in many states expressly prohibit workplace harassment based on ethnicity or country of origin. If you are being made fun of or are the target of obnoxious remarks because you are Black, Arab, Hispanic, or even German, you are being harassed and it has no place in the workplace.

If the harasser or even the boss tries to tell you that you are making too much of it, they're wrong. In Helga's case, the boss and even the personnel manager, who surely knew better, told her to "lighten up" and just ignore it. But as I told her, *they* don't get to decide what constitutes harassment, *you* do. According to the website lawyersandsettlements.com, "Harassment is any form of unsolicited, deliberately offensive behavior."[27] It is not the harasser but the target who gets to decide whether it is harassment. If it makes you uncomfortable and the harasser refuses to stop, it is considered harassment legally whether they agree or not. For the boss or personnel manager to tell Helga to "lighten up" or ignore it was a dereliction of duty as well as rude and inconsiderate.

Sometimes you may be told things by management that aren't even true. April, the professor I mentioned above, was told by the university's (female!) lawyer that what her colleague was doing wasn't legally harassment. April knew better and refused to withdraw the complaint. Since that time, several other lawyers have confirmed that April was right and the university's lawyer, who after all was being paid to protect the *university*, was wrong. Don't be intimidated by people who have their own agenda. Don't back down if you believe you are right and have evidence to back you up.

Be careful, however, about whom you turn to for help. The Department Chair or boss may or may not be sympathetic. If you think they are part of the problem, go up the line. But the company's lawyers, as in April's case, may be more interested in protecting the company than you. Even the Human Resources director, as in Helga's case, may not take you seriously. If you do not get satisfaction within the company, you may have to seek help outside. Some suggestions appear below.

Sometimes women are treated as if they brought it on themselves and are reluctant to speak up. Psychologists call this "blaming the victim." This attitude is comparable to what often happens in domestic violence cases.[28] The batterer often blames the battered. Even the victims often say to themselves, "What did I do wrong?" But those who are being harassed or battered are not at fault, the harasser or batterer is. Don't fall for this line of unreasoning. If you are being harassed or bullied, you have a right to protest and object to inappropriate behavior. If no one at your company is willing to take you seriously, you may have to do what battered wives have to do—permanently get out of the situation.

TAKING ACTION

Speak up

Here's what the experts recommend for dealing with harassment. First tell the harasser in a calm but firm manner that what he is doing makes you uncomfortable and you want him to stop. That may sounds obvious but it doesn't always happen. In fact, one analysis found that it is not the usual response of choice, avoidance is (in spite of the fact that avoidance is the technique least likely to be effective).[29] If the harasser is your manager or boss, you may be afraid to tell him to stop for fear of losing your job. If the harasser is a co-worker, you may still be reluctant because you either don't want to rock the boat or you may even think you just have to accept it because it won't do any good to speak up. In the case of sexual harassment, some women even think such behavior is "normal" and may simply suffer in silence. Some may be afraid or embarrassed to speak up because many women have been socialized to believe that it's "not nice" to be confrontational. But if someone is being rude to you, you are not obligated to be "nicesy nice." The harasser is acting inappropriately, not you.

Sometimes merely speaking up is enough. In the documentary, "Dangerous Propositions," one woman tells of a time when a co-worker would continually greet her by smacking his lips and staring at her breasts.[30] She finally got fed up and told him she didn't want him to do that anymore. This clueless guy was actually surprised and said, "I thought you women liked that." After this conversation, he stopped the offensive behavior and left her alone. You may think this story is a fluke but it's not.

Dr. Diamond, who is Jewish, recalls a workplace situation many years ago when she was working in offices to support herself while attending college. She had just gotten a job after many months of looking. Some of her co-workers were tradesmen and were accustomed to using phrases such as "jewing them down" or "kike" as well as other terms derogatory to Jews. Because she needed the job, Diamond tried to bite her tongue and accept these terms, but after the second day of her employment, she just couldn't do it. She went into the back, where these men worked and asked them if they knew the meaning of the words. Basically they said, "No, these are just expressions we've been using all our life." She explained the derogatory meanings to them and how she, as a Jewess, felt hearing them. To their credit, they apologized and never (almost never) used the terms again.

According to *What to Do When You Don't Want to Call the Cops: A Non-Adversarial Approach to Sexual Harassment* by Joan Kennedy Taylor, the most effective way to deal with harassers is to communicate with the harasser.[31] "Communication with those you are having problems with is not just one of several useful tools—it is by far the best tool, as was indicated by [a] 1992 *Working Woman* survey," writes Taylor. She goes on to cite a formal study of university faculty which found that the tactic that resulted in the most satisfactory outcome was talking to the harasser without using threats or verbal attacks.

Taylor also reports that assertiveness is especially useful when you need or want to maintain a positive relationship with the harasser and avoid being aggressive or putting him down.[32] This, she says, is often called "facework." Though fighting or getting nasty with the harasser may be emotional satisfying, it is not the best way to communicate. Taylor cites Wendy Grossman's quote about what she calls "a well-known Internet saying": "Never wrestle with a pig. You both get dirty, and the pig likes it." This advice is totally consistent with what most communication and relationship experts say. You will get your message across better if you are firm but polite. Though this approach doesn't always work, it's the place to start.

Consider alternative options

Sometimes it takes a more forceful and creative approach when the harasser is not likely to respond to rational or polite entreaties because he is a bit mentally off. Felicia, a receptionist at a county office building and a young, attractive married woman, was being harassed by a bum who kept wandering into the building. After her employer laughed it off, Felicia told her husband Al. When the bum wandered in again, Al was ready for him. Al came up to the bum and in a menacing tone said: "This is my woman. You better stop it and leave her alone." The bum never returned.

In a milder vein, I once had a male student who was also a bit disturbed (though not in a dangerous way). One day when I had accidentally left my briefcase in the classroom, he came running after me to tell me that I had left my "purse" there. When he said to me, "You'd lose your head, dear, if it wasn't attached," I was dumbfounded! No student had ever talked to me that way before—or since. Because I was talking with other students and have a policy of never dressing down a student publicly (thus using "facework"!), I waited till the next class to take him aside privately and tell him in the sternest voice I could muster (and, trust me, that is *very* stern!) that what he did was inappropriate and that he better not *ever* talk to me that way again. And he never did. He was the very model of decorum in the classroom for the rest of the semester.

When the harasser is on a power trip and won't stop even after you ask him to stop, it may take an even more forceful approach to get rid of him. In the book *Back Off! How to Confront and Stop Sexual Harassment and Harassers*, the author, Martha J. Langelan, tells the story of Camille, an office manager at a law firm.[33] An attorney from next door kept coming over to bother her at her desk, gradually escalating to invitations to lunch and dinner. Because she was young and naïve at the time, she kept politely refusing in the ladylike fashion she had been taught. When she was offered a job at another firm, she thought she was rid of him. To her astonishment, he showed up there, saying he was "very disappointed in her." Camille finally wised up and realized that being polite wasn't going to cut it. She asked him to step out into the corridor and let him have it. Leaving her "ladylike disposition on the doorstep," she told him that if he ever bothered her again, she would go to the police and have a restraining order sworn out against him. She never heard from him again.

Too bad Camille didn't do it sooner when the polite approach fell on deaf ears. If being polite doesn't work and the harasser is persistent, especially, as in this case, when he is not even a co-worker that you can report to your boss, the threat of legal action can be *very* persuasive. But a warning here, be fully prepared to follow through on your threat if the creep doesn't get the message.

Prepare your case

If telling the person to stop doesn't work and he continues with the harassment, whether sexual, racial, or any other kind, here's what every guide to dealing with harassment will tell you to do. Carefully document the wrongdoing, bullying or harassment in as much detail as you can. Keep a journal with date, time, exactly what happened and what was said, names of witnesses, if any, and any other relevant details. Describe your response to the harassment. Did you ask the person to stop? How did he respond? Write down how the harassment affected you, including its effect on your health, your emotional state, and your job performance. Ask around to see if others witnessed it or know of similar incidents involving this person.

Collect any evidence relevant to your case. This could include offensive letters, notes, photographs, pictures or cartoons. If you can't confiscate them, make copies of them or describe them in detail in your journal. Note the dates of any offensive material that was posted on a bulletin board. Get a copy of your company's sexual harassment policy and use the specifics in preparing your case.

The Nolo Press book, *Sexual Harassment on the Job,* suggests that you get a copy of your work records before you tip your hand.[34] That way, if the boss tries to retaliate by transferring or firing you, claiming poor job performance, you have evidence that it's not true.

Put it in writing

Next write a letter to the harasser in a detailed but calm, professional way. Here are some ideas for what to include in this letter based on suggestions at womenemployed.org:[35]

- State the basic facts of what happened, e.g., "you commented on my appearance at the meeting" or "You brush against me in the hall."
- State how the behaviors made you feel, e.g., "My stomach turns to knots when I come to work" or "I'm thinking of asking for a transfer."
- State what you want to happen next, e.g., "I want our relationship to be professional" or "I want you to stop making comments about my appearance."

If this letter doesn't stop the harassment, take your letter to your boss, your boss's boss (if your boss is the problem), the personnel department, or other appropriate office. If you're not sure who is the best person to talk to, speak to someone in the personnel office, or, if at a school or college, ask a trusted professor. Many victims are afraid to speak up for fear of retaliation from the harasser or other negative repercussions. In some cases, the fear is justified but often is not. Donna, an undergraduate student at a large university, was angered when one of her professors had the nerve to tell her that her boyfriend wasn't right for her. Since she sensed that the professor was implying that *he*, in contrast, *was* right, she decided to take action. She sent him an e-mail that told him off in no uncertain terms *and* sent a copy to the Chair of that department. As it happens, this particular professor was well-known for such inappropriate behavior and he knew it and knew the Chair knew it! He quickly sent her a profusely apologetic letter. Donna didn't need to fear that he would change her grade once the Chair knew about the incident. Don't be afraid to speak up. In many companies and universities, the lurking fear of a lawsuit alone is enough to make them take you seriously.

If even the boss or others in charge refuse to take you seriously, state in writing to the harasser or bully that you want him to "cease and desist" and send a copy to the boss or personnel department. If they think this is funny or try to intimidate you, then they are acting foolishly. "Cease and desist" is a legal term and suggests you may be taking the problem to a new level and may even have consulted a lawyer. Most companies don't want to risk law suits so by hinting that you know the law, you are suggesting that you may be ready to file a legal complaint with the EEOC and/or get a lawyer. They won't want this! Even if you *are* bluffing, they don't know it and they may not want to find out the hard way. See the Resources section below for a guide to writing cease-and-desist letters.

In the case of larger companies, chains or franchises, also consider the possibility of "going upstairs" by sending a detailed letter of complaint to the CEO of the parent company by registered mail. Most big companies don't want trouble. By sending a letter to the CEO, you are announcing yourself as someone who can make trouble and may even file the dreaded lawsuit. But once again, be careful with this approach. Be prepared to actually go to a lawyer. If they call your bluff, you had better be prepared to follow through or you will look foolish and lose even more power.

Seek allies

If there are witnesses to your harassment, find a neutral third party, such as a Human Resources representative to get statements from them in writing. That's safer than doing it yourself because otherwise you run the risk of being accused of manipulating the witnesses. But often there are no witnesses. Talk to your friends about the harassment and how it made you feel. Then you will at least have witnesses to the effect of the harassment on you. If you have no evidence that you were upset or offended, the investigators will be skeptical and your case weak.

Talk to co-workers but don't put them on the spot. You don't want to jeopardize their jobs. But some of them may have seen the harasser bothering other women (or men) so they could back up your claim that the person who harassed has a history of it. The Nolo Press book, *Sexual Harassment on the Job,* suggests that former employees are also a good resource. Some of them may have left for that very reason.

Consider alternatives

If you can afford it, you might also seriously consider spending a few hundred dollars to actually have a lawyer write the "cease and desist" letter. Nothing like a letter from a lawyer to make people sit up and take notice! If those in charge continue to harass you or try to fire you, the lawyer will just have more grist for the legal mill. It will be a powerful and damning piece of evidence if you do decide to file a law suit or report the company to the EEOC.

This tactic can also be effective with harassment or bullying outside the workplace. Daphne and Joanne had created a fan site for an actor they admired. It was a fun and creative hobby un-

---

Strength in Numbers

Here are some tips adapted from the Nolo book on "getting strength from numbers," in other words, seeking allies:[36]

- Find out who cares about the problem. Talk with co-workers and get them to find out who cares about the problem.
- Agree on a plan. Who do you need to deal with in the company? What are suggestions for improving the situation? Decide what the best tactic is—a letter, petition, meeting with the boss, or some other action.
- Take action. Involve as many people as you can. That gives you a strong group.
- Spread the word about your successes. Others may join you. You might use your group to learn more about the issue.
- Keep it going. A support or advocacy group can give workers a collective voice. There's likely to be women in the group who have experienced sexual harassment and can add their insights to the group.

The Nolo list was adapted from *The New 9to5 Office Worker Survival Guide* published by 9to5, National Association for Working Women, another useful resource for women in the workplace.

til Denise, a "rival" webmaster who apparently thought she "owned" the actor, flipped out and posted scurrilously defamatory comments about them on her fan site. Because this was not the first time Denise has harassed them (it had actually been going on for over a year), Daphne and Joanne decided they had had enough and hired a lawyer to send Denise a "cease and desist" letter that included a hint that they would sue her for defamation if she didn't knock it off. It worked. The defamatory comments came down and they never heard another peep out of her.

An additional possibility is to take your complaint with all its details to your local newspaper. If your situation is unusual or outrageous enough, it may capture the interest of the paper. In Helga's case, the paper might have seen harassment of a *German* as a novel situation and therefore as a "human interest story." Here's a real life case where going to the newspaper was an effective tactic. Two women lecturers in the Geology Department of a large university in Southern California had gone up through all the levels of bureaucracy at their school with their complaint that one of their colleagues had dropped his pants when they were in his office. Though he never denied that he has done this, he claimed that they "played rough" in his department and it was all in good fun. Obviously the women didn't think so. But because they were merely part-time lecturers and the man was the darling boy of the department and up for tenure, the department turned a cold shoulder to their protests. When even the president of this campus refused to take action, they went to the *LA Times* with their story! The story splashed all over the newspaper was so embarrassing that the university had no choice but to deal with it. Public humiliation is sometimes more effective than the threat of legal action. The tacky professor was denied tenure. And, as a satisfying coda, one of the women was later able to get a tenure-track job at another university in California so she was not irreparably harmed by her boldness.

RESOURCES FOR BULLYING AND HARASSMENT

The Internet is a good resource for information on these issues. Look at the websites dealing with harassment and bullying in the workplace and see what information they have to offer.

One good site that may help you is bullyinginstitute.org. It has information about psychological as well as legal issues. It also tells you how to find a lawyer who specializes in workplace and employment issues and has links to a discussion forum. Information and research about the productivity cost to companies for allowing bullying and harassment can also be found on this web site. You may even want to include some of the research in your letter to the CEO or Human Resources.

There are also many books on bullying and harassment. I have listed several below that you can find at your local library or order online. *What to Do When You Don't Want to Call the Cops: A Non-Adversarial Approach to Sexual Harassment* by Joan Kennedy Taylor offers some especially useful options that are less drastic than launching an expensive and potentially traumatic law suit. But the others below may also be helpful, so check out several from the library and see which one best fits your situation.

Lastly, if the harassment or bullying continues but you do not choose to follow up with the legal options, you should consider looking for a new job where you will be treated fairly and with respect. Consider telling the bosses why you are leaving. If they joke about that, you will know you have made the right choice. However, keep in mind that there are consequences to exiting, particularly if you exit under strained circumstances. Be prepared to deal with them.

Conclusion

Asking for raises and questioning policies or evaluations can be nerve-wracking, but if you prepare carefully ahead of time and keep your cool, these situations can often be handled in a satisfactory manner. Even if you don't get what you want the first time, you will have gained information and experience that will help you shine the next time. If you are being bullied or harassed, confronting the perpetrator with resolve and assertiveness may solve the problem. Taking further necessary action, even if only to leave that situation, will empower you. Being a timid mouse or a victim gains you nothing. Acting to protect yourself gains you what really counts—self-esteem and a belief in yourself.

RESOURCES

BOOKS

Work

Richard M. Bramson. *Coping with Difficult Bosses*. New York: Simon & Schuster, 1994.

Robert M. Bramson. *Coping with Difficult People: The Proven-Effective Battle Plan That Has Helped Millions Deal with the Troublemakers in Their Lives at Home and at Work*. New York: Dell Books, 1988.

Patricia King. *Never Work for a Jerk*. New York: Barnes and Noble Books, 1987.

Amy Stark, Ph.D. *Because I Said So: Recognize the Influence of Childhood Dynamics on Office Politics and Take Charge of Your Career*. Deals with how to overcome negative childhood influences that may affect your workplace relationships and performance, including how to develop personal power. New York: Pharos Books, 1992.

Attorney Barbara Kate Repa. *Your Rights in the Workplace*. Berkeley, CA: Nolo Press, 2007. Nolo Press is one of the most reliable sources for information about legal issues and how to be your own lawyer.

Bob Rosner. *Working Wounded: Advice that Adds Insight to Injury*. New York: Warner Books, 1998. Tips from Rosner's newspaper advice column.

Muriel Solomon. *"What Do I Say When . . ." A Guidebook for Getting Your Way with People on the Job*. Englewood Cliffs, NJ: Prentice Hall, 1988.

Deborah Tannen. *Talking 9 to 5: Women and Men in the Workplace; Language, Sex and* Power. New York: Avon Books, 1994. Dr. Tannen's best-selling books on communication between the sexes are solidly based on research.

Bullying and Harassment

Robert Alberti and Michael Emmons. *Your Perfect Right: A Guide to Assertive Living.* San Luis Obispo, CA: Impact Publishers, 1995. Many psychologists consider this the best book on learning how to be assertive.

Mary Boland. *Sexual Harassment in the Workplace.* Napierville, IL: Sphinx Publishing, 2005.

Linda Gordon Howard. *The Sexual Harassment Handbook.* Franklin Lakes, NJ: Career Press, 2007.

Gary Namie and Ruth Namie, Ph.D. *The Bully at Work: What You Can Do to Stop the Hurt and Reclaim Your Dignity on the Job.* Napierville, IL: Sourcebooks, Inc., 2000.

Stanlee Phelps and Nancy Austin. *The Assertive Woman.* San Luis Obispo, CA: Impact Publishers, 2002.

Attorneys William Petrocelli and Barbara Kate Repa. *Sexual Harassment on the Job: What It is and How to Stop It.* Berkeley, CA: Nolo Press, 1999. Nolo Press is a reliable guide to legal matters.

Robert Sutton, Ph.D. *The No Asshole Rule: Building a Civilized Workplace and Surviving One That Isn't.* New York: Warner Business Books, 2007. In spite of its provocative title, most people on Amazon gave this book a 5-star rating. It discusses the problem from both the boss and the employee's perspective and suggests that having jerks in the workplace costs the company money.

Joan Kennedy Taylor. *What to Do When You Don't Want to Call the Cops: A Non-Adversarial Approach to Sexual Harassment.* New York: New York University Press, 1999. Based on interviews and research, it includes some views not found in other books on the topic.

Susan Webb. *Step Forward: Sexual Harassment in the Workplace: What You Need to Know!* New York: Master Media, 1998.

WEB SITES

Workplace Problems and Issues

Anonymousemployee
www.anonymousemployee.com
"Helping you solve your problems at work" is their tag line. Info on bullying, harassment, health and safety issues, poor communication, wrongful termination and much more.

Workplace911
www.workplace911@wordpress.com
A blog to deal with workplace issues and questions, created by Bob Rosner, author of *Working Wounded* and Sherrie Campbell. Its tagline is "24/7 emergency workplace help."

Women Employed
www.womenemployed.org
Resources and information for issues that women face in the workplace.

9to5, National Association for Working Women
www.9to5.org
Resources that include information about workplace rights and sexual harassment.

Diamond Associates
www.diamondassociates.net
Management training and resources for both business and nonprofit organizations. Dr. Diamond publishes an online newsletter and is the author of several books.

Bullying

Workplace Bullying Institute
www.bullyinginstitute.org
This nonprofit organization, started by the authors of *The Bully at Work*, offers many resources, including short articles, research studies, speakers, coaching, training professionals who help victims, information about legal issues, and links to related sites.

Bad Bossology
www.badbossology.com
Lists many books and links that provide information to help protect "people and companies from bad bosses."

Video of Robert Sutton discussing his book, *The No Asshole Rule*.
www.youtube.com/watch?v=QAThL4TJfaA

Sexual Harassment

Women Employed
www.womenemployed.org/docs/Sexual%20Harassment.pdf
A good summary of what sexual harassment is and what to do about it can be found in this PDF.

Free Advice
http://employment-law.freeadvice.com/sexual_harassment/62/
Offers free legal advice about sexual harassment matters on the page above.

Equal Employment Opportunity Commission (EEOC)
www.eeoc.gov
Information on what sexual harassment is and what you can do about it legally.

Chooselaw.com
http://articles.chooselaw.com/business/view/How-To-Write-A-Cease-And-Desist-Letter.158.html
How to write a cease-and-desist letter.

UPDATES

For updates on books, web sites, web site URLs and links (they sometimes change), articles and other relevant information, check the web site for my book:
www.standuptoauthorities.com

CHAPTER

5

Services from Hell: Surviving Lawyers, Contractors and Other Professionals without Getting Ripped Off

Melissa contracted with a marble firm to do a bathroom remodeling. The job was supposed to take two weeks; it ended up taking "3 months of hell." For starters, the contractor didn't have a permit. The workers tracked dirt on her new carpet and left a glue gun on her new marble sink. She was taken for over $6,000 for a simple remodel of a new tub and three marble walls. "I wouldn't recommend them to Satan himself," she concludes.
—from at the web site of Contractors from Hell[1]

THERE ARE MANY KINDS of professionals that people deal with on a regular basis—from accountants to plumbers, from attorneys to interior decorators. I can't possibly discuss all the different kinds individually in one chapter of one book. What I can do is pick some representative samples to use as models for the kind of questions you should ask and the approaches you should take. Because both lawyers and contractors can be intimidating and it's easy to get ripped off by both, I've chosen them as the two main examples.

Many of the general principles carry over from one professional service to another, whether accountant, plumber, contractor, lawyer, or any other. When using professional services, keep the following list in mind. If your project is complicated or expensive, make a written list as a reference:

- Know what you want; think things through ahead of time
- Ask for references
- Talk to previous customers
- Check for credentials or licenses
- Get a written contract
- Make sure you understand the contract
- Get second opinions or other bids
- Don't be afraid to ask questions and demand answers if something doesn't seem right or you don't understand what's happening
- Expect respectful treatment from the professional; if you don't get it, go elsewhere
- Keep informed; get frequent updates of your case or project
- Consider alternative options, if necessary

Justice on a Trial Basis: Dealing with Lawyers

Many attorneys are competent and do their best to win your case. But, as with any profession, a few are incompetent, lazy or dishonest. Shakespeare famously wrote, "The first thing we do, let's kill all the lawyers," but you don't need quite such a drastic solution if your attorney doesn't pursue your case with "due diligence." However, dealing with problematic lawyers could fill a whole book and it does—*Mad at Your Lawyer?* by Attorney Tanya Stearnes. If your lawyer is, for example, guilty of malpractice, you have the right to sue him or her. But I'm not a lawyer and I can't tell you how to do it. You would need to read this useful book from Nolo Press. What I *can* do is give you some general tips on how to pick a lawyer, how to communicate with him or her, and a few guidelines for deciding whether or not you are getting ripped off. Then, if you do feel you've been cheated or mistreated, go to this Nolo book for more in-depth information.

CONSIDER ALTERNATIVE OPTIONS

I'm listing this suggestion first because you may be able to resolve your legal problem without even using a lawyer. So my first tip: look at the Nolo Press catalog! Nolo, which specializes in "do-it-yourself" law books, is a wonderful informational resource. You can use the many legal books from Nolo as guides to either avoiding the costs of lawyers by doing it yourself or by giving you enough information to know whether your lawyer is doing the right things. All of its legal books are written by attorneys. Some of the many titles include *Nolo's Sample Will Book, Living Together: A Legal Guide for Unmarried Couples; 101 Law Forms; Beat Your Ticket: Go to Court and Win; Divorce Without Court;* and *Patent It Yourself*. See the Resources section below for other titles.

Nolo's web site is truly a treasure trove. Besides hundreds of books on areas ranging from starting a business to doing your own divorce, from planning your estate to adopting a child, there are printed forms, software, blogs, lawyer referrals and more. I used a Nolo book on how to form a nonprofit corporation for my organization, Resources for Independent Thinking (RIT), and found the directions clear and thorough. Because there were many steps in the process, I saved thousands of dollars in legal costs for RIT and only spent $150 to have a lawyer make sure the articles of incorporation would pass muster. RIT was incorporated with a minimum of fuss.

If your legal problem is simple enough (and is a civil issue rather than criminal), one of the Nolo guidebooks may be enough. However if your problem concerns criminal law, whether misdemeanor or felony, you probably need to hire a lawyer. If you are charged with a felony, don't even consider defending yourself. The law is way too complicated for that. But keep in mind that the Nolo books can help you understand the legal process and help you decide whether your lawyer is handling your case appropriately.

PICKING A LAWYER

Picking a lawyer isn't any easier than picking a physician or any other kind of expert. In fact, it's harder. Lawyers aren't necessarily as benign as physicians and they cost a lot more. Possibly a greater percentage of incompetent ones too. From public defenders who are overworked and underpaid and cheapo attorneys rushing through their cases in a superficial way to ambulance chasers just out for your money, picking a lawyer is a roll of the dice. And they don't all have law degrees from a prestigious school such as Harvard. So it's really hard to know what you are getting beforehand unless you have solid information. Unfortunately, it's easy to get a dud.

Referrals from people you know

If you can get a recommendation from a trusted friend, go for it. Or maybe your friends or work colleagues know someone who has had a similar problem and can recommend a good lawyer. Ask about their experiences. But keep in mind that people are different and their experiences may not be the same as yours.

Find a lawyer with the right specialty

It's important to find the right kind of lawyer for your problem. As with any complex discipline, lawyers specialize. There's criminal and civil, that's easy. But there are many kinds of civil specialties. Check out the ads in the phone Yellow Pages under attorneys. My lawyer's specialty is "entertainment," which includes publishing and the arts. Other specialties include real estate, divorce, contract, business, intellectual property rights—the list goes on. However, you may not want to just pick out your lawyer cold from the phone book. Their Yellow Page ads tells you nothing about their competence or ethics.

Check with your state or city bar association. It may provide referrals. The San Francisco Bar Association, for example, will provide referrals for injury cases with a free ½ hour consultation or $25 referrals for other cases, which includes a ½ hour consultation.[2] In a consultation, the lawyer will discuss your case with you and give you an idea of its merit and whether he or she is willing to take it on.

There may be other sources for referrals, depending on the kind of case. I found my lawyer through the San Francisco Council for the Arts. Nolo Press has a list of lawyers across the US (see below). Do an Internet search for organizations that might provide referrals of the kind you need. But be careful of online referrals. They may be little more than glorified ads. Though referral organizations have to be approved by the state bar association, that alone doesn't guarantee either competency or integrity on the part of any individual lawyer. Skip the ones that charge the lawyer for a listing, suggests Nicholas Carroll, author of *Dancing with Lawyers*.[3] He also suggests checking out the directories of lawyers at many public libraries (Martindale-Hubbell is the most extensive directory). Though the lawyers often write their own entries, you can at least learn something about them. Some list specialties, for example.

Carroll also suggests checking out the National Lawyers Guild. Their politics are leftist but, because they are idealistic, they are less likely to have sold out than some lawyers and they don't force their politics on clients. Some chapters of this organization give referrals and some don't. I once called the Guild in connection with a friend's case and found the attorney who answered the phone to be very friendly and helpful even though he was unable to provide a referral for my friend's location. He even asked me to call him back and tell him how the case turned out. To say to the least, I was impressed!

Ask for a consultation

Most lawyers are willing to give you a brief consultation for free. Some will answer your questions over the phone. But ask before you make the appointment. Beware someone who wants to charge you a regular hourly rate for a consultation. Dennis had a serious problem with a publisher and wanted to bail out of the contract. A business associate recommended Beulah. Dennis didn't know he should ask ahead of time about consultation fees and found out the hard way that Beulah did charge full rates. She looked over the case, then decided not to take it but billed him $250 anyway. To add insult to injury, Nolan, the lawyer she referred him to turned out to be a sleazeball who took Dennis's money and did nothing, absolutely nothing with it. Ouch! More on that later.

Size of the firm

One important consideration for choosing a lawyer is the size of the firm. If you have a simple problem, a small firm or even an individual lawyer may be fine and even preferred. If you think you have a big time law suit on your hands or you have a complex business problem, for example, you may want a bigger firm that will have the firepower and specialists you need. However, keep in mind that the bigger the firm, the more it will charge and the more likely it is to put an emphasis on billing rather than performance. According to attorney William Gore, "You may be shuffled from attorney to attorney/assistant depending on who is available—all charge you to re-learn the case. The most efficient attorney relationships are one-on-one but these can give A service or F service, depending on the quality of the attorney."[4] Generally, the more the firm's capabilities, the greater the cost of the services. However, suggests Gore, when it comes to severe personal injury suits, you do need a firm that is big enough and well-funded enough to carry the litigation.

Cost

If you have a civil case and money is a problem for you, there are several options. Many cities offer sliding scale law clinics for people who can't afford the usual rates. You can, for example, look in the Yellow Pages or in the front of your phone book White Pages for your local Legal Aid office. You can also look on the Internet. But keep in mind all the guidelines I mentioned earlier. In California, you can get lots of useful information about low cost options by going to the web site of the California Courts Self-Help Center (see URL below). Look for something similar in your state. If you are really poor and desperate or have a complex case that is beyond your means, another possibility is to call a big law firm that specializes in the area of your case and see if they are willing to take on the case pro bono (for free). Many big firms do a certain percentage of cases on this basis. Maybe your case is the one they'll take on but don't get your hopes up. Most pro bono cases are the high profile ones.

WHAT TO LOOK FOR AFTER YOU MEET THE LAWYER

You should assess the lawyer's behavior and attitude during the initial free consultation. You don't have to accept him or her just because they agreed to consult with you.

- *Respect for you*
  This should be your first consideration, suggests Gore. If the lawyer talks down to you or is rude or curt, you've got trouble already. You're not looking for a buddy but you *are* looking for an ally. An ally is civil and respectful. You're the potential client; the lawyer will be working for you. Don't put up with anything less either in the first meeting or later.

- *Rapport*
  If the lawyer makes you uncomfortable, that's a bad sign. He doesn't have to be your "best friend" (and shouldn't be) but there has to be some basic rapport. "You should feel compatible with the lawyer," writes Judge Thomas C. Warren. "You need to get along and have confidence in each other."[5] If you don't hit it off, he suggests, find another lawyer.

- *Credentials*
  Make sure the lawyer has a degree from a creditable law school. Look up the school on the Internet if you don't recognize the name or affiliation. It doesn't have to be the Harvard Law School or Boalt at U.C. Berkeley to be good (and many attorneys from the "second tier" are hard working and effective) but there are lots of third rate schools out there, to say nothing of the shady correspondence schools offering questionable degrees. Ask yourself, do you really want an attorney who hasn't worked hard for that degree? If you don't have access to the Internet or aren't sure how to do the search, ask a librarian to help you search for information.

- *Local connections*
  Nicholas Carroll, author of *Dancing with Lawyers*, suggests that you may want someone who has lots of local contacts because they will have an easier time navigating the

shark-infested waters of the legal system. But watch out if you have a controversial issue or problem. If what you need is someone who is willing to buck the system, too many local connections could make his or her loyalties questionable.

QUESTIONS TO ASK IN THE INITIAL INTERVIEW

Both Carroll and Gore suggest several questions that should always be asked in the first meeting. "You also need to explain who may be involved to be sure that there are no conflicts," advises Gore. "Then you bring a complete factual picture for the lawyer." Also bring related documents and reports.

- *What are my legal options?* This may take more than one visit.
- *What is your experience in this area of the law?* Ask them what previous cases they have handled.
- *Can you give me a chronology, event by event, of what is likely to happen, the time and costs involved and what are the likely outcomes at each stage?* "Get the lawyer talking," suggests Gore. "This will quickly give you good information to help you choose between attorneys (plus it will scare you about how expensive and out of control litigation can be). When doing the lawsuit/project chronology, ask the lawyer to explain what is the likely response from the other side and its costs and time."
- *What are the odds?* In Carroll's opinion, realistic lawyers will quote you a ballpark figure, with the understanding that it is a guess, not a guarantee.
- *How much will it cost?* Ask the attorney to expand on the fee structure and the estimated cost of each part of the process. Ask for a chronology of expenses here too.
- *How long will it take?* The lawyer may hem and haw, but try to get a reasonable estimate. Push for a chronology of events here too.
- *What about the retainer?* The lawyer will tell you whether he or she wants cash up front or a deposit or retainer (an upfront amount against the fees to be charged). A retainer is not unusual, but if they ask for full payment ahead of time, start looking for another lawyer. Paying upfront is

risky, says Carroll, because the money has a way of evaporating. It's not standard operating procedure for reputable lawyers. Gore agrees. "Unless it's a small matter, no full payments! Always ask for estimates—even just for the next event. Lawyers tend to underestimate but then they feel guilty and give the benefit of the doubt to the client when they have overbid—it does help to keep the bill down." He adds: "Questions to ask are whether you have to pay for time on the phone or traveling or if an associate has to be brought up to speed. The issue is whether you pay only for time or if you pay for time that has value to you and the case. The attorney should be sensitive to this and want to try to only charge for time that has value to the case."

PSYCH YOURSELF UP

If you've never dealt with a lawyer before, the visit may seem a bit intimidating. So mentally prepare yourself. You want to appear calm and serious, reasonable and nonflaky. In his book, Carroll discusses several approaches to the "dance."[6] The one that doesn't work is the "democratic" approach. "Lawyers," he writes, "are notoriously class-conscious." They're unlikely to want to be your friend and they won't see you as their equal so don't even go down that path. The approach Carroll cites that is most likely to work for you is the "business attitude." This is a no-nonsense, direct, to-the-point approach that is focused on results. Some examples that Carroll suggests: "If the cost exceeds my budget, I won't buy it," "I need to know that results can be expected, how much it will cost, and when it can be done." Being direct and to the point will save you money too because lawyers charge by the hour, usually in increments such as 6 minutes (1/10 of an hour) or 15 minutes. Money or not, the lawyer will appreciate the fact that you know how to get down to business.

PUT IT IN WRITING

To avoid being intimidated by a lawyer, Carroll recommends the same tactic I do. Make a list of what you want to talk about before the meeting. Put the facts of your problem on paper, says Carroll. Having your facts well-organized saves you money because it'll take less time to explain. You'll also be less likely to be side-tracked by the lawyer's agenda rather than yours if you have a list to follow. When you are talking to the lawyer, go down the list of points one by one. Being organized will also help the lawyer see that you are serious and business-like, a quality most of them appreciate. It also fits in with the "business attitude" approach that Carroll recommends.

DRESS FOR YOUR SUCCESS

On this subject, Carroll and I have somewhat different philosophies. He says if you normally wear a suit, OK. If not, don't. "Employees should never develop the idea that you are trying to impress them," he archly points out.[7] I understand why he says this but I'm going to hedge on this. You don't have to wear a three piece suit if that isn't your normal attire but wearing something that makes you look serious is always appropriate. My advice is to wear something nice that makes you comfortable. This doesn't have to be a suit but, unless you are very forceful, I would strongly advice against wearing anything too casual like sweatpants or jeans, even if it *is* your normal attire. If you are a woman, I don't care what Carroll says. Women need to dress seriously if they want to be taken seriously. No jeans. No T-shirts. And please, no frilly or flirty dresses. This is business. On the other hand, dressing too severely or too "masculine" is not a good choice either. Lawyers may have their biases and stereotypes too, and you don't need *that* extra baggage.

WATCH YOUR LANGUAGE

Talking to a lawyer is not the time to be shy. If you are normally reserved and soft-spoken, says Carroll, you should make an extra effort to be sure that lawyer understands you are serious. Don't be reticent. Don't be a supplicant. If you think you may become tongue-tied or if you are easily intimidated, the list you have prepared will help you be more forceful and look more serious.

Remember my advice from Chapter Two. Don't apologize; don't speak in a quiet, deferent voice. Watch your posture and body language as well. Don't slouch; don't be fidgety and nervous. Be as assertive and crisp in both verbal and nonverbal language as you can muster. Not only will attention to these details make you look more serious, it may help you to avoid being taken advantage of by the lawyer. If you don't act like a victim, you are less likely to be one.

BRING BACKUP

If you are shy or nervous about talking to a lawyer or you are very upset about your problem, bring a trusted (and assertive) friend or relative along. The friend can help keep things moving if you falter or the lawyer gets sidetracked. If you are at risk for being very emotional because you are distraught, the friend can help you explain your situation to the lawyer. The friend may also be able to spot weasel words and other signs that the lawyer may not be right for you. "It's also good," adds Gore, "to have a witness as to what you are being told."

BE AN ACTIVE PARTICIPANT

Make a conscious decision to be an active participant. Don't just passively accept whatever the lawyer says. Talk to the lawyer about your case, recommends Tanya Stearnes, author of *Mad at Your Lawyer*.[8] If you are willing to learn and the lawyer doesn't help, demand better. Continue educating yourself about the case. Ask for and read the files. Always read the letters the lawyer sends out on your behalf. Most lawyers will send you copies to approve. If yours doesn't, ask her to do so. The letters are supposed to be aggressive but you need to make sure they are not over the top.

"These matters are basically team work and the client is an important part of the team," asserts Gore. "Also people (including lawyers) make mistakes. But they make less if all the team is working together and covering each other. Attorneys like to have their work understood and appreciated, so definitely discuss what is happening so that you are informed and your attorney knows that you care and understand what is happening. Finally, you and your attorney need to agree on matters. If you don't agree, then change attorneys until you have one who shares your view of what is important and what isn't."

Offer to help with any legwork that doesn't require legal training, for example, looking up information on the Internet or at City Hall. This has two benefits—it'll save you money and it sends the message that you are serious about the case. If you are actively involved, the lawyer may give more attention to the case, says Stearnes.

KEEP INFORMED

Your lawyer should tell you from the outset what to expect and what his role will be. He should explain what is going on, what kinds of complications might arise and discuss with you the best ways to cope of problems if they do occur. He should keep you informed at each major step. If he doesn't, ask that he do so.

Check to make sure documents are filed in time. It isn't unusual for lawyers to miss filing deadlines. Don't be shy about establishing deadlines for each step. Some lawyers get easily sidetracked on other cases.

TAKE NOTES

At meetings with your lawyer, always take notes. This helps you keep up with what is happening so that you stay in the loop. It also tells the lawyer that you are monitoring her performance.

Stearnes also recommends keeping a telephone log. Write down details of everything you agree to locate and provide, whether in person or by phone.

Send the lawyer a memo to confirm the details of any phone conversation.

HAVE COPIES OF EVERYTHING

Copy everything, keep everything. Give copies of all pertinent documents to your lawyer, not originals. Ask the lawyer to send you everything—copies or scans of letters she sends out, depositions, etc. This material will help you keep up with case. It'll help you know that the lawyer is actively doing something for you. If you need a second opinion or if you have to change lawyers, having all this material will help you get down to business right away with the new lawyer.

CLEAR UP JARGON

If your lawyer uses arcane language you don't understand, ask that he say it in plain language. Insist that he explain difficult points of law. Carroll says you should be able to understand 95% of what is said. If the lawyer tells you that it's too complicated to explain, he is being condescending. He's essentially saying "don't worry your little head." Don't let him get away with it. If he can't make himself understood to you, get another lawyer who can.

PUT IT IN WRITING AGAIN

First of all, you should expect a written contract from your lawyer stating what the expectations, i.e., what she intends to do for you, what the fees will be, and so on. Poor Dennis didn't realize that this was standard. Because he was desperate, he dealt with Nolan, the second lawyer, only over the phone and without a contract. Bad idea! He got screwed again. The lawyer asked for a retainer and then did absolutely nothing for him, despite numerous calls. A contract would have made it clear that something was wrong. We'll return to this case later.

Written communication, whether letters or email, is crucial, suggest both Carroll and Gore. Carroll recommends sending follow-up letters to the lawyer at each step, with words like "I'm writing to make sure I understand."[9] This serves four functions: it's a way to make sure there are no misunderstandings; 2) it keeps the lawyer's nose to the grindstone; 3) it documents the conversation; and 4) it lets the lawyer know you are more sophisticated than the average customer. If you're computer savvy, send PDFs by email. This will have more weight than just an email message alone and be faster than a mailed letter. The letter (in whatever form) should be written in a matter-of-fact, straightforward manner with no fancy stuff. If you are using the U.S. Post Office, send it certified, return receipt requested. Email functions well as a written record so it's also a good way to communicate, points out Gore. However, keep in mind that each letter or email costs you money. The lawyer is always on the clock and that includes the time reading your letter or email. But insisting on some kind of written communication so you have documentation of what you have been told is a good idea.

PHONE CALLS, YOURS AND THEIRS

Chances are you'll be talking with the lawyer over the phone. Be prepared ahead of time. If there is information the lawyer will need, have it ready by the phone. Remember that the billing clock is ticking. Make a phone log with dates; take notes about what is discussed.

If you call the lawyer, be succinct and to the point. Don't pester and call every day. You need to keep up with the case but things don't happen every day even if the lawyer is pursuing your case diligently. Don't keep changing your mind about what you want.

If you call the lawyer and have to leave a message, expect a return call by end of the next business day, maximum (unless he is on vacation). If he doesn't return your call in a reasonable amount of time, drop him. Communication is vital to a successful case. After the initial phone consultation, poor Dennis was rarely able to reach the lawyer by phone. Email wasn't much better. He should have dropped the lawyer long before he did.

SEEK SECOND OPINIONS

If you have a complex case or you are not certain about how well the lawyer is handling your case, you may want to seek a second opinion. No two attorneys handle complex cases the same way, says Stearnes, so she recommends considering this option.[10] Unless you want to pay big bucks, the analysis, which may only be an hour of time, will be cursory rather than thorough, but at least it lets you know if your lawyer is on right track. If the second lawyer points out serious problems that make sense, then you can think about whether to change lawyers.

Second opinions are especially important on complex matters, says Gore. "Usually only another attorney can evaluate what is really happening or likely to happen in complex litigation. Big businesses use in-house counsel to monitor their out (of) house counsel."

CONSIDER ALTERNATIVE OPTIONS

If you are not happy with your lawyer and/or you are running out of money, consider other options. These include self help books, sliding scale clinics and small claims court.

- *Self-help books*
  Nolo Press catalog (www.nolopress.com). No more need be said. It's all there.
- *Low cost self-help clinics*
  Look them up on the Internet or have a librarian help you find them. See the Resources section below for more tips.
- *City, county and state agencies*
  With certain kinds of problems, governmental agencies may be able to help. Do an Internet search using key terms that include "government agency," [your state], and [your problem] or ask a librarian to help you.
- *Small claims court*
  If your case is a relatively simple one that involves a dispute, you can consider using your state's version of small claims court. Filing the claim is easy and cheap. The most common cases are car accidents, property damage, landlord/tenant rent deposit disputes, and collection of money owed. In California, the filing fee depends on how much money you are asking for; anywhere from $30 to $75. You can collect up to $7500 in damages in California.[11] Check what is allowed in your state either on the Internet or through your local library.

Though the basic procedure is simple, detailed tactics are beyond the scope of this book. Once again, the ever reliable Nolo Press has a book on how to file in small claims court (see below). You can check it out from the library or buy a used copy online. There are also several web sites that give you basic information, including Nolo (see URLs below).

Be aware, however, that even if you win, that doesn't necessarily mean you can collect. If the loser is unwilling to pony up, you will have to know the person's bank account number and pay the Sheriff's Department to levy the fine before you can collect. Dennis won his suit in small claims court against the neglectful lawyer but never saw a penny of it. Though Dennis' lawyer was able to put a lien on Nolan's house, Dennis couldn't afford to pursue legal means any further and didn't have enough information to go to the Sheriff.

An example of creative letter writing as an alternative

It may also help to get creative and try to think of what else could help your case. I have a friend, let's call him Gene, who once had a landlord who refused to clean the halls of the apartment building. The roach infestation soared, garbage piled up in the trash areas, and the building reeked with an overwhelming stench. None of Gene's complaints to the landlord did any good. So he took photos, refused to pay the rent, and sued in court.

For unrelated reasons, Gene also had to file for bankruptcy. Because he was stressed about his living conditions and about a serious illness in the family, he missed an important filing deadline. To bolster his request for an extension on the filing rather than denial of his petition, I wrote a letter attesting to his good moral character and to the effects of extreme stress on one's ability to deal effectively with tasks, even important ones. As a psychology professor, I was able to bill myself as an "expert." I even added research references for good measure. The extension was granted and his petition went forward. I can't know whether the letter was the deciding factor but I'm sure it helped. Be creative about what might help your case—and think about what friends may be able to help!

CONSULT WITH OTHERS

Chances are that your problem or issue is not unique. You may be able to get assistance or information from a special interest group attuned to the area of your problem. You can look either locally (try your newspaper or ask a librarian to help you) or go searching on the Internet. In just a short time searching, I found groups dedicated to problems resulting in everything from divorce and bad contractors to medical and aging issues.

YOUR RIGHT TO PROTEST—AND TO FIRE YOUR LAWYER

If lawyer is unpleasant or cuts you off, don't put up with it. The lawyer is supposed to be on your side. If that isn't his or her attitude, get a new lawyer. Customers with money and experience, says Carroll, have standard responses; the one Carroll likes best is to stand up and walk out without a word. You want a lawyer who works *with* you, not against you. Remember there are lots more lawyers out there.

If lawyer is doing a bad job, you not only have a right to fire her, you should do so. What's the point of spending money on an incompetent lawyer who isn't doing what needs to be done to resolve your case?

Here are some warning signs to watch out for:

- Failure to return phone calls or communicate with you for extended periods of time
- Persistent failure to meet filing dates or other deadlines
- Failure to do the work paid to do
- Criminal conduct, alcohol or drug abuse
- Failure to pay settlement proceeds

Nolan, Dennis's second lawyer, managed to qualify on at least two of the above warning signs sign. He didn't return phone calls and didn't do any of the work he said he would do. Dennis finally got fed up when the problem for which he needed the lawyer reached a crisis point. He regretted not bailing on this loser sooner because by the time he did get a competent lawyer, the problem was so out of hand that it required years of haggling before the case finally went to arbitration. Dennis did win the arbitration but if he had not gotten screwed over by Nolan, he might have been able to resolve it sooner and at considerably less cost.

If your lawyer is not communicating with you, contact him and insist on being told what is happening on the case. If he fails to respond or you have other evidence of incompetence, don't be like Dennis and wait till your problem reaches crisis proportions or worse yet, you lose in court. Change lawyers. It will cost extra money but better that than a botched job, says Stearnes. If your lawyer refuses to return your call, refuse to pay the bill.

If you do fire the lawyer, file a complaint with your state's lawyer discipline agency. Dennis filed a complaint with the state bar, not only because of Nolan's neglect (it's technically called "abandonment") but because he didn't return Dennis' retainer either. Dennis eventually got his $750 retainer back from a fund specially designed for this problem. Meanwhile another person also filed a complaint against Nolan. Facing the possibility of being disbarred, Nolan resigned rather than run the risk. Thus Dennis' complaint served two useful purposes: he got his money back and Nolan couldn't screw anyone else—at least not by pretending to act as a lawyer.

If the lawyer makes a big enough mess of your case and it's fairly high profile, you can always sue for malpractice. Here's where reading a book like *Mad At Your Lawyer?* comes in. If you are considering suing your attorney, you need more advice than I can provide, so check out Stearnes's book.

Projects from Hell: Handling Contractors and Other Home Repair Professionals

Contractors and plumbers have a bad reputation and there's a reason why. Though many of them are conscientious, hard-working and honest, everyone has heard the horror stories about the bad ones—scams, rip-offs and shoddy workmanship. Fortunately there are many resources for protecting yourself against being ripped off. Whether you're starting from scratch or just rehabbing your home, whether you have a small problem or a major overhaul of your plumbing or wiring, you're asking for trouble if you don't make use of these resources.

First of all, any public library will have several books on dealing with contractors or doing your own contracting (see below for some titles). Many city planning and permit departments have brochures on how to pick a contractor or architect. These departments often have knowledgeable staffs who can help you. Make use of these resources. You might also talk to local neighborhood or preservationist groups or the city historical society. They are likely to know the local contractors and can tell you which ones are trustworthy.

Joanne's neighborhood group, for example, had several stories to tell about sleazy contractors. One contractor who couldn't get a permit to take down some interior walls had his workers come in illegally at night and take the debris from the demolished walls out through the windows. Another contractor tried to get around an ordinance prohibiting cutting down a certain species of tree by chopping them down on weekends. A resourceful observer with a camcorder brought that ruse to a halt. The contractor was fined $10,000 a foot for each tree he cut down. "The bad guys do get creative," says Joanne.

Another excellent resource is the web site of Contractors from Hell (CFH) created by Jody Costello. This web site (contractors fromhell.com) lists guidelines as well as vivid horror stories to help you know what to watch out for. It also includes articles and a blog as well as links to other useful sites.

The subject of contractors provides a role model that can help you formulate ways to deal with other kinds of home services, so I've provided a synthesis here of the advice gleaned from Consumer Reports, several other books, the CFH web site, and the strategies in my book. This advice is appropriate whether you need a housing contractor, architect, plumber, electrician, roofer or other service professional for your home. For more details about what to be aware of and what questions to ask, read one of the relevant books listed below or check out the web site references.

PLAN AHEAD OF TIME; THINK THINGS THROUGH

- Know what you want. Take time to think over what you want as clearly and thoroughly as possible, says Consumer Reports.[12] What is your "wish list"? Be as specific as possible.
- Think carefully about your budget and how you are going to pay for it. Loans? Where will they come from? How will you secure the loan? Being clear on these details will help keep you from being tempted to go beyond your budget.
- Clarify what you want—explain your ideas each step of the way. Misunderstanding is the biggest problem with contractors, says Consumer Reports, not dishonesty.
- Know your right and obligations; make sure you understand what you are signing.

GATHER INFORMATION

Learn something about the kind of repairs or rehab you will need. Use one of the books below, search the Internet, or ask friends who have gone through the same problem. The more informed you are, the less likely you are to get scammed or bamboozled. You can also ask more knowledgeable questions, which, in turn, will tell the contractor that you're not a pushover.

Look into the kinds of materials you want to use. Check on quality, color, name brands, etc. Decide what's right for your budget. Then you can be specific about exactly what you want and expect. You should decide, not the contractor, otherwise you can end up with low-quality products that boost the contractor's profits. When Lewis and Darlene suffered a fire in their rented condo, the contractors provided by the insurance company gave them a bid that they accepted without question. They didn't realize they should have looked carefully at the quality of the products the contractor bought, so they ended up with flooring and carpets that were considerably inferior to what they had before.

Fixed price bids are especially vulnerable to the risk of low-quality scamming but any construction project would benefit from careful and specific listing of exactly what materials you want and expect the contractor to use. Georg Buechi, a reputable contractor and designer in Northern California, suggests that, whether it is a fixed price bid or other kind of bid, all specs on construction items be carefully spelled out down to the precise name brand, models, items numbers, etc. of all the wood, flooring, tiles, carpets or any other material going into the construction or rehab.[13]

Lewis and Darlene learned their lesson the hard way. Don't make their mistake. Know exactly what you want and insist on it.

PSYCH YOURSELF UP

The right attitudes are important to keep you from becoming a victim. Adopt a buyer beware attitude, warns Consumer Reports. Don't assume you will be ripped off but don't be passive either. Be prepared to ask questions and demand answers. If you don't get the right answers, consider another contractor.

You need to be assertive and business-like without being obnoxious or aggressive. With the information you've gathered, you can come across as knowledgeable and confident rather than uncertain and confused. This attitude sends an important signal to the service professionals that they shouldn't try to scam you.

BRING BACKUP

If you are a naturally shy or reserved person, consider having an assertive friend with you the first time you meet the contractor. If you are a woman and handling the problem by yourself, this is doubly important. Like some auto mechanics, unethical contractors may think a woman is fair game and try to bamboozle you.

PICKING A CONTRACTOR OR OTHER SERVICE PROFESSIONAL

First and foremost, look for credentials and references. But that's not enough. Just because someone has a license doesn't mean he/she can be trusted to follow the laws and perform ethically. You'll have to dig deeper. How deep you need to dig depends on the job. If it's a $75 repair, you don't have to go through the entire list below! If you are getting a complex, expensive rehab or construction, it will pay you to be very thorough and use most or all of the following guidelines.

Here is advice based on the guidelines offered by CFH, the books listed in the Reference section, and the professionals I have talked to. Use them according to your needs.

- Make sure that you verify that the contractor, plumber or other service professional maintains a permanent mailing address, email address, published business phone number, fax number, and a cell phone, or voice-messaging system. If the contractor doesn't have a business phone or address published in the phone book, forget him fast. The contractor working out of his truck is one of the warning signs listed at CFH[14] Ask each contractor to provide you with a copy of his license, writes Steve Gonzalez, author of *Before You Hire a Contractor*.[15] It's one of the five essential steps he lists in picking a contractor. He also suggests asking for the driver's license to make sure the name matches the license. You can also check with your State's regulatory agency that governs the licensing and enforcement of building contractors to make sure that the contractor's license is legit *and in your state*. No out-of-state contractors! If the contractor doesn't have a license, you are running a big risk of being scammed, with little recourse. And if you think the licensed ones are bad, says CFH, many of the unlicensed ones are even worse.
- Use an unlicensed contractor only if his reputation is absolutely rock-solid. There's an exception to the rule about making sure the contractor has a license—*if* you know the person well or he has excellent references. There *are* unlicensed constructors who are reputable and competent. I have a good friend who is one such contractor (for small

renovations). His work is cheaper *and* better than most regular contractors. If you get a reference from someone who can be thoroughly trusted, who has good judgment, and who has used the unlicensed contractor before, the contractor may work out OK for small jobs. However, be aware that in some states, there is a legal limit to what an unlicensed contractor may do. In California, it is $500. Naturally, many of the same guidelines below still apply for evaluating the contractor overall. Be *very* careful of this option.

- Ask for references from previous clients. If the contractor, plumber, or other service professional hems and haws and won't provide any, find someone else. A good service professional will have references.
- Better yet, ask people you know for references, if you can. "Nothing is better than personal references from people a client trusts," says Buechi. "It is impossible for a client to know everything a good contractor knows (unless being a contractor him/herself) and it is impossible to control every step that is being done on even a small-scaled project," he advises, so finding someone you can trust is crucial.
- Follow up on at least 3 references. "Ask for both recent (12 months) as well as the last three years," suggests CFH.[16] Choose referrals with projects similar to yours, advises Gonzalez. Look up these homeowners and ask for a personal interview. Ask questions about the quality of the workmanship, cost overruns, communication problems, and so on. The books listed below will give you detailed questions to ask.
- Visit one of the contractor's current projects. Do the activities appear to be professional and the people courteous?
- Ask for copies of the contractor's insurance coverage. This is another one of Gonzalez's essential steps. This should include worker's compensation, general liability and property damage. If a worker is injured on your property and the contractor doesn't have insurance, warns CFH, you'll be responsible for the medical bills. Ouch!
- Make sure the subcontractors or independent contractors are licensed too. Obtain their license numbers and check their status with your Contractors State License Board.

- Educate yourself on the permit process so you don't need to take the contractor's word on whether a permit is needed or not. Check to make sure that the necessary permits have in fact been taken out. Some contractors will tell you that they did but pocket the money for the fees instead.
- Make sure the contractor has a clear complaint record, says Gonzalez. Check for a history of complaints with your state's Contractors Licensing Board or regulatory agency. Find out if there is a complaint history or any legal actions taken against the contractor. However, warns CFH, "No record of complaints against a contractor does not necessarily mean no previous or current consumer problems."[17] They found out the hard way that complaints can take months to surface. Check and check again.
- Check with the Contractors State Licensing Board. They are a major resource, says Buechi. "They have done a lot to protect consumers by establishing certain rules contractors have to follow in the way they write contracts etc."[18] The website for the California CSLB is clear and easy to navigate. Find the comparable board for your state. "Contractors have to present everything in writing," continues Buechi. "The client has 3 days to rescind a signed contract. The maximum down payment is $1,000 or 10% of contract amount. Every contract has to include a checklist for homeowners, and more." Don't neglect this important resource for your protection.
- Check with the Better Business Bureau because some people may not complain to the Contractors Board. If there are any complaints, regardless of whether resolved or not, move on, suggests CFH. But keep in mind that the BBB is not necessarily the best, let alone, the final authority on complaints.
- Be cautious of someone who advertises heavily in the local newspapers, Sunday newspaper inserts, mass-mailed coupons, or other mass media, warn several of the sources. If a contractor spreads himself too thin, your project may suffer. The really good contractors develop word-of-mouth referrals from customers and have plenty of work to keep them busy the next several months says CFH. The good ones are worth the wait.
- Ask for a list of the contractor's or plumber's suppliers. Contact them to verify his credit standing and reputation.

Gonzalez suggests that this may also be an additional source of references.

- Get at least three bids using the same set of plans so that the bids are comparable. This is true, regardless of the kind of service. In a *Kiplingers* article on how to choose a plumber, for example, Sean O'Neill also suggests that you should take at least three bids.[19]

  If you only get one bid, you may become the victim of a dishonest service professional. Here's one such story, as reported by Ripoff Report™:

  "Upon being called to our home to investigate a simple clogged sewage pipe, he described a horrifically broken, root-clogged drain pipe system, scaring my wife so much that she started throwing toilet paper in the trash can and running down to the basement after flushing to make sure it hadn't flooded again.

  This plumber gave my wife a $23,000 estimate it would cost to replace her 'badly damaged' sewer line. In the meantime, he and his plumber henchmen acted like aggressive salesmen and told her she wouldn't be able to go 'number two' without causing flooding."[20]

- If the job is going to be an expensive one, check out the contractor's lien history with the County and court records for lawsuits. If you find anything, look for someone else.

- Listen to your intuition, suggest several sources. If you get a "gut" feeling that there is something suspicious about the person for any reason or you feel uncomfortable with him, even though he passes on all the points above, move on. There are other contractors and plumbers out there.

  Here's a story about someone who wisely followed this rule. Denise, an attractive blonde, needed to call a plumber the day after Christmas because she had a backed up drain. The guy immediately gave her the creeps. Though she was modestly dressed, he kept giving her the once-over. He gave her a $700 estimate and said he would be back the next day. Instead she called her father and asked him to contact the plumber who he had previously used. The problem turned out to be less serious than the creepy plumber claimed and cost only about $125 to fix. Unprofessional behavior of any kind is a red flag telling you to call in someone else.

GET IT IN WRITING

Don't trust verbal agreements or your memory, warns Consumer Reports; get everything in writing. A written contract is a must. But don't sign anything until you have read it very carefully and completely understand the terms. For more information on construction contracts, check out the Consumer Report book or the CFH web site. Get estimates in writing as well. This makes it harder for the contractor or plumber to jack up the prices later. If they try to do up the price without ironclad reasons, you should dump them.

Be sure to get a plumber's written, on-site estimate, asserts Sean O'Neill in his article on how to hire a plumber (see reference below). He suggests refusing to pay more if the plumber goes over that estimate. O'Neill tells the story of a couple who discovered a drippy kitchen faucet and a leaky shower in their newly purchased home, in Chester, N.J. They called the first plumber listed in the Yellow Pages. The plumber gave them an estimate of $500 but the total actually billed was $900.[21] This is unethical, so don't stand for it.

EVALUATE WHAT THE CONTRACTOR OFFERS YOU CAREFULLY

If a deal sounds too good to be true, both CFH and Consumer Reports agree that it probably is. Here are some of the warning signs they both give.

- Beware big discounts in exchange for huge cash deposits. Once the contractor has your money, you are at his mercy. If he skips out with your money, you're out of luck.
- Offers cut-rate deals on material "left over from other jobs."
- Offers rebates if you use your home for a "model" to sell other projects. Contractors with good reputations don't need to do that.
- Suggests that they trade their labor for products or services you might have in your company.
- Offers discounts for finding other customers.

Services from Hell

- Asks for cash for anything.
- Asks you to get the required building permits. That's their job. If they want you to get it, this may mean that they don't have a legitimate license. Not a good sign.
- Asks for payment for the entire job in advance or accepts cash payments only. "Yikes! Don't you dare!" warns CFH.[22] Every source I read insists that you do not *ever* pay cash. Furthermore, write the check to the company, not to the individual. Your cancelled check is legal proof of payment.
- Tries to pressure you into signing the contract. The salesperson or contractor tells you the "special price" will only be available if you sign the contract today. Sounds like one of those sleazy late-night commercials to me. Legitimate bids will have expiration dates but not in one day! Most are good for at least 30 days. Never sign a contract before you have a chance to read it over carefully.
- Rings your doorbell and says he "just happened to be doing work in the neighborhood and noticed that you needed (a new roof, driveway resurfacing . . . or whatever)." He then claims that he has all the equipment and can do it at an amazingly low price. This is a well-known scam. You'll shell out money, he and his men disappear, and you've been had. The work will be shoddy and you will have no recourse.
- You are asked to sign a completion certificate for the job "by appeal, threat, trick" or before the job is properly completed. Never sign off until the job is done to your satisfaction. Use a punch list to make sure everything has been done and done right. If the job is especially complex and expensive, consider hiring an independent inspector to assess the work.

MEETING WITH THE CONTRACTOR OR SERVICE PROFESSIONAL

- Pay attention to the contractor's response and reaction to your questions, says CFH. If the contractor or service professional weasels or objects to your questions, consider that a red flag. Ethical service professionals don't mind answering questions.

- "The contractor starts talking about 'problems' he has had with certain customers—pass on this one because you'll likely be his next problem," warns CFH.[23] He may be making excuses to cover up whatever you may uncover in your interviews. If he has had a problem with a customer that has not been resolved satisfactorily, this is another warning sign. Ethical contractors want happy and satisfied customers and work to resolve issues.
- Ask about how situations with unsatisfied customers were handled.
- If a salesperson asks you to sign a contract before meeting the contractor, walk out the door and never come back. This is *not* how it is done.
- If the service professional yells at or threatens you in any way at any time, tell him to leave immediately, call the police and file a report, urges CFH. Ethical contractors don't act like this. But, according to CFH, this kind of behavior is not uncommon. Don't be intimidated. Filing a police report will help protect you from possible retaliation.
- Be specific about the quality of materials as well as name brands, colors and other details. Don't let the contractor decide because he may be tempted to use low-quality materials to increase his profits.
- Require lien releases after each payment. If the contractor has a problem with this, it's another red flag.
- Think of any other relevant questions that need answering.
- Make final payment only when the job is completely finished to your satisfaction.

PUT IT IN WRITING AGAIN

If problems or conflicts arise, documentation is crucial. Keep a record of all letters, conversations, invoices, and so on. If you need to take the contractor to court, this information will be important evidence on your side.

- Take photos of questionable work.

- Notify the contractor in writing. Be specific about your concerns without ranting. Be neutral but to the point.
- If the contractor doesn't respond, send a second letter and ask for an explanation or a face-to-face meeting.
- If the contractor does respond, have him put in writing what he intends to do to remedy the situation.
- Follow up with a letter stating your understanding of what will be done and the time frame in which it will be done. Send the letter certified mail, return receipt requested.
- If the contractor still fails to resolve the problem or quits before a job is finished, send him a certified letter stating the specifics of his negligence or abandonment.

SEEK OUTSIDE HELP OR SECOND OPINIONS

If you run into a problem with the contractor or have concerns that are not addressed in a satisfactory manner, consider the following alternatives:

- Hiring a professional inspector to give you a second opinion. If you have been abandoned or are the victim of negligence, hire a forensic contractor to assess the situation and give you an estimate of what it will take to correct the situation.
- If the contractor fails to cooperate or address your concerns, file a complaint with the Contractor's Board in your state.
- If there are significant problems that have not been addressed or there are defects pointed out by a third party, consider hiring a lawyer. If the cost of remedying the problem is not too large, you can also consider small claims court (see section on lawyers, this chapter).

If you are vigilant and proactive, you can avoid some of the worst pitfalls of dealing with contractors and other service professionals. If you run into serious problems, you should seek further information from the books or web sites listed below.

Other Professional Services

"And now for something completely different," to quote the illustrious Monty Python . . .

Publishing

These days lots of people have something to say. Since the advent of the Internet, many of them now have a place to say it. But what if you want to see your ideas in print? It's obvious why I have a soft spot for people who want to publish a book or communicate an idea. It's not as hard as you think but it's not easy either. There's a smart way and a not-so-smart way. You'll get plenty of doors slammed in your face, lots of rejections. The authorities *will* say no to you. How do you deal with that? Quite frankly, there are so many books readily available on this topic that it would be pointless of me to discuss it at length. What I *can* do is give you a few pointers and recommendations that will lead you to the information you need to do it right.

But before you get started, here's some important advice—make sure you are a good writer (or have a brilliant editor). Many manuscripts are relegated to the slush pile of rejected books because the writing is clumsy, pedestrian, boring, full of errors or otherwise wretched. Have a friend who will be honest with you, or better yet, an independent consultant, evaluate your writing before you start metaphorically knocking on publishers's doors. One book that I know of, for example, is so full of egregious grammatical and spelling errors that no editor would surely have accepted it. It's from a press I never heard of and I strongly suspect the author published himself because no one else would touch it. Don't embarrass yourself. If you are not a good writer, get professional help or shut up.

- The first tip: Get a good book on how to get published. There are a lot out there; I've listed below a few that got good reviews on Amazon. [It's always smart to check out the reviews before you buy a book of any kind.]
- Next tip: Get an agent. Publishers don't want to be both-

- ered with would-be authors. Send your manuscript in without an agent and, chances are, it will be relegated to the bottom of the slush pile at best. The books below will tell you how to find an agent.
- Don't go to an obvious vanity publisher such as Vantage Press. That's where *you* pay *them* to publish your book and sign away your rights. They claim "You retain full ownership" but one web site calls this "the vanity/subsidy press 'Big Lie.' "[24] Forget this! No bookstore will touch these kinds of books and you'll look like a twit. There are better options.
- If you get turned down by the publishers you try or you just want to control the process yourself, consider self-publishing. Rather than throw your money away on the vanity presses, invest in a book on self-publishing and do it yourself. You'll get a lot more bang for your buck.
- Get a good book on marketing your book. Even if you have a conventional publisher, they won't or can't do much promotion. If it's not the kind of book that will be a best-seller, major publishers won't spend much money or time on it. If you have a small publisher, it won't have the budget. If you want to sell the book, you'll have to do it yourself.
- If you can't afford to self-publish, consider publishing it on the Internet. The self-publishing books below will tell you how to do it.

One of the reasons I wanted to include this section (besides loving the idea of helping people get their ideas out) is to include the story of M.J. Rose. She had many doors slammed in her face when she tried to get her unusual erotic novel, *Lip Service*, published.[25] The publishers couldn't figure out who the audience was for her book and were afraid to try anything exotic and different. That didn't stop her. She refused to take no for an answer. So she published it herself on the Internet, did her own publicity and was then able to publish it in conventional book form. Her efforts were so successful that a major book club picked up her novel. Ten years later she has published 11 novels and a book on how to get your book published. She has also been interviewed, written up many times, and has a handsome website to promote her books . . . I love do-it-yourself success stories!

The authorities (in this case, editors) were wrong about Rose's book and they'll be wrong again. Consider some of the best-sellers that were at first turned down by publisher after publisher. Most famously rejected, of course, were the Harry Potter books. Several publishers have no doubt been kicking themselves in their metaphorical pants ever since. Then there is *Atlas Shrugged* by Ayn Rand and *The Feminine Mystique* by Betty Friedan. Both were rejected over and over. Too unconventional, too "radical." Publishers, like Hollywood producers, prefer what is safe. But Rand and Friedan persisted, eventually found publishers, and both became best sellers and are still in print today, decades after the original publication.[26] Maybe your book won't be a mega-hit like these examples but if you have something to say and have written it well, be persistent. Don't take no for an answer and you *will* find a way to get your book published.

Conclusions

The key to avoiding being bamboozled and abused is knowledge and assertiveness. Know what you want ahead of time and have a plan. Check out credentials, learn what you should expect from a reputable service professional and then insist on it. Don't be intimidated. Don't allow them to treat you badly. Always remember that *you* are hiring *them*, not the other way around.

REFERENCES

BOOKS

Lawyers

Attorneys Paul Bergman and Sara Berman-Barrett. *The Criminal Law Handbook: Know Your Rights, Survive the System.* Berkeley, CA: Nolo Press, 2007.

Attorneys Paul Bergman and Sara Berman-Barrett. *Represent Yourself in Court: How to Prepare & Try a Winning Case.* Berkeley, CA: Nolo Press, 2008.

Nicholas Carroll. *Dancing with Lawyers: How to Take Charge and Get Results.* Lafayette, CA: Royce Baker Publishing, 1992. Though Carroll's book has been endorsed by experts, he does point out that he is not an attorney and that his book offers generalities, not specific solutions. It is, however, a very useful guide.

Attorney Joseph L. Matthews. *The Lawsuit Survival Guide: A Client's Companion to Litigation.* Berkeley, CA: Nolo Press.

Kay Ostberg and Adrian Helm. *Using a Lawyer . . . And What to Do If Things Go Wrong: A Step-by-Step Guide.* Westminster, MD: Random House, 1990. Recommended by Nicholas Carroll. Available free from HALT if you join (see URL below).

Attorney Tanya Stearnes. *Mad At Your Lawyer? What to Do When You're Overcharged, Ignored, Betrayed or a Victim of Malpractice.* Berkeley, CA: Nolo Press, 1996.

Also see Chapter Nine for more books on dealing with the legal system.

Contractors

In addition to the titles below, there are also books on remodeling and being your own contractor. Check out the reviews on Amazon or Barnes and Noble for suggestions or see what your local library has in its catalog.

Carmen Amabile. *How To Hire, Manage, And Fire Your Contractor.* Clinton Township, MI: LWP Publishing, 2008. Not yet rated on Amazon as of this writing but it *is* more up-to-date than other titles.

Paul Bianchina and the Editors of Consumer Reports. *How to Hire the Right Contractor: Getting the Right Prices, Workmanship, and Scheduling for Home Remodeling.* Yonkers, NY: Consumer Reports Books, 1991. Consumer Reports is always a reliable source of information.

Steve Gonzalez, C.R.C. *Before You Hire a Contractor: A Construction Guidebook for Consumers*. Ft. Lauderdale, FL: Consumer Press, 1994.

Tom Philbin. *How to Hire a Home Improvement Contractor Without Getting Chiseled*. New York: St. Martin's Press, 1996.

Duncan Stephens. *The Unofficial Guide to Hiring Contractors*. New York: MacMillan, 1998.

GETTING PUBLISHED

The books below are the ones that got the best ratings on Amazon. There are other good books but these will get you started. You should read the reviews for yourself and see what you think will work for you. Many of them are available from local libraries.

How to Get Published

Sheree Bykofsky and Jennifer Basye Sander. *The Complete Idiot's Guide to Getting Published*, 4th edition. New York: Alpha Books, 2006. Good overall but, according to one reviewer, a little weak on how to do a book proposal.

Susan Rabiner and Alfred Fortunato. *Thinking Like Your Editor: How to Write Great Serious Nonfiction—and Get It Published*. New York: W.W. Norton, 2003. The reviewer at Amazon especially liked the chapters on writing a book proposal. You may want to read or buy both of these books.

How to Self-Publish

Peter Bowerman. *The Well-Fed Self-Publisher: How to Turn One Book into a Full-Time Living*. Atlanta, GA: Fanove Publishers, 2006.

Dan Poyter. *Dan Poynter's Self-Publishing Manual, 16th Edition: How to Write, Print and Sell Your Own Book.* Santa Barbara, CA: Para Publishers, 2007.

Jennifer Basye Sander. *The Complete Idiot's Guide to Self-Publishing.* New York: Alpha Books, 2005.

How to Promote Your Book

David Cole. *The Complete Guide to Book Marketing.* New York: Allworth Press, 2004.

John Kremer. *1001 Ways to Market Your Books*, Sixth Edition. Taos, NM: Open Horizons, 2006.

Brent Sampson. *Sell Your Book on Amazon: The Book Marketing COACH Reveals Top-Secret "How-to" Tips Guaranteed to Increase Sales for Print-on-Demand and Self-Publishing Writers.* Parker, CO: Outskirts Press, 2007.

Steve Weber. *Plug Your Book! Online Book Marketing for Authors, Book Publicity through Social Networking.* Falls Church, VA: Weber Books, 2007.

WEB SITES

Lawyers

Referrals

American Bar Association
www.abanet.org
A highly credible source of lawyer referrals.

Martindale-Hubbell Law Directory
www.martindale.com ®
This well-regarded legal network is one good place to look for a lawyer referral. Includes ratings of lawyers.

Nolo Press Lawyer Referrals
www.lawyers.nolo.com/
If your town is on this list, with a lawyer who specializes in your problem, this would be a reliable source.

Nolo is a private business with a (legal) reputation to maintain and is not likely to have sleazy lawyers on its list.

Self-help

Nolo Press
www.nolo.com
Nolo Press is *the* resource place for self help. In addition to the catalog of books available, Nolo also has many free articles with advice or tips on a variety of common issues including small claims court, family law, business law, wills and estate planning, and much more. Look for the "Nolopedia" list of articles by scrolling down the top page.

California Courts Self Help Center
www.courtinfo.ca.gov/selfhelp/smallclaims/scbasics.htm
Basic information on how to file in small claims court. Read this and, if you need further information about the court in your state, use the search term: "[your state name] self-help small claims court."

California Courts Self Help Center
www.courtinfo.ca.gov/selfhelp/lowcost/
Offers tips on low cost options. Check this out and then see what your state offers. Use the search term: "[your state name] low cost self-help."

Chooselaw.com
http://articles.chooselaw.com/business/view/How-To-Write-A-Cease-And-Desist-Letter.158.html
How to write a cease-and-desist letter. Use on people who are harassing you.

Dancing with Lawyers
www.dancingwithlawyers.com
The book is available through this web site. It also has some short articles and tips for a variety of legal situations.

Consumer Protection and Rights

HALT (Help Abolish Legal Tyranny)
www. halt.org

HALT distributes books, guides and brochures to help consumers deal with the legal system. If you join, you can get a free copy of *Using a Lawyer . . . And What to Do If Things Go Wrong: A Step-by-Step Guide* (cited above).

Articles

Nolo Press
"How to find an excellent lawyer"
http://www.nolo.com/article.cfm/ObjectID/796DE8B4-2417-4175-80714E5DCCE20C75/
If the link above doesn't work, do this Internet search: "How to find an excellent lawyer" Nolo Press."

Entrepreneur.com
http://www.entrepreneur.com/startingabusiness/startupbasics/legalissues/article58326.html
Tips on how to pick a lawyer for a business.

"Mistakes to Avoid Before You Hire a Lawyer"
www.consumerlawpage.com/article/howhire.shtml
Good questions to ask a lawyer.

"How to Hire a Lawyer"
www.expertlaw.com/library/consumer/howtohire.html
Excellent advice about what to avoid in lawyers as well as what to look for.

"Hiring a Lawyer"
www.calbar.ca.gov/state/calbar/calbar_generic.jsp?cid=10581&id=2165
Includes some info not found in the above articles.

Contractors and Other Service Professionals

Contractors From Hell
www.contractorsfromhell.com
Their byline is "Helping Homeowners Avoid—And Deal With—A Home Remodeling Nightmare With The Contractors From Hell Since 2000." A wealth of information, including tips, horror stories, links to other sites, a newsletter, and articles to help you avoid or deal with "the contractor from hell." Some of the articles are listed below.

Ripoff Report ®
www.ripoffreport.com
According to the web site, "Ripoff Report® is a worldwide consumer reporting Web site and publication, by consumers, for consumers, to file and document complaints about companies or individuals." Includes articles, videos, and reports that cover contractors, plumbers and other services, as well as telemarketing and other scams.

Angie's List
www.angieslist.com
Ratings of contractors, service companies and health care providers across the country, based on consumer ratings. Their promise: "Unbiased ratings and reviews, companies don't pay to be on Angie's List, our staff reads every review before you do." Articles on how to pick contractors, roofers, and plumbers as well as other useful information. A well-designed site that is user-friendly.

Diamond Certified
www.diamondcertified.org
If you live in the San Francisco Bay Area, this web site provides ratings of many kinds of service professionals and services. A rigorous standard is applied to all applicants, who are also rated on a strict customer satisfaction survey.

Articles

"The Right Way to Fire Your Home Remodeling Contractor"
http://contractorsfromhell.com/firing_your_contractor.html

"Consumers Need to Know: Home Construction Contracts"
http://contractorsfromhell.com/home_construction_contracts.html
Information about what should go into a contract.

"What You Need to Know About Hiring a Plumber"
www.angieslist.com/Angieslist/Visitor/PressDetail.aspx?i=704

A useful article by Sean O'Neill from *Kiplingers*, reprinted on Angie's List.

"Questions for Interviewing a Plumber"
www.waterchoices.com/interview-questions.pdf
A useful PDF form with questions to ask a plumber and a line to fill in the answer. It can be adapted for use with other service professionals.

"How to Hire a Contractor, Plumber, Painter or Electrician"
www.ehow.com/how_110416_hire-contractor-plumber.html
A bit brief but adds a few tips not included above.

"How to Hire an Architect"
www.ehow.com/how_111123_hire-architect.html

"How to Hire an Architect"
www.aiachesapeakebay.org/clients/hireArchitect.cfm#hire
Takes a different tack than the e-how article above; this is from a chapter of the American Institute of Architects and deal more with the esthetics and planning.

"Ask Questions Before You Hire an Electrician"
http://realtytimes.com/rtpages/20021212_electrician.htm

Publishing Your Book

There are pages and pages of web sites with tips on how to self-publish or get your book published. Lots of them want to sell you their services. That's not necessarily bad, but before you pay money for anything, read one of the books above and get the whole picture. Here are a few web sites that are not so commercial.

Write and Publish Your Book
www.writeandpublishyourbook.com/
Lots of articles and tips on writing both fiction and nonfiction

Published.com
www.published.com

A "Free Directory of Writers and Artists" with many useful links.

How to Publish a Book
www.howtopublishabook.org/
Videos, interviews with writers and other resources.

RJ Communications
www.rjcom.com/faq/
A useful FAQ that answers many questions about self-publishing, including the differences between vanity and subsidy publishing vs. self-publishing.

And for inspiration, check out M.J. Rose's web site:
www.mjrose.com
One of my favorite success stories about refusing to give up.

UPDATES

For updates on books, web sites, web site URLs and links (they sometimes change), articles and other relevant information, check the web site for my book: www.standuptoauthorities.com. Or you can use the titles or words in the references as search terms to do your own Internet update search.

CHAPTER
6

All the News That's Unfit to Print: Thinking Critically about the Printed Word and Other Media Sources

"The press has become the greatest power within the Western countries, more powerful than the legislature, the executive, and the judiciary."
  —Aleksander Solzhenitsyn, Nobel Prize winner in literature[1]

"The media don't encourage critical thinking."
  —Dr. Paula Caplan in
  You're Smarter than They Make You Feel[2]

SIGNIFICANT NEWS STORIES that affect millions of people are routinely left out of mainstream US newspapers. Political coverage is usually biased. Scientific research is frequently reported in the popular media in simplistic, distorted ways. Glitzy entertainment passes for news. The media are bamboozling us and most of us don't even realize it.

Concern about the credibility of the media is nothing new. Complaints of "yellow journalism" go back at least as far as the 1890's and the criticisms of William Randolph Hearst's newspapers.[3] The idea that the media distort and misrepresent is not new; what *is* new is the pervasiveness and subtlety of the distortions. The problem has not gone unnoticed. Books criticizing the media, whether newspapers or government reports, textbooks or television, could fill a large bookcase. "You are being lied to," say the critics. "Misinformation," "disinformation," "whitewash," "unreliable sources," and "cultural myths" are only some of the words being used to describe the state of the media today. "Spin" has become the norm. If we don't want to be fooled by this barrage of misinformation from the mainstream media, we need to be critical thinkers. We have to be willing to question and to seek alternative information if we don't want to be fooled by so-called experts of the media.

Most of us are already a little skeptical of journalists. Chances are, you agree that people shouldn't believe everything they read in the papers. One study looking at which experts and authorities are perceived as most trustworthy found that only 24% of the men surveyed in 2008 trusted journalists.[4] Women were even more skeptical; only 15% trusted them. Yet in spite of your skepticism, there's a good chance you're not aware of all the ways that bias can sneak in, even when the media don't consciously intend to deceive you. Journalists and other writers are clever with words—that's one reason why they became writers. Editors sometimes have different agendas than the journalists and even journalists have to submit to their editors. If you're not informed, critical, and wary of the media, you may be hoodwinked by the press without even realizing it.

NEWSPAPERS AND TELEVISION NEWS

Despite the study cited above, another study done by the *Times Mirror* found that North Americans and Western Europeans trust newspapers and TV news so much that many readers and listeners consider the media even more believable than their churches.[5] This study also found that more people get their news from television than any other source. At the same time, the majority of people in these countries think TV and newspapers are often unfair and one-sided.[4] These contradictory attitudes may be shared by many of us, if not in what we say, then in what we actually do when reading news stories. In practice, many of us are largely uncritical about media news when we actually read it. We don't recognize how distorted and selective the media are nor do we realize how much news is left out or outright censored. "All media," critic Marshall McLuhan once wrote, "exist to invest our lives with artificial perceptions and values."[6] Avoiding being seduced by the media means taking the responsibility to be critical of these perceptions and values, as well as the information presented.

POLITICAL BIAS IN THE NEWS

The myth of a neutral press is just that—a myth. Most newspapers, TV news, and news magazines have a political point of view, even if they don't announce it. We all filter our information through the lenses of our own biases and opinions. Why should the media be any different? True, some news sources (and individuals) are better at being objective than others but no one is totally exempt from bias. But watch out for sweeping generalizations about what the political distortions in the media actually *are*. Liberals think the media is biased in favor of conservatives. Conservatives think it is biased in favor of liberals. They're both partly right. It just depends on what media you're talking about. *Washington Post*? *New York Times*? Liberal. Fox News? Conservative. And what about PBS? That depends on the program. It's not as simple as some people think it is, as some of the examples below will demonstrate. There's plenty of disinformation, political and otherwise, across the political spectrum.

MEDIA DISINFORMATION

NEWS MAY BE . . .

Highly selective

For starters, the press is highly selective in what it chooses to reports. "Junk food" stories of the latest celebrity naughtiness often make bigger headlines than news with substance. But these stories are merely annoying and distracting. More disturbing are problems such as the overemphasis on the lurid "if it bleeds, it leads" stories that distort both the amount and sources of violence. Violence makes the front page; stories about science or good deeds are often relegated to the back pages. This is true for violent people as well as violent events. Highly respected CBS reporter Daniel Shorr once said, ". . . In the mid-Nineteen Sixties, covering urban unrest for CBS, I perceived that television placed a premium on violence and the threat of violence. I found that I was more likely to get on the *CBS Evening News* with a black militant talking the language of 'Burn, baby, burn!' than with moderates appealing for a Marshall Plan for the ghetto. So I spent a lot of time interviewing militants like Stokely Carmichael and H. Rapp Brown."[7] It hasn't gotten better since then.

"Prefab"

A more subtle distortion is the overreliance on the "prefab news" of government and corporate press releases. Most print media are highly predictable, churning out a similar mix of wire service copy and prefabricated puffery. Many stories are simply handed to reporters, not ferreted out by clever and enterprising investigators. A study by the *Columbia Journalism Review*, for example, found that more than half of the news stories reported in a typical issue of the *Wall Street Journal*, were "based solely on corporate press releases."[8] The releases present only the corporation's or government's spin on events.

"Inoffensive" to sources and advertisers

Because of their dependence on government and private institutional sources of information, reporters who offend their sources by presenting other points of view may not last long. Reporters have to be nice to their sources. Journalists who are adversarial or even just skeptical find that they are no longer invited to press conferences or that their sources have suddenly dried up.

The media must not only worry about offending their sources of news, they have to be concerned with their advertisers as well. Most of the revenue for newspapers and magazines as well as TV news comes from advertisers. That's true for public television as well as the private networks and cable stations. A significant portion of the funding for PBS comes from large corporations. Liberal/progressive watchdogs of the media, such as Norman Solomon, Jeff Cohen, Martin Lee and other writers for Fairness and Accuracy in Reporting (FAIR) have provided many examples of corporate pressure not just on network programming but on PBS as well.[9] PBS, often seen as a bastion of liberalism, has actually given much more time to conservative than liberal political talk shows in the past several decades. The conservative McLaughlin Report, for example, has been a long-time mainstay of PBS, and in the past was solely sponsored by General Electric. When some PBS subscribers complained about this imbalance, a few PBS stations began to air the Kwitny Report. But when Jonathan Kwitny, a former ace reporter for the *Wall Street Journal*, began to criticize government actions, WNYC, the PBS station that launched the show, cancelled his program.[10]

THE NEWS MAY . . .

Omit important stories

The selective reporting of the press *disinforms* by what it leaves out—points of view left underrepresented, issues not dealt with, and stories censored or not followed up. How many of us have heard about the US using depleted uranium in Kosovo, Iraq and Afghanistan, a practice potentially creating dangerous radiation for centuries to come?[11] We've all heard about the benefits of the psychiatric drugs Prozac, Paxil and Zoloft, but how many of us have heard about the dangers?[12] The Project Censored web site at Sonoma State University, dedicated to publicizing under-reported news stories, tells us the rest of the story. The web site includes, for example, a story about how drug companies influence physicians and health organizations to push medications for depression and other mental health related problems, discussing how drug companies promote the idea that these medications are magic panaceas for all kinds of problems. This, even though a federal research study in 1999 cited in this article found that the newer antidepressants were only effective about half the time and outperformed placebos (fake pills) only 18% of the time. The article also points that the drug industry spends $5 billion annually on sales reps while giving fantastic perks to doctors who promote these medications. This story was only reported in the alternative press. Nor did the mainstream media cover in any significant way the dangerous side-effects of many psychiatric drugs, or the organizations, such as the International Center for the Study of Psychiatry and Psychology, that provide information about the dangers of these drugs.[13] Only in the last few years have the side effects of such drugs received any coverage from the mainstream media and then only minimally.

Omit controversial or "inconvenient" points of view

The problem with media disinformation gets worse. Sometimes there is direct pressure on journalists to leave out certain controversial or inconvenient points of view in their coverage. In *Into the Buzzsaw: Leading Journalists Expose the Myth of a Free Press*, editor Kristina Borjesson brings together 19 chilling essays by major journalists, many of them award-winners, that detail their personal experiences with cover-ups, self-censorship and pressure to curtail reporting.[14] Dan Rather, one of the most prestigious names in TV journalism, for example, talks of how he was pressured to avoid asking "tough questions" about the war in Iraq. ". . . anyone who tells you that he or she did not feel this pressure," he writes, "I think is either kidding themselves or trying to deceive you."[15] Willing to include himself in the criticism, he adds that if he had not conformed, he would have been branded "unpatriotic" or worse. "It's an obscene comparison—I'm not sure I like it—but there was a time in South Africa when people would put flaming tires around people's necks if they dissented, and in some ways, the fear is that you will be necklaced here. You'll have a flaming tire of lack of patriotism put around your neck. Now it's that fear that keeps journalists from asking the tough questions . . ."

Rather is far from alone in his rebuke of the media. Former Fox Network producer Charles Reina points out how the Fox TV "Fair and Balanced" news is shaped everyday by an executive memo that lists what stories will be covered and how they will be covered.[16] An expose by Jane Akre of a powerful and controversial growth hormone used on cows was squelched when the chemical company's lawyers threatened to sue. But that's not the end of the story—she and her colleague were fired, sued by Fox because they were whistle-blowers, and forced to go through years of devastating and expensive litigation.[17] Pulitzer nominee John Kelly offers a troubling account of how the CIA is committing serious crimes, including assassination, torture and other violations of human rights, but the media remain silent out of fear. When CBS, ABC and the BBC dared to air even a small part of what was going on, they were met with an attack by the CIA. The press got the message; journalists were reassigned to less sensitive desks. The cover-ups and carnage continue, reports Kelly. And, as he says, "The US media won't be there to cover it."[18]

Conservative commentators get in their licks too. Don Feder of Accuracy in Media (AIM), for example, has frequently written about what the liberal press leaves out of its reporting. One of his favorite targets is the *New York Times*. "The problem with *The New York Times'* coverage of the financial crisis involving huge mortgage lenders Fannie Mae and Freddie Mac," he writes, "isn't so much what it reports as what it refuses to cover."[19] In his view, the "liberal media" imply that the mortgage crisis was caused by greedy bankers. "Here's what *The Times* isn't telling you," he continues. "It was Jimmy Carter who first pushed Fannie and Freddie to lend to high-risk borrowers . . ." Feder even quotes Bill Clinton as saying "Responsibility with the Democrats rests more in resisting any efforts by Republicans in Congress or by me when I was president to put some standards on and tighten up a little more on Fannie Mae and Freddie Mac." These are only some of the things, he asserts, that the *Times* has not included in its coverage of the mortgage crisis, as well as many other topics.

Libertarian media also have a point of view about what gets left unsaid. On a *Reason* TV You Tube video, for example, George Mason University economist and author Robert Russell agrees with the point that the current mortgage critics is not just the fault of greedy bankers but provides a fuller, more balanced picture of the many influences, governmental or otherwise, than Feder or many others.[20] You don't have to agree with everything Russell or Feder says to see that the causes of the 2008 mortgage lending crisis are more complex than what many of the news media sources imply or report.

The point of all these examples is, of course, that you can't get the whole "video" from only one "frame." If you only read or watch one source, or only the side you agree with, you won't see the whole picture. You won't know what is being left out. You won't have all the information you need to make an informed decision.

The examples of stories and information left out of the news potentially affect millions yet few people know anything about them. Here is the lesson: Don't assume that the mainstream media have given you the whole story—ever. Always assume there is more to the story, and that there are many other stories untold. When it comes to the potential political bias of news coverage, don't depend on only one source and never assume *any* side has given you the whole story. To avoid being seduced and bamboozled by the mainstream media, you need to be a critical thinker and seek alternative information. Otherwise you may be consuming pabulum instead of solid food.

Key Tools for Standing Up

Since we don't directly confront the "experts" of the media, we have to "stand up" to them in a different way. I've talked about *why* we need to be critical of the media. Here's some suggestions for *how* to do it.

MEDIA ALTERNATIVES

Seek alternative information

What's the alternative to reliance on TV and newspapers? First of all, don't rely on only one or two sources of news. If you want to get the full story, try nonmainstream sources and compare what they say against what the mainstream is saying. If you are concerned with political slanting of news sources, read critiques from many points of view, not just the ones you agree with. Then decide for yourself. A variety of magazines, cable or satellite programs, and Internet sources offer alternative information. A few examples are listed below. Even if you don't have time to read these alternative sources every day or every week, an occasional peek will keep your perspective better balanced.

If you are American or Canadian, watch or read European or other English language broadcasts from abroad. TV cable and satellite services, for example, offer BBC news and *Deutsche Welle* (a top German news network broadcasting in several languages, including English). Both also have web sites. They frequently report stories not presented in the mainstream American press and offer different perspectives on world news. I've often been amazed at the important and highly relevant news about the USA, as well as the rest of the world, reported on these stations but not on American TV or newspapers. In 2008, for example, at an event organized by Iraq Veterans Again the War, dozens of veterans testified about crimes they had committed during the course of battle, many of which were promoted by the orders or policies of superior officers. Though the BBC predicted that this event would dominate world news, there was an almost total blackout in the American press.[21] The BBC also frequently carries information about abusive conditions in other countries that doesn't make it into the mainstream American press.

Project Censored, created by the journalism department at Sonoma State University in California, publishes its pick of 25 "censored" stories every year—important and newsworthy stories that are underreported in the mainstream media. The Project publishes a book about these stories every year as well as reporting the stories on its web site. One of its picks for 2003, for example, was the news that the U.S. government was handing out millions of dollars worth of weapons to rogue nations well-known for torture, looting, and outright murder.[22] The source of the news was the *Bulletin of the Atomic Scientists*, a well-known and prestigious publication in its field. In spite of this, it was reported in the *Utne Reader,* an alternative magazine, not the *New York Times* or other leading newspapers. One of the stories for the Project's 2009 report deals with worldwide slavery. "Twenty-seven million slaves exist in the world today, more than at any time in human history," says its web site. "According to the US State Department's 2004 Trafficking in Persons Report, the FBI projects that the slave trade generates $9.5 billion in revenue each year."[23] But how many of you have ever read a news report about this colossal violation of human rights?

The Project Censored web site and books can help you be better informed, but keep in mind that, like any other organization, it has its own agenda. Read and judge accordingly.

No matter what your own politics are, keep in mind that no one point of view has a monopoly on truth. Don't just rely on *Time* or *Newsweek*. Don't just read sources with ideologies compatible with your own. Remember to separate the message from the messenger. Some of the best muckraking is found in the independent press so check them out. Progressive and left of center sources include magazines such as *Mother Jones* and *Z* and the web site for the organization, Fairness and Accuracy in Reporting (FAIR). A politically different but equally nonmainstream and muckraking point of view can be found in the libertarian magazines, *Reason* and *Liberty*. For a conservative look at the news, try the online sites of Accuracy in Media (AIM) and the Conservative News Service or the venerable magazine standard *National Review*. For a liberal look at the news, try *The Nation* magazine.

Many large city newsstands carry the magazines mentioned above. If you can't find them in your area, check out their web sites. I promise that you'll find news you won't find in your local paper. It's up to you to decide the trustworthiness or usefulness of the stories they present but whatever you decide, it's likely that they will make you think and give you new insights.

> *"Today, I read 30 different publications, most of them obscure periodicals from both the left and the right. I never want to be deceived again."*
>
> —Howard Bloom, media critic[24]

For other sources of alternative information on the Internet, check out newswatch.org. It objectively describes a broad range of national and international news services and media criticism sources across the political spectrum and provides links to them. Then browse as you choose.

One eye-popping online alternative is Disinformation (disinformation.com), which has published a series of provocative and wide-ranging anthologies, including *You Are Being Lied To* and *Everything You Know is Wrong*.[25] You don't have to agree with everything they report (and you won't) to realize that there is more to the picture than what the mainstream media feed us. Nor is does Disinformation report from one point of view only. There is something for everyone in these volumes from liberal to conservative, from progressive to libertarian.

If you are interested in computer or digital media, try The Register (theregister.co.uk) for an irreverent but insightful look at issues such as copyright infringement, free speech, and encroaching governmental programs. The Register also covers other stories that bring home important lessons (often humorously) about the human condition.

How to Judge the Printed and Spoken Word: Evaluating Newspapers, Television News, Magazine Articles and Books

It's obvious that we can't always take what we hear and read in newspapers and TV at face value. But alternative sources are not enough. What else can we do to help us be more critical and careful about what we hear and read, not just in the news but in magazines and books as well? Here are some suggestions for critical evaluation of media reports. By following these guidelines, you can decrease your chances of being seduced and bamboozled by the printed and spoken word.

EVALUATE THE REPUTATION OF THE SOURCE

Is the newspaper well-respected, with a good reputation, such as the *New York Times,* the *Christian Science Monitor* or the *Washington Post*? Or is it an entertainment-oriented or sensationalistic paper like the *New York Post*? Is it your small home-town paper that has limited resources and possibly less than top-quality writers? Supermarket checkout line tabloid? While good stories can and do show up in any of these kinds of papers (well, maybe not the tabloids . . .), the more controversial or important the topic, the more discerning you need to be about the quality of the newspaper. However, keep in mind, that even the best newspapers are not always objective and fair in their coverage. In fact, many media critics think that all of the corporate newspapers are highly biased. Unfortunately, in the newspaper game, it's all relative. That's why reading multiple sources of different kinds is critical if you want to avoid being hoodwinked by the media. Compare what different sources say about the same topic. Then you can decide for yourself what (if any) sources make the most sense to you.

Is the book from a well-known publisher such as Macmillan or Oxford University Press, or even a well-established small press such as Ten Speed Press in Berkeley, or is it self-published? I think self-publishing is a viable option but I'm a bit more wary of information from self-published sources because it hasn't passed though any review process at all. Not that the big name presses don't publish nonsense. They do it a lot. You have to add up the whole equation of critical thinking factors to get a proper perspective.

EXAMINE THE PURPOSE OF THE SOURCE

How likely is the magazine to present solid information rather than glitzy entertainment, pop psychology, pop science or otherwise tell people what the publication thinks the audience wants to want to hear? Is the article, for example, in an entertainment-oriented magazine or a science-oriented magazine (e.g., *People* vs. *Discover*). While even the science-oriented ones may have articles that are less than totally accurate, they are more likely to have writers who have science backgrounds and therefore report science news more accurately. Beware of magazines whose main purpose is entertainment—unless, of course, entertainment is what you're looking for!

WATCH OUT FOR A BIASED AGENDA

Does the magazine or the newspaper have a political or social point of view? Be aware of that point of view and take it into account when judging the conclusions the writers come to. Overtly ideological publications, such as the liberal *Nation*, conservative

National Review, progressive *Mother Jones*, and libertarian *Reason* are obvious, but others may be more subtle. Even *Time* and *Newsweek* have their own political slants. Local newspapers may have a slant too, as their editorials will inform you. Don't reject or accept information just because of a publication's bias, but be aware of it as you evaluate the articles and take that slant into account. Keep in mind the lens through which the source views its information.

EVALUATE THE EXPERTISE OF THE JOURNALIST OR WRITER

Does the writer have a background in the topic of the article? If the topic of the article is a specialized one, even newspapers may tell you that the journalist is, for example, the science writer for that paper. Some newspapers include bios of the writers. If not, see if the author has a web site. Assess how relevant the writer's credentials are. Articles about scientific research written by the newspaper's science writer are more apt to be accurate than one written by a cub reporter who just got a degree in journalism last year. When I've compared articles by newspaper science writers to those penned by other journalists, I've found that the science writers are more likely to describe studies in a scientific way. They are, for example, more likely to mention the research methodology (e.g., that it had a control group to which the experimental group was compared; a necessary scientific ingredient) so you can judge for yourself whether it is meaningful research or just fluff. They're also more likely to present opinions of other scientists unconnected with the research, including disagreements with or critiques of the research. This is especially important if the research area is controversial, as, for example, with gender-related studies. One source of good online science writing is the BBC web site (bbc.co.uk).

Good magazines will tell you something about the credentials of the writer. See if the bio information sounds relevant to the topic. If no bio is given and the article is about a topic that requires specialized knowledge, take the writer's conclusions with a proverbial grain of salt until you have further information from knowledgeable sources. See if the writer has a web site with relevant info about her or his credentials. Read other articles by other writers on the same topic.

Creditability of the author is even more important for a nonfiction book. We tend to take books more seriously than magazines and assume that authors have some background in the topic. This isn't always the case. Look to see if the author's credentials are relevant and appropriate to the level of the book. The more serious, scholarly or controversial the topic, the more important credentials are. If, for example, the topic is a scientific one, check to see whether the author has an advanced degree in a relevant science from an accredited university. If the topic is human behavior, does the writer have a psychology or other social science background or degree? Does the author have an academic affiliation?

Let's compare two books on gender differences in communication, by way of example—John Gray's best-seller, *Men Are from Mars, Women Are from Venus* and Deborah Tannen's best-seller, *You Just Don't Understand*. Both have Ph.D's that are relevant—Gray's is in psychology and Tannen's in linguistics. But Gray's is from a school that is not only nonaccredited but discredited as well (it was closed down by the State of California); Tannen's degree is from the prestigious University of California at Berkeley. Gray is not affiliated with any school; Tannen is a professor at Georgetown University in Washington, D.C., an eminently respectable school.[26] These facts alone don't prove that one book is better than the other, but Gray's questionable credentials should raise a red flag that warrants further consideration and wariness.

Has the author written previous books related to the topic? Even if the author doesn't have a relevant degree, similar books tell us that the author has some specialized knowledge. For example, Alfie Kohn, author of *The Brighter Side of Human Nature*, a book about social science research on altruism and helping behavior, doesn't have an advanced psychology degree. He has, however, written eleven psychology- and education-oriented books, including *No Contest*, a book about studies on cooperation, and *The Case Against Standardized Testing*. This is all information that you can glean from his web site.[27] His book, *No Contest*, also won an award from the American Psychological Association, another strong clue that the author has merit.[28] Furthermore, he writes in a measured tone that is neither simplistic nor glitzy, and references every study he cites.

EVALUATE THE SOURCE OF THE INFORMATION CITED

Who is the writer citing? Does the writer tell you about the credentials of those cited in the article? If research is being reported, is the study done at a reputable, accredited university? Did the studies being mentioned appear in a reputable peer-reviewed scientific or scholarly publication? ("Peer-reviewed" mean a body of experts in the field review the research article for the journal and find it acceptable. To help determine if a particular journal is peer-reviewed, refer to the journal itself—either to an individual issue of the journal or to the publisher's web site.) Or was it done by some institute you never heard of? Look the organization or publication up on the Internet and see what you learn. Does it sound solid or does it sound fly-by-night or ideologically one-sided? Does it have links to known reputable organizations and individuals? For example, let's say that *Cultic Studies Review*, a publication you never heard of, was cited in an article on cults. If you look it up on the Internet, you will find it associated with Margaret Singer. Dr. Singer, as several web sites will reveal, is considered a leading expert on cult groups, is the author of the highly praised *Cults in Our Midst*, a retired professor at the University of California at Berkeley, and a clinical psychologist.[29] Chances are high that this publication is solid and worthwhile. Or, on the other hand, is the citation to an advocacy group with a particular political or social agenda? One popular talk show host, for example, likes to cite the Family Research Council (FRC) as a source of social research. The FRC turns out to be a highly politicized conservative advocacy group with its own specific social agenda concerning abortion and homosexuality.[30] It is not even remotely neutral, much less scientific.

Does the author cite a source for the information or study? In magazine articles and books, is a bibliography included? If there is no bibliography, you have no information about where the evidence came from and no way to independently verify the information. Most reputable nonfiction authors will use a bibliography so be skeptical if there isn't one. A case in point once again is John Gray's book, *Men Are from Mars, Women Are from Venus*. There is no bibliography so the reader cannot know whether his claims about alleged gender differences are based on actual research evidence or just his personal opinion. In Gray's case, much of what he claims is, in fact, not based on the latest scientific research about gender.[31] The points that he makes about gender differences in communication that *are* based on research have no citations either, so the reader has no way of separating the reasonable wheat from the opinionated chaff. In contrast, Deborah Tannen's book, *You Just Don't Understand,* which is also about gender differences in communication, does cite scientific research sources for her assertions. So you could verify Tannen's conclusions for yourself if you wanted to.

ANALYZE FOR HIDDEN ASSUMPTIONS

Watch for hidden assumptions behind the arguments in an article. Look for vested interests or hidden bias. Sometimes the writer's hidden assumptions color the claims and conclusions he or she makes. Biases can lead them to unwittingly select and interpret what they write to fit their preconceptions. A person with politically conservative views talking about drug policies or research on families, or a person with politically liberal views presenting statistics on gun control each bring their ideological baggage into the discussion. The statistics they report and the slant they put on their arguments are likely to be influenced by their political views. Liberal advocates of gun control, for example, typically don't mention the statistics on how many lives have been saved because the victim had a gun, while the conservative advocates of anti-drug laws don't discuss the increase in crimes of violence as a result of such laws. Before accepting conclusions, consider the ways the experts's biases may be affecting their presentations. Make a habit of reading opposing points of view to be sure you're getting a more balanced picture of the issue under consideration. If the two sets of evidence don't jive, dig deeper.

ASSESS THE TONE OF THE WRITING

Is the tone emotionally charged or factual and neutral? Is the information presented in a sensationalistic, lurid or glitzy way? Does it use loaded terms or buzzwords? Does it try to be glib, "cute," and entertaining rather then informative? Much that passes for writing today is designed to grab your attention and sell books and newspapers rather than to inform. Be alert for writing that tries to sway your opinion or your emotions by the use of less than objective tones or that is lacking in factual content.

If the tone of the book, book cover, or article is flashy, lurid, or gushes too much, watch out. Self-help and diet books, for example, are notorious for glitzy writing and sensationalistic promotion. Every year's crop of pop psychology books are touted as "phenomenal breakthroughs" in understanding some aspect of human behavior. They often have flashy, cute titles such as *What Every Woman Should Know about Men*, *Men Who Hate Women and the Women Who Love Them*, or *Men Are from Mars, Women Are from Venus*. In an independent survey asking clinical psychologists to rate popular self-help books, the first two titles were rated as "not recommended" while Gray's best-seller (which was published after the survey was done) has increasingly drawn major criticisms from psychologists and many unhappy readers.[32]

An example of lurid promotion is *Body Language* by Julian Fast. The front cover of one of the editions shows a woman sitting in her chair, accompanied by the question, "Does her body say that she's a loose woman?" On the back cover, it asserts "Read *Body Language* so that you can penetrate the personal secrets of both intimates and total strangers."[33] This statement manages to be lurid, sleazy, and deceptive all in one sentence. It promises far more than it can deliver; no psychologist yet has come up with a way to have X-ray vision into a person's psyche! Anyone who promises you a sure-fire way to read other people's minds or manipulate them, as this promo slyly implies, is bamboozling you. Beware if the promos are appealing to base motives such as manipulating or tricking people. Reputable books don't do that.

LOOK FOR LOADED LANGUAGE

The use of loaded language, particularly in writings about social or political concerns, is common in both newspapers and magazines. Watch out for selective use of language and politically dubious phrases. Beware of the use of emotionally charged words and obvious spin. The way language is used can also give you a clue to the political orientation of the writer. Was someone "taken" to jail or "thrown into" jail? Was a demonstration described as a "civil disobedience protest" or a "riot?" Was one side in a war called "freedom fighters" and the other "terrorists?" There's often a slant to the description of groups, favorable for the ones that the writer likes and not favorable for the ones the writer doesn't like. For example, the pro-gun control group, Handgun Control Inc., may be called a "citizens' lobby" or a "public interest group" while the anti-gun control National Rifle Association may be called a "lobbying juggernaut," "radical gun lobby," or "most feared lobby."[34]

Are there hidden negative or positive connotations of words that slant the story in one political direction or the other? Words such as "civil liberties" and "watchdog," for example, have positive connotations while words like "extreme", "radical," "agenda," and "fundamentalist" have negative ones. Be on the alert for buzzwords. There are many recycled clichés being presented as truisms. Some examples include the phrase "believed to be" used as if everyone knowledgeable shares the same belief. "Believed to be" by whom? We don't know. Or "bailout" used to describe taxpayer money going to souring investments of wealthy financiers or "extremists," meaning political groups the government disapproves of.

Politically charged labels and images may be used to subtly sway people. Certain designations used gratuitously, may result in deception or reinforcement of stereotypes, for example, saying "pro-abortion" instead of pro-choice;" "anti-abortion" instead of "pro-life," or calling the Green Party or the Libertarian Party "extremist." Former President Lyndon Johnson used this kind of political spin to good (and famously notorious) advantage against Republican Barry Goldwater in a highly controversial ad from the 1964 presidential election. Capitalizing on comments made by Goldwater about the possibility of using nuclear weapons in the Vietnam War, the ad shows a little girl pulling petals off a daisy. When her count reaches nine, an ominous male voice starts counting down to a missile launch. When he reaches zero, there is a flash and mushroom cloud from a nuclear explosion. The ad was widely criticized as unfair and deceptive but helped insure Johnson's win.[35] Don't fall for this kind of emotional trickery.

Watch out for words that neutralize controversial events through the use of euphemisms. George Orwell, in his classic novel *1984*, called this "double-speak," coining such examples as "war is peace." Standard examples include heinous acts of repression described as "controversial measures," or "collateral damage" used as a substitute for "number of civilians killed." "Regime" is bad but "change" is good. Goodbye, "coup d'etat," "assassination," and "overthrow;" hello, "change." Listen also for new lingo that may sound OK at first hearing but should really make us do a double-take. "Homeland" security? Shades of the Nazi "Fatherland" or the Soviet "Motherland." Ouch.

CHECK FOR UNATTRIBUTED ASSERTIONS

Watch out for suspicious or vague sources. Reporters citing unidentified sources, especially government ones, like "top U.S. officials" or "according to Western diplomats" leave us wondering about the reliability of the sources. Who knows if it's reliable; we can't tell. Or "believed to be" or "considered to be." By whom? Exactly who is doing the "believing" or "considering"? Such phrases allow the reporter to generalize at will as if it were common knowledge when it might only be a handful of people or even a lie. In November 1984, for example, based on unnamed U.S. intelligence sources, most major media reported that Soviet MIG fighter jets were being unloaded in Nicaragua. The story turned out to be a hoax.[36] Critical thinking texts call this trick a "proof surrogate."[37] It sounds like proof is being offered but no references that can be tracked down are actually there. Don't trust attributions when there is no findable, let alone reliable, source indicated.

WATCH OUT FOR UNBALANCED SOURCES AND SELECTIVE REPORTING

It's not uncommon for the media, particularly television, to cite only one source or cite only from a narrow range of "experts" (e.g., only government sources, ignoring popular movements). After a 40-month investigation, FAIR reported, for example, that *Nightline*, which is considered by many to be one of the best news programs on TV, was out-of-balance to an extreme.[38] Of all the

U.S. guests, 80 percent were professionals, government officials, or corporate representatives. Only 5 percent represented "public interest" constituencies (environment, peace, consumer organizations, etc.). Less than two percent were leaders of labor or racial/ethnic groups. The report also documented that 89 percent of the U.S. guests were men and 92 percent were white. Thus, concluded the FAIR report, "Minorities, women, and those with challenging views are generally excluded." Why should upper middle class white men with mainstream views do almost all the commenting? What about other perspectives? Don't those people's opinions count? Regardless of your political ideology, these questions raised by the FAIR report are worth considering.

Ask yourself what sides are being reported and what is being left out. If the story is about a labor dispute, for example, are both the union and management quoted equally? If there is a panel discussion about abortion on TV, are there women on the panel and not just a group of middle-aged men? Or if there is a story about astrology, for example, are both the pro- and anti-astrology sides quoted equally? Michael Shermer, publisher of *Skeptic* magazine and author of *Why People Believe Weird Things*, for example, has been the token skeptic on many television programs about psychic phenomena and the paranormal. In more cases than not, he gets merely a quick sound bite while the pro-psychic people get the lion's share of the program. Many TV producers assume the audience wants to hear that psychic phenomena are real—it's so much more colorful and interesting, or so they imagine, than "boring" science. So skeptical scientist Dr. Shermer often gets only crumbs of time. Yet what he has to say is backed up by research and logic while the other side merely has assertions without evidence. That's not reporting, that's entertainment. Don't be fooled by such one-sided presentations.

Checking for balance is especially important if the topic is controversial. For example, when journalist John Stossel put together an ABC-TV special several years ago about the origins of gender differences titled "Boys and Girls Are Different," it was obvious which side he wanted us to believe.[39] Instead of a balanced program on the question of whether nature (genetics) or nurture (the environment or culture) influenced gender-related behavior more, his show clearly took a side. On the pro-genetics side, he interviewed respected neuro-psychologist Doreen Kimura. Did he interview equally respected scientists who take a more socio-cultural position on the origins of gender roles, such as biologist Anne Fausto-Sterling, anthropologist Peggy Sanday, or social psychologist Carol Tavris? No. He interviewed political activists and feminists Bella Abzug and Gloria Steinem, who are intelligent and respected, but have no scientific credentials or special knowledge of the scientific issues involved. Not very balanced and very not fair. Don't be swayed by such one-sided programs.

In reporting scientific news, many reporters with no science background assume that if someone has a Ph.D. or M.D., they are speaking the "truth" and that no further exploration is necessary. This practice is especially rampant on TV. As an example, see the story about Dr. Randy Thornhill that I describe below. Even though Dr. Thornhill's book on the history of rape is highly controversial, no reporter asked questions, let alone expressed skepticism, of his position.[40] They should have because many scientists think his book is decidedly *un*scientific. That's why it's a good idea to be wary of articles written by a journalist who is not identified as a science reporter and to be *really* wary about any program on TV that does not have both sides fairly represented.

CHECK FOR DISCREPANCIES BETWEEN HEADLINES AND ACTUAL CONTENT

Watch out for what Lee and Solomon call "headline hanky-panky." Newspapers often use deceptive headlines and titles that don't jibe with ensuing articles (e.g., "Thatcher Salutes Reagan Years" when the text quotes her as saying "Poor dear, there's nothing between his ears").[41] Or the article proclaiming "Math gene found" when what the article really described was the researchers' belief that the gender differences they found probably had a genetic basis. Not the same thing as saying "math gene." No reputable scientist would ever say that any complex behavior was caused by *one* gene.[42] More on this story later. But don't blame the writer of the article for outrageous headlines. Headlines are picked by the editors, not by the reporters. Just don't be fooled into accepting the idea promoted in the headline without reading further.

DON'T BE SUCKERED BY STATISTICS

"There are three kinds of lies: lies, damned lies, and statistics."
—attributed to Benjamin Disraeli and
popularized by Mark Twain[43]

Statistics reporting is often a numbers racket. Rigged statistics, inflated or deflated estimates of attendance at political rallies, contradictory tallies, and numerical tricks are commonplace. Here are some examples. Each month, the Federal Bureau of Labor Statistics releases national unemployment figures. According to Lee and Solomon, these statistics, which are reported by the mass media, hide the true extent of U.S. unemployment.[44] The count doesn't include those who haven't looked for work for over a month or those who are forced to retire early. It also inflates employment numbers by counting those who work only one hour as week as fully employed.

Be wary of statistics cited by those with a zealous political or social agenda. Information about controversial issues such as drugs, for example, is often distorted to suit political ideologies. On July 23, 1998, then US Drug Czar Barry McCaffrey, in trying to prove that illegal drugs are dangerous, said: "The murder rate in Holland [where hard drugs are legal though regulated] is double that in the United States. The per capita crimes rates are much higher than the United States . . . That's drugs!" However, what the Dutch Central Planning Bureau of Statistics (1996) and the FBI Uniform Crime Report Data (1998) will reveal is that the Dutch murder rate is 440 percent *lower* than the US murder rate.[45] Oops, Mr. McCaffrey, run that by me again.

WATCH FOR POLLS MADE TO ORDER

Polls have gotten very sophisticated in their sampling methods over the years. They have reliable techniques for getting a representative sample even with fairly small numbers of participants. No more predicting that Alf Landon will win the Presidential election over Franklin Roosevelt (a classic example of a major polling goof from the 1930's!) But does that mean polls can all be trusted now? Not necessarily. Pollsters sometimes slant their questions to get the desired answer, i.e., the answer that will make their sponsor happy. In their critique of the media, *Unreliable Sources*, Lee and Solomon provide this classic example of how the Roper Poll worded a question to get the desired answer (the sponsor was the Television Information Office). "How do you feel—that there should be no commercials on any children's programs or that it is all right to have them if they don't take unfair advantage," resulting in the report: "Roper finds three out off our Americans approve principles of commercial sponsorship for children's television programs."[46] A more neutral—and more honest—way to ask the question would have been: "Which do you agree with more: It's OK to have commercials on children's' television; or It's not OK to have commercials on children's television." The original version was slanted to get the results the sponsor wanted because it lacked parity—the two questions were not comparable. The second, more neutral version, in contrast, does have balanced and comparable questions. The moral: Think twice about accepting the results of a poll if you don't know the question. If you *are* given the question, look carefully to see if it is neutrally worded or whether it is subtly slanted toward a certain point of view.

I once saw this in action for myself. One night I received a phone call from a polling group asking for my opinions on the "blight" in the town I live in. "Blight," I thought it myself, "What blight?" My town is an older city in California but very charming. There isn't any "blight." I knew what was going—this company was sponsored by developers who were chomping at the bit to tear down the old buildings and put in their new high rise buildings on the waterfront. If the poll had been fair, it would have first asked *if* I thought there was blight in my town. But the questions were worded so as to assume that there *was* blight. Critical thinking texts call this a "loaded question."[47] The answer is already assumed or "loaded" into the question. The poll was a sham and a scam, all in the name of "civic redevelopment."

DON'T BE SWAYED BY ANECDOTES

Anecdotes do not constitute proof. The purpose of anecdotes is to illustrate by example, not to prove the case. "Proof," from a scientific point of view, requires carefully controlled and replicated studies. No single study, let alone a single anecdote, ever "proves" anything in science. But lively anecdotes, particularly from one's own personal experience, often seem so much more real and compelling to people than something as dryly abstract as a research study done at some far away university. Here's a kind of example I've heard many times: "I raised my kids in a nonsexist way. But my little boy loves toy guns and my little girl adores Barbie dolls. Gender differences must be innate after all." No matter that I tell them how social science research provides abundant evidence of cultural influences on gender roles.[48] No matter that increasing research evidence demonstrates that peers may often be a more important source of socialization than parents.[49] If some people read an anecdote that matches their experience, they will accept it much more readily than contrary research conclusions. This is an example of what psychologists call the confirmation bias—we unconsciously look for evidence to back up what we already believe, and don't look for or don't accept evidence that would contradict our cherished beliefs.[50] This is not critical thinking.

Self-help articles and books are among the worst offenders in the use of anecdotes. Many self-help books are not based on reliable scientific evidence but simply on the author's biased anecdotal experiences. Watch out for a book based mainly on testimonials, a small number of interviews, or a few clients seen in therapy. Most authors of good self-help books will describe the research evidence and provide a bibliography and/or citations in the appendix. Be cautious if this information is not provided. (See Chapter Three for my guidelines for choosing self-help books.)

BE CAUTIOUS ABOUT CONTROVERSIAL TOPICS

Articles on controversial topics such as gun control, affirmative action, gender research, or environmental issues are notoriously one–sided. Don't rely on just one source. Don't just read the side you already agree with. Nobody is right all the time; there really are two sides to many issues.

Don't assume that TV documentaries or newspaper articles will present both sides of controversial issues fairly. Psychological reports in the popular press tend to be made uncritically and with a definite bias toward the reporting of sensational findings. This is especially true if the topic is controversial. When the book, *The Natural History of Rape: Biological Bases of Sexual Coercion* by evolutionary biologists Randy Thornhill and Craig T. Palmer was published, it made the front page of many newspapers. Its thesis: Men are natural rapists! The fact that the book had many serious flaws and was criticized by other evolutionary biologists, did not keep it from being front page news.[51] The newspaper article I read in the *San Francisco Chronicle* at least provided criticisms of the book on the inside page continuation of the article, which is more than TV viewers got when Thornhill was interviewed on a national news program. Instead of having a balanced presentation with scientist Thornhill on one side and another scientist on the opposing side (for example, fellow evolutionary biologist Jerry Coyne or evolutionary anthropologist Sarah Blaffer Hrdy), this program, with an eye toward entertainment rather than fairness, offered a feminist lawyer specializing in rape cases.[52] Though a professional with an important point of view, she was in no position to refute Thornhill's research assertions, so his claim to being scientifically accurate went unchallenged.

BE CAUTIOUS ABOUT MEDIA REPORTING OF RESEARCH

Many articles about scientific research found in newspapers and magazines are simplistic and distorted. They are often written by reporters who are ignorant of the methods of science. These writers may not even know what information is important and what is not. If the study is about medical or psychological research, for example, we need to know whether there was a control group (a comparison group that was comparable to the experimental group but was not subjected to the experimental condition or drug) and a random or representative sample and what the sample size was. If there is no control group, we have no way of knowing whether a drug, for example, had a real medical effect or whether any effect was simply a result of expectations or self-fulfilling prophecies. If the group is not representative, i.e., if it is not similar to the larger population in important characteristics, then generalizations from the sample to the population are not appropriate. If the sample size was very small, we need to be wary of generalizing to the larger population. Without such information, we cannot evaluate whether the data was conducted in a scientifically acceptable way and thus whether the data should be seriously considered. A good reporter will also include opinions from other scientists in the field, indicate whether there is any controversy about the findings, and cite the original source. Without information about where the study was published, we cannot apply the credibility test that I suggested earlier.

Articles about psychological studies are often reported in a simplistic, sensationalistic way that distorts and misrepresents the original research. When, for example, psychologists Camille Benbow and Julian Stanley found a large gender difference in the math scores of mathematically talented boys and girls on the Math SAT (Scholastic Achievement Test), their discussion in the original journal stated that they believed that the gender difference had a biological basis (for the record, a highly controversial conclusion that many researchers question).[53] This precipitated one newspaper headline to scream "Math Gene Found," a far cry from what Dr. Benbow and Dr. Stanley actually said.[54] Several years later, after an interview with Benbow, one reporter wrote a newspaper article with the headline, "Male math skills linked to brain damage in womb."[55] Since I was teaching at the same school (Iowa State University) as Dr. Benbow at the time, I asked her what she thought about the headline and the article. She sighed and explained that the article was a distortion of what she had said. What she actually described to the reporter was a study about the effect of different amounts of testosterone on prenatal male and female brains. She assured me that she did not use the phrase "brain damage!" She was distressed with both the interviewer and the paper (remember that editors set headlines, not reporters) but indicated that such reporting goofiness was a common occurrence with her research.

CONSIDER ALTERNATIVE EXPLANATIONS

When evaluating claims or conclusions presented in articles, always consider alternative explanations. Many people accept the first explanation they hear, without thinking it through. Instead, think about alternative interpretations before coming to a conclusion about complex issues. Formulate hypotheses that offer reasonable explanations of characteristics, behavior, and events. Look for alternative ways to explain events besides the ones given. Consider whether another theory can explain the evidence as well or even better. Look for explanations that require fewer assumptions.

In her book, *You're Smarter Than They Make You Feel*, psychologist Dr. Paula Caplan gives one such example where considering alternatives was called for.[56] A reporter for the *Toronto Star* cited a researcher who had announced that he had found differences between the brains of homosexual and heterosexual men. The reporter left out an important piece of information: the brains of the homosexuals studied were from men who had died of AIDS; the brains of the heterosexuals studied were not from men who had died of AIDS. This crucial information should lead a critical thinker to ask: Could the differences be due, not to the differing sexual orientations, but to the fact that one group of brains was diseased and the other was not?

Another example where seeking alterative explanations is warranted is cited in the book *Critical and Creative Thinking* by psychologists Carole Wade and Carol Tavris.[57] One research study announced that there was a correlation between living together before marriage and later getting a divorce. Does this mean that cohabitation leads to divorce? Not necessarily. Dr. Wade and Dr. Tavris suggest another more plausible alternative. Perhaps those willing to live together before marriage are less traditional and thus more willing to consider divorce if irreconcilable problems arise.

When it comes to reporting of alleged biological differences, caution is definitely called for. Biology and behavior, as I frequently tell my students, is a two-way street. Biology can affect behavior (e.g., intelligence has a genetic component, testosterone is necessary for aggression) but behavior and environment can affect biology (e.g., stimulating environments can increase IQ, aggressive behavior can increase testosterone level).[58] For example, asserts Dr. Robert Sapolsky, an award-winning biology professor at Stanford University, though a certain level of testosterone must be present for aggression to occur, testosterone alone is not enough. Aggressive behavior can increase testosterone level.[59] Recent research on neuroplasticity also provides evidence of this two-way street. It shows us just how "plastic" the brain is and how environment and stimulation can change the structure of the brain.[60] The media frequently report simplistic views of human behavior, especially when it comes to biology. Apparently they believe that "anatomy is destiny" sells.

The Bottom Line

"The old saw says, 'Let a sleeping dog lie.' Right. Still, when there is much at stake it is better to get a newspaper to do it."[61]

—Mark Twain

We don't have to believe that newspapers or other media sources always lie to recognize that we need to be wary of the media. We can never let down our critical thinking guard. Be wary, be critical, read more than one kind of source, and never forget that there's always more to the story. It takes work to regain the power that the media takes away from us but it beats being bamboozled and manipulated.

RESOURCES

BOOKS

General Critical Thinking

Judith Boss. *Think: Critical Thinking and Logic Skills for Everyday Life.* New York: McGraw-Hill, 2009.

Paula Caplan, Ph.D. *You're Smarter than They Make You Feel: How the Experts Intimidate Us and What We Can Do about It.* New York: Free Press, 1994.

Brooke Noel Moore and Richard Parker. *Critical Thinking.* New York: McGraw Hill, 2007. (many editions).

Media Critiques

Kristina Borjesson. (Ed.) *Into The Buzzsaw: Leading Journalists Expose the Myth of a Free Press—Revised and Expanded Edition.* Amherst NY: Prometheus Books, 2004.

Bernard Goldberg. *Bias: A CBS Insider Exposes How the Media Distort the News.* New York: Harper Paperbacks, 2003. This one has a more conservative slant than the others. But as one reviewer said on Amazon: "If you're open-minded and can avoid both mindless aversion and mindless adherence, you can benefit and learn from some of the very valid points made in this book. Don't listen to the emotional ravings of either extreme. Decide for yourself, if you can handle it."[62]

Bernard Goldberg. *Arrogance: Rescuing America from the Media Elite.* New York: Warner Books, 2003.

Martin A. Lee and Norman Solomon. *Unreliable Sources: A Guide to Detecting Bias in the News Media.* New York: Carol Publishing Group, 1990. This is an excellent book with a wealth of information and many good tips. However be aware that its political slant is leftist/progressive and judge accordingly.

Russell Kick. (Ed.) *You Are Being Lied To: Disinformation Guide to Media Disinformation, Historical Whitewashes and Cultural Myths.* New York: Disinformation Company, 2001.

Russell Kick. (Ed.) *Everything You Know is Wrong: Disinformation Guide to Secrets and Lies.* New York: Disinformation Company, 2002.

Russell Kick. (Ed.) *Abuse Your Illusions: Disinformation Guide to Media Mirages and Establishment Lies.* New York: Disinformation Company, 2003.

Russell Kick. (Ed.) *You Are STILL Being Lied To: The NEW Disinformation Guide to Media Distortion, Historical Whitewashes and Cultural Myths.* New York: Disinformation Company, 2008.

Alexandra Kitty. *Don't Believe It: How Lies Become News.* New York: Disinformation Company, 2005. Very positively reviewed on Amazon, it discusses how to verify information and evaluate sources.

Richard Paul and Linda Elder. *How to Detect Media Bias & Propaganda.* Sonoma, CA: Foundation for Critical Thinking, 2006. This short piece is available as a free PDF at www.criticalthinking.org.

Douglas Rushkoff. *Coercion: Why We Listen to What "They" Say?* New York: Riverhead Books, 1999. Though confusing the word "coercion" with deceptive persuasion, it offers a useful critique of how the Internet as well as other media "short-circuit our better judgment."

John Stauber. *Toxic Sludge is Good for You: Lies, Damn Lies and the Public Relations Industry.* Monroe, ME: Common Courage Press, 2002. A positively reviewed book at Amazon that shows how much corporate press releases and other PR pieces affect what gets reported in the media.

WEB SITES

Media Watchdogs

Newswatch
www.newswatch.org
It objectively reports on a broad range of national and international news services and media criticism sources across the political spectrum and provides links to them.

The Real News Network
www.therealnews.com
With the slogan "The future depends on knowing," this fledging news organization is attempting to report on what the mainstream media leaves out.

Disinformation
www.disinfo.com

This site criticizes many aspects of the media and publishes several anthologies, including *You Are Being Lied To, Everything You Know is Wrong,* and *Abuse Your Illusions*. It has a Disinformation Store with 5 pages of DVDs and eight pages of books about deceptions and lies perpetrated on the public. A variety of different points of view are represented.

What's the Harm
www.whatstheharm.net
"Not all information is created equal" says the FAQ for this web site—so true that is. This site is designed to make the point that you can easily be injured or killed by neglecting to think critically about information. It has collected information about over 225,000 people who have been injured or killed as a result of someone not thinking critically. The topics range from colon cleansing to scientology, from faith healing to satanic ritual abuse. Whether the information you are considering comes from the media or everyday conversations, this site offers a critical look at many controversial topics.

Snopes
www.snopes.com
With the tag line "Rumor has it," Snopes is *the* place to find out if the stories you read on the Internet or in your email are true or "urban legends." Many stories are simply made up. It also includes info about many kinds of scams and frauds.

Project Censored
www.projectcensored.org
This project at Sonoma State University reports on the 25 most underreported important stories of the year. The info is available both in book form and a summary on the web site.

Fairness and Accuracy in Reporting (FAIR)
www.fair.org
FAIR criticizes the media from a politically progressive/liberal point of view.

Accuracy in Media (AIM)
www.aim.org

AIM criticizes the media from a conservative point of view.

However keep in mind what newspaper columnist Walter Goodman once said about FAIR and AIM. He noted that neither organization has ever had talk shows or documentaries from anything other than their own perspectives. He goes on to say that both groups perform a useful service and are provocative but each side only see the bias in the other side. AIM sees the "liberal" press as in control of TV and FAIR sees it as controlled by big business. Goodman has a point.[64]

Alternative magazines that offer nonmainstream points of view

Many of these magazines can be found on larger city newsstands and in bookstores such as Barnes & Noble or Borders, as well as independent bookstores. All of them have a web site.

Libertarian

Reason
www.reason.com

Reason TV
www.youtube.com/user/ReasonTV
www.reason.tv
Videos hosted by TV actor and comedian Drew Carey. Libertarians even-handedly slam both Democrats and Republicans, liberals and conservatives.

Liberty
www.libertyunbound.com
There are several magazines named "Liberty." This is the web site of the libertarian one.

Progressive (left liberal)

Mother Jones
www.motherjones.com

All the News That's Unfit to Print

This is the leading publication for left of liberal points of view.

Z Magazine
www.zmag.org
www.zmag.org/zvideo [video productions]

Other sources of critical thinking about the media

Open Directory Project: Media Literacy
www.dmoz.org/News/Media/Media_Literacy
Many links to web sites dealing with media literacy and crtical thinking about media and ads for both adults and young people.

Media Literacy
www.medialiteracy.com
Many resources for teaching media literacy, including articles and free downloads as well as kits to buy. Good for teachers and parents as well as other interested individuals.

News Biased Explored
www.umich.edu/~newsbias.html
Many resources for critical thinking about media bias, including articles and links to web sites examining media bias from different points of view.

UPDATES

For updates on books, web sites, web site URLs, articles, and links (they sometimes change or become obsolete), and other relevant information, as well as a blog, check the web site for this book: www.standupto authorities.com. Or you can use the titles or words in the references as search terms to do your own Internet update search.

PART III

I am Not a Number: Questioning Bureaucracies and Institutions

Introduction and Overview

> *"The biggest evil against Freedom is no longer the "evil dictator." Most of them are gone now and they only exist in a few places in the world. No, today the biggest evil against personal freedom and the pursuit of happiness is the Bureaucracy that stifles free-enterprise, freedom and free people."*[1]
>
> —Lance Winslow

"I AM NOT A number, I am a free man" exclaimed Patrick McGoohan defiantly in *The Prisoner*, a 1968 British cult classic TV drama about a secret agent who was kidnapped and held prisoner by unknown forces. Though none of us have suffered through the fictional mind games and travails faced by Prisoner #6 in this powerful allegory about the relationship between the individual and society, most of us have felt the brunt of mind-numbing institutions or been frustrated by dealing with uncaring people in irrational bureaucracies. "Just treat me like an individual" many of us have wanted to shout. "Don't keep passing the buck. Give me an answer." Many of us would like to know how to navigate the system and get around the frustrating stupidities of bureaucracies.

But learning how to survive the system isn't the whole enchilada. In their book, *Beating the System: Using Creativity to Outsmart Bureaucracy*, Russell L. Ackoff and Sheldon Rovin point out a second reason for learning how to beat the system. "Without this knowledge," they write, "we run the risk of becoming accustomed to being beaten by systems that are supposed to serve us. Many of us already accept, and are even inured to systems abuses because we feel nothing can be done about them. This threatens our quality of life and the extent to which we can exercise control of our lives."[2] In other words, if we just give up and accept defeat, it will have a more general negative effect on our psyches and our ability to deal with problems. From a psychological point of view, this is sound. The more we give up and don't try to deal with our issues and problems, the closer we get to what psychologists call "learned helplessness," a state in which we think that no matter what we do, nothing will help us.[3] This state can become a self-fulfilling prophecy. If we think nothing will help, then we won't even try to find solutions; we won't act on new strategies. We'll just continue feeling sorry for ourselves and stew in our own self-imposed pitiful state. Fighting back is good for the psyche as well as the soul.

OK, you say, "Let's fight bureaucracy. I'm up for it. How do we do it?" In dealing with institutions and bureaucracies, both private and public, the problems we face are a bit different than in the workplace or in the physician's office. It may not just be one boss we have to deal with in a one-on-one situation. It's more likely to be a chain of rules and regulations that seem to have a life of their own. This is especially true in government bureaucracies but occurs in private institutions too. Those you ask for help may claim, "I can't help you; I have to follow the rules," or some similar bit of sidestepping. Or they may try to enforce petty, stupid rules that make no sense.

Bureaucracies are a pervasive fact of modern life. Students have to survive educational bureaucracies to graduate from college. Business people have to deal with mind-numbing red tape at City Hall. Nearly everyone has complaints about a customer service line or computer tech support. All of these bureaucracies have elements in common and, at the same time, many differences. There *are* principles that apply to all bureaucracies. Rather than repeat the general advice over and over again, I've opted for a separate introduction to this section (unlike the first two) that emphasizes some of the key common elements. At the same time, each kind of bureaucracy has unique differences that call for different tactics. That's why in this section of the book, I have divided the issues into three separate chapters, each with its own specifics: education, government, and consumer services.

Here are some general principles that are relevant to all manner of bureaucracy.

Key Tools

- *Remember that you have a right to question*
  Don't assume it can't be done. Don't assume the rules can't be broken. Rules within bureaucracies are broken all the time. Recognize your right to question the rules when they make no sense or their observance would have bad or even immoral consequences.
- *Prepare your case and the evidence*
  You won't get anywhere with hostile rants or tearful pleading. You have to provide proof or make a cogent argument. If you or your child is being bullied or harassed at school, write down what happened and when. If you have a complaint about a faulty product or think that a rule is being enforced against you inappropriately, think through your argument logically and in detail. Describe the problem dispassionately.
- *Put it in writing*
  Bureaucrats like paper. They want to see it in writing; they want to see it documented. As I've said in other chapters, a complaint in writing is much more powerful and persuasive than a merely oral one. You are creating a "paper trail" that lets the bureaucrat know that not only are you serious and determined, you have evidence to back you up. Like the medical note from Adela's physician (see Chapter Two) that gave her a good excuse for forgetting to pay the traffic ticket, paper gives substance to your claim.

- *Seek allies*
  When dealing with bureaucrats, it's often helpful to have others on your team to back you up. If you're just one person, you may be only an annoying gnat to be brushed aside but several people are harder to ignore and harder to deal with. Whether several people go together to talk to the bureaucrat or merely sign a petition, it lets the bureaucrat know you are not alone. Allies also allow you to organize a boycott, strike, or demonstration in situations where one of these could be an effective tactic.
- *Be persistent*
  If the bureaucrat says no, go above her head. If you have to come back to her, say Ackoff and Rovin, find another way to put your request. If necessary, continue with emails, phone calls, or faxes till you wear them down. But be careful of looking like you're harassing them. Don't go too far and don't ever be nasty.
- *Get another opinion: Go up the chain of command*
  At the lowest rung of the bureaucratic ladder, the clerks have little discretion to do anything other than follow the rules. They don't want to take chances and it's easier and safer to robotically follow the rules anyway. No thinking involved. Some of them may even enjoy their tiny fiefdom and get off on giving you a hard time. It may be all the power they have. If the first tier says no to your request or is blasé about your complaint, go up the line. Ask for the supervisor, boss, principal, dean or whatever higher level administrator is appropriate.
- *Get another opinion: Get outside information*
  You are probably not the first person to encounter a problem with the bureaucracy that is making your life miserable. Look for resources and advice for dealing with this issue: books, the Internet, friends who have experiences with this bureaucracy.
- *Seek alternative solutions: the creative way*
  Try to think of ways to get around the rules of the bureaucracy. Look for a way to redefine the rules or the description to fit what you are doing or what you want. If you have a problem with the letter of the law, think of a way to fulfill the spirit instead. Engage in "creative" writing or thinking. Just make sure it doesn't involve law-*breaking* . . . That's not what I'm advocating at all.

In some cases, depending on the company and the rule, you could just do it. Or as Ackoff and Rovin put it, "Act first, ask permission later." If you'll get praised for your initiative, even though you risk a slap on the wrist, do it anyway, suggests Denise Kersten in her *USA Today* article, "How To Bend the Rules of Corporate Bureaucracy."[4]

- *Seek alternative solutions: the drastic way*
  If discussing or arguing your issue doesn't work with the supervisor or administrator, you may have to use more forceful alternatives. If the complaint is serious enough, the threat of public humiliation and/or a law suit is one possible avenue to pursue. Public humiliation can include getting a story in the school paper or the local newspaper or TV news, or organizing a demonstration, strike or boycott. For local consumer complaints, the threat of flyers or picket signs proclaiming the company's wanton disregard of your issue is a highly effective way to get the attention of the business *really* fast. If you opt for contacting the media, learn how to write an effective press release. See sidebar in this chapter for some tips and a sample press release. The Resources section tells you where to find additional advice about press releases and publicity.

  If you want to generate publicity for your cause beyond just a one-shot protest, you should invest in a book or two on how to get publicity. There's lots more to a serious effort than just sending out a press release. A book especially designed for social/political causes is *Making the News: A Guide for Nonprofits and Activists* by Jason Salzman. From compiling a media list to writing an op-ed piece, it's full of useful information that will help you be much more effective with your message. Most books on getting publicity emphasize the business angle and how to sell your product or service so I have only included books below that are useful for protest events.

These general tips on how to wrestle with bureaucracies are just a beginning. Read the next three chapters for more specific guides to surviving the landmines of bureaucratic red tape, uncaring administrators, and robotic customer service reps. Additional tips on dealing with paperwork and endless forms are in the chapter on City Hall. Good luck.

RESOURCES

BUREAUCRACY

Russell L. Ackoff and Sheldon Rovin. *Beating the System: Using Creativity to Outsmart Bureaucracies.* San Francisco: Barrett-Koehler Publishers, 2005. Full of clever ideas and delightful vignettes.

PRESS RELEASES AND PUBLICITY

There are lots of books on how to get publicity but many are aimed at marketing a product or service. The books below are ones that may be useful for protests, causes, and social activism, especially if it involves more than a one-shot protest.

Books

Josephine Bellaccomo. *Move the Message: Your Guide to Making a Difference and Changing the World.* New York: Lantern Books, 2004.

Jeff Crilley. *Free Publicity: A TV Reporter Shares the Secrets for Getting Covered on the News.* Dallas, TX: Brown Books Publishing, 2002. Presenting the reporter's point of view, this book got a 5-star recommendation from almost all of the reviewers at amazon.com. See his URL below.

Ellen Ratner and Kathie Scarrah. *Ready, Set, Talk! A Guide to Getting Your Message Heard by Million . . . On Talk Radio, Talk Television, and Talk Internet.* White River Junction, VT: Chelsea Green Publishing, 2006.

Jason Salzman. *A Guide for Nonprofits and Activists.* Boulder, CO: Westview Press, 1998.

Web

Here's Internet information on how to write a press release and/or get publicity.

WikiHow
www.wikihow.com/Write-a-Press-Release
An excellent summary of the basics.

Publicity Insider
www.publicityinsider.com/release.asp
Offers some additional tips and examples worth looking at.

www.ehow.com/how_8793_write-proper-press-release.html
Another pithy summary.

Google Templates Press Release
docs.google.com/templates?q=press+release

Jeff Crilley Free Publicity
www.jeffcrilley.com/index.htm
Crilly offers tips on getting publicity and writing press releases. You can watch his video or buy his book at this site too.

How to Write a Press Release: A Hypothetical Example

Contact: Jane Smith [name]
For Immediate Release: [date and year]
Telephone: 555-555-5555
Email: saynotobullies@yourfreemailservice.com [organization or organizer's email] [THIS IS NOT A REAL ADDRESS!!-SP]
Web site: [organization's web site, if available and relevant]

**TIRED of SCHOOL YARD BULLIES BEATING UP YOUR CHILD?:
One Group Fights Back**
[pithy, attention-grabbing headline]

Are our kids targets for bullies? A group of concerned parents calling themselves "Stand Up to Bullies" is fed up with Midland School's lack of response to their fears about bullies in the school yard. A protest is planned from 10am to Noon, Tuesday, October 16 at 1212 Elm Street at the main entrance to Midland School. All concerned citizens are invited to join the protest. Picket signs and coffee will be provided.
[The lead paragraph includes the who, what, when, why, where and how of the story. Everything the reporter or newspaper needs to know in a nutshell]

After repeated attempts to get school officials at Midland School to get serious about the problem of bullying in their school and take action, Jane and John Smith decided to take action themselves. After meeting with other parents whose kids are being beaten up and bullied at Midland, they formed "Stand Up to Bullies" to raise public indignation and support. "It's outrageous that Principal Jones claimed nothing can be done," said Ms. Smith. "Our son Devin is picked on every day. Some days they steal his lunch money. Other kids have the same experience. I want to know why the school won't do anything about it."
[Additional succinct, to-the-point information about how the problem originated, what has been done about it so far, and a quote from a member of the group. All written in third person]

The protest is scheduled to last from 10am to Noon. The group will provide further detailed information about the unsuccessful attempts to resolve the problem with Midland School. A petition condemning the lack of action will be also be circulated. "Stand Up to Bullies" invites all concerned citizens to join in the protest and become a part of the group.
[Additional details about the event and what can be expected]

For further information or to schedule an interview with members of "Say No to Bullies," contact Jane Smith at 555-555-5555 or email her at saynotobullies@yourfreemailservice.com.
[where to get more information]

###
[signals end of press release]

Hypothetical Press Release for a Speaker

Contact: Robert Jones [name]   For Immediate Release: [date and year]
Phone: 555-555-5555
Email: rjones@communityauthors.com [organizers email address]
Website: www.communityauthors.com

**LOCAL AUTHOR SAYS YOU DON'T HAVE TO TAKE IT ANYMORE:
STAND UP TO EXPERTS AND AUTHORITIES**
[attention-grabbing headline, reference to speaker]

Should you take a lie detector test? Do you want your doctor to actually listen to you and take you seriously? Do you want to learn to separate the valuable wheat from the bogus chaff in media reports? Dr. Sharon Presley, author of *Standing Up to Experts and Authorities: How to Avoid Being Intimidated, Manipulated, and Abused* answers these questions and many more in her talk at the Wynona Community Center. Dr. Presley's book offers a how-to toolkit that provides specific techniques to help people stand up to and deal effectively with experts in a wide range of contexts. She will be speaking Tuesday, May 4 at 7pm. The Center is located at 1212 Main St. Tickets are $5. All welcome.
[The who, what, when and where, plus something important about the speaker]

Dr. Presley will discuss specific settings in which authorities or experts can bamboozle people, including institutions (e.g., schools, bureaucracies), the workplace (e.g., dealing with bosses, evaluations, and raises), media (e.g., news programs, magazines, self-help books), and services (e.g., medical care, lawyers, customer service, contractors, psychologists). She will also discuss how to stand up for your rights and the rights of others with the police and other government agencies.
[Info about the specifics of the talk]

Michael Shermer, author of *Why People Believe Weird Things*, says "I love this book! I wish I would have written this book! This is skepticism for the real world, an introduction on how to think, a manual for the survival of the human race. Sharon Presley is the Ralph Nader of bad ideas, the consumer advocate of bogus claims and phony experts."
[endorsement of speaker's point of view or speaker]

After the talk, Dr. Presley will answer questions from the audience about authority situations they may face. She will also be available for book signing.
[additional details about the talk and what can be expected]

Sharon Presley, Ph.D. is a social psychologist and former college professor who has frequently written and spoken on obedience and resistance to authority. More information about Dr. Presley can be found at her professional website www.sharonpresley.com or the book website www.standuptoauthorities.com.
[info about the speaker]

For more information about the event or to schedule an interview with Dr. Presley, contact Robert Jones at 555-555-5555 or though the sponsoring organization's website at www.communityauthors.com
[who to contact for more info about the event]

###

CHAPTER
7

Not Another Brick in the Wall: Surviving "Education"

We don't need no education.
We don't need no thought control.
No dark sarcasm in the classroom.
Teacher, leave those kids alone . . .
All in all you're just another brick in the wall.
—from "Another Brick in the Wall"
by Pink Floyd[1]

WE'VE ALL FACED THE bureaucracies of educational systems. Many of us have had bad experiences through no fault of our own. At all levels from grade school to college, decisions are made by teachers, principals, and administrators that aren't always good ideas. Many times the decisions made are not what's in the best interests of the students but rather what will save face, make money, be politically correct, avoid potential law suits, or in some other way further the interests of the schools or colleges. I've seen and read about many examples over the years. Sometimes it feels as if the musical group Pink Floyd had it pegged right: "All in all, you're just another brick in the wall."

> **Key Tools**
>
> - Right to protest
> - Prepare your case
> - Put it in writing
> - Seek allies
> - Seek outside opinions
> - Explore alternatives
> - Be aware of body language

K-12 Schools

QUESTIONING SCHOOL POLICIES

There are many fine schools where parents, teachers and principals work together to create a good educational environment for students. Unfortunately there's also a lot where the education isn't the best and the policies leave something to be desired. If you think a policy is inadequate or just plain wrong, you have a right to protest. If a teacher is treating your child in a demeaning way or other students are harassing your child, you have a right to speak up and demand that it stop.

However, a word of caution. There are also parents who think their little Tommy or Marcy can do no wrong and that every bad grade or problem is the teacher's fault. Stories abound of parents who narcissistically think the world revolves around them and their child and that *everything* must be the school's fault. No wonder some developmental research shows that young adults are more narcissistic than ever before.[2] But late-breaking bulletin here: Sometimes the teacher is right and the kid is wrong. Keep in mind that there are two sides to every story. Be prepared to listen to the teacher and others in the system, not just simply demand your own way. Being willing to listen makes you look like a reasonable person, not just a crank or narcissist. Being reasonable rather than aggressive is also more likely to get you what you want.

Ritalin as an example of dealing with school policy

The use and misuse of Ritalin is one of the most common conflicts that parents face in dealing with schools so I use it here as an example of how to handle both this problem and others that may arise. The keys are to question, get outside opinions, and seek additional and alternative information.

One of the big decisions many parents are faced with in elementary school is whether to allow Ritalin to be given to their child who has been diagnosed Attention Deficit Disorder (ADD) or Attention Deficit Hyperactive Disorder (ADHD). Pediatrician and family therapist Lawrence Diller, M.D. writes that the num-

Not Another Brick in the Wall

ber of children and adults diagnosed with ADD has risen from about 900,000 to almost 5 million since 1990[3] Is there a growing epidemic or it is a case of growing overdiagnosis? That may depend on what experts you read. However, here's a clue: The USA produces and consumes 90% of the world's Ritalin.[4] Canada and European countries don't come close to the percentage that the USA uses. No wonder that Diller suggests it is cultural. We Americans love to solve our problems with drugs. So much easier than therapy or hard work. So heck, let's drug our kids too . . .

Many experts, including Diller, note that we don't even know what ADD really is nor is there is any real test for it. Other experts such as psychiatrist and anti-establishment critic Peter Breggin, M.D. go a step further and assert that diagnosis is often simply an excuse to control "difficult" children, such as daydreamers and those who annoy parents or teachers. He further asserts that Ritalin is dangerous for children, can have horrendous side-effects and that better alternative treatments exist.[5] Moderates like Diller suggest that Ritalin can be useful for some children some of the time but must be used cautiously. Yet in many school districts, those who sing hosanna to the wonders of Ritalin are the only ones allowed to be heard. In some districts, parents are told they have no choice to give Ritalin to their ADD-diagnosed child or the child will be kicked out of school. What should parents do if faced with the diagnosis? What if they decide not to medicate? Then what?

Whether you want to allow your child to take Ritalin or a similar drug is a choice only you should make—not a teacher, not the school, not even a psychiatrist. Diagnoses are often made by untrained teachers or administrators who are not therapists, let alone experts. Do not listen to them. If you are uncertain about whether you want your child to be given Ritalin, inform yourself about the pros and cons. Read several books about Ritalin from different perspectives. Some books on the topic are listed below. Ask for a second opinion from a developmental specialist who is not a psychiatrist; many psychiatrists are all too eager to prescribe drugs. (See my comments in Chapter Three) If, after reading the different points of view, you decide that Ritalin is not in your child's best interests, you will need to know how to fight back because you are very likely to be pressured to give it to your child whether you want to or not. Even if you decide it's a good idea, you need to think about how long your child should take it and when to quit.

However, I want to stress here that parents need to be aware of the responsibility that a decision to resist Ritalin entails. An alternative solution may require time and effort as well as courage. The therapeutic alternatives suggested by the behavioral psychologists or the suggestions from Dr. Breggin (see below) require dedication and possibly even letting go of other uses of time and money. Some people would say "sacrifice" but if you think the extra time and effort to help your child is worth it, then it's not really a sacrifice. Just be aware that opposing the school's pressure to drug your child (or opposing any school policy, for that matter) has costs.

RESOLVING CONFLICTS WITH SCHOOL POLICY

In his book, *Talking Back to Ritalin*, Dr. Breggin advocates a conflict resolution model that seeks mutually satisfying win-win solutions. This approach, points out Dr. Breggin, can serve as a model for other conflicts with school personnel. Here's what Dr. Breggin suggests.[6]

- First build rapport with your child's teachers and other resource people at school. Express your concerns while trying to work out more child-oriented alternative solutions (see Breggin's books and other books below for specific ideas).
- Second, listen carefully to the teachers in order to understand their concerns about your child. Try to find out if their motives are benign or tainted by some other agenda (e.g., simply controlling the child's annoying behavior). Don't come on so strong that you make the teacher defensive.
- Third, Dr. Breggin warns against going down the path of psychological and psychiatric evaluations. He advocates against letting the school or their psychologist evaluate your child. If an evaluation is necessary, pick a private consultant who does not have reputation for being enthusiastically pro-Ritalin. You want a fair appraisal, not a railroading to suit the school's agenda rather than yours. Get the opinion of an objective expert outside the system.

In the video "Generation Rx," (see below) there is an example of parents who used this approach.
- Fourth, if possible, have a family member go to school to observe your child. Explain that you want to observe the problem so you will understand it more clearly. The family member can then get a better idea whether the child is simply too rambunctious or has another behavioral problem that needs to be dealt with.
- Fifth, pay attention to the improvement of your child's reading skills and enjoyment. "The vast majority of academic problems in preschool and early elementary school children," says Breggin, "can be corrected through improved reading skills."[7] Read to them; take them to the library and museums. If necessary, get them tutors. Developmental research backs up Dr. Breggin's advice. Children whose parents read to them do better in school; the more the parents read to them, the better is the child's vocabulary and reading ability.[8]

You should also look into the exact nature of the laws, rules and regulations regarding what the school may or may not do. You may even have to seek legal consul. In some states, the stranglehold of Ritalin believers is so strong that your refusal may be perceived as "child endangerment" and Child Protective Services might be brought in to the picture. An example of this is given in the A&E video "Investigative Reports: Generation Rx: Reading Writing and Ritalin."[9] A couple who felt that their son was being harmed by Ritalin not only refused to continue giving it to him but took him out of school and sought alternative treatment. At the insistence of the school, Child Protective Services investigated them for child endangerment. Though they were cleared of the charges, the experience was an ordeal. If you go against your child's school, be prepared to stand your ground.

Look for alternative ways to deal with your child's learning and behavioral problems. Alternatives that you may want to explore include home schooling, increasing physical activity, and creating a more tranquil home environment. In the A&E video, "Generation Rx," for example, one couple found a child behavioral psychologist (one trained to deal with overt behavioral problems) who helped reorganize their son's environment to help him stay calm and focused.

You may not be able to send your child to a school like the Albany Free School, an experimental school that gives individual attention to every student and treats every child as an individual, but there are lessons to be learned from its experience. The school has created a real community, with genuine concern for each child's emotional health. "To conclude distressed children simply have faulty brain chemistry and to categorize millions of them as though they are in some way defective is to take the easy way out," says Chris Mercogliano. "It provides the basis for a thinly veiled Orwellian social policy that threatens the futures—and the very souls—of our nation's children."[10]

BULLYING AND HARASSMENT AT SCHOOL

Bullying and harassment are big problems on school campuses. A survey by the National Institute of Child Health and Human Development found that 29% of the 15,000 children studied have been involved in bullying either as the bully or the victim.[11] Some schools take it seriously; some do not. But regardless of the school policy—more on that later—your child should not assume she or he simply has to put up with it. It is wrong and letting it go on may damage your child's self-esteem and possibly expose her to danger. Be there for your child. A study by the Kaiser Family Foundation and Nickelodeon TV found that most children did not find conversations on this topic with their parents helpful because the parents didn't take it seriously.[12] Do take bullying seriously because it can have a considerable negative effect on your child.

Prepare your case and put it in writing

Here's what the experts say about what students can do to help themselves. Either you or your child should write down the date, time, location and what was said. This provides documentation and specifics that make your complaint more convincing and real. If there were any witnesses, try to get a statement from them or at least talk to them. This is just as true if the teacher is the bully or harasser.

Most teachers are dedicated and responsible educators. But

some do step over a line. One of my students, the mother of a girl in high school, told me that one of the male teachers had been spouting sexist comments, e.g., girls weren't as good at math as boys, in her daughter's class (which research shows is not in fact true).[13] No teacher has any business putting down their students, either as a group (e.g., girls) or individually. If the teacher is making sexist or racist remarks, it should not go unchallenged. Sexist or racist remarks in the classroom are harassment and violate public policy as well as the law. If the teacher is making fun of a particular student or disparaging him or her in front of other students, it is not appropriate and needs to stop. It is still bullying even if the teacher is doing it. Bullying by the teacher is way outside what is permissible in the classroom.

Psych your child up

Encourage your child to develop an assertive attitude. Tell him that it's OK to politely but firmly tell the harasser to stop. Underneath their bluster, bullies are cowards looking for an easy target. Don't let your child be one. There are many books and several web sites that can give you and your child further good advice about how to deal with bullies. They also have suggestions for how to help your child understand this issue as well as how to deal with it. Some resources are listed below.

Tell your grade school child that she doesn't have to let bullies call her names. Tell her to stand up to them and say: "You're not nice. Stop it." If your boy is being bullied by a group of other boys, tell him to quietly but firmly tell them to stop. Even if they don't stop, acting afraid only encourages the bullies more. Sometimes your child may have to run away to get to safety, but he doesn't have to do it in a fearful way that will feed the bully's ego.

Tell your teen that she doesn't have to be rude or aggressive if someone she doesn't like asks her out. She can just say no; she doesn't have to give a reason. If someone tells an offensive joke, just politely say: "That joke offends me. I don't want to hear it."

If the teacher is the one making the offensive remarks, the child can quietly but firmly tell the teacher in private that she finds the remarks offensive or hurtful. If the child is afraid to stand up to the teacher, then proceed to the next step. It's hard for young children to stand up to a powerful authority figure such as a teacher. But don't just accept it; bullying or harassment by the teacher is a reprehensible abuse of power and it needs to stop.

Encourage confident body language

In Chapter Two, I mentioned the power and importance of nonverbal language. It's just as true for your child as for you. Bullies look for easy targets. One of the clues they use is body language. If your child is fearful and cringing, this will just make the bully more likely to target him. Encourage your child to have a posture that suggests confidence, not defeat, suggest SuEllen Fried and Paula Fried, Ph.D., the authors of *Bullies, Targets & Witnesses*.[14] They recommend that you consider enrolling your child in martial arts such as karate, tae kwon do or tai chi. Children have blossomed, they report, when exposed to the kind of respect and centering engendered by such disciplines. Any good martial arts program will emphasize the ethics of fighting; that the purpose of the training is to *avoid* confrontation and aggression if at all possible.

Martial arts training is just as relevant for your daughter as your son, maybe even more so. Girls also need to learn to project confidence and assertiveness because they are often stereotypically seen as powerless and weak targets by bullies and harassers. Most martial arts center have girls as well as boys enrolled so she won't feel out of place.

Report the harasser

Encourage your child to go to an adult and ask for help. Don't delay. Most experts say that it is a bad idea to either ignore the harassment (that only encourages bullies) or to make threats or retaliate. Retaliation is fighting on the bully's level and is likely to make things worse instead of better. "Escaping isn't always possible, and bullies can enjoy trying to trap you," writes Adam Hibbert, author of *Why Do People Bully?*, a book written for grade school children.[15] "It may also encourage them to think of you as an easy target."

Be prepared for some teachers not to be helpful. There are teachers who have the attitude that "boys will be boys." Bypass these dinosaurs. Bad behavior that hurts others is never acceptable, whether done by boys or men, girls or women. Some teachers may deny that there is a problem or not be sympathetic. A researcher quoted in *Bullying: How to Deal With Taunting, Teasing and Tormenting* by Kathleen Winkler said "Kids say that when they tell the adults about bullying, adults don't take them seriously, or they make them feel responsible for going back and working it out."[16] This is a cop-out at best and cowardice at worst. Adults in a school situation are responsible for protecting children. If they fail at this obligation, they should be held accountable.

Seek allies among the children, teachers and counselors

A Canadian research project found that 79% of the bullying in the playground and 85% in the classroom had witnesses.[17] Have your child ask other children if they are also being bullied or harassed. Or maybe there were witnesses who saw your child being harassed. Get their stories, if you can. However, in many cases, it may be advisable to get the other children's parents permission to talk to them. If several students are being bullied, it is harder for the principal to dismiss it as a fluke or try to sweep it under the rug.

A word of caution here: children, especially younger children, can be highly suggestible when questioned.[18] If you ask a child, your own or others, about what they witnessed, do not ask leading questions or you may not get reliable answers. So instead of saying, for example, "Did you see Joe hitting my son Timmy?" it's better to ask: "Did you see another child bothering Timmy? Do you know who it was? What was he doing?"

If there is a sympathetic teacher, it might be a good idea to enlist his or her aid in presenting your case. The teacher may be aware of the problem and add credence to your complaint. However, in some cases it might be a good idea to speak to a counselor instead. If there are many teachers or the bully is in another grade, your child's teacher may not have seen anything useful. Or, if you suspect the teacher has handled a bullying situation poorly, you need to go elsewhere. Keep a record of the conversations you have with anyone you talk to about the issue, whether child, teacher, counselor, or principal. It's important to be as precise and accurate as you can about what you hear from other children as well as what adults say to you. "Take the time to repeat what you hear and ask if you have heard the reply correctly," recommend Fried and Fried.[19] "Let them know that you are taking notes for accuracy rather than trusting your memory." Dating documentation is very important, suggest these authors. You never know when you might need it.

Seek allies among other parents

If other children have been the victims of bullies, seek out their stories. Talk to their parents about the negative consequences of bullying or harassment on children. Inform yourself about the toll that bullying takes so that other parents will not respond with what James Garbarino, Ph.D. and Ellen deLara, Ph.D., authors of *And Words Do Hurt Forever*, call the "myths about school safety."[20] Encourage other parents to come with you to PTA and school board meetings, and to teacher conferences. Try to get other parents to come with you when you present your case to the principal, and, if necessary, the Superintendent of Schools or Board of Education.

Seek information about the policies before you talk to the principal

Find out if school has a bullying or sexual harassment policy. If not, demand that it have one. If the school gets federal funding, it is required by law to have a sexual harassment policy.[21] Then demand that the school follow the policy. Go to the principal with the written policy in hand if you can. Present the evidence in writing and ask her to enforce the policy or you will report her to the Board of Education or to the newspapers. Be gutsy (but polite); your child's self-esteem and well-being is at stake here.

Go up the chain of command

If the principal refuses to do anything about the bully or harasser, you may have several options. First investigate the Board of Education policies on harassment or any relevant State laws. If you think you have found breaches of policy, marshal your evidence and take it to the Superintendent of Schools in your district. If the breach is serious enough, consider reporting it to your local newspaper. Even if you aren't sure that a breach of policy has occurred but the school refuses to stop the bullying, you should report it to someone up the line. You can consider threatening to sue (that'll get their attention) but be prepared to follow through. You may have to. Many school districts are notoriously unwilling to admit that anything is wrong in *their* schools, doggedly pushing problems under the rug.

Consider alternatives

There are a number of possible alternatives to explore. Garbarino and deLara suggest that if school safety is a major concern, you call in an outside evaluator. Someone who is familiar with how schools work may be able to see things more objectively and be able to make suggestions for change.[22] If the problem is rampant, consider going to the newspapers or local TV channel. Explore the possibility of a protest demonstration. Remember what I said about the power of public humiliation. If that's what it takes to get administrators to take the problem seriously, you should use it.

When all else fails, consider legal action

If the situation is outrageous and the school refuses to protect your child, a law suit may be the only way to get them to listen. In the video "Dangerous Propositions," a high school student in Minnesota, who was the victim of sexual harassment by other students, is interviewed. Some of the boys circulated a list of the 25 "most fuckable girls" in her school. Some of the girls were (foolishly) flattered but she was not. When she went to the principal's office, the response was to offer *her* counseling rather than take action against the boys. Incensed, she refused. She finally filed a law suit against the school and won, justifiably so. Her school was apparently more concerned with protecting itself than protecting this abused student.

Alternatives to legal action

Sometimes people with reasonable complaints and good cases still lose. Life isn't always fair and entrenched bureaucracies don't always budge. If you get no satisfaction from the power structure and you either choose not to sue or you can't afford to hire a lawyer, consider alternatives. If the school will not protect your child from bullies, harassers or violence, then consider other options. Explore moving your child to another, safer school. If you can get other parents involved, try a public protest and notify the local newspapers and TV stations.

Is home schooling an option? There is an abundance of resources for home schooling on the Internet. If bullying, harassment or violence is a big problem at your school, see if other affected parents would be interested in joining together in a home schooling effort. Some home schooling resources are listed below.

VIOLATIONS OF STUDENT RIGHTS

School administrators often want the easiest policy, not the best policy. They want "easy fixes" just like so many people do. Sometimes these so-called easy fixes not only violate student rights but just plain common sense and common decency. A wonderful book titled *Guerrilla Learning: How to Give Your Kids a Real Education With or Without School* by Grace Llewellyn provides a vivid example.[23] When Hafidah Collins refused to submit to a strip search, an indignity that violated her Muslim beliefs, the New York school demanded that her father instruct her to submit. The father's response was to remove her from the school. A good solution but not one that is practical for every parent and child.

Seek information: Be aware of your rights (or lack thereof)

The sad truth is that teens and children have fewer rights than adults in a school situation. The school staff can search a student's locker nearly anytime they have even a shred of an excuse. That goes for backpacks, purses, and clothing. In college, fortunately, the administration would have to have much more "probable cause" than in high school. But if you are a teen or your child is, does this mean you are at the mercy of the principal? Not necessarily.

Find out what your rights are. Searches, for example, require "reasonable suspicion." Only under limited circumstances are general searches of all students permitted. But the court decisions are nuanced and complex. I'm not a lawyer and can't give you advice about what your rights actually are. I *can* recommend a book that can answer some of your questions about rights of teenagers in schools. *Teen Rights (and Responsibilities)* by Tracy Truly, J.D. covers a wide variety of issues, including searches, freedom of speech, birth control, rights of religion in school, and many others.[24] She is a practicing attorney and discusses court cases that bear on the various issues. You can also get information about school laws from your local school district administration or an attorney familiar with school law.

School records are another potential source of conflict. First of all, parents have the right to access their child's records until he or she is 18. This has not always been the case. A child's dossier is not merely a report about attendance or grades. In many school districts, teachers can put comments in a child's record, These comments can follow a child throughout grade and high school. It may be a good idea to know what's in the dossier because there are circumstances under which it can be viewed by others in spite of the fact that it is supposed to be confidential. What you don't know *can* hurt your child.

If you are a teenager or your child is, be aware that, unlike TV cop shows, the principal does not have to "miranda-ize" or read a teen her rights if she is under suspicion or questioned.[25] What a teen says can be used against him, regardless. Encourage your child to be very careful of what he or she says if confronted under such circumstances. Even a teenager is not obligated to answer any and all questions that a principal may ask. There is, however, a risk that the student may be suspended for failing to answer questions. Carefully weigh the pros and cons of answering questions when legal issues are involved.

However, if a teen in school is arrested by a police officer, then he or she does have a right to an attorney and the police are obligated to tell them this. As a general rule, warns Truly, if the police are involved or the teen is being questioned about activities that could lead to being arrested, don't talk![26] Ask to call the parents or an attorney. The police or the principal may try to persuade the teen to waive his or her rights. Don't do it.

Truly's book contains many resources for further information about the issue she discusses, including web sites, organizations, agencies, and recommended books. She also includes a state-by-state appendix of laws pertinent to teen rights, including age of majority, compulsory school attendance, parental consent in regard to abortion, and many others. If you have an issue concerning student rights, be informed.

Seek allies

If you encounter a policy that is outrageous or questionable, talking to the principal (whose idea it probably is) is unlikely to get you very far. In spite of this, you probably should try to talk to him or her, using some of the suggestions above. It's a good idea, however, to find other parents who are outraged and bring them with you. Harder for the principal to face down a group than an individual.

But if you get the cold shoulder, consider contacting the nearest branch of the American Civil Liberties Union (ACLU) and ask their opinion about the legality of such policies or suggestions for dealing with the problem. You could also try to interest your local newspaper in the story. In the Collins case, the parents could have tried using the discriminatory religious angle to embarrass the school. As I've already suggested, public humiliation is often a useful tool against recalcitrant and unsympathetic administrators.

The ACLU is a strong advocate of student rights, not just the rights of adults. It recognizes that student rights are routinely violated by schools and provides resources to help deal with these violations. Here's what I found on its web site:[27]

> "Constitutional violations are far too common in public schools across the country. Articles about controversial subjects written for student newspapers are censored. Lockers and backpacks are searched without reasonable suspicion.
>
> Minority students are disproportionately shunted in lower track programs. Majoritarian religious practices are officially sanctioned by teachers and school administrators. Female students are excluded from certain extracurricular activities, and gay students are intimidated into silence."

The ACLU has long been in the forefront of the right of free speech and free expression for students. One particularly outrageous case it took on in 2006 was the case of 7th-grader Toni Kay Scott of Napa California, who, according to the ACLU web site, was "sent to the principal's office not because of a revealing see-through top, spiked collar or platform heels—but because her socks featured a picture of the Winnie-the-Pooh character Tigger." The school had a highly restrictive dress code that prohibited any kind of images on the clothes or belongings of the students. Toni's younger sister also got into trouble for wearing a T-shirt that said "Jesus freak." The Northern California ACLU filed a law suit against the Napa Valley Unified School District. "They are enforcing a 'school uniform' under the guise of a 'dress code' and that's in violation of the California Education Code," said Sharon O'Grady, an attorney at Pillsbury Winthrop Shaw Pittman LLP, the firm representing the plaintiff, along with the ACLU. The case was decided in 2007.[28] The school lost, the students won. The dress code was rescinded. Sometimes the good guys do win.

Resources provided by the ACLU web site include listings for local ACLU branches as well as publications such as "Making Sense of Student Drug Testing: Why Educators Are Saying No" and "Ask Sybil Liberty About Your Rights to Free Expression" (student rights to free speech).

Colleges and Universities

College bureaucracies sometimes promote patently dumb policies that don't work. Furthermore they often don't care whether the policies make sense. Apparently others think this is a widespread problem too; I have a button on the bulletin board in my office that reads "It doesn't have to make sense. It's University policy." Once in place, the policies can take on a life of their own. In such bureaucracies, individual complaints often fall on deaf ears.

Question policies

Questioning university policies can be like trying to hold on to a greased pig. Administrators can be slippery and evasive, saying one thing to you and another behind your back. Or they may stonewall you or simply say no. Quite frankly, if you protest, you *will* lose a lot of the time. But not always. It may be worth it to at least explore possible courses of actions before you assume nothing can be done and give up.

Minor policies, particularly if they violate other rules, are usually easier to deal with than major policies; here there is a greater chance of success. I often teach a lab class at my university's satellite campus. Because it was an interactive lab class, there is a strict limit of 12 students in the class. The department's catalog specified certain prerequisite classes that had to be taken. In addition to statistics and a previous experimental class, the students were required to take a class in the subject matter of the lab. Because two of the students did not meet that last criterion one quarter, I dropped them from the class. They howled in protest to the administrators at the satellite campus because they had been told they did not have to meet that criterion. When I met with the adviser who "waived" the criterion for the students, she claimed that the required course was not taught often enough at the satellite campus. I was outraged. First of all, I had recently taught the required class at the satellite campus. Secondly, I did not believe that this adviser, who had no connection with the Psychology Department, had the right to change my Department's policies. I complained both to my Chair and to the Dean of the satellite campus. The Chair agreed with me and the adviser was never allowed to pull that trick again. In this case, merely speaking up was enough to solve the problem.

Sometimes the policies are flexible if only you dare to question them. Laura, a student of mine, applied for our school's Social Welfare Graduate Program but was turned down before the application deadline was even reached. I urged her to go to the head of the program and politely ask why she was rejected. She was told that she needed to have intern and volunteer experience (she had none). But Laura's sincerity and her articulate explanation of why she wanted to be in the program impressed the professor in charge. Laura was given another chance and told to submit additional letters of recommendation from several more professors. Since Laura was one of my best and most conscientious students, I had no problem writing her a glowing letter. She got accepted. The moral of the story—be persistent and don't be afraid to question policy.

Questioning the policies of individual professors can be pretty tricky. In most universities, professors have the freedom to decide what texts to use, how to teach the course and, within reasonable limits, how to grade. However, sometimes what they do *is* clearly beyond reasonable bounds. Teachers who openly harass or humiliate their students, either individually or as a group, who engage in racial or sexual attacks or harassment, or who have patently unfair ways of grading step over the line. Harassment is against most university policies and should be reported first to the Chair, then further up the line if necessary. I make some suggestions below about how to handle this.

Unfair grading is a tougher one to call. From my many years of experience, I know that there are some students who think professors who simply have high standards are being unfair. But if the *entire* class thinks the professor is unfair, then there may be more to it. This is still a tough one to deal with because, without plenty of evidence, the Chair is likely to side with the professor. Suggestions for dealing with unfair grading are listed below.

However, there are other unfair policies that can be protested. I recently heard of a case in which the professor, first of all, piled on way more homework than could be reasonably done in the quarter. Even the good students were complaining. Then he decided to eliminate one lab report *and* add a final exam that was not on the syllabus. That's a big no-no. Professors have some leeway and can postpone due dates or eliminate work or exams with good reason, but adding work not in the syllabus is considered a breach of contract; in this case, the syllabus is the contract. I advised the student to seek allies among the good students in the class and go together as a group to discuss the problem with the Chair of that department. In this case, I knew that the professor was new to this school and may not have had much teaching experience. This could be a situation where the Chair could give guidance to the new teacher and resolve it in a satisfactory way.

Go up the chain of command

Sometimes the problem is inappropriate policies within the department. In this case, going over the head of the department chair is sometimes the solution. Selena was a history major in a small Western university. She discovered that there were three courses she needed to finish her major but only one had been offered in the last three years and that one, only in the summer. When she complained to the Chair, he brushed her off, giving her no indication of when these courses would be offered. She went straight to the president of this school and, armed with evidence that the classes were required but never offered, she threatened to sue. Funny thing—*that* definitely made an impression on the president. Suing the university is bad press and administrators hate that. The president told the Chair he had to offer the courses.

The Chair, in a frankly remarkable show of arrogance, then tried to offer all three classes at the same time. Selena wasted no time in going back to the president. The Chair was forced to relent but told her that she would have to find enough students to fill the classes or he would cancel them. As it turned out, when the other history majors found out about the courses, they *begged* her to be on the list for the classes. When graduation ceremonies rolled around, all 42 of the (finally) graduating history majors gave Selena a rousing round of applause! The morale of this story: don't be afraid to complain at the highest level, be persistent, and, oh yes, the threat of a law suit can be an effective part of your arsenal also.

Another story where the threat of public humiliation was used to good effect is related in *Beating the System* by Russell L. Ackoff and Sheldon Rovin. Bill, a graduate student and research assistant in a large university, took his black Labrador dog Jesse to his office on most days. When Jesse wanted to go out, he would wait by the elevator till someone came along. Most people recognized him and pushed the ground floor button for him. This usually worked but sometimes Jesse got off at the wrong floor. A professor on this floor complained to the university vice president. Bill attached a notice to Jesse's collar. The professor complained again. Bill then suggested to the vice-president that the local paper might find the expulsion of the dog an interesting news story. The vice-president, recognizing that this would make the university look bad, talked to the professor, who reluctantly agreed that such notoriety would be undesirable. Jesse got to stay. As Ackoff and Rovin point out, "Organizations like nothing less than having their dirty linen washed in public. The threat of exposure often can make an organization accept what it would otherwise reject."[29] They add that you should not assume that punishment will follow even it is threatened. That too would make the school look bad.

Seek allies

Another important tool is to have allies. There really *is* strength in numbers so seeking out others to form a united group front against outrageous policies can be very effective. Here is another wonderful example from *Beat the System*.[30] The living quarters provided for married students at one large university had deteriorated over time. The apartments were run down, the basement where the washing machines were located was so rat-infested that the machines couldn't be used, and many refrigerators were malfunctioning. Complaints by individual students were ignored. Finally the students had enough and an action group was formed. They went on a rent strike. At first there was no response from the administration. But then the students managed to get sympathetic articles into the school paper. Next, the local media picked up the story. Finally the administration responded, asking them how long would the strike go on. The response—as long as it takes. The university gave in to all demands and fumigated the basement, put in new refrigerators (it turns out that were a bunch in the university warehouse all the time), and cleaned up the apartments. The student group also demanded that there be no repercussion on their grades.

Consider alternatives

In the chapter on work, I told the story of two women adjunct faculty lecturers who had been harassed by one of the male professors. They took their complaint first to the Chair, then to the Dean, but to no avail. Even going up the line to the president of the university did no good. But when they took their rather colorful story (of how the professor had dropped his pants when they were in his office) to the *LA Times*, bingo. The story was so embarrassing that the university had no choice but give in and to deny tenure to the tacky professor.

Public humiliation is a powerful tool against unsympathetic administrators. They don't like to look foolish. If there is a policy or problem that the school is failing to address, if all other avenues of appeal have been exhausted, then consider taking the story to the local papers. But be sure to have well-documented evidence as well as testimony from several people so that the paper doesn't dismiss the story as one cranky student's issue.

DEALING WITH PROBLEM PROFESSORS

Most professors do the best they can to provide what most students want—an education. But they are human beings like everyone else and some of them can make mistakes or be abusive. If the professor says or does something inappropriate in class, students are usually afraid to say anything for fear of reprisals. I've heard lots of stories over the years but it is unfortunately rare for students to have the courage to stand up. In most cases, however, the student's fear of reprisals is unfounded.

Speak up

Sometimes all it takes is saying something to the professor. Lillian, a pleasant and reasonable professor, once made a remark about Muslim head scarves that unintentionally offended one of the Muslim students. The student came to me because she was afraid to confront the professor directly. I assured her that the professor didn't mean to be offensive. When I told Lillian, she took it very well and realized that she had to be more careful of what she said. This is the best case scenario and sometimes it actually works!

But problems don't always resolve themselves so well. At a school I taught at many years ago, one male professor was notorious for overtly staring at the women's students' breasts in class. It was so obvious that even the male students felt uncomfortable and told me so. Understandably, none of the women wanted to go to this professor's office hours. The professor had been reprimanded several times by the chair of the department but to no avail. He had tenure so he didn't care.

What might have been effective (if the students could have

been convinced that there would be no reprisals): going to the president of the school *en masse* and demanding that this professor be told to stop it in no uncertain terms or they would go to the local paper and/or sue. Even if it was a bluff, the president might not want to take a chance. Unfortunately, to be quite honest, the response of many universities to this kind of inappropriate behavior is to desperately try to sweep it all under the rug. There is no guarantee that the president would have responded appropriately. However if he did, it might have had some effect. The professor thought he could get away with his little number because he was tenured, but even he has to bow to pressure from the president of the college.

BULLYING AND HARASSMENT

In the chapter on work, I told the story of Donna, a female student who was offended by a remark made by one of her professors. She told him so in an email and sent a copy to the Chair. This protected her against the possibility of reprisals from the professor. If he were to try to give her a lesser grade, she has documentation about protesting the harassment. But since the offender knew that the Chair knew about the email, she had little to worry about.

Another professor at a school I once taught at had a long history of coming on to his students but he was apparently careful to not step over a line and be totally overt in suggesting anything clearly sexual, let alone a *quid pro quo*. Roberta, a student of mine and an excellent one, complained to me about him. He kept calling her and sending her emails. She finally felt so uncomfortable that she stopped coming to class but was afraid to report him in spite of my assurances that he couldn't get away with changing her grades. If I had heard the story of Donna, I would have suggested to Roberta that she send an email to the Chair as Donna had done. This professor knew he was under suspicion (there had been many previous complaints) and would have been smart enough to leave her alone really fast. Since he even left messages on her answering machine, she could have saved them, as well as his emails, as evidence against him. In Roberta's case, she had enough evidence to actually file a complaint with the university. Too bad she didn't because it just might have been the nail in this predatory creep's coffin to finally get him fired, as he deserved.

Consider alternative explanations

On the other hand, sometimes a behavior that the student interprets as bullying is simply a case of misunderstanding and miscommunication. Students can be very subjective about their teachers. If they don't like the teacher's personality or are not getting a good grade in the class, they may imagine that they are being mistreated when they are not. They sometimes react irrationally and emotionally.

Ann once had a student who complained to her about her teaching but was not very clear about what the problem was. Ann patiently tried to understand and react appropriately to the student's issues. But Wanda, a Nigerian woman in her thirties, continued her complaints across several different times. Each time she came up and stood very close to Ann; each time her tirade became more shrill and loud. She complained that Ann "disrespected" her and as evidence, she noted that Ann flinched and backed away from her. But because of the location of the desk (in a corner), Ann felt trapped and literally backed into a corner. Flinching was an automatic reaction to this feeling of being psychologically trapped, not a reaction to the particular student. Wanda, because she was from a culture where "personal space" norms allowed her to stand closer to someone else than Americans would find comfortable, had no clue she was violating an American norm.[31]

If you feel a teacher is not respecting you, be sure *you* are not the problem before you begin complaining. You have to be willing to listen to the teacher's side too. Wanda wasn't really willing; she felt too sorry for herself (her grade was not what she wanted it to be) to listen. Dennis, another student who wouldn't listen, didn't like the professor's politics, or at least what he imagined the politics to be. He even went ranting to the Chair of the department about the alleged bias of the professor. Though the professor was outspoken about social issues, he was not known for expressing a *partisan* point of view. No one else in the class complained that the professor was biased, even in the standard anonymous evaluations of the professor at the end of the course. Dennis, it turned out, was taking an off-campus class for anger management. Apparently it didn't help much. Being self-centered and self-absorbed and wanting your own way, regardless of other considerations and other points of view, is not appropriate nor is it likely to get you what you want. Be honest with yourself. It'll get you further in the long run.

Prepare your case

Use the harassment guidelines suggested in the chapter on work here too: document individual incidents, including description of what occurred and when, what was said to the harasser and what his response was. If the harasser has sent you an email, so much the better. Get written statements from witnesses or other victims, if any. Describe the detrimental psychological effects the harassment has on you. In Roberta's case, she felt so uncomfortable that she was no longer willing to come to class. That could have affected her grade. Because she had told me about how uncomfortable this harassment made her feel, she had additional proof that the harassment had a negative effect on her. Don't be afraid to talk to a trusted professor. It'll strengthen your case.

Seek allies

Though speaking up and letting the Chair know what has happened may stop harassment in some individual cases, stopping harassment in the long run is much more difficult. Many professors who are sexual harassers are still teaching, unfortunately, so unless they do something really overt and outrageous, they will not be fired. One suggestion is group action—organizing some of the students who have been targets of this unwanted attention. Complain as a group to the Chair, then complain to the Dean and to the President, demanding that something be done about the professor. Threaten to go to the local papers with your story. Remember that administrations fear public humiliation. Without that pressure, they might just sweep things under that proverbial rug again.

CHALLENGING A GRADE

Question the grade

Before you get confrontational, make sure that the grade is not just simply an error or misunderstanding. When a teacher is dealing with lots of students, unintentional mistakes do occur. Over the years I have been teaching, I have changed student grades several times because a simple typo occurred when the grades were recorded. If you have a grade issue, ask the professor in a polite way whether the grade is correct before you fly off the handle.

Sometimes students start getting anxious before the grades are even final because they don't understand the process. At my university, many professors post the grades for each exam or written work on an Internet system called Blackboard. At least once a year, some student goes into a panic because he or she gets confused and thinks that Blackboard has computed a percentage that puts the points they have earned into a lower grade category than they were expecting. One year I received the following email from such a student. Connie wrote: "I am sorry to bother you; however, I have a question on my grade on my paper. It said that I received a 75% on my paper on Blackboard . . . I am sorry but I do not understand how I received such a low grade." She assumed incorrectly that Blackboard automatically calculated her grade based on the percentage of the total score. In her panic, she forgot that I had said at the beginning of the course that I graded on a curve (took the overall performance of the class into account in assigning the letter grades). She was, in fact, earning a B, not a D, as she imagined. Ask the professor first before you assume the worst.

If, however, after you have made sure that there is no mistake, you still feel that the professor has given you an inappropriate grade, first make sure you have a good case. Don't complain just because you simply *want* a better grade. Bring in your exams or your paper. Ask the professor to explain how she or he arrived at the grade. Be prepared to go over specific parts of the exam or paper. If the professor sees that you actually understand the material better than what your written answers show, he or she may be willing to adjust or negotiate the grade a bit. When students have come to my office and pointed out specific answers, for example, I have sometimes been willing to give them more credit after they have explained their answers more clearly. If you are reasonable, make a good case, and you are persistent, it can sometimes pay off. The chances of a teacher trying to punish you for questioning are small. If they do try, you have even more evidence to use against them. Contrary to some student opinion, professors can't get away with giving you any old grade they want.

Prepare your case and put it in writing

If talking to the professor doesn't help and you are certain that the teacher is being unfair, marshal your argument. Construct a logical argument with any evidence that supports your case, e.g., your grades on previous exams or papers in the class, other students with similar paper or exam grades getting a better course grade, other students complaining about unfair grades, and so on. If you have a specific reason why you think the professor is treating you this way, write out an explanation. A word to the wise: comments such as "He doesn't like me," or "The professor is biased against men" are very weak. You'll have to do better than that.

Then find out what the procedures are at your school for contesting a grade. You can start with the Chair of the department that offers the course in question. If that doesn't get you anywhere, every college has grievance procedures for challenging grades. In my department, there is a Fairness Committee that meets to hear student complaints. Ask around—the Department Office, the Dean's Office—till you find the office that can officially help you with your complaint. Find out how far up the line any decisions can be challenged. Then present the case that you have carefully written out with as much detail as you can muster.

Conclusion

If you or your child has an issue with the school, don't just let it slide. Your or your child's well-being in school is too important to give up on. Prepare your case carefully with as many specifics as you can. In educational bureaucracies, seeking allies is possibly even more important than in ordinary workplaces. Bureaucrats respond to group pressure more than bosses do. Don't be afraid to complain and protest. Don't be afraid to use the threat of public humiliation. It's your education and they are your servants, not your bosses. They work for you, not the other way around. Don't let yourself or your child become "another brick in the wall." Dislodge the metaphorical brick and throw it though the symbolic window of apathy. But be prepared to take responsibility for the proverbial shattered glass of consequences.

RESOURCES

BOOKS

Ritalin

Peter Breggin, M.D. *Talking Back to Ritalin: What Doctors Don't Tell You about Stimulants for Children.* Monroe, ME: Common Courage Press, 1998.

Peter Breggin, M.D. *The Ritalin Fact Book: What Your Doctor Won't Tell You.* Cambridge, MA: Da Capo, 2002.

Richard DeGrandpre, Ph.D. *Ritalin Nation: Rapid-Fire Culture and the Transformation of Human Consciousness.* New York: W.W. Norton, 2000.

Lawrence Diller, M.D. *Running on Ritalin: A Physician Reflects On Children, Society And Performance In A Pill.* New York: Bantam Books, 1998.

Chris Mercogliano. *Teaching the Restless: One School's Remarkable No-Ritalin Approach to Helping Children Learn and Succeed.* Boston: Beacon Press, 2003.

Sydney Walker III, M.D. *The Hyperactivity Hoax: How to Stop Drugging Your Child and Find Real Medical Help.* New York: St. Martin, 1999.

Sharma Olfman. (Ed.) *No Child Left Different.* Westport, Conn: Praeger 2006.

Educational Alternatives

Cheryl Corder. *Home Schools: An Alternative.* Tempe AZ: Blue Bird Publishing, 1990. This book lists many resources for further information about educational alternatives.

Harassment and Bullying in School

Allan L. Beane, Ph.D. *Protect Your Child from Bullying: Expert Advice to Help You Recognize, Prevent, and Stop Bullying Before Your Child Gets Hurt.* San Francisco: Jossey-Bass, 2008.

Allan L. Beane, Ph.D. *The Bully-Free Classroom® Over 100 Tips and Strategies for Teachers K-8.* A CD-ROM and workbooks for children in the classroom are also available. Minneapolis, MN: Free Spirit Press, 1999.

Barbara Coloroso. *The Bully, the Bullied, and the Bystander: From Preschool to High School—How Parents and Teachers Can Help Break the Cycle of Violence.* New York: HarperResource, 2003

SuEllen Fried and Paula Fried, Ph.D. *Bullies, Targets & Witnesses: Helping Children Break the Pain Chain.* New York: M. Evans and Company, 2003.

James Garbarino, Ph.D. and Ellen deLara, Ph.D. *And Words Can Hurt Forever: How to Protect Adolescents from Bullying, Harassment and Emotional Violence.* New York: The Free Press, 2002.

Adam Hibbert. *Why Do People Bully?* Chicago: Raintree, 2005. Aimed at a grade school level, this book helps kids understand bullies as well as suggesting how to deal with bullying.

Debbie Stanley. *Everything You Need to Know about Student-on-Student Sexual Harassment.* New York: Rosen Publishing Group, 2000.

Trevor Romain. *Bullies are a Pain in the Brain.* Minneapolis: Free Spirit Publishing, 1999. This award-winning book is aimed at ages 8–13. An accompanying DVD activity kit for educators is also available.

Kathleen Winkler. *Bullying: How to Deal With Taunting, Teasing and Tormenting.* Berkeley Heights, NJ: Enslow Publishers, 2005. This book is aimed at teenagers.

Other

Russell L. Ackoff and Sheldon Rovin. *Beating the System: Using Creativity to Outsmart Bureaucracies.* San Francisco: Berrett-Koehler Publishers, 2005.

Traci Truly, Attorney at Law. *Teen Rights (and Responsibilities): A Legal Guide for Teens and the Adults in Their Lives.* Napierville, IL: Sphinx Publishers, 2005.

WEB SITES

Student Rights:

ACLU
www.aclu.org/studentsrights/index.html

Student Press Law Center
www.splc.org
The SPLC, an advocate for student free press rights, provides information, advice, and legal assistance at no charge to students and the educators who work with them.

Free Child
www.freechild.org/student_rights.htm
This web site provides links to many resources for student rights, including the issues of free press, school uniforms, and Internet censorship.

Underground Action Alliance
undergroundactionalliance.org/resources.php?r_section=9

Committee Opposed to Militarism and the Draft
www.comdsd.org/pdf/hs_1.pdf
Provides a PDF titled "High School Students' Rights: What Every Student Should Know."

Ritalin and Other Drugs Given to Children:

Peter Breggin
www.breggin.com
Dr. Peter Breggin's web site, with articles about the misuse of Ritalin, as well as other psychiatric drugs.

Doc Diller
http://docdiller.com/
The web site of Lawrence Diller who, in addition to *Running on Ritalin,* has written several other books of interest to parents.

Drug Free
www.drugfree.org/Portal/drug_guide/Ritalin
Neutral description of Ritalin and its side effects.

Bullying and Harassment in Schools (Children and Teens):

Teen Advice at About.com
teenadvice.about.com/od/sexualharassment/Dealing_with_Sexual_Harassment_at_School.htm
Links to many resources for dealing with sexual harassment at school.

Stop Bullying Me
www.stopbullyingme.ab.ca

Bullies.org
www.bullying.org

No Bullying.org
www.nobully.com
Resources for administrators, teachers, parents and students

iSafe
www.isafe.org
A nonprofit organization dedicated to Internet safety for youth.

National Youth Violence Prevention Resource Center
www.safeyouth.org
A Federal resource for communities working to prevent violence committed by and against young people. Bullying is one of many topics.

Alternative Schooling and Educational Resources

Free Spirit Publishing
www.freespirit.com
The catalog is full of self-help books for grade school kids and teens, with books that tackle issues running the gamut of problems that children face today, including bullying, teen depression, and learning to be assertive and independent. Its books give advice on many topics, including character building, self-esteem, and dealing with grief, with "materials that are practical, positive, pro-kid, and solution focused." A wonderful resource.

Autonomy in the Family
www.autonomyinthefamily.com
Offers resources for raising children to be independent and critical thinkers.

Homeschool World
www.home-school.com
The official web site of *Practical Homeschooling* magazine.

Home School Central
homeschoolcentral.com
Many resources for the new or continuing homeschooler.

Homefires
www.homefires.com
The web site for the online homeschooling journal *Homefires*.

Homeschool Home Educators Resource Directory
www.homeeddirectory.com/

UPDATES

For updates on books, web sites, web site URLs and links (they sometimes change), articles and other relevant information, check the web site for my book: www.standuptoauthorities.com

CHAPTER
8

Your Call Is Not Important to Us: Getting What You Deserve From Consumer Services

Ron Burley bought an expensive monitor for his computer. When it died after only three weeks, the Customer Service rep told him to box it up and ship it back. Two weeks went by and no word. When he called the company's repair center, he was first told the monitor had been misplaced. Then he was told it had internal damage and he would have to pay for the repairs. But they messed with the wrong guy. Burley surfed the Internet till he found the fax number for the vice-president of sales for the company. Then he faxed a polite letter (twelve times!) with the details of what had transpired. He wrote that he felt a responsibility to make sure no other customers would have to go through what he had. He said he would stand outside his local computer store and pass put flyers telling people about the irresponsible tech support for this company. Though he never heard directly from the company, the next day a new 20-inch monitor arrived on his door step.[1]

W<small>E'VE ALL HAD</small> bad experiences with products or services—the headphones that don't work right, the customer support rep who says nothing can be done about the problem, the contractor who cheats you, the tech support person who mindlessly repeats the same script over and over again even though it doesn't help. What most people do about this problem is—nothing, nothing at all.² They don't complain to the company, they don't write letters, they just accept their bad luck and discard the product or hang up on the support call. Some do complain to the company's customer service but if they get no satisfaction there, they just give up. This reaction is a bit like what psychologists call "learned helplessness"—a preconceived idea that no matter what you do, nothing will make a difference."³ It's a self-fulfilling prophecy. If you give up and think nothing will work, it won't—because you'll do nothing. But there are ways to significantly improve your chances for compensation if you bought a defective product, or have been cheated, or are otherwise unhappy with a product or service that doesn't live up to its claims.

It may not be easy. According to Ron Burley, author of *Unscrewed: The Consumer's Guide to Getting What You Paid For*, customer complaints are up 30% since 1990 but research indicates that less than 1% get resolved to the customer's satisfaction.⁴ Don't be discouraged by this. One reason so few complaints get resolved happily for the customers—they're using techniques that don't work. Quite frankly, if you are dealing with a particularly recalcitrant company or you're not sure of your ability to pull off these ideas, you may want more information than will fit into this book. That's why I have the list of recommended books below. They're readily available in libraries on or online. But in the meantime, many of you will find that these tips below will do the trick.

There are two categories of techniques that can be effective, depending on the circumstances—the conventional and unconventional. I'll tell you about both and let you decide. You can start off with the more conventional ideas suggested by others (see below), and if they don't work, you can always try the more unconventional ones advocated by John Bear and Ron Burley. Burley, who is cynical about customer service (and is largely right in being so) makes a point that's essential to keep in mind—the most effective techniques are those that affect the company's bottom line. If you make it expensive for them to ignore you, you significantly improve your chances. Don't be naïve, he urges, and assume that any company, particularly the bigger ones, really cares about individual customers. Not in this day and age of rising costs, decreasing budgets, and—let us not forget—corporate greed. Your call is in fact *not* important to them!

YOUR RIGHT TO PROTEST

You don't have to succumb to a sense of futility and just give up. If you are a shy or nonconfrontational person and are reluctant to complain, don't run away. If you bought defective goods or you didn't get the service you paid for, you've been cheated. Why should you allow yourself to be cheated? Why should you be a victim?

Sure, you might decide it isn't worth it. I bought a box of pens at a large office supply store recently while visiting a friend. I thought the price was a bit steep so I checked that online price for this company when I got home. I had been mischarged by about $4. But I couldn't find the receipt (even I screw up sometimes) and the store was not in my neighborhood. I let it go—no proof and too far away to go back and complain for a mere $4. But if I had found the receipt, I would have been on the phone complaining, ready to fax a copy of the receipt and demanding a refund by mail just as a matter of principle. Maybe for $4, you'd decide it isn't worth it to complain but what if it were $40 or $400? The big companies count on people not bothering to complain. Don't play their game.

> **Key Concepts**
> - Recognize your right to protest
> - Gather your evidence
> - Put it in writing
> - Be assertive but calm
> - Tell them how your complaint will cost them money
> - Go up the chain of authority if necessary

Sometimes all it takes is a little protest. Alicia took her husband's overdue books back to the library. She was annoyed because he was supposed to be receiving an email alert from the library and it never came. This was in fact his second attempt to get the alert to work correctly. Even though she knew it was his responsibility to know when the books were due, the nonfunctioning email overdue notice irritated her. When Alicia got to the library, she found a librarian (not a clerk) and complained (politely). The librarian not only sent a notice to library administration but canceled the $8 fine that had accumulated. OK, so librarians are probably nicer and more reasonable than many managers. But you don't know till you try, so don't be shy about speaking up.

Then again, maybe you're the opposite kind of person. You're really steamed at getting cheated. You don't want to just protest, you want revenge. You want a pound of flesh. Forget that too, warns Burley. Yelling and screaming are also counterproductive. This won't get you what you want either. In fact, this kind of behavior will just stiffen resistance. Keep in mind what your goal is—to be compensated for the defective product or service. As Burley says, "Revenge has no value." However, he suggests, if the company *thinks* that's your motive, it might work to your advantage . . . But, just to give you another point of view, Bear's book *Send This Jerk the Bedbug Letter* has a whole chapter on rather creative and amusing ways of getting even.

BE PREPARED: GATHER YOUR EVIDENCE

First make sure you save all receipts, invoices and warranties for any goods or services you buy, whether in a store or online. Put them in a safe, designated place. If you make arrangements over the phone for services with the phone company, for example, *always* write down the confirmation number and the name and number of the agent or representative to whom you spoke.

GATHER OTHER INFORMATION

For certain kinds of consumer problems, there may be pertinent information or helpful tips on the Internet. Well-explored complaint areas include car repair and travel. I've provided some specific examples below but you might want to check on your own. You can also check out some of the books listed below from your local library, depending on how serious your problem is. They'll give you useful additional ideas.

When you are ready to make your complaint, gather all the pertinent information so that it is accessible when you make your call or write your letter. If you get easily flustered, outline your case in simple, succinct terms. Decide what will provide an adequate solution and write it down. Think of it as a "script" to follow. Have a pen and notebook or blank paper ready to take notes.

MAKE A PHONE CALL

Placing a phone call to Customer Service is often the first step. Here is a synthesis of Burley's unconventional (but highly effective) tips, my ideas, and some standard suggestions from other books.

What to do and say

- Make sure your "script" and evidence are ready. Psych yourself up to be assertive but calm. Make sure there are no distractions (e.g., TV, kids).
- First get the name of the person you are speaking to and his or her agent or representative number. Though Burley suggests getting the physical location and internal call back number, Shannon Wirchniansky, a customer rep trainer, says that most centers are told not to give out such information.[5] Instead be nice and try to establish rapport. Wirchniansky points out that reps get a lot of abuse from customers, even though the reps may not be the one who created the problem. She advises using a "partnership" approach. "My suggestion," she says, "would be to start the conversation focused on the idea that you are looking for resolution and the person that you reach on the other line is someone who can help you get the answers you need." Beka Wildman, another consumer rep trainer, suggests that a limited amount of small talk can facilitate the conversation.[6] But don't go overboard. Keep focused on your goal, both warn.
- Set the right tone. Being apologetic or indignant are both bad tactics, says Burley. You may note that his advice squares with what I've said elsewhere in this book. Of course it does. It's what any expert would recommend. Being angry puts people on the defensive and doesn't

make them want to give you what you want. No matter how angry you are at the company or perhaps another rep you've spoken to, being rude will not help you. Being apologetic isn't much better. Why should you be apologetic—the company is at fault, not you. Being apologetic sets you up for failure, for having the door slammed in your face. As I said in Chapter Two, being overly polite when it is not appropriate simply makes you look weak. Being appropriately polite and calm but assertive will go a lot further. And if the rep is nice to you, thank him or her. Wildman maintains that if you treat the rep well, he or she will treat *you* well.

- Take control of the conversation. The customer rep, says Burley, expects you to obey the script. They are thrown off by someone who is quietly unrelenting, he continues. Though Burley insists that you should never let them put you on hold, other experts disagree. Wildman says that they don't *have* to put you on hold. Instead you can say to the rep: "No, thank you, I'd rather have you on the line with me." Or occasionally, a rep may suggest a callback. Don't let them call you back. It may never happen. Ask for a supervisor instead.

    However, some call centers are set up so that the rep must follow the script and are not trained beyond it. In that case, they will have to seek clarification on how to handle the situation so putting you on hold is what they will have to do to give you the answers you want. "Often, if given the chance to research appropriately," says Wirchniansky, "an agent will come back with good information on how to resolve the issue. If pressured to stay on the line, they cannot do the research needed and may be less willing to find a satisfactory resolution for you because you are preventing them from doing their job." You'll have to decide what the best choice is for your situation.

- If the person you are dealing with refuses to help you or to pass you on to a supervisor, says Wildman, just hang up and call back. When you do call back, get the name of the person you are speaking to. Then you might say, suggests Wildman, "Tanya, I've called before and haven't received much help. I'm hoping you can change that." If Tanya doesn't have the authority to help you, don't get mad. Just say you understand and ask to passed up the

chain of command. When you do talk to a supervisor, make sure to mention the name and number of the unhelpful rep to her. But keep in mind that the policies are not set by the agents. Don't blame them for something that is not their fault.
- If a customer really feels he or she has been wronged by the agent on the line, then, agrees Wirchniansky, either pushing for the escalation, or calling back and going straight to a supervisor is the right thing to do. If you recognize that the agent is trying to help, but the company policy is what has made you mad, suggests Wirchniansky, "explain to the agent that it's not related to how he or she handled the call, but you would like to speak with someone in management about the company policy. This will open the door for the escalation much easier. (It always benefits the customer to communicate that they understand the agent is trying to help them, within the limitations of the company policy, and their assistance is appreciated. They are just doing the job they were trained to do, and the grudge is really with the company, not them)," she continues. "The agent is then able to communicate to a supervisor that they discussed the situation and company policy, but the customer would like to express their feelings. It sets a different tone. It takes the personal aspect of the conversation out. This approach also has the potential to open more doors as well. Hearing that the agent did their best but the policy stinks in your situation, might inspire the agent to do more research, or try to pull strings. At this point, you're seen as a partner in the process. (They may not agree with their company policy as well, and because you were so professional, they may go the extra mile. This really does depend on the situation or the agent, but if anything, it might get late charges removed, get better deliver times, or a price break, etc.)"
- If you can't understand what the rep is saying because she is mumbling or has a thick accent, ask to be transferred. Don't fail to get the info you want because you are worried about hurting someone's feelings. Their job is to communicate and if they can't do that, you have the right to speak to someone who can. Just be polite about it. Ranting about their accent or their nationality will *not* help

you get what you want and is rude, uncivilized behavior. Remember that the rep is just trying to earn an honest living. "As the customer, this is an important perspective to maintain," says Wirchniansky. "Most really do want to help you, and they are human."
- Take notes. Note the time and date of each phone call. Make sure you get the rep's name, and, if you talk to a supervisor, her name too. Write down what she says and make a note of the time and date.
- Tell your story. State your problem clearly, succinctly, and calmly and in a logical step-by-step sequence. Use the script you have prepared if necessary. "Very important here to focus on the facts and events, rather than the he said/she said details," says Wirchniansky. "The more that you show all you want is a resolution and to get out of their hair, the easier it is for them to focus on resolution."
- State the solution you want. Clearly say exactly what you want the company to do to solve your issue.
- Ask for satisfaction. Say no more at this point, asserts Burley. "The one who speaks first, loses," he writes, only partly tongue-in-cheek. If you hear the dreaded words, "It's against our policy" or I can't help you," then proceed to the next step.
- Don't waste your time with the rep, at this point. If he can't give you the information you want or solve the problem, ask for a supervisor. Reps are generally following a predetermined script. They have little information outside of the script and even less authority to make decisions not in the script. Supervisors have much more discretionary power.
- Restate your case calmly to the supervisor. Don't forget to write down her name and what she says. If she says no, then time to move up to the next level.

Here's a story from "7 Things You Should Always Say to Customer Service" by Burley.[7] It illustrates how getting the kind of information suggested above can help you if something goes wrong. When he called to confirm a family vacation flight he had booked, he was told that they couldn't find his reservation. But when the rep asked him who he had spoken to, it was easy. Thanks to his standard practice of asking for the rep's name and chatting her up, he was not only able to recall her name correctly, he was able to mention her two kids by name. Faced with indisputable proof that—despite what their records said—he'd had an extended conversation with their reservations agent, the company was forced to rebook his flights. Get names, take notes—crucially important advice.

What not to say

In his article "7 Things You Should Never Say to Customer Service," Burley gives advice about words you shouldn't use with customer service.[8] These are "lawyer" (if you threaten at this point, you have closed the door to further negotiation, except with the expensive suits); "job" (don't threaten to get someone fired; you need the agent as your ally, not your enemy) "bankrupt" (same deal, don't threaten); any of form of obscenity (they'll hang up on you and put a note in your file so no one will ever take you seriously); "never" (if you aren't going to buy their products, why should they do anything for you?); "media" (only the higher-uppers will care about this, not customer service); and "kill" (this should need no explanation, please!) I've mentioned his companion article, "7 Things You Should Always Say to Customer Service" above. Much of the advice is already incorporated in this chapter but you can find both articles and read them for yourself at the URL in the Resources section below.

PUT IT IN WRITING

If the phone call doesn't work, you have several choices. If your gripe is with a local company, you can consider showing up in person to speak to the manager or owner. If it's not local, then you may need to put it in writing. Remember that the written word has more power than merely oral complaints on the phone. Here's what the conventional experts say about writing effective complaint letters. Some of this may seem obvious but years of teaching have taught me never to assume that even smart people always know the right thing to do in a given situation.

Before you write the letter, you have to know to whom the letter should be addressed. Write to a specific person, not a department or title. "To whom it may concern" doesn't cut it. That's a straight ticket to the circular file, say the experts. You need to address it to someone who can solve your problem, someone who has the authority to make decisions. Clerks and even managers don't generally have the discretion, leeway, or power to meet your demands. The person in a position to help you is usually the owner, president, chair, or CEO of the company.

You can look up the CEO's name on the company web site or call the company. Look for the "About" or "Contact" button on the web site. If you have trouble locating the name, your local library will have standard reference books such as *Standard and Poor's Register of Corporations, Directors and Executives* or *Dun and Bradstreet Directory*. If the manufacturer is not in either of those, try the *Thomas Register of American Manufacturers*. If these don't work or you get confused, ask the librarian to help you. They are trained to know how to find information.

- Use standard business letter format. No colored papers, no fancy fonts. The letter should be typed on white paper using good old-fashioned standard fonts such as Times New Roman or Ariel. Your full return address and phone number should be somewhere in the letter either as a letterhead, if you have one, or at the end of your letter. Put the addressee's full name and address at the beginning. You want it to look serious and business-like, not like a crank letter.
- Have a strong opening paragraph that gets to the main point right away. No windy preambles. Begin with a clear and succinct statement of the problem that gives a good reason for action on the part of the company. Begin the letter with a "good reason to read it," say John Bear and Mariah Bear in *Complaint Letters for Busy People*[9].
- Be calm and reasonable, polite but assertive. Tone down the rhetoric. Sure, you're mad because you didn't get satisfaction over the phone but don't threaten or swear. If the first letter doesn't work, you can adopt a stronger tone later but the first one should be civil. Just state the problem in neutral, unemotional terms.
- When stating the problem, organize your complaint in a concise, logical, coherent fashion. Make an outline first if that helps. What you want to avoid is a rambling "fruit salad" that goes off in irrelevant tangents. Line up your facts and present them in a succinct, orderly fashion. State,

for example, what damage was done, why you want a refund, what you see as a solution, and so on.
- Don't be too wordy. Write naturally but don't go on and on. Avoid being pompous, whiny or rambling.
- Know your rights. Look up the company policy on the Internet or by making a phone call to Customer Service. If they give you a runaround, ask for the Legal Department. State the relevant rights in your letter.
- Back up your complaints with documents. Attach copies of receipts, warranties, and so on.
- Ask for what you really want. State your expectations clearly. Don't be afraid to ask for more than what you expect. Maybe you'll get it.
- State ways the company could lose your business.
- Set a deadline for the company's response.
- Close politely but firmly.
- Proofread your letter. Careless typos and misspelled words make you look less serious and weaken your letter. If you're a bad proofreader (and many people are), ask a friend or relative to read it.
- Send the letter return receipt requested. Then they can't say later that they never received it.

COMPLAIN IN PERSON

If your complaint is with a local company, you may consider showing up in person to make a complaint. Don't bother with the clerks and salespeople. They can't help you. If it is a large company, ask for the sales manager or the supervisor. If it is a smaller store where the owner is likely to be present, go straight to the owner.

- *Prepare your case*
  If you have already made a complaint call, you already have your case prepared. If not, then follow the suggestions above. Otherwise, review your case and bring copies of any relevant documents. Prepare a script if you are the shy or nervous type.
- *Psych yourself up*
  Prepare yourself mentally to be calm but assertive. Go

over your script one more time, if you need to. Take a deep breath and relax.
- *Dress for your success*
Follow the suggestion from Chapter Two—choose whatever apparel is appropriate to the situation and makes you comfortable. For most stores, dressy casual will work. For banks or financial institutions, you may want to wear a suit. But please, no ratty jeans, no Goth look, no overly frilly, flowery pastels or cutesy-poo costumes. You want to be taken seriously. Wear something that will put you on the same level as the person you will be speaking to. Most managers of most stores do *not* sport all-black clothes (with some interesting exceptions . . .) nor do they wear, for example, oh so-very-cute teddy bear sweatshirts. You shouldn't either.
- *Fine tune your approach*
Decide on what approach to take. Several techniques are suggested below. Make sure you have the right props.
- *Build rapport*
When you first make contact, introduce yourself and thank them for their time. This establishes a pleasant rapport and makes you look reasonable and civil.
- *Watch your language*
Remember to speak in a calm, firm voice. No whines, no belligerent rants, no apologies. Watch your body language too. Shoulders back; don't slouch or wring your hands. Make eye contact. The more credible you sound, the more seriously you will be taken.
- *Bring backup (if necessary)*
If you are a shy, nonconfrontational or nonassertive person, don't be afraid to bring backup to keep you from feeling intimidated. A friend or relative who can stand by your side and make sure that you are not bowled over by a nasty or blustery supervisor might be a good idea. And that way, you have a witness to whatever is said or promised. If you are female, especially if you are shy, this is even more important. Sexism isn't dead and male managers may still try to intimidate you if you are female.
- *State your case*
Present the manager or supervisor with the dry facts. Don't go on and on about how mad you are, how bad you feel, how upset you are. They're not likely to care.

- *Ask for satisfaction*
  Tell the manager what you want—a refund, a new product. If he starts in about how it's "against policy" or otherwise gives you the runaround, then tell him what you intend to do if you don't get your problem solved. And what you intend to do should be something that can hurt the business (without actually threatening to do so). Owners, managers and supervisors may not care about *you* but they *do* care about their bottom line. See the suggestions below.

WHAT IF ALL THIS FAILS?

You've called the Customer Service Department of ZQ Store or written XY Corporation but to no avail. Are you down for the count? Not necessarily. Depending on how much money is involved or how badly you want a solution, you can up the ante. If you're dealing with a significant amount of money, there are a number of ingenious techniques that have suggested by the experts. Just be sure you have exhausted more civil means of gaining satisfaction first. The down side to the following ideas: they're a bit more aggressive and may occasionally backfire. They may even be seen as harassment. But experts like Burley and Bear have used them to good advantage.

What rarely helps, according to Bear, is taking the complaint to your local Better Business Bureau. He cites a number of studies that show that the BBB is ineffectual at best.[10] It often simply took the company's word for it that the problem had been resolved. Get the picture? And after all, the BBB is a creation of business owners, not consumers.[11] My take—don't waste your time with the BBB. There are far more effective techniques to obtain satisfaction.

Large techniques for small businesses

Burley has several techniques for dealing with small businesses. I'm not going to describe them all here. You may want to read his clever and engaging book for yourself. Here's two of the more intriguing ones.[12]

- *"Town Crier"* or Picketing

Burley isn't the first to suggest picketing a store (which is essentially what this technique is) but he has it honed to an art. If you've gotten the bum's rush from a local business, exercise your freedom of speech. Tell the owner or manager politely that since you were not able to get your request honored, you intend to stand outside his place of business near the door exercising your right to free speech and passing out flyers describing how you've gotten mistreated or cheated by his business. Do *not* threaten; do *not* suggest that you are trying to hurt the company or put it out of business (this could get you sued). Instead, suggests Burley, say that you feel it is your civic duty to tell people how badly the company has treated you so it will not happen to anyone else. Show the manager or owner the flyers—or at least have them with you in a manila envelope. There's a good chance you won't ever have to pass them out.

Burley recounts the story of how he bought a car one weekend and then discovered after the fact that the car dealer had been advertising a $1500 discount for any car bought that weekend. No salesperson had divulged this to him. He went back to complain and was told that he had to ask for the discount at the time. He was also told "That's our policy" by the sales manager. So he made up some flyers with the headline "Akamai Motors lies to its

---

Making Up a Picket Flyer for the "Town Crier" Tactic

Based on examples from Ron Burley's book, Unscrewed.

- State your complaint about the company, e.g.," XY company lies to its customers," in large print
- Give a succinct and truthful summary in one sentence, e.g., "They advertised the product at one price [be specific about amounts] and sold it to me at a higher price [name the price]."
- Give your name and a way to contact you. You do *not* want to use your normal private email. You can always use a disposable free email address from Yahoo or Hotmail.

customers" and a brief description of what had happened to him. Burley pointed out to the manager that if even only a few customers went elsewhere, it would cost the company far more than the amount he was asking for. The sales manager, reports Burley, looked like a "frightened rabbit." He went out and came back with the "good news" about the "misunderstanding" a few minutes later. Burley left with check in hand.

- *"Spokesperson for the competition"*
  This works well with local companies that have stiff competition, reports Burley. Compose a letter succinctly describing the case, as above. State that you don't understand why you are being treated so poorly when it would be so much easier to resolve the problem. Fax it to the head of the company, stating that you intend to send this fax to all their competitors (give specific names of competitors in town, if you can).

Beating Big Business

Burley suggests a different approach for big companies.[13] With small ones, he says, you tell them what you are going to do before you do it. With the big guys, you do something to attract their attention first, then you negotiate. Again, I won't describe all of his rather creative techniques. You should really read this creative book for yourself if you want to explore these ideas further. The first one below is probably the most useful. If you're clever, you may think of other variations for the second one. But be careful here. This could be interpreted as harassment and get you in trouble. Don't be heavy-handed, if you use these techniques.

- *"Faxing for Dollars"*
  Send a succinct but polite fax stating your case and what will resolve the problem to every available fax number within the executive offices for the company. Be sure to include your phone number and email. Then hit "redial"— again and again. The idea here is to tie up the fax lines till they respond. You will have to be clever about finding the appropriate fax numbers but a bit of time on the Internet with the right search terms will probably do the trick. For

example, you might do a search on "fax vice president of sales [name of the company]." If this doesn't work or the company web site doesn't have the number, look for press releases or other documents online that are likely to have it.
- *Online customer product reviews*
  If your problem is a product that didn't work right or other unsatisfactory transaction with a company, there may be blogs online where you can post your complaints. This is especially useful for highly competitive products such as computer equipment, software, and financial information. Burley bought a computer printer that, unbeknownst to him, did not have a printer driver that was compatible with the latest version of Windows. After getting the runaround from the store where he bought it and the manufacturer, he placed a review on the product review page of the manufacturer. Then he went to get himself a sandwich. A phone call came in from the senior supervisor of the sales department before he could even finish the sandwich. Burley reports that certain kinds of online reviews are closely monitored by the sales departments of such products. Wildman suggests forwarding a copy of the review to the company itself. The review should contain all the relevant info I discussed above—names, numbers, dates, and so on—and should, of course, be polite, short, and not a rant.

Other creative ideas

If you're creative and clever and don't mind being just a tad aggressive, there are some other ideas that have been effective, Maybe you'll get inspired by these examples and come up with some variations of your own. Just remember—no nasty stuff, no threats, nothing harmful.

John Bear offers some out-of-the box solutions in *Send This Jerk the Bedbug Letter*. Coming up with something creative or attention-getting (as long as it doesn't have the appearance of threat) may do the trick, unless of course, the company is extremely stodgy or is a government office. Government agencies require a different approach (see Chapter Nine), If this approach appeals to you, you should read Bear's book. The true stories he relates are hilarious as well as clever. Let me just give you a flavor of it.

Send your letter via an unusual, attention-getting method, suggests Bear.[14] The 144 foot long letter on a series of taped-up paper tablecloths might not work in these post–Unibomber, hyper-security days but there's always the singing "gorillagram." Or you could adapt the following story. Bear reports a suggestion made by the head of a large airline. If you have a complaint against an airline, succinctly hand-write your complaint on the rival airline's stationery while in flight. It'll work, promises the airline executive.

Unusual packaging or unusual contents may backfire so consider carefully before you go down this road. However, if you use the "gorillagram" method, for example, and notify the media, you might just get the right kind of attention. See the Introduction to this section of the book for how to write a press release.

Here's another clever idea cited in Russell Ackoff and Sheldon Rovin's book, *Beating the System*[15]. A young physician just starting his business set his office phone to ring at his home as well. The office phone number was only one digit off from a radio station request call-in number. He began getting the station's request calls in the middle of the night. Because changing his number at this early point in his career could be costly, the physician politely asked the station manager to change the call-in number instead. The manager refused. The physician found the name and home phone number of the station owner. Then when someone called in with request for the radio station, he or his wife would give them the owner's phone number. "In a very short time," note Ackoff and Rovin, "the calls ceased."

WHAT IF EVEN THIS FAILS? SEEK ALTERNATIVES

Many of the techniques above are likely to work, especially for local businesses. But what if they don't? You could just give up. But if this business has treated you so badly, why should you let them get away with it? You can still stand up to them, even if only for the principle of it. Here are some options.

- *Sue the local company in Small Claims Court.*
  The maximum amount you can collect varies from state to

state. In California, it's $7500, an amount that covers many consumer complaints. Companies don't like this because they are required to send an officer from the company. More information about this option is given in Chapter Five.

- *Contact your local TV, radio or newspaper action line*
In the San Francisco Bay Area where I live, there's the TV action line "Seven on Your Side." Many cities have similar "on your side" action lines. Do an Internet search on "TV action line" plus your location if you're not familiar with the one in your area. Many newspapers also have complaint columns. If your complaint fits in with the column's theme, by all means, write. Seeing the company's name on TV or in the local paper in a bad light may be enough to get the problem solved. The *San Francisco Chronicle*, for example, carries two different complaint columns—one for travel issues and one for public services. See what your paper offers.

- *Lodge a formal compliant with an appropriate state or federal government agency*
This may not help your resolve your personal complaint but at least there's a chance that someone official will look into the more serious cases of fraud and misrepresentation. Look up your state's consumer protection division on the Internet or ask a librarian to help you. Some of the web sites cited in the Resources section also have these listings.

  If you're not sure what agency you need to contact with your complaint, you can contact the Federal Citizen Information Center at 1-888-8 PUEBLO (1-888-878-3256) or use the web sites in the Resources section at the end of this chapter. It'll give you current phone numbers for many consumer organizations.

- *Get a lawyer*
If you have money to burn or the complaint involves a major and expensive problem, you might consider this. But suing is not only the most expensive way to attempt a solution, it isn't even the technique most likely to get what you want. Except in major cases such as a class action suit, the main value of a lawyer is the *threat* of a law suit. Companies don't know whether you're bluffing. But this is a really last resort and probably even marginally helpful

only if you are dealing with small companies. The big companies have more money and better lawyers than you do. To a big corporation, the threat of a law suit is a mere gnat to be effortlessly swatted away.

Specific Applications for Service-Related Complaints

In this section, I explore some common service-related issues and apply this chapter's techniques to them. There's no way I can cover every kind of complaint category but these examples may give you some good ideas about how to handle your situation. For additional examples, a book that gives succinct and useful suggestions for many complaint areas is the Readers Digest book, *Fight Back and Win: What to Do When You Feel Cheated or Wronged*. At 467 pages, it's truly encyclopedic, covering everything from landlords and tenants, travel and car concerns, and insurance tangles, to workplace worries, estate planning, protecting your privacy, crime and punishment, and more. It includes sample letters as well as addresses of places to take your complaint to, if necessary. This is the kind of book your local library is likely to have so look for it there. For complaints that involve legal issues, such as legal rights, how to sue, and using small claims courts, as well as legal forms for many different problems, see the Nolo Press web site listed below. Nolo Press, as I say in Chapter Five, is a treasure trove of legal self-help books, articles and forms.

The following section on tech support is written by long-time IT consultant Art Smith, who runs a web services business (www.arttecho.net).

TECH SUPPORT: NAVIGATING THE MAZE

Tech support can be a nightmare; almost everyone has a horror story about futile attempts to get a vendor to fix a customer's problem. I've collected my own experiences over the years and combined that with some research to come up with some of the top customer complaints about tech support:

1. Unable to find out how to get support; support phone numbers are often hard to locate in a vendor's Web site.
2. Difficulty getting an individual to talk or write to.
3. Support reps following a rigid script, forcing the customer to "jump thru hoops" before the issue gets assigned to someone who can actually fix it.
4. Outsourced call centers—hard to understand accents, deceit over names ("Hello, my name is William..." in a thick Indian accent).
5. Excessive wait times while listening to sappy music on hold.
6. Boilerplate responses to E-mail support requests. It's common for some companies to look for keywords in the customers request without actually reading the content of the message, and then sending back pre-packaged instructions on how to use the feature that's not working.

THE SUPPORT LANDSCAPE

The availability and quality of tech support offered by software and hardware companies varies from nothing at all to excellent. The best example of nothing at all is Microsoft™ (www.microsoft.com); they only offer self-help or paid support services. On the other end of the spectrum is GoDaddy (www.godaddy.com); while they're not perfect for technical people, they are totally accessible, putting their phone number on the top of their Web page.

Let's start with #1, finding out how to get support. Most large companies will have a phone number buried somewhere in their Web site. A good example is my ISP, a large telecommunications company. Starting at their home page, I can click on a "DSL Support" link. That takes me to a page listing several categories and an "Ask Us" E-mail support link, but no phone number. Clicking on a "DSL Support" link on this page takes me to a page with yet more categories and a link that says "Call Us" that finally takes me to a page with phone numbers. Each page I had to "drill-down" through was cluttered with numerous options, requiring careful reading and thinking. The process can be mind-numbing and is designed to discourage phone calls. It's a good idea to locate this number and write it down before you have a problem. If your problem happens to be a nonworking Internet connection, you'll have to call the company's main number to get the support number.

SELF-HELP AND THE FAQ

From the ISP's (and other companies') viewpoint, there's a good reason for trying to deter you from calling. Over 90% of support calls turn out to be something customers could theoretically have figured out for themselves. That assumes the customer is willing to learn what things such as "FTP passive mode" mean. If you're a bit adventuresome and have the time, you should give it a try. Look for FAQs (Frequently Asked Questions) in the support section of the company's Web site. The FAQ has become the industry standard format for conveying information about common problems customers encounter. For example, if you have software that's misbehaving and giving you error messages, write down the text of the error message and see if it's covered in the FAQ. There's a better than even chance it'll be there, along with the fix. If the fix is easy for you to understand, simple to carry out, and solves the problem, then you're done.

If it's not covered in the vendor's support FAQs, don't despair. Your answer might be found on the Internet. Try searching for the error message or symptoms on your favorite search engine, such as Google, Yahoo, etc. If you get some hits, take a look and see if there's anything that wasn't covered by the vendor's support site. If you do find something that seems useful, it's important to not stop at the first hit. Examine several sites and look for a consensus of opinion. The Internet is a wild and wooly place, full of all sorts of junk. I've seen tech advice sites be wrong on more than one occasion. Some support sites will actually have volunteers answer questions if you sign up as a member. This is quite common in the Open Source world where Linux and Open Office come from. In any case, you'll want to be careful about who you sign up with, so do an Internet search on their site or company name and look for reputation issues. If no one on the

Internet seems to have had any experience with the company, avoid them. In general, you should stay away from any site or company that has no reputation.

However, if you don't have the time or inclination for searching FAQs, or if your issue is not covered, or if the fix in the FAQ doesn't work, then you're going to need some personal attention either via E-mail or telephone. Whether you use the E-mail or phone option, it's important that you carefully document what's happening. Include the text of any error messages, a list of symptoms, and what might be triggering the problem. For example, if your computer crashes only when running some programs but not others, make a note of what programs cause the problem. If you don't include this information in your support call or E-mail, the support rep is likely to dismiss your problem with an "Unable to Replicate" status. Then you'll have to start all over.

E-MAIL SUPPORT

If you have the time and/or patience, you can start with E-mail support. This is often easier to locate on a company's Web site than a phone number. Your first response will probably be an automated reply telling you that your support request has been received. Don't delete this message; it may contain a "Trouble Ticket" number or incident number that you're going to need later. After that, you may get one of several responses:

1. No response at all.
2. Exactly how to fix the problem, and it turns out to be easy for you to do.
3. Exactly how to fix the problem, but it's too complex for your level of knowledge.
4. "Unable to Replicate," sometimes accompanied by a request for more information, but often telling you that problem is not on their end so it must be either your computer or else you're doing something wrong.
5. A lame boilerplate response. For example, if you're having trouble downloading something, the support staff may not actually read your message, but see the word "download" and send you a link to the download instruc-

tions that you've already read and are following to the letter.
6. An actual dialog, where the support staff is working on your issue.

There are other possibilities, but these are some of the most common ones. If you problem isn't solved by E-mail, you're going to have to call for help. In any case, even if your issue is resolved, don't delete any E-mail messages related to it, particularly if there is a Ticket, Case, or Incident number involved. You may need them later if the issue crops up again, or if something similar happens.

PHONE SUPPORT

If E-mail support doesn't help, or if you don't have time for it, you're ready to try phone support. Assuming you've located the correct support number, you might encounter:

1. A phone menu that attempts to give you advice, but no way to talk to a human, e.g., "If you're having trouble with Web browsing, press 1. If you're having trouble with E-mail, press 2, etc." Then you get recorded instructions on how to set up or use the company's product or service.
2. A multi-tier support structure, where you first have to speak to a nontechnical person who asks a lot of questions, many of them unrelated to your issue.
3. Being on hold with music that's either too loud or annoying, punctuated every few minutes with a recording telling you "All our representatives are busy assisting other customers. Your call is important to us, please stay on the line . . ." If you're lucky, they might also give you an estimated hold time.
4. A recording telling you to describe your problem and leave your phone number for a call back. This is rare these days but is still sometimes encountered with smaller companies.
5. An actual human who's ready to help you.

I've run into #1 above with some cable companies and a major ISP. In both cases I discovered by experimentation that it's sometimes possible to break out of the "Menu Jail" by repeatedly pressing the "0" key. I've encountered the same problem with voice response systems; in that case I've been able to eventually get a person by repeatedly saying things that were not on the menu. It even worked when I cursed it and called it an "idiotic robot." It probably doesn't matter what you say, as long as it's not one of the menu choices. You may have to repeat the bad choices several times to get the robot to give up on the menu and connect you to an operator of some kind.

With #2, the multi-tier system, the person you end up talking to is there to screen out the easy problems. Be patient with them and go ahead and answer all their questions. If they can't solve your problem, they are supposed to "Escalate" your issue to the next tier, usually called something like "Level 2 Support." At this point, you should make sure you get the Ticket or Incident number if the call rep hasn't already given it to you. Be aware that some support departments will issue a new number when an incident is escalated. If your call to this first level support is getting nowhere after a while, you can always request "Escalation" to a specialist who is almost certainly going to be more knowledgeable.

For #3, there's not much you can do except be patient. Perhaps this is why Microsoft made the solitaire game a standard part of Windows©.

If you run into #4, a "Leave a message" recording, you want to be succinct and brief with your message. While waiting for a call back, you might want to try to locate another phone number in case they don't return your call. I had this problem with one company a few years ago, and was able to locate the main corporate phone number and eventually get through to a support person.

When you finally arrive at # 5, a real person, there are additional issues to deal with.

TALKING TO SUPPORT

The complaint I hear most often is that the support tech has a thick accent and is hard to understand. You've most likely connected to an outsourced call center in India. If you can't understand the call rep, there are two important things to keep in mind: It's not your fault, and it's not their fault. The vendor is trying to save money on support, while still giving you someone to talk to. The call rep in India is just trying to make a decent living in one of the most impoverished places on Earth. That said, you still have a right to speak to a rep that you can understand. You can always politely ask for a supervisor or someone with better English.

Once you're in conversation with someone, you're halfway there. The first thing to do is get the rep's name or ID number. As the conversation proceeds, take notes, focusing on what diagnosis the rep arrives at, and what they suggest you do to fix your problem. In some support departments, the call reps are under pressure to get off the phone so they can handle more calls per day. If your problem hasn't been solved yet, or you are otherwise unsatisfied with how the call is going, you can always ask to speak to a supervisor. In any case, you'll always get better results by being patient and polite; no matter how frustrated you are, yelling or insults will only make things worse.

Whether the call is successful or not, save all your notes in case the problem recurs or you have to complain to management. If your problem doesn't get solved after all attempts with tech support, it's time to start utilizing the ideas and techniques presented elsewhere in this book.

It *is* possible to get good results with tech support. It may require some work, patience, and persistence on your part but it can be done.

HEALTH INSURANCE

To your great dismay, you open the letter from your insurance company and discover it has rejected your claim or covered far less of it than you were expecting. Give up? No way. First look at the explanation of benefits. Sometimes this is a bit dense but if you persevere, you can usually find the answer. Maybe it was rejected because they claim you haven't met your deductible or the service is not covered. If you still don't understand the claim or you disagree with the explanation, it's time to apply the techniques in this chapter. Don't wait to complain. Many companies have a time limit on appealing a claim rejection.

Gather your evidence

Find the booklet with the descriptions of benefits and look to see what you coverage is. Check state law online. Health plans are required to follow state and federal law for handling complaints. If after reading the booklet, you still don't understand why your claim was rejected, round up the invoice from your physician with the date of service and description of the procedure. Have the denial of claim form ready when you proceed to the next step.

Make your phone call

If your employer provides your insurance, you might first call the Human Resources Department for a copy of the policy. Ask a benefits specialist to explain the provisions. They may then refer you to the insurer.

Call the claims department of your health insurance company. Be sure to write the name of the person you speak to, her title, and the date and time. Write down everything the representative says, including what she says the next step will be. Put these notes and your evidence into a folder. Ask for a clarification of the rejection. Sometimes it can be as simple as needing more information. Make sure you understand exactly what information is required and from whom. Occasionally, for example, says Readers Digest, a physician may not give the reason for the consultation. Getting the physician to clarify the reason may be enough to solve the problem. If you are still told that your claim is rejected, get the name of a specific supervisor to send a letter to. They'll probably tell you to just send in a complaint form from their web site but insist on the name of a real person.

Write a written appeal

If a simple phone call doesn't resolve the problem, then the next step is a letter. Following the advice given previously in this chapter, explain why you think the claim should be covered. Be sure to include all the pertinent information about date of service, procedure, physician's name, what the rejection letter said, and a summary of your phone conversation. Make copies of the invoices, making sure you keep the original of everything, and send the appeal return receipt requested, to the name of the appropriate supervisor at your insurance company.

In the article "Fight for Your Health Care," Lori Andrews offers some advice from Jennifer C. Jaff, an attorney who is the executive director of Advocacy for Patients with Chronic Illnesses.[16] Jaff recommends requesting your entire claim file. The file will tell you the specific rationale for the rejection. You can then tailor your appeal to the plan's criteria for denial or acceptance and make sure that you have the right supporting documents. If, for example, the file says the treatment was "unnecessary," you can then attach copies of medical records as well as a letter from your physician that explains why you need this treatment. If the file claims the treatment was "experimental," you will need to show that the treatment is, in fact, medically accepted. An Internet or library search on medical journals with articles showing that the treatment is effective will provide you with backup.

Seek allies

Andrews also suggests that if you have a chronic condition such as cancer or diabetes, or other medical issues such as Crohn's disease, contact an association that provides support for your problem. These organizations can be found on the Internet or though an associations directory at your local library. The organization may be willing to go to bat for you. AARP, for example, went to bat for Flora Turbin when she was denied payment for an epidural treatment for back pain that should have been covered. It filed a class action suit on behalf of her and 2.5 million other participants that led to a settlement. Flora received $3,790 as her share.

These organizations often have discussion boards where you might find how other people have dealt with a similar situation. University medical web sites may also offer information about such organizations and discussion boards.

Write another letter

If the first letter doesn't work and the company still claims your policy doesn't cover the claim, ask for the specific provision in the policy that supports its position or other documentation of their position. Insist that the company honor its commitment to you.

If this doesn't work, seek other options

If there is no response or you are still not satisfied with the response, there may still be several options. One is to contact the consumer protection division of your state insurance department. Call to get the name of the person who investigates these kinds of claim, says Readers Digest.[17] Enclose copies of all the correspondence between you and the insurance company. Make sure your name, address and daytime phone number is included, in case the investigator has questions. Explain why you think your claim should be covered and ask the investigator to contact the insurance company. If there is ambiguity in the terms that could favor you, suggests Readers Digest, contact from the state may encourage the company to pay your claim to avoid further trouble and expense. After all, most claims never get this far so you have announced yourself as a "troublemaker." They don't know how far you will carry this. The insurance company typically has 30 days to respond to the state. The state department should send you a copy of the insurance company's response.

If the insurance company still gives the state department a runaround, you could consider the "faxing for dollars" technique but that probably works better with product businesses rather than insurance companies. If your insurance policy has an arbitration policy, that might be the next step. If retaining a lawyer is too much for your budget, read one of the books suggested below to get tips on how to proceed. But be aware that the decision of the arbitrator is final and if you lose, that's it. If the policy doesn't include an arbitration clause, then you can consider a conventional law suit. If the amount of the claim is too small to justify the cost of a lawyer, then either represent yourself or take it to small claims court.

Another option is to request an independent medical review (IMR). This decision is binding on the health plan but not you. About 40% of IMRs are resolved in favor of the patient. In California, IMRs are offered by the State Department of Managed Health Care.[18] The Department of Insurance also regulates a smaller number of plans. Patients are Powerful is a group that can help you locate the appropriate agency in your state (see its web site in the Resources section below). You can also try an Internet search using the term "health care complaints [your state]" or ask a librarian to help you.

LANDLORDS AND TENANTS

Most renters and landlords are reasonable (or at least OK). But renter/landlord issues are one of the most common complaint areas that make it to court. Landlords sometimes get renters who don't pay their rent or trash the place. Renters sometimes get landlords who won't make repairs or who keep the security deposit after the renter moves out. Both can find useful advice in the Nolo Press books on landlord and tenants' rights listed below. Since my book is aimed at the "underdog," I'm going to discuss the tenant side.

Most landlords are more than willing to make needed repairs. After all, the condition of the property affects its value. But there are plenty of sleaze balls out there too. You've probably heard stories but there are plenty on the Internet if somehow you have missed hearing about such unpleasantries.

Look at the lease or rental agreement

Look for the relevant sections about security deposits or repairs. Make sure you comply with the requirements. If you think you have done so, then contact the landlord and ask for repairs or for your security deposit. Nolo Press provides forms for such requests.

Make a phone call

The first step is calling to voice your complaint or request your deposit. In most cases, this is the last step too. If you are moving out, Readers Digest suggests that you ask the landlord to do a walkthrough to see for herself that the apartment is in good condition. But if that doesn't work . . .

Write a letter or send a form

If the verbal request gets you nowhere or you want to be more formal to be on the safe side, you can write a letter. Look back at the suggestions above for how to write a complaint letter. Succinctly summarize the problem, remind the landlord of your previous requests for repairs and set a deadline, suggests Readers Digest. It should also spell out what you intend to do if the problem is not resolved or the security deposit not returned. You may also use a form from Nolo Press. It has several that are relevant, including "Tenant's Demand for Return of Security Deposit" and "Tenant's Notice of Needed Repairs." As of this writing, the cost is $4.99; a reasonable price that is easily worth it if you have trouble writing, want to make sure you have covered all bases, or otherwise feel the need for formality. Be sure to send the letter or form return receipt requested so the landlord can't claim you never notified her.

The three options Readers Digest lists if the repairs are not done or the deposit not returned:[19]

- *Repair the problem and deduct the cost from the rent*
  Unless you have the right training, better to have a licensed repair person fix the problem. That way the invoice gives you proof too.
- *Withhold the rent until the landlord fixes the problem* (this is called a rent abatement)
  If the cost of repair is high, you can withhold some or all of the rent until the repairs are made. In most cases this can't exceed the amount by which your apartment value is reduced. You should put the amount you withholding in a separate bank account. If it goes to court, this shows good faith and demonstrates that you weren't simply refusing to pay. If you want to pursue the rent abatement option, it might be a good idea to head for the library for one of the Nolo books.
- *Move out under the doctrine of "constructive eviction"*
  This is reserved for the most drastic cases, ones in which the apartment is essentially uninhabitable. Before you elect this option, consult a lawyer or one of the Nolo books.

Gather evidence

Whether the landlord refuses to return your security deposit or fails to make needed repairs, you'll need to have evidence to back up your claim. Here's what Readers Digest recommends before you move out of an apartment. Photograph or videotape the apartment to show that the apartment is clean and undamaged. Record the plumbing and electrical systems to show that they are in working order. Flush the toilet, turn the lights off and on. It's good advice if you have an uncooperative landlord who refuses to do needed repairs too. Record the problem either through photos or videotape so you'll be prepared if you have to go to court. Other evidence that could be relevant includes the rental or lease agreement, telephone records, return receipts of letters sent, and affidavits from other tenants or witnesses.

Here's one of the stories I found on the Internet in which the tenant made excellent use of evidence. A person I'll call Robin had to countersue the landlord. Because the landlord refused to repair the apartment, Robin decided to move out. The landlord claimed that he did not give sufficient notice so withheld the security deposit. But Robin had been very careful to gather evidence. Here is what Robin writes on the blog:

> "My evidence: photos of leaking ceilings, date and time-stamped phone message from him confirming my notice of leaving; affidavits from 3 neighbors (one, a police detective!) attesting to the threats posed by his insane son who screamed and pounded on walls all hours of the night, [the] son who he'd stashed in the apt. downstairs, and, the best, my "LCD's" ("local call detail" from the phone company), which showed the dates and times of all of my calls to him to try and rectify the situation over 7 months. 14 calls in 7 months. All documented."[20]

Robin was smart. He not only recorded evidence as he went along, he enlisted witnesses in his apartment building and kept phone records. So instead of having to pay the landlord's demand of $3000, Robin won $435 from the landlord.

Alternative options

You can consider some of the options noted in the first part of this chapter, such as contacting the local TV ombudsman. But frankly, your best bet might be the last resort. . . .

Your last resort

For most people getting a lawyer is too expensive for the amounts usually involved. But for issues with landlords, small claims court is a viable option and one frequently used for this purpose. See Chapter Five for information about suing in small claims courts.

TRAVEL

Travel is another area that generates many complaints. One of the leading experts on dealing with travel complaints is Christopher Elliott, the ombudsman for *National Geographic Traveler* magazine. He has a nationally syndicated column and a helpful web site. According to Elliott, 99% of grievances get resolved if you follow the right techniques.[21] The other 1% are the ones he deals with. If the tips below don't work, you can take your issue to him by sending an email (see below). Here's some advice adapted from his web site and from *Fight Back and Win* as well.

Gather your evidence

Keeping careful records of any trip is a good idea but is especially important if something goes wrong. Make sure you have all receipts, emails, brochures, tickets (and even screen shots of your reservations, if necessary) before you leave on your trip. Know the difference between a deposit, a prepaid reservation and a confirmation. The latter doesn't guarantee you a reservation unless you arrive at the stated time. Take your receipts with you as you travel; use them as evidence in case of a dispute. The hotel can't claim that you don't have a reservation if you have an email printout. If you run into problems with a hotel room or car rental, take photos of the "bedbug-ridden hotel room or the rental car with a chipped windshield," says Elliott.

Don't wait to complain

Mention your grievance before you check out, deplane or disembark, says Elliott. The person you speak to may have the power to resolve your issue. If you wait, he continues, you'll have to deal with an outsourced service rep who has "50 ways of saying no."[22]

If you arrive at a hotel and the clerk claims there is no room available, stand your ground. If you used a credit card for the prepaid reservation or deposit, the hotel is legally obligated to provide a room for you even if you arrive after midnight, says Readers Digest. If it is only "confirmed" (made without a credit card or a deposit) you have to arrive by the stated time. If the clerk is refuses to help you, ask for the manager. Remain polite because the hotel can toss you out if you become violent. Show the manager your reservation documents (credit receipts, confirmation number, etc). Don't leave the desk till an acceptable room has been located either in this hotel or elsewhere.

If you don't find the room acceptable, say so right away. If you have been promised a nonsmoking room or the room is dirty or doesn't otherwise match what you have been led to expect, immediately explain why it is unacceptable and, if necessary, ask for a manager. If you are told that another room is not available, politely ask when an acceptable one will be ready and that you be moved to it as soon as it is ready.

Here's a summary of one of the many stories on Elliott's web site: Mary Jane, who was traveling to attend a wedding, obtained a Las Vegas hotel reservation though Hotwire. When she arrived, she was told that there was no reservation in her name. A phone call to Hotwire uncovered the information that the hotel had not properly completed the reservation. It was a holiday weekend so she was told no rooms were available. Though Hotwire found another hotel for her, it was a $62 cab ride outside of town and she missed most of the wedding events. All Hotwire did for her was give her a $50 "compensation" for her inconvenience.

Elliot told her that what Hotwire did was inappropriate. It has an obligation to find her a comparable hotel in Las Vegas, not outside of town. If it was in fact the hotel's mistake, the hotel has an obligation to find her a room. He suggested that in a situation like this, you stay in the check-in area till you have a room key in your hand. The hotel will try to get you to leave, says Elliott, but don't do it. In this particular case, Elliott's intervention netted her a $571 credit, which covered her hotel and cab fare.

Write a letter

If talking to the person behind the counter at the airline, car rental or hotel doesn't work, Elliott recommends that the next step be a letter. "Talk [on the phone] is cheap," he says and doesn't leave a usable paper trail (because you don't have access to it, even if they do). Go right to a letter for the next step.

Make the letter tight and polite. Get to the point in 500 words or less, with no ranting. "The two most common mistakes that people make with a written grievance are being vague about the compensation they expect and being unpleasant," says Elliott.[23] The more business-like your letter, the more likely it is to be read and acted upon. Include confirmation numbers, dates and other relevant information. If documents are appropriate, attach copies. Proofread the letter for spelling errors. Sloppy writing, as I point out above, will result in you being taken less seriously.

If the hotel or rental agency is part of a chain, complain to the parent company. You can contact the customer service department but you should try to get the name of a specific person, if possible (see above for tips for contacting executives). If it is independent, find out the name of the owner and write directly to him or her.

Elliott, like Ron Burley, recommends sending copies of your letter to all relevant people, whether in the company or a government regulatory agency. "When they see you've shared a grievance with a few other folks, it will give the complaint more weight," writes Elliott.[24] See his web site listed below for tips on whom to contact. This includes the Department of Transportation's Aviation Consumer Protection Division, a link to a list of state attorney generals (for hotel complaints), the American Society of Travel Agents and the Federal Trade Commission (for dishonest advertising).

Though Elliott doesn't suggest sending a letter to executives within the company till the second letter (if it is needed), you may want to follow Ron Burley's advice and send copies the first time around. "Every travel company has a vice president of customer service or a manager who is in charge of dealing with passengers or guests," says Elliott. "That's who needs to hear from you next. These executives go to great lengths to keep their names and contact information from becoming public. But a quick online search will reveal the contact person."[25] Elliott lists many of them on his web site.

Whether you send a written letter, email or online form, make sure you keep a copy of what you wrote. If you use regular mail, be sure to send it return receipt requested. Then be patient, advices Elliott. It may take 6 to 8 weeks for the wheels of bureaucracy to grind out a response. If the company turns you down, get it in writing, not by phone, and move on to the next step.

Notify your credit card company

If you do not get what you paid for with your credit card—for example, the hotel room or car you reserved, contact your credit card company. Not getting what you paid for may violate a contract the hotel or rental agency has with the credit card company. You may even be entitled to a refund, says Readers Digest. You can also consider officially contesting the charges, as a last-ditch option. If you've really been ripped off, maybe consider it as a "first-ditch" option.

Seek relevant information

If your complaint is with a major travel company, Elliott's web site may be able to help you. He has a file of tips for dealing with these companies on his web site. One of the best tactics for dealing with a big company is to convince it that that it didn't follow its own rules. "Airlines have what's called a contract of carriage: the legal agreement between you and the company. Cruise lines have ticket contracts. Car-rental companies have rental agreements, and hotels are subject to state lodging laws," says Elliott.[26] If the contract is not on the company's web site, ask the customer service department of the company for it.

If none of the above works

If the airline, hotel or rental agency still refuses to accommodate you, you have several choices. First you can seek an ally—such as ombudsman Elliott at his web site. It's his job and he's very effective. Because of his position, he carries some weight and the big companies don't want to look bad in his column or on his web site. As I have said in other chapters, embarrassment and humiliation can be effective weapons.

Going to court is tough. Most cases aren't worth retaining a lawyer and small claims court claims require filing in the same state as the company being sued. If it's a hotel or agency within your home state, you can consider this option but otherwise, it won't help you.

Readers Digest suggests that it may be worthwhile to contact the office of consumer protection in the hotel or agency's home state. A record of complaints may prompt the attorney general to bring a lawsuit on behalf of you and others with a similar problem.

Last but certainly not least, you can use the Burley technique "faxing for dollars" (see above) or Elliott's "Hail Mary." Elliott's last-ditch measure is "a respectful but insistent letter overnighted directly to the chief executive officer along with the disappointing string of "nos" you've received. This is a little-known loophole in the system. Something Fed-Exed to the top exec has an excellent chance of being read by that person," says Elliot.

A final thought

Think twice about using sites such as Hotwire to book your hotel reservations. Elliott recommends using a travel agent to help you find an acceptable hotel in your price range. Though these sites may often provide good prices, they're what's called "opaque" sites—in other words, a pig in a poke, because you don't know what you are getting till you arrive. One person complaining on Elliott's site, for example, ended up in a dirty, smelly room in a Spokane hotel. Because the fees are nonrefundable, he was stuck. If you are traveling abroad, you can find advice about hotels from travel books such as the Rick Steves series (he gives you unbiased, down-to-earth reviews) and that way avoid the booking commissions *and* unpleasant surprises. Looking for hotel reviews on the Internet is another way to avoid the worst hotels.

In Conclusion

Don't be a victim. Stand up and fight back. By carefully marshalling your evidence, being persistent and, if necessary, creative, you *can* make your call or letter important to them, whether they like it or not. Whether you do something to affect their bottom line or are just simply persistently annoying, you are not only more likely to get what is rightfully yours, you'll feel more empowered in general and that's good.

RESOURCES

BOOKS

Russell L. Ackoff and Sheldon Rovin. *Beating the System: Using Creativity to Outsmart Bureaucracies.* San Francisco: Berrett-Koehler Publishers, 2005.

John Bear, Ph.D. *Send This Jerk the Bedbug Letter: How Companies, Politicians, and the Mass Media Handle Complaints.* Berkeley, CA: Tenspeed Press, 1996.

John Bear and Mariah Bear. *Complaint Letters for Busy People.* Franklin Lakes, NJ: The Career Press, 1999.

Ron Burley. *Unscrewed: The Consumer's Guide to Getting What You Paid For.* Berkeley, CA: Tenspeed Press, 2006.

James M. Kramon, Esq. *You Don't Need a Lawyer.* New York: Workman, 2005. Advocating that you "think like a lawyer" rather than hire one, this handy little book has 84 sample complaint letters ranging from an HMO, restaurant, or credit card company to car manufacturer, garden service, or school principal. Also includes a fairly up-to-date contact info for federal, state and credit reporting agencies.

Ellen Phillips. *Shocked, Appalled, and Dismayed! How to Write Letters of Complaint That Get Results.* New York: Vintage, 1998.

Attorney Janet Portman and Marcia Stewart. *Every Tenant's Legal Guide.* Berkeley, CA: Nolo Press.

Reader's Digest. *Fight Back and Win: What to Do When You are Cheated and Wronged.* Pleasantville, NY: Reader's Digest Association, 2001.

Marcia Stewart, Attorney Ralph Warner and Attorney Janet Portman. *Every Landlord's Legal Guide.* Berkeley, CA: Nolo Press,

WEB SITES

Federal Citizen Information Center
www.pueblo.gsa.gov/complaintresources.htm
1-888-8 PUEBLO (1-888-878-3256)
As the URL suggests, a list of government resources for complaint issues.

About.com: U.S. Government Information
usgovinfo.about.com/library/weekly/aa043099.htm
Information about agencies, bureaus, and commissions that accept and investigate consumer complaints and reports. This site may be a little easier to use for some people than the previous one.

Consumer Action
www.consumer-action.org
Thorough and useful guidelines about how to complain.

Consumer Affairs
www.consumeraffairs.com
A private organization with information and resources for consumer complaints.

Consumer Watchdog
www.consumerwatchdog.org
Acts as a consumer advocate, with articles about violations of consumer rights and other corporate misdoings.

Ron Burley
www.ronburley.com
Information about Burley's book *Unscrewed,* as well as his radio commentary, A Piece of My Mind.

Two AARP articles by Ron Burley
"7 Words You Should Never Say to Customer Service"
www.aarp.org/money/consumer/articles/seven_things_never_say.html

"7 Things You Should Always Say to Customer Service"
www.aarp.org/money/consumer/articles/seven_things_always_say.html

Wikihow
www.wikihow.com/Write-a-Complaint-Letter-to-a-Company
Great tips about writing a complaint letter plus useful links.

Complaints Board
www.complaintsboard.com
A web site with tips, stories, and articles on a wide range of complaint issues, including suggestions on how to write complaint letters. You can also submit complaints and see warnings from others. The articles include "Avoid Telephone Bill Scams" as well as others on how to protect yourself in the wake of rampaging Internet scams.

Consumer Reports
www.consumerreports.org/cro/index.htm
CR has provided unbiased, tested consumer products ratings since 1936 (they accept no advertising). One way to avoid problems is check the product's ratings out before you buy. CR covers a wide range of products, from health and drugs to appliances, from garden products to food and electronics.

Ripoff Report®
www.ripoffreport.com
According to its web site: "Ripoff Report® is a worldwide consumer reporting Web site and publication, by consumers, for consumers, to file and document complaints about companies or individuals." Also reports on Internet and telemarketing scams.

Nolo Press
www.nolo.com
The place for self-help resources about legal issues, including books, articles and forms. See Chapter Five for more info about Nolo.

Christopher Elliott
www.elliott.org/help/how-to-fix-your-trip/
Elliott is the ombudsman for *National Geographic Trav-*

eler magazine. His web site has many tips for helping you deal with travel grievances, as well as many anecdotes.

Smarter Travel.com
www.smartertravel.com/travel-advice/Finding-help-with-your.html?id=10443
Another useful web site with information about how to complain over travel issues, with links to complaint agencies.

Patients are Powerful
www.patientsarepowerful.org/hmo.cfm
Provides information about how to file HMO complaints in the U.S. It also provides the contact information for the Joint Commission on Accreditation of Healthcare Organizations (JCAHO), which wants to hear about health care complaints.

Joint Commission on Accreditation of Healthcare Organizations (JCAHO)
www.jointcommission.org/GeneralPublic/Complaint/
You can go to the Joint Commission directly with your complaint.

Kaiser Permanente Thrive Exposed
www.kaiserthrive.org/kaiser-permanente-horror-stories/
A web site dedicated to collecting and exposing complaints about Kaiser's HMO.

Art Techo
www.arttecho.net
This web services site offers info concerning tech support and how to deal with it, as well as other consumer issues about computer services.

UPDATES

For updates on books, web sites, web site URLs and links (they sometimes change), articles, and other relevant information, as well as a blog, check the web site for this book: www.standuptoauthorities.com

CHAPTER
9

You Can Fight City Hall: Tackling Government Bureaucracies and Interacting Effectively with the Police

Unbeknownst to Carol and her neighbors, an architectural firm bought a residential home and set up shop. Suddenly the neighbors noticed a lot of people going in and out of that one house. Parking became nonexistent, and traffic on their quiet street increased dramatically. Carol and her neighbors realized that the business was responsible for all the changes they saw. The neighbors also discovered that their neighborhood was not zoned for such activity. In fact the neighborhood was not zoned for business at all. Carol and her neighbors didn't just wring their hands and quietly endure it. They fought back. They formed a neighborhood group, did their homework, went to meetings of the City Council with their case. It took persistence but their hard work paid off. The firm was forced to move.

Fighting City Hall

COMMUNITY PROBLEMS

MOST OF THE TIME ordinary citizens (unless they own their own businesses) don't pay much attention to their local government or it to them. Maybe we read about some squabble on the City Council or Board of Supervisors about redevelopment, zoning variances, or city ordinances but probably don't too get worked up over it. Maybe we glance at the newspaper article about some other problem that the city is having but don't follow up on it. We exist in what seems to be parallel universes. Then comes the day when the universes collide, when one side becomes aware of the other side. This may occur when a zoning law is violated or other changes occur that affects you and your neighbors in a negative way. Or you seek a permit of some sort, have a dispute with a neighbor, unknowingly break some local code or law, or find that someone else is breaking a code or law that impacts you directly. You suddenly find yourself facing down the multi-headed hydra of city bureaucracy. Now what? Depending on the situation and how your local government is structured, you may be either dealing with a bureaucrat, a commission, the city council itself, or perhaps all of them. Any way you slice it, it can be daunting or even intimidating.

If your neighborhood issue is crime prevention, the tactics you need to use are somewhat different than what is listed below. With this problem, the police can be your ally—get in touch with them. Many police jurisdictions have community policing units. A good book that provides many helpful tips and guideline is *Safe Homes Safe Neighborhoods: Stopping Crime Where You Live* by Stephanie Mann and M.C. Blakeman. Also see the web sites referenced below.

NEIGHBORHOOD COMPLAINTS: A MODEL

One of the most common and effective ways to deal with problems that affect the whole community or neighborhood is to form a group or association. Such groups have been formed for many reasons, including crime prevention, neighborhood cleanup or other problems that interfere with positive community functioning.

The following ideas are based on what Carol and her neighbors did and what they suggest to others in a similar situation. Other types of situations where the tactics detailed below will work include getting speed bumps put on your streets, dealing with badly run elder care homes, getting better lighting for the neighborhood, keeping developers honest, and so on. Note that these are all problems that affect the entire neighborhood, not just you. This is not a tactic to use for your neighbors with the dog that barks too much.

Get information

Think a simple call of complaint will end the problem? Sometimes, but frequently not. The first thing to do is become acquainted with the structure of your local government and the chain of command. Find out what city department oversees your issue—zoning, health codes, employment, development, human services, parking and traffic, and so on. Next, find out what the local laws are concerning your issue. If your issue is, for example, zoning, find out whether businesses are allowed to operate in your neighborhood. In some cities, there are neighborhoods that are designated "Mixed Use." Under this regulation, certain businesses are allowed in residential neighborhoods. If your neighborhood is not zoned for business, you have something to work with. For zoning issues, the department is usually either the Zoning Department and/or the Planning Commission. If your issue is parking regulations, find out if there are specific rules for the residential areas in your neighborhood. If you are concerned with developers and their projects, most cities have a Planning and Development Department. For other kind of problems such as speed bumps or lighting, track down the right agency by looking at the city's web site or calling City Hall.

Seek allies

Find out whether you have an active local neighborhood improvement group. Ask around, search the Internet using the term "[your city] neighborhood association," ask at the library or even call City Hall. If you are lucky enough to have one, present the problem to them and get their help and support. You can fight City Hall, but it is much easier and more likely to be successful if you do it as a group or a collection of groups. You don't need to get lawyers. Lawyers can break the neighborhood piggy bank and sometimes do more harm than good. Let the people who don't know any better spend their money on lawyers. All you need is a pack of irate, determined neighbors.

If you don't have a neighborhood improvement group, seriously consider putting in the time and effort to start one yourself. See the Resources section below for links to two detailed articles on how to form a group. Neighborhood groups normally form around an issue that affects everyone. Begin with the people on your street and fan out from there. Decide on the size of your neighborhood, i.e., how many blocks it will include. Once you have a group formed, register with the city, if possible. Hold meetings. Pass petitions around your neighborhood and collect as many signatures as possible.

Put it in writing

Begin a neighborhood-wide letter writing campaign. A caveat here. *Do not* use form letters that you circulate around the neighborhood. Those carry little weigh with bureaucrats. *Do* ask people to write down in their own words how they feel about the issue, which demonstrates a much more genuine concern than form letters.

Be patient. The issue won't be solved overnight or in one meeting. Nothing related to government ever does.

Seek allies in government

You should try early on to win the support of the council person who represents your neighborhood. Either make an appointment for representatives of your group to meet with the council person or invite him/her to your neighborhood meeting. Since you are likely to end up in front of the council, it will be to your benefit to have the support of your council member. Solving any neighborhood problem or crisis is likely to be a long drawn out affair, stretched over months, and you need all the help you can muster.

City bureaucracies

The most likely progression of events in a conflict over zoning laws is to begin in the zoning or planning department, then you'll be referred to the planning commission and finally go before the city council. Once you are at the city council level, you will most likely have three or more hearings in front of them before a final decision will be made. Sometimes the matter will end at the Planning Commission level. However, there are some issues that may take several years to get resolved, so you must be persistent and patient.

Prepare your case

Be persistent. Be a very squeaky wheel. Be very detail oriented. Know the rules, know the code. If you think there is a code violation, spell it out in detail, citing the exact line and number of the code. Cite any other relevant rule or regulation that is relevant to your case.

Present each commissioner and/or councilperson with a packet containing copies of letters, petitions, and photographic evidence to back up your claims each and every time you go before them. Doing it once is not enough. Your campaign will involve letter writing to each and every bureaucrat, commissioner and councilperson. You will need to flood them with packets of signatures and information beforehand each time they hear your case. Most of the time, you will be giving them the same material over and over again. If it is close to election time, use that to your advantage. Get people from your neighborhood to work in the candidate's campaign offices. They can remind the candidate of the neighborhood issues. The businesses trying to misuse your neighborhood surely will! You can do the same.

Stick to the laws and the facts when writing letters or presenting your facts in person. Don't be verbose or offensive in either your writing or your speeches. Show your indignation at the situation, but don't shout swear words at either the offender or at the government body who you are in front of. Do not call commissioners or council people names no matter how frustrated you are with them. This will only alienate them and defeat your purpose. Make your letters short, preferably one page, and succinct. Stick *strictly* to the facts.

Present your case

Try to get as many people as possible to write and speak at the council meeting. At the same time be aware that there is sometimes a limit placed on the amount of time each speaker is given to make a presentation, and sometimes there is a limit to the number of speakers that a group is allowed. If there is a limit, have your best speakers go first. If you have someone in the group who is longwinded and/or a poor speaker (and every group has them!), make sure they are among the last to speak. Don't let them waste precious time. Don't let them make a bad impression on the council. In a situation of this kind, first impressions make a difference and so does order of presentation. Those who go first will have the most impact.

Write out the most critical and important arguments in your case and make sure those are presented in the first speaker's presentation. The other speeches from your group can then expand on the topic. Because the first speech has the most impact, it needs to be the best.

Have allies at the city council or agency meeting

Pack your audience with supporters. If your neighborhood group can get other neighborhood groups to join you, so much the better. The issue then becomes a city-wide issue. When it comes to zoning laws, gathering allies isn't hard to do, and you will make an even bigger impression on the city council. Nothing gets a city council or planning commission's attention faster than several hundred people, all wearing the same color, coming into the meeting, sitting together and staring at them. You don't want the officials to go to sleep on you. This will wake them up! What you will be trying to do is get your government to enforce the laws that they have constructed or sworn to uphold. They are voted into their offices and they need to be reminded that they can be voted out.

Find other allies

What if it turns out that your neighborhood is zoned for mixed use and you and your neighbors are unhappy about it? Get your group to campaign to have the zoning changed in your neighborhood. Use the same tactics. This will take longer and require more persistence and commitment from you and your group, and you may need to call on help from other neighborhood groups, but it is doable.

Persistence and joining with other groups paid off for Carol's group when they joined with two others to fight a planned Safeway expansion. This expansion could have not only driven many of the local Mom and Pop merchants out of business but could have caused real traffic and noise problems. Because this was one of Safeway's more prosperous stores, corporate headquarters decided to expand a modest size store on a busy street into a gigantic store that would include a deli, a drug store, a Chinese cafeteria, a dry cleaning place, a flower shop, and a bakery (such stores already existed on this street). To accomplish this, Safeway would have had to demolish the small house (which they had bought under the table) that was adjacent to the parking lot. The roof top parking lot would have been level with the homes on the intersecting street. To say that the people in the neighborhood were upset was an understatement.

"We really slaved on this one," reports Carol. "The tactics were the same [as the architecture firm incident], but we had to keep hammering at the city to uphold the law and to do the bidding of the residents, that it was their duty." For five years, the groups had to fight sleazy politicians who were in Safeway's pocket, and then watch a councilwoman have her career destroyed because she sided with Carol's group. But all their hard work finally paid off. The resulting changes in the store were the ones approved by the neighborhood groups. They even stocked what the residents asked for. But, adds Carol as a word of caution, if the store had not been such a cash cow for Safeway, it probably would have just closed the store as a punishment and moved elsewhere. Assess *your* situation carefully.

Seek alternatives

Another possible alternative for dealing with certain kinds of community problems is to contact the media. If they think your problem will make good copy, they may investigate. City Hall is not immune from embarrassment and humiliation. The *San Francisco Chronicle,* for example, has a column that reports problems such as broken street lights and sidewalks, and other public facilities that don't work. The paper finds out who is responsible for the appropriate facility and publishes his or her name, phone number and photograph in the newspaper. This puts the official on the spot, in public view. But if and when the problem is finally resolved, the paper publishes the person's name again. If the problem doesn't get resolved in a reasonable amount of time, the "Chron Watch" publishes the information again. First, a carrot and stick. Then a (possible) pat on the back. You might urge your local paper to follow suit.

SIDESTEPPING BUREAUCRATIC RED TAPE

If you or your group needs to visit a department or a commission, schedule your appointment for when the agency first opens. You want the bureaucrats you need to deal with to be as refreshed and as stress-free as possible to increase the chances that they will hear you out. Find out ahead of time what documents or information you need to bring with you. Make sure you have all your papers with you and in order. If you know that you will have a wait time before you see the individual you are to meet with, bring something to read. Some departments are known for being crowded, for example, permit departments. Reading while you wait will lower your stress level so you will be calmer when you finally talk to the bureaucrat.

If there is paper work involved, e.g., applications or other forms, check to see if the forms are available online. If so, you can save time by downloading the forms and filling them out at home. Check online to see if questions you have can be answered there instead going to the department or agency.

If the clerks you are dealing with are discourteous, or if you are having trouble communicating with them, go to someone else if you can, or ask to speak to the supervisor for the help you need. If you yourself do not speak English well, ask for an interpreter. One may be provided. Be sure you understand *everything* that you are told. It's OK to ask the clerk or supervisor to repeat what they have said.

If you have a form to fill out, be sure you fill out *everything* that pertains to you and your situation. If something doesn't apply, draw a line through it and write N/A (not applicable) on it. *Never* leave blank spaces where an answer is required. Forms with blank spaces are often rejected as incomplete. It's a smart thing to make a copy of the form and fill out the practice form first. Also make and keep copies of everything you ever give to government officials. If something gets lost, or if someone says the form or document wasn't received (losing documents is not unusual in bureaucracies), you can then quickly produce the document and give it to them again.

When mailing anything to a government department, make sure that you send it with a return receipt requested with signature. You will then have proof that you sent the document and that it was received. Keep the receipt too. Whenever possible, hand deliver documents to the office instead of mailing them, and *get a signed receipt*.

When dealing with Commissions and City Councils, there is usually a deadline before the hearing date for documents (such as your packets of information) that will be presented at the meeting. This allows time to get the packets into the hands of the officials so they have time to review your case. Make sure you know what that deadline is. On the day of the hearing, bring extra copies of your packets with you, enough for each commissioner or councilperson, "just in case." Be sure to give a packet to the City Clerk and also to the City Attorney. Always make sure everyone in your group has his/her full packet to refer to, if needed. Here's another hint. Always be nice to the receptionists, secretaries and administrative assistants. They're the gate keepers and they have the power to make things tough for you if you treat them poorly. Don't do that!

"SHREDDING" THE PAPER: ANOTHER TAKE ON BUREAUCRATIC PAPERWORK FOR BUSINESS AND HOME OWNERS

As any businessperson, home owner or contractor knows, paperwork hell is part of the price paid for operating a legitimate business or for home construction. Government red tape, permits, permissions, licenses—the forms go on and on into infinity. So do the horror stories—the Internet is full of them. In the space of this one chapter, I can't possibly do justice to the complexity of the modern bureaucracies today's business people need to deal with. There aren't any general rules that will work in all cases. The bureaucrats are far too inventive, each in their own Kafkaesque way. I can't even suggest any good books that cover all the possibilities that business and home owners face. All I can do here is pass on a few tips that I've garnered from interviews and from applying my book's strategies. Good luck.

- *Ignore the initial contact*
  Needless to say, this will not work for every form you are sent or for every circumstance. If a specific form is sent to your specific business or organization, then, alas, you better fill it out. If it involves fees or taxes, you *really* better fill it out. But generic forms that merely request information can often be ignored. Kevin, who has run an eating establishment in a Western city for many years, has frequently ignored such forms. Many times he never gets a second request.

  Bureaucrats love to send out endless forms, even when they are not really necessary and no one cares. If the rules say send it out, it gets sent even if no one ever evaluates the forms or follows up. Use your own judgment about whether ignoring routine forms will work for you. You can always turn one in at a later date.

- *Look for alternatives*
  Many times there are ways to get around the rules if you're clever. Look carefully at the wordings or the definitions. Is there a way to reinterpret the definition or rule to fit what you want to do, a way to change the vocabulary of your request? Try to understand why the rule was originally established so you can see how you can fit the spirit, if not the exact intent. "If you want to get around it or change it, you've got to understand why it exists," says David Brown, author of *Organization Smarts*.[1]

  Denise wanted to add a new bedroom to her house but she was told she that couldn't get a building permit for a bedroom. After reading the regulations carefully, she realized that the rule's concern was not with an addition per se but having too many people in one household. She wasn't trying to add people, only a guest bedroom. She refined her description of what she was planning to add to the house. She described it to sound more like a den. After all, that's what it functioned as when guests weren't there! Permit granted. Be creative and clever; it may pay off.

  If there's a blank on some bureaucratic form that you don't want to fill out because you think it's intrusive or annoying, don't leave it blank. You could just write "n/a" but you could also get creative. Well, depending on what the blank is asking, of course . . . Years ago I had a temporary job processing registration forms at my university. Someone apparently didn't like the question about "religious affiliation" and filled in "Aztec snake worshipper." Citing "Jedi" as a religion, which started as a joke, is now allowable in Great Britain, so why not?[2]

Gene recalls the time that his campus organization had to respond to a lot of what he considered pointless questions. The organization was also obligated to provide bylaws. Since it only had five members, this was not really at the top of Gene's to-do list. So he found a boilerplate bylaws form and tacked it on to his application, along with some rather imaginative additions. When he found that the organization was required to say that it would abide by the directives of the president of the university and the Board of Regents, he couldn't resist the temptation to add ". . . and the Governor and whoever else thinks they have a right to tell us what to do." He never got one complaint or request to redo the form. Probably no one ever read it, or if they did, they didn't care. I'm not recommending this kind of tactic, but it does illustrate that you can often get away with more than you might think when the request is merely for pro forma information.

- *Seek exemptions*

If you want to go through the proper channels, find out who can grant your request and try to get around the rule. Set up a meeting and, following the procedures I've outlined elsewhere, prepare your case. Make it succinct, clear and to the point. Explain why the rules don't apply to your case. Make it easy for them to grant your request.

When filling out government forms, if you think the rule doesn't apply to you, you can just write "exempt." Kevin did this when he was confronted with a form that demanded that he give his zoning permit number. But he had previously been told by another department that he wasn't required to have a zoning permit for this particular project. No room on the form to explain that so, because he knew that every blank *must be filled in* (see my comments above), he simple put "exempt." It worked. He never heard a peep after he returned the form. The bureaucrats don't want to work hard (unless it involves money) so as long as you answer the question with something remotely plausible, they're often happy.

- *Be agreeable*
  Find out what the bureaucrat wants. Pleasantly go along with him. Be nice. Be agreeable. Chat him up. Kevin calls this "side-tracking" but I'll just call it building rapport. The bureaucrat or inspector will write his report; after all, he has to write down *something*. He'll tell you to do things. You'll say you'll do them. What happens after that . . . you decide. As long as his form is filled out, he's happy. A caveat here: this advice is not intended for important regulations that are reasonable to comply with, e.g., rational health and safety codes. This tactic is for makework rules and regulations that only exist to keep the bureaucrats busy.
- *Push back*
  Be careful about this one. You have to do it in a polite, reasonable way. If an inspector or other authority is bugging you about some alleged infraction, size him up. If he is young and inexperienced, he may be strict about the rules. If he is older and more experienced, he may be more flexible. If you think the authority may be flexible, you might get away with challenging the rules if you do it in a way that makes sense to him.

  Lenora's luncheonette is a popular hangout that offered tasty hot dogs and hamburgers at a reasonable price. So that the hot dogs would start warming up and not require as much cooking, she routinely left them by the side of the grill to await customer orders. The health inspector insisted that any sausages not in the refrigerator must be kept on the grill itself. Lenora knew that the sausages would shrivel up from the heat and be uneatable if she complied. So she challenged him. "What do you know about sausages?" she asked. Of course he knew nothing. So she explained what would happen to them and why, with sausages, it was safe to disregard the bureaucratic rule. He backed off and wrote down "no significant health violations found."

  Lenora is good at chatting people up so she can get away with this kind of maneuver. She is always pleasant and smiling, never rude. "Sometimes," she adds with a twinkle in her eyes, "I just talk them to death and they give up." She knows how to push back and build rapport at the same time.

- *Turn the tables*
  Don't present yourself as an adversary. Sometimes you can turn the tables and make yourself look like you and the bureaucrat are on the same side. "I can appreciate where you're coming from. I want the same thing." These are phrases that Kevin has often used to great advantage. Try to find out what the inspector or the bureaucrat wants. Give some thought to how to present yourself as an ally before you confront this person.
- *Be persistent*
  Keep appealing the rules or the complaint. Don't give up. Keep looking for a way out or around. Sometimes you can wear down the bureaucracy or, in the case below, your opponent who is using the bureaucracy against you.

  Kevin's establishment is open late and sometimes attracts a rowdy clientele in this college town, especially on weekends. He does his best to keep them quiet but once they step outside his business, he has little control over them. A neighbor complained about the noise, trying to get his business to close at 10pm. Since a large chunk of his business occurs after 10pm, this was not acceptable. The use permit department paid him a visit. Kevin pointed out that the disturbance was occurring on public property, not inside. Nonetheless, he had to go through a series of hearings. Always civil and polite, he kept explaining that this was a mixed zoning area, after all, and that he did everything he could to control the noise. He persisted in the hearings and appeals, never giving in to the unreasonable demand. Finally he simply wore the complainant down and she gave up. "Government is good for that," he notes wryly. The final resolution: Kevin put up a sign asking customers to "Let the students sleep and study." His business continues to gladly serve the student community after 10pm, and they continue to happily scarf down his tasty late night edibles.

A Different Side of Government: Dealing Effectively with the Police

Police officers have a tough job. They have to deal with the worst element of our society, often putting their lives in danger. They represent powerful authority figures for good and occasionally for the not-so-good. The guilty revile them but even the innocent may fear them. It's easy to be intimidated by a police officer in uniform. Uniforms, as research shows, have the power to compel obedience even when the uniforms aren't relevant to the situation (recall my example in Chapter One).[3] When they *are* relevant, the impact can be even greater. So knowing how to relate to the police in an effective way can be very important.

Citizens have dual roles in regard to the police. Sometimes citizens are the clients, for example, when you register a complaint about noise or are the victim of a crime. Sometimes you're an eye witness. Other times, citizens are the subject, for example, if you're suspected of a crime. The way you deal with the police is different, depending on what role you are playing. Different concerns and caveats come into play so your behavior may be quite different as well.

CITIZEN AS CLIENT, VICTIM OR EYE WITNESS

If You Have a Complaint to Register

If your neighbors are having a wild noisy party late at night or you see someone suspicious, it's simple. You just call your local police department and they'll dispatch an officer to check things out. But other kinds of complaints can be trickier. If you suspect your neighbor is abusing his kids, you see someone suspicious in the neighborhood, or you're witness to a crime, you may have to deal with the police more extensively than through a mere phone call. This interaction may not be as simple as you think.

If You Are Interviewed by the Police

If you are an eye witness to an auto accident or a crime, the police may want to talk to you. Under these conditions, you may not find the police too intimidating. Nonetheless, it's important to remain calm. Eye witness reports can be unreliable so it's crucial that you think through the questions they ask carefully.[4] They need for you to tell them what you saw as unemotionally and objectively as possible. Be succinct and to the point. Don't jabber on about irrelevant side issues. Just answer what they ask as calmly as possible.

If you are unsure about the events when the police first talk to you, ask for more time. "Individuals who are unprepared to talk about certain events," write Bergman and Bergman-Barrett in the *Criminal Law Handbook*, "may become confused and answer incorrectly, especially when confronted by police officers."[5] If you later want to change your story, it may be met with suspicion or used against you, if a crime has been committed. Which brings us to ... how to talk to the police, and when *not* to talk to the police, if you are under suspicion.

CITIZEN AS SUSPECT OR "PERSON OF INTEREST"

If You Are Confronted by the Police

You may find yourself in the position of being questioned or stopped by a police officer some day. If you are questioned by the police, knowing how to interact appropriately and effectively with them will be useful, perhaps even crucial, to keeping you out of trouble.

When they question people, police officers sometimes get two opposing reactions: polite, perhaps fearful acquiescence or surly defiance. Neither is optimal, to say the least. Whether you are pulled over for speeding or being interviewed about a crime, you need to be calm but alert, polite but not obeisant. Being surly and defiant is, need I say, really unwise with people who have guns and can arrest you if you give them a hard time. But being too acquiescent may hurt you too.

Sometimes the police try to deliberately rattle people into

confessing to some crime they imagine the person has committed. If you are innocent, stay calm and keep your wits about you. And whatever you do, don't talk too much! Sandra had rented a car because she was visiting from another state. Because the rented car was different from her own, she had turned on the knob for the headlights only to the parking light position, without realizing that it took one more turn for the correct driving position. Because she was driving along a well-lit boulevard, she didn't notice the difference. But it was late at night in an upper-middle class neighborhood. The police pulled her over because driving with only parking lights looked suspicious to them. The two officers questioned her in a very intimidating manner, demanding to know where she was going and asking for the address. Sandra, recognizing what they were doing, did not allow herself to be rattled. She calmly explained that she was from out of state and produced the rental car papers.

But Sandra took it a step further. Putting on her most innocent manner, Sandra expressed surprise that her headlights weren't on (true enough) and told them that her own car was a Volkswagen (also true) that had headlights that turned on in a different way. Nothing she said was untrue but her "flustered female" guise added to her credibility in this situation. The police had to let her go. I don't recommend that you play games with the police—way too risky—but being too nervous and scared keeps you from presenting yourself in the best light and being surly is just plain dumb. Instead, be calm and alert and don't let yourself get flustered (unless you want to look that way . . .).

If you are being questioned by the police about a crime, pay attention to the kinds of questions they are asking you. It's one thing if they are asking you details about a crime you have witnessed, another if they are asking you questions that imply you might be a suspect. Do not be naïve and assume that because you are innocent, you are not a suspect. Don't assume that they will even *tell* you if you are a suspect. The police are *supposed* to tell you but that doesn't mean they always *will*.[6] If you think it's possible that you are being treated like a suspect, cooperate only to the minimum and call an attorney without further delay! You know you are innocent but they don't. They may try to wring as much information out of you as they can before they tell you that you are a suspect or worse yet, arrest you. Don't be naïve; innocent people get arrested all the time.

Dr. Elizabeth Loftus, an award-winning research forensic psychologist and the leading expert on eyewitness testimony, tells a chilling story in her book, *Witness for the Defense,* about an innocent man who was questioned and ultimately arrested because he vaguely fit the description of the killer the police were looking for.[7] Steve Titus knew he was innocent and since the police never told him he was a suspect, he babbled on. Though everything he told them was the truth, they were still able to use what he said against him. In this case, because of faulty eyewitness testimony (a whole story in itself), he was actually convicted of a crime he did not commit. It took two years to clear his name. If you think this is a weird fluke, you may want to read Dr. Loftus's book. She has many other scary stories like this and so do other forensic writers. Don't think it couldn't happen to you.

If you are being questioned by the police in a way that might suggest that you are a suspect, shut up. Demand that they tell you whether you are a suspect. If they weasel or do anything besides say no, absolutely not, tell them you have nothing more to say without your attorney present. "Prosecutors can be counted on to use your words against you," write Attorneys Bergman and Bergman-Barrett in their *Criminal Law Handbook.* "Even a seemingly innocuous explanation may appear to link you to a crime when your words are recounted by a police officer."[8] You are not legally obligated to answer police questions, no matter what they claim. You have the right to refuse to answer. Don't let them intimidate you into believing otherwise. Instead, remind them that you have a right to have an attorney present and then call one immediately! If they try to tell you that you don't need an attorney unless you are arrested, don't believe them. Sometimes the police deliberately wait to officially arrest someone because people are less likely to call an attorney if they have not been read their Miranda rights.[9] The police may then try to pump people for information before an attorney shows up. And contrary to what you may imagine from watching TV, the police are not obligated to read a "Miranda warning" unless you are in custody and they intend to officially interrogate you.[10]

If you are poor and can't afford a lawyer, don't assume that a public defender is at your deposal when you are questioned. You are not entitled to a public defender until you are actually arrested.[11] If the police insist on interrogating you before they arrest you (this is common), don't cooperate. Just keep insisting that you have nothing to say without a lawyer present. The police will either let you go or arrest you. The latter is not so good but at least you'll get a lawyer. But let me warn you, getting a public defender is a roll of the dice. Maybe you'll get a decent one but most are underpaid and overworked and some are incompetent or inexperienced.[12] Only the District Attorney's Office has all the resources of the State to draw on, not the Public Defender's Office. (See Chapter Five for more information on dealing with lawyers.)

The rules for what you *are* obligated to tell a police officer who wants to question you are complex and vary from state to state. I am not an attorney so I can't give you definitive answers, only broad guidelines. According to Bergman and Bergman-Barrett, a police officer can ask you questions even if you have done nothing wrong. You are, however, not generally obligated to answer or to allow a search. Even if you are pulled over for drunk driving, you have a right to refuse to answer questions, though you must submit to a sobriety test if the officer requests it.[13] On the other hand, if the officer asks for identification, it's probably a bad idea to refuse. Don't walk away from an officer without asking whether he or she intends to arrest or detain you. If the officer says that you are not free to leave, then don't!

However, be aware that the police may treat your refusal to answer questions with suspicion and even hostility. It's often OK to answer very straightforward questions that will immediately provide you with an alibi or otherwise remove you from suspicion. If you are too forceful in standing up for your rights, say Bergman and Bergman-Barrett, you run the risk of "contempt of cop." You don't want to be roughed up or arrested for resisting arrest. If you are careful about what you say, at least in response to straightforward questions, it may be OK to talk to the police. You have to make a judgment call.

If you are under suspicion for a crime and the police ask you to submit to a so-called "lie detector" or polygraph test, don't assume that because you are innocent that you will pass the test. If you are nervous or easily flustered, you could fail the test. The polygraph doesn't measure "lies," it only measures anxiety and emotional response.[14] Many innocent people fail the polygraph test because they are understandably upset about being questioned for a crime they did not commit. In fact, in a series of three studies, researchers found that the rate of "false positives" (falsely labeling innocent people as liars) was 45%![15] It could be you. So before you agree to a lie detector test, you'd better either be the calmest, most unruffled person you know or have your attorney present. Of course, if you have an attorney present, he or she is likely to tell you not to take the test in the first place!

In his book, *Tremor in the Blood,* psychologist Dr. David Lyyken, an expert on research about polygraphs, tells many chilling stories about innocent people who failed lie detectors tests. One such example is the sad story of Floyd Fay, an innocent man arrested on a charge of aggravated murder. Though he failed two polygraph tests, his attorney never offered any evidence to refute the validity of such tests. Fay was convicted and sentenced to life in prison. In prison, Fay had the good sense and good fortune to hire a public defender who not only engaged Dr. Lyyken as an expert witness on the unreliability of polygraphs, but also managed to find and extract a confession from the real culprit. But, by this time, poor Fay had wasted two years of his life in prison.[16] Lyyken has many more such stories in his book. Please believe me, it happens a lot.

Dr. Lykken also has a chapter on "How to Beat the Lie Detector." Detailing this method goes beyond what I think is appropriate for this book nor would it be appropriate for me to advocate doing so. However, if you are ever in a position where you are forced to take such a test, you may want to be aware that such information exists. You can also find videos on YouTube that discuss these methods. The best video on the topic was done by professional skeptic and author Michael Shermer.[17] He demonstrates how unreliable the polygraph is by actually being tutored in a technique for beating it, then letting himself be tested. He passed even when he was lying. I use this video when I lecture about polygraph tests in my Forensic Psychology class. It's a real eye-opener.

If you are actually arrested for a crime, obviously the first step is to obtain an attorney. You can learn more about your rights and what to do at each step by reading the *Criminal Law Handbook* by Attorneys Paul Bergman and Sara J. Berman-Barrett. It's complicated so you need to read the experts in this area. Reading their book will also help you evaluate how well your attorney is serving your interests.

However, be aware that even with the Miranda warning, many arrestees ignore the warning and talk to the police anyway.[18] I know that may seem odd to you but it really does happen. It might be helpful to understand the reasons why this can happen so if you're ever in this situation, you'll feel less pressured to talk. Once a suspect is in police custody, it's easy to feel vulnerable and out of control. The police take advantage of this psychological unease. Many suspects feel intimidated and talk in order to please the jailers. Police often use the "good cop-bad cop" routine to get the suspect to talk to the cop they think is on their side. But never forget that cops are on the cops' side, not yours. Even if the police promise leniency if the suspect talks, say Bergman and Bergman-Barrett, they may deny it later and the judge will believe them over the suspect in a heart beat.[19] You may find this hard to believe but police pressure can be so great that a few people even confess to crimes they have not committed.[20] The bottom-line: don't talk to the police once you are in custody unless your attorney is present, period. Don't give in to the pressure; they can and will twist your words!

In summary, my advice for dealing with the police: if you are a witness to a crime or have a complaint to report, be calm and to the point, don't rattle on and on. If you are questioned by the police, be calm, don't talk too much, don't submit to lie detector tests, and you just might want to keep your attorney's number on speed dial on your cell phone!

FIGHTING SPEEDING AND PARKING TICKETS

Not only can you fight City Hall, you can fight speeding and parking tickets too. Will you always win? No. Will you win sometimes? Yes, if you follow the techniques below.

The Internet teems with ads for books on fighting tickets but the most reliable ones come from Nolo Press. It has two books: *Fight Your Ticket and Win in California* and *Beat Your Ticket: Go to Court and Win* (for everywhere else), both by Attorney David W. Brown. Other books and web sites with information are listed below.

Your right to protest

First of all, decide whether you have a chance to beat the ticket. If you do, go for it. For starters, getting a ticket doesn't necessarily mean you're guilty. Brown points out, for example, that situations in which red-light runners are caught on camera are problematic.[21] Nearly 30% are so blurred that they are unusable in court. Nevertheless, in San Francisco and Los Angeles, for example, every car is photographed and the registered owner gets a ticket, period. The person getting the ticket has to prove the evidence is unreliable. Guilty till proven innocent. Mariette knows this first hand. After a visit to LA, she received a red-light violation. She knew she didn't do it so she read the ticket carefully. The violation had occurred three hours *after* she had turned in the rental car. The rental car agency had screwed up. So she made the agency send her a fax with the time the car had been turned in and printed out a similar receipt from the company's web site as well. She sent a letter and copies of the two receipts, return receipt requested, to the appropriate place for claiming that she was not the driver. Mariette was told she was off the hook and the Red Light Enforcement Bureau (RLEB) would go back to the rental agency for more correct information. Unfortunately, however, she never received the written confirmation she was promised. Instead she received an unpleasant letter from Superior Court claiming she had not paid her ticket, and, eventually, a nasty letter from a collection agency. It took a phone call from her attorney to the rental company and a letter to the LAPD RLEB to get the matter settled.

There may be mitigating circumstances. While visiting his accountant in an unfamiliar city, Dean got a parking ticket because he failed to see a sign that said one hour parking only. Because it was down the street from the parking slot and not easily visible, he thought the ticket was unfair. But he didn't have a camera with him and ended up not having time to go back and take a photograph. The judge told him that if he had the photo, the ticket might have been dismissed. Be alert for such circumstances and be prepared to provide supporting evidence. A cell phone with a camera would be a real plus in such situations.

In about a third of the states, speed laws may not be absolute. That means, says Brown, that if you were driving just a little above the speed limit and can convince the judge that you were driving safely, the ticket might get dismissed.[22] Or if you are given a ticket for an "unsafe lane change," you might be able to show that you changed with reasonable safety. If no accident was involved, you have a chance.

If, however, you are accused of a felony violation such as drunk driving or hit-and-run, get a lawyer. The consequences of getting convicted are way too serious to fool around arguing with the judge.

When the officer stops you

Everyone who writes on this topic says the same thing. Don't lose your cool. Don't yell or rant. Don't cry or get hysterical. Above all, don't try to bribe the officer. Don't accuse him or her of being prejudiced against you because you are black, old, young or whatever. This will just ensure that the officer will write the ticket to prove that he gives out tickets to everyone equally, says Attorney Mel Leiding, author of *How to Fight Your Traffic Ticket and Win!!!*[23] Don't appear to suck up to him either by excessive use of the term "sir." Having a good attitude toward the officer is crucial, Leiding adds, just don't overdo it. If you are surly, you increase your chances of getting a ticket rather than just a warning. If there were several possible violations, you'll be sure to get a ticket for all of them if you mouth off. If you are nice, maybe you'll be lucky and only get a ticket for speeding.

It's important not to admit to anything, says Leiding. Let the officer start the conversation. If she asks you a tricky question, such as "Do you know why I stopped you?" don't say yes and don't say no. Be vague and noncommittal, e.g., "I'm not really sure." If the officer says "Do you know how fast you were going?" say "I believe I was doing the speed limit. " That can mean– what was safe for the conditions. *Don't* say that you didn't know what speed you were going. That'll look bad. Of course, if you were going 100 miles per hour, this won't work. Just take your lumps because you probably didn't have any business going that fast anyway (unless there was a medical emergency and no ambulance—but you better be able to prove it!) Bottom line: You don't have to answer the officer's questions about the facts surrounding the supposed violation, says Leiding. Better to be vague, stupid or noncommittal than admit guilt to an officer who is taking notes for use in court.

If you are pleasant to the officer, without ranting or whining, you may be able to ask for a warning instead of a ticket (well, not for going 100 miles an hour . . .). Leiding suggests saying something like "You're probably right, Officer, but I'm usually a safe driver and would like to keep my record clean." If your record is *not* clean, don't say this because he'll check and then you're really in trouble for lying.

Gather information

The first step is to read the wording of the exact law you are breaking. Look for the number on your ticket that corresponds to the law (often called "statute" or "vehicle code section"). Now go to the Internet or to your local library. You can do a search on the Internet using your state name and the name and/or number in quotes from the ticket. The librarian can help you research your state vehicle code. Just be sure that it is up-to-date. Once you find the law, study it carefully to see what the prosecution has to prove to convict you. Many laws are so convoluted that you may find, upon examination, that what you did was not, technically speaking, a violation. Derrick learned this while attending college in New York City. As many students do, he had a local job. But the cop on the beat noticed that he had California plates on his car and gave him two tickets—allegedly for having improper registration and insurance. The cop didn't know—and probably didn't care—that Derrick was a student; he thought Derrick was scamming. Fortunately for Derrick, this cop's partner was a nice guy and told Derrick to take the tickets to the Clerk of the Court and check out the wording of the law. Turns out the tickets were technically for not having *any* registration or insurance. But Derrick's car was properly registered and insured in California, which he was readily able to demonstrate. For good measure, he brought along an affidavit proving that he voted in California too. The Clerk of the Court dismissed the two tickets before Derrick even got to court.

Once you have found the exact wording, break it down into its component parts. The law requires that the state prove that you violated *every* part or clause. One example Brown uses is a U-turn violation.[24] So, for example, if the law states that the U-turn is in a "residence district," you can challenge it if the location is not in fact a residence area. Other possible challenges—the car approaching was more than the required distance away (e.g., 200 feet) or that an "official traffic-control device" was present at the intersection. Being a literalist pays in court; it's what the lawyers do.

Gather evidence at the scene. If appropriate, photograph the scene to support your case that the code does not apply in your case (e.g., a traffic light is present) or that mitigating circumstances were present (e.g., obscured parking signs, good weather that creates safer driving conditions). If you're not sure what's relevant at the time of the ticket, take pictures anyway if you can—a good reason to have a camera in your cell phone or to carry a cheap digital camera in the car. If you are involved in an accident, even more reason to have a camera to provide evidence. Other evidence could include witnesses or a diagram of the intersection.

If your case is complex or not clear-cut, the next step is to research previous case decisions. Judges put weight on precedent. You'll need to find law books that are annotated with case decisions. They can be found in law libraries, many court houses, and some public libraries. If you pursue this route, one of the Nolo books listed below may be of great help.

Go to court

If you decide the situation or the law is sufficiently ambiguous that you have a chance to win, then, by all means, go to court. First off, if the officer who gave you the ticket is a no-show, you win in most states. But don't count on it, says Brown. Maybe he'll be on vacation but the cop usually shows up. So be ready with your evidence and argument.

Here are some methods that Brown suggests, depending on your case.[25]

- *Prove a necessary element of your ticket is missing*
  As with the example above, if you find any element or part of the code is missing from your situation, your ticket should be dismissed
- *Challenge the officer's subjective conclusion*
  If no accident occurred, you may have a shot at this defense. For example, if the officer was not in a good location to view traffic or, in the states that are flexible about the speed limit, that what you did was safe under the circumstances. Here's where taking photos of the scene may help you.

- *Challenge the officer's observation of what happened*
  In a dispute between what the officer claims happened and your version, guess who the judge is likely to believe. Right. So have evidence to back you up. This can include statements of witnesses or a clear, easy-to-understand diagram that shows where your vehicle and the officer's vehicle were in relation to other traffic and locations (especially if the alleged violation was in an intersection). Photos of the location are especially useful if there are factors present that may have obscured the officer's vision.
- *Prove your conduct was based on a legitimate "mistake of fact"*
  This refers to circumstances beyond your control that prevented you from being aware that you were violating the code. For example, Dean's failure to see a parking sign that was many feet from his car in a neighborhood he was not familiar with. Photos will help here.
- *Prove your conduct was "legally justified"*
  Depending on the circumstances, you may be able to argue that what you did was justifiable and reasonable. For example, a hornet flew into your vehicle and caused you to make a lane change without signaling, or you had chest pains and were racing to your doctor's office. Best to be able to prove it, of course . . .
- *Prove your conduct was necessary to avoid serious harm*
  Emergencies not of the driver's making are recognized in all 50 states. If, for example, you can argue that your action was necessary to avoid a serious accident, the judge may dismiss the ticket.

Here's what *doesn't* work, according to Brown: arguing that the violation didn't hurt anyone, claiming the officer was picking on you, or sobbing that your [mother, spouse, child] was ill.[26] Ignorance of the law won't help you either; however, in a few circumstances, it may help mitigate the fine. Derrick also got a ticket for having a bumper sticker in his back window (the officer *really* didn't like young people, according to the guy's partner). In California, this was not a violation but in New York it was. The judge was obligated to say that ignorance of the law is not a legitimate excuse, but only fined Derrick $5. The $5 fine was worth it, says Derrick, to see the disappointed look on the cop's face when he got off with a mere $5 fine and two dismissed tickets.

The above should be enough to help you decide whether you can fight your ticket or not. There's much more that could be useful to know if you do want to contest it, but that's beyond the scope of this book. Brown's book, for example, gives you sample questions to use to cross-examine the officer who gave you the ticket, how to draw useful diagrams, when to get a lawyer, and URLs for finding the state vehicles codes of all 50 states and the District of Columbia.

Conclusion

If you have a community issue, don't fall into a pit of despair and helplessness and assume "you can't fight City Hall." Fighting City Hall isn't easy; it takes hard work and persistence, but it *can* be done. You won't always win but, if the stakes are important enough, it's worth trying. If you are innocent and are interrogated by the police, know your rights and insist on them so you don't fall victim to the possible abuses of the legal system. Standing up to legal authority is never easy but if you don't stand up for yourself, who will?

RESOURCES

BOOKS

Bureaucracies

Russell L. Ackoff and Sheldon Rovin. *Beating the System: Using Creativity to Outsmart the Bureaucracy.* San Francisco: Berrett-Koehler, 2005. Though this is aimed mainly at corporate bureaucracies and institutions, it provides many creative suggestions for dealing with the bureaucratic mind. Highly recommended.

Neighborhood Organizing and Improvement

Michael Greenberg. *Restoring America's Neighborhoods: How Local People Make a Difference.* New Brunswick, NJ: 1999. Interviews with community leaders who have successfully dealt with problems such as arson, violence, neglected neighborhoods, and other serious community problems.

Michael Levine. *Fight Back: How to Take Back Your Neighborhood, Schools, and Families from the Drug Dealers.* New York: Dell, 1991. Unfortunately, many urban areas need this kind of advice.

Stephanie Mann and M.C. Blakeman. *Safe Homes, Safe Neighborhoods: Stopping Crime Where You Live.* Berkeley, CA: Nolo Press, 1993. A practical guide to effectively working with the police to decrease crime.

Peggy Robin. *Saving the Neighborhood: You Can Fight Developers and Win.* Rockville, MD: 1990. Lots of practical information on community organizing, with a variety of different cases from saving old buildings to saving the suburbs. Though the resource guide in the back is out-of-date, it can give you a place to start looking for additional resources.

Police and the Legal System

Attorneys Paul Bergman and Sara J. Bergman-Barrett. *Criminal Law Handbook: Know Your Rights: Survive the System.* Berkeley, CA: Nolo Press, 2007.

Attorney David W. Brown. *Beat Your Ticket: Go to Court & Win.* Berkeley, CA: Nolo Press, 2005. Extremely thorough and reliable advice from the premiere source for legal self-help.

Attorney David W. Brown. *Fight Your Ticket & Win in California.* Berkeley, CA: Nolo Press, 2007.

Attorney Mel Leiding. *How to Fight Your Traffic Ticket and Win!!!* Anaheim, CA: Avenir International Publishing, 2006. A quick summary of advice that is a bit pricey for this slim volume compared to what you get from Nolo (and the poor grammar is a real turnoff). However, he does have very good advice about what to do and say when the officer stops you that is not present in the Nolo books.

Dr. Elizabeth Loftus and Katherine Ketcham. *Witness for the Defense: The Accused, the Eyewitness and the Expert Who Puts Memory on Trail.* New York: St. Martin's Press, 1991. An easy-to-read account of Loftus's experiences as an expert witness, with chilling stories that will change how you think about eyewitness testimony.

David Lyyken. *A Tremor in the Blood.* New York: Basic Books, 1998. Detailed research about the unreliability of polygraphs and voice-stress analyzers by one of the most prominent researchers on this topic.

WEB SITES

Community Groups

City of Tallahassee
www.talgov.com/dncs/neighborhood/h2guide2.cfm
A detailed guide to forming and maintaining a neighborhood group.

Northside Planning Council
www.northsideplanningcouncil.org/groups/howto.pdf
An even more detailed PDF on how to organize a neighborhood group is available at this site.

Crime Prevention

City of Mobile Community Services Division
www.cityofmobile.org/mobilepd/html/divisions/enp.html
One example of a police effort to reach out to the community to prevent and fight crime. "The goal" says the web site is "to address problems in our neighborhoods before they generate crime and disorder. We do it

through alliances with neighborhood groups, crime prevention programs and youth programs."

Fighting Traffic Tickets

There are dozens of sites on the Internet telling you how to beat traffic tickets. Here are a few of the better ones.

The following four sites are recommended by Attorney David W. Brown, author of the two Nolo books on fighting traffic tickets.
www.motorists.org
www.mrtraffic.com
www.speedtrap.org
www.radartest.com

Also helpful:
"How to Fight a Traffic Ticket"
www.wikihow.com/Fight-a-Traffic-Ticket

"How to Fight Your Traffic Ticket and Win"
www.beattraffictickets.com
Advice from Attorney Mel Leiding about what to say if you are stopped for speeding and what to do to beat the ticket.

Faulty Eyewitness Memory

"Make-Believe Memories"
faculty.washington.edu/eloftus/Articles/
AmerPsychAward+ArticlePDF03%20(2).pdf
An article by Elizabeth Loftus on the dangers and distortions of false memories.

"Interview with Elizabeth Loftus"
www.pbs.org/wgbh/pages/frontline/shows/dna/interviews/loftus.html
PBS interview with Loftus, in conjunction with its program "What Jennifer Saw," a dramatic example of the dire consequences of faulty memory.

"Interview with Elizabeth Loftus"
www.injusticebusters.com/04/Loftus_Elizabeth.shtml

"Remembering Dangerously"
www.csicop.org/si/9503/memory.html
An article by Loftus on the dangers of repressed memory syndrome, a diagnosis that has been much abused in legal cases.

The Dangers of Polygraphs (So-Called "Lie Detectors")

"Polygraph"
en.wikipedia.org/wiki/Polygraph
Wikipedia article on the history and legal history of the polygraph.

"Lies, Damned Lies and Polygraphs"
www.salon.com/april97/news/news2970410.html
A short summary of some of the problems with polygraphs.

"The Truth About Lie Detectors, Says David Lykken, Is That They Can't Detect a Lie"
www.people.com/people/archive/article/0,,20079233,00.html

Polygraph (lie detector)
www.skepdic.com/polygrap.html
Description of research about the polygraph.

Michael Shermer Tests the Polygraph Part 1
www.youtube.com/watch?v=GLL3wtgBiFA
This YouTube video (plus the second part) shows how the polygraph works and how it can be beaten. Professional skeptic and author Shermer learns how to lie and still pass the test. A good reason to be skeptical of, as well as cautious about, polygraph testing.

UPDATES

For updates on books, web sites, web site URLs and links (they sometimes change), articles and other relevant information, check the web site for my book: www.standuptoauthorities.com. Or you can use the titles or words in the references as search terms to do your own Internet update search.

PART
IV

What's Next?

CHAPTER
10

Won't Get Fooled Again: Wrapping It Up and Taking It with You

> *Then I'll get on my knees and pray*
> *We don't get fooled again*
> *Don't get fooled again*
> *No, no!*
> —The Who from "Won't Get Fooled Again"[1]

NOW THAT YOU'VE READ this book, you're better armed against bamboozling, manipulating, abusive, arrogant, or just plain incompetent experts and authorities. You have tools for questioning, techniques for confronting, and encouragement to stand up to them. Is that it? Do you have it down pat now? Or will you "get fooled again?" Learning how to stand up to experts and authorities, like any other skill, is not merely an end product, it's an ongoing process. You have to continue to be alert and on your guard and to practice your skills. The techniques in this book don't necessarily come automatically, even after you learn them. You have to hone them, practice them, and continue to sharpen your critical thinking about the messages of experts and authorities.

Some of you may already be practiced in assertiveness and standing up for yourself and just needed a few tips in areas you hadn't thought about before. You bought this book for those tips. Maybe you won't need all of the suggestions below. Maybe you already have the right mindset. That's good. But frankly, many of you may find the advice below helpful. I have to remind myself to follow my own advice from time to time. Perhaps you will too. I'm also willing to bet that a few of the books in the Reference section below could give you something new to think about. On the other hand, if you're *not* practiced in assertiveness, the suggestions below may really help you. I certainly hope they will.

THE RIGHT MINDSET

If you don't want to be fooled again, you do need the right mindset. That means being alert to the "seduction of the situation." Pay attention to your surroundings and what other people are doing. Think about how the social situation may be affecting you. Are you just going along with the authority? Allowing experts to pressure you? "Be mindful" of your social situation, as Buddhist monks suggest.[2] Don't just go around in a fog.

Having the right mindset means:

- always be willing to use your critical faculties. Listen careful to what the experts are saying and watch for manipulative techniques or emotional appeals. Don't just accept what they hand you—ever. Give it some thought. Look for flaws in their thinking; think of alternative possibilities.
- have the courage to stand up for your rights. If you are being taken advantage of, why should you allow it? Always demand your rights—unless doing so would make things worse. (You don't have to be a martyr.) But remember that if you act like a victim, you're likely to become one.
- feel good about yourself and have confidence in your ability to make good decisions. Everyone can learn to make good decisions. Don't sell yourself short.

If you make yourself less vulnerable to influence, it will help you have more confidence. You'll feel better about your ability to stand up for yourself. You'll feel more encouraged to buck authority and question experts. If you have trouble feeling this kind of confidence, some of the suggestions below may help you.

Positive Things You Can Do to Be Less Vulnerable to Influence by Experts and Authorities

CULTIVATE A SENSE OF SELF-WORTH AND BUILD POSITIVE ATTITUDES ABOUT YOURSELF

Many of you don't need this reminder. If so, you can skip this section. But if you sometimes doubt yourself or ever feel that you are a "dummy," here's some suggestions for you.

Keep in mind your special talents, the times when others thought you were special. Nourish a secret "inner core" of self that can't be violated. If you feel good about yourself, you won't be as vulnerable to manipulation and emotional appeals by others.

Because of a bad divorce, Jeanette's self-esteem was at an all-time low. Her husband had left her for another woman and she had no marketable skills. Jeanette's friend Mandy reminded her that she had raised two decent children who had never had drug problems or brushes with the law. Any mother would love to have children like hers. Keeping this in mind helped raise Jeanette's self-esteem and self-worth. She also felt better able to stand up for herself in other situations.

Think of all the times that you were right about an important issue. We've all been wrong sometimes and we've all been right sometimes. Think of the good things you've been able to accomplish. Keep a balanced perspective and don't sell yourself or your abilities short.

If you do have continuing self-esteem issues, there's some excellent books that may help. Dr. Nathaniel Branden is a psychotherapist who is *the* expert on the psychology of self-esteem and has written many books on this topic. Two that might be helpful to you are *The Six Pillars of Self-Esteem* and *Honoring the Self: Self-Esteem and Personal Transformation.* Neither is one of the many superficial, simplistic books of rah-rah affirmations of dubious value. Dr. Branden not only discusses why self-esteem is crucial to healthy psychological functioning, he gives practical steps on how to increase your self-esteem. For more information about these two books and others he has written, see Dr. Branden's web site (www.nathanielbranden.com) or read the reviews on Amazon.com. I have listed several more by Dr. Branden, as well as other books about building self-esteem in the Resources section below.

Another approach to building your feelings of self-worth and defeating negative attitudes about yourself is though a relatively new area called "positive psychology."[3] As the name implies, it emphasizes the positive aspects of human behavior rather than the negative behaviors, such as aggression, that earlier psychology was so obsessed with. Psychologist Dr. Martin Seligman, who is one of the leading researchers in this new area has written a highly recommended book titled *Authentic Happiness: Using the New Positive Psychology to Realize Your Potential for Lasting Fulfillment.* Check out the reviews on Amazon.com and see if this sounds like a useful book for you.[4] He also wrote *Learned Optimism*, another excellent book that can show you how to approach life with attitudes that will contribute to your health and happiness. Realistic optimism, the research shows, is linked with better health, greater achievement, and generally better outcomes.[5]

One way to assess your character strengths (and nearly everyone has some!) is to take the Values in Action Signature Strengths survey at the Values In Action web site listed in the Resources section below. Creativity, zest and enthusiasm, self-control, humor, honesty, love of learning, and bravery are only some of the character traits measured. If you are down on yourself, you may find that you have more strengths than you realize. The web site also has many other tests that you may find interesting or helpful. Since the web site was partly developed by Dr. Seligman, it has good credentials.

BUILD YOUR SELF-CONFIDENCE

If you lack self-confidence or have excessively negative attitudes, fears or anxieties that make you vulnerable to pressures from authority or make you doubt your ability to make independent judgments, seek professional counseling or at least seek advice from an appropriate book. Books based on cognitive therapy usually offer sensible and effective techniques that can help you change negative beliefs that make you doubt your own abilities. There are many good ones available but therapists especially recommend the books by David Burns, M.D. See the Reference section below for titles by Dr. Burns, as well as other suggestions.

Self-efficacy (a person's belief in his or her ability to succeed in a particular situation) is an essential ingredient in self-confidence. The most effective way to develop self-efficacy, says psychologist Dr. Albert Bandura, the leading researcher on this topic, is through "mastery experiences."[6] Performing a task successfully strengthens our feelings of self-efficacy. Other experts, such as Dr. Branden, agree. Develop a skill that you can succeed at. If you already have a skill, keep that in mind when you feel as if you can't do things right. Perhaps there was time when you were able to stand up to an authority figure. You lived through it, didn't you? Remember your successes, not your failures.

Then, suggests Dr. Bandura, think about a time when others praised your skill in a particular area. Or when others said something positive about you that helped you reach your goal. Build on that, instead of your self-doubts. Learn to cope with self-doubt by concentrating on what you do well, rather than what you imagine you're not good at.

Kendra is an example of this advice too. She once felt she had no skills and couldn't do anything. Then she learned to use a computer. When she first started, she had to ask her son to tell her how to turn on the computer. Now she is so skilled that she maintains a web site and does most of the graphics for it. This has enormously boosted her self-esteem and self-efficacy.

BUILD ASSERTIVENESS SKILLS

If you have trouble being assertive in the face of authority or are overly timid or passive, find an assertiveness training group, a counselor with a background in such training, or at least read a book on assertiveness training. In a nonthreatening situation, practice using the techniques you learn so you won't feel so awkward or timid when you really need to stand up for yourself.

Take a course

Local adult schools often have such classes or perhaps classes in confidence building. If you feel more confident, you'll be able to stand up for yourself better. In classes, you get to practice the techniques so they become more natural to you. Check around for what's available. Don't overlook martial arts training, such as aikido, as a way to build assertiveness. Part of the philosophy of many of these courses is confidence-building.

Read books

If you can't take a course on assertiveness training, the single best book to read is *Your Perfect Right: Assertiveness in Your Life and Relationships* by Robert Alberti and Michael Emmons. It has gradual, realistic step-by-step activities and exercises for learning assertiveness, better decision-making, and coping with fear and anxiety. Both professionals and laypeople familiar with this book praise it highly. Said one reviewer on Amazon: "This is a highly motivating guide for learning how to act in your own best interests without behaving in an obnoxious Me First manner."[7] I agree. This book is *not* about how to manipulate others, it's about how to stand up for *you*. The reviewer goes on to say: "It's about choosing how to respond, exercising personal rights without denying the rights of others, with the win-win result of making all your relationships more equal."

Practice

If you are not able to attend a class, find ways to practice being assertive. If it's hard for you, try it in baby steps, in a setting that's not too overwhelming. Then you can slowly build up by being more and more assertive in more intimidating situations, as your fear lessens. Psychologists call this technique "desensitization." *Your Perfect Right* will give you some exercises to try.

KNOW WHAT YOUR VALUES ARE

Know what your values are; develop and maintain a sense of commitment to principles that are important to you. If you recognize what your values are and why they are important to you, it will make you less likely to knuckle under to some authority who's trying to get you to do things that are not consistent with your values.

One way to think about your values is to look at the Values List at www.rit.org/valueslist.html. I've compiled a list, from many sources, of important values that people may hold, such as independence, family, freedom, honesty, creativity, happiness, self-esteem and justice, as well as many others. There's an exercise there to help you clarify what's important to you. If, for example, family is important to you, then doing anything that might harm your family is something you want to avoid. What if your son's teacher is urging you to allow the school to give your child Ritalin or Straterra (both are drugs for ADHD) and you're not sure. Your spouse is insistent too. But then you learn about the negative side effects. Recognizing that your son's health is more important to you than placating the teacher or your spouse will help you stand your ground.

Howard made that kind of decision. His son's psychiatrist had run through several different drugs over a period of four years and none of them helped. Howard wanted an alternative nondrug therapy but his soon-to-be ex-wife thought otherwise. They were locked in a bitter battle over their son's medication. The boy didn't want to continue them nor did the father but the mother insisted. Since his son's grades had actually worsened, not improved over time, even the child's teachers, guidance counselor, and psychologist all thought that it was time to come off the medication. Because of the divorce proceedings, the family was under a court order to continue the medication until a psychiatrist would prescribe another kind of treatment. Howard could have given up. But he valued his son's well-being too much. Instead he searched out information and actively fought the psychiatrist's diagnosis. He found a new, more open-minded psychiatrist who did not assume a drug-centric approach was necessary and was willing to work with him. The mother backed off when even the family pediatrician agreed it was time for the boy (who was now a teenager) to come off the drugs.

Or another example—your boss wants you to "fudge" a report. You value your family's well-being. At first you think—"I better do what he wants because I need my job. Where would my family be if I lost my job?" Then you reflect a little more. What would your family think of you for lying? Is that the role model you want to set for your children? How will being dishonest affect your self-esteem? You may decide it's not worth it to go along with the boss when you think of the long-term consequences to your values.

Another way to strengthen a commitment to your values is to join with others who share your values and who are willing to stand up for the values that are important to you. Find allies at work or school. Join an organization that supports your values. If there's a social or political issue that's important to you, get active. Join a group and work for social change. You'll get experience doing something meaningful to you, as well as building your confidence in your abilities. It'll make you less vulnerable to pressures from others.

Acting morally

I admit it. I am unabashedly in favor of acting morally. Not the go-to-church-(or other house of worship) on-Sunday, sin-on-Monday kind of morality. I hate hypocrites. Nor do I mean the fire and brimstone, telling other people how to live their lives—what they can "ingest, smoke, listen to, or sleep with" kind of morality. No one has a right to tell you how to live your life, as long as you aren't harming other people. I'm talking about living in accordance with what the Christian religion calls the "Golden Rule;" or what philosopher Immanuel Kant called the "categorical imperative." The Golden Rule suggests that you treat other people the way you want to be treated. You want to be treated with respect and fairness. So that's the way you should treat others too. Kant's advice is to ask yourself—if everybody acted the way you want to act, would the world be a good place to live? Would you want everyone else to act the same as you? If not, why do you think it's OK for you to break moral rules and not everyone else? French existentialist Albert Camus might have called it "bearing witness to the truth." Whatever your religion or lack thereof, do you want to be able to say "I did the right thing"? The most basic moral rule, no matter what your religion or philosophy, is not to harm innocent people.

But lots of people compartmentalize their values and morals, overlooking them when it becomes inconvenient. Philosophers and theologians alike will tell you that you pay a price for moral hypocrisy. So will psychologists. Going against your conscience will take its toll on you in the long run, making you feel bad about yourself, eroding your self-worth.

Unfortunately, many otherwise good people let their fears or their awe of authority overwhelm their conscience. This is understandable, if not admirable. But if you are one of the many people who do try to act morally yet find yourself caught up in fear, uncertainty, and pressure to act immorally, stop and think about the consequences. If you see something inappropriate, troubling or potentially harmful going on in your workplace, school, or other social situation, talk about it with someone outside that situation that you trust. Seek allies within the group. If you don't stand up, who else is going to? If something bad happens to others because you did nothing, how will you feel in the long run?

Suppose, for example, your friend at work is being sexually harassed by the boss. She asks you to help her. You know what the boss is doing is wrong but you're afraid that you'll get fired if you report what you've seen. But ask yourself—do you really want to work for such a sleazy boss? Is that the right way to treat your friend? What would you want your friend to do if you were the one in her situation? As I suggested above, you may pay a price later on. Maybe you'll lose a good friend. Probably you'll feel guilty. Look at the long-term picture, not just your short-term fear.

Darlene faced a complex moral dilemma. She attended a private Christian high school. Her religion taught that homosexuality was wrong and she agreed. But the other kids were bullying a friend of hers without mercy after they found out that he was gay. She didn't want to be ostracized for standing up for him, but she didn't like the way they were treating him either. Even though she disapproved of her friend's homosexuality, she knew that the New Testament taught that Jesus said "Love your neighbor as yourself" and "He who is without sin among you cast the first stone." She couldn't reconcile those gentle teachings of Jesus with the cruel behavior of her classmates and finally took a courageous moral stand for her friend, if not his sexual orientation.

BUILD CRITICAL THINKING SKILLS

There are many reasonable definitions of "critical thinking" but I like the one offered by psychologists Carole Wade and Carol Tavris because it emphasizes the positive side to critical thinking. Too often people think that being critical means just tearing some argument down: "Critical thinking," they write, "is the ability and willingness to assess claims and make objective judgments on the basis of well-supported reasons. It is the ability to look for flaws in arguments and resist claims that have no supporting evidence. Critical thinking, however, is not merely negative thinking. It also fosters the ability to be creative and constructive—to generate possible explanations for findings, think of implications, and apply new knowledge to a broad range of social and personal problems. You can't really separate critical thinking from creative thinking, for it's only when you question what is that you can begin to imagine what can be."[8]

No one is a perfect critical thinker all the time. Not me. Not even authors of critical thinking books. Build your critical thinking skills. Practice analyzing and discussing arguments, looking at the pros and cons of important issues. Build creative arguments and counter-arguments for these issues. When talking with an expert—physician, contractor, educator or others—remember to ask questions and carefully evaluate what you see or hear. Take the time to get a second opinion.

Read books

There are many books that teach good critical thinking skills. If you're ambitious, there's several good textbooks that can help you. You don't need to read the whole book to learn new skills. Pick out the parts that interest you.

The text I use when I teach this class, *Critical Thinking* by Professors Brooke Noel Moore and Richard Parker, is written in an engaging, humorous style that's easy to read and understand. Pick out the chapters that appeal to you. Some are a bit technical but the ones on credibility, rhetorical devices (verbal techniques for fooling you), and causal explanations are especially useful. Any edition can help so you can get a copy cheap online.

Another engaging text I've found is *Think: Critical Thinking and Logic Skills for Everyday Life* by Judith Boss. It's jam-packed with useful, down-to-earth ideas. Topics include marketing and the mass media, how emotional appeals are used to trick you, why arguments persuade you, and much more. It's colorful and easy to read but quite substantial.

There are a growing number of excellent popular books that

have plenty of substance and useful information. First of all, there's a crop of books that ask you to examine your own thinking for faulty reasoning. Four that I can especially recommend are the following: *Don't Believe Everything You Think* by Thomas Kida; *Mistakes Were Made (but Not by Me): Why We Justify Foolish Beliefs, Bad Decisions, and Hurtful Act*s by Carol Tavris and Eliot Aronson; *How We Know What Isn't So: The Fallibility of Reasoning in Everyday Life* by Thomas Gilovich; and *What People Believe Weird Things: Pseudoscience, Superstition and Other Confusions of Our Time* by Michael Shermer. No one is immune from these kinds of cognitive fallacies. These books are likely to make you humble when you see all the ways that even smart people can be fooled by their own thinking. It's a good wakeup call and the ideas will help keep you on your mental toes.

Take a course

Maybe you're the type who benefits from a more rigorous application of text material. Merely reading a text may not be enough for you. Nearly every college campus has critical thinking classes. Most allow people to audit or take courses that don't count toward graduation so you don't have to be officially enrolled. My school, for example, has an "Open University" program for this purpose. But here's a tip—take the course in a psychology, sociology or English department, not philosophy. Philosophy courses in *anything* are way too hard for the average person and very abstract. Courses in other departments tend to be more practical and down-to-earth.

Practice

Practice evaluating evidence, opinions and advice. Don't swallow newspaper stories about controversial issues whole without exploring the alternative press. Look at different points of view regularly. Explore your own ideas. What basis do you have for them? Because your parents said so? Because that's what you've always believed? Not very critical. Evaluate these ideas, using critical thinking principles. Maybe you'll decide they do make sense; maybe you'll decide to do more thinking about them. Stretching your mind is always a useful exercise, no matter what you decide.

READ DIVERSE OPINIONS

If you don't want to be fooled by the media, politicians or other so-called experts, you need to read opinions and ideas from many different sources, not just the ones that make you comfortable. If you subscribe to or read news magazines, occasionally read some from viewpoints other than your own. Look at the sources I listed in the reference section of the media chapter. If there's an important issue that you need to make a decision on, whatever it may be, read more than one point of view. This will help you build your critical thinking skills.

Read different kinds of sources. Don't just read what you agree with. Be as well-informed about opinions you disagree with as your own. If you're a liberal, read a conservative point of view occasionally. If you are conservative, do the reverse. If you're a libertarian or progressive, you're not immune from this advice either. Analyze the pros and cons of different opinions. Be open to the possibility of changing your opinions. Have I already said no one is right all the time? Well, let me say it again. No one is right all the time. Not you. Not me. Not your favorite pundit or radio talk show host. Not anyone.

When watching TV news or reading a newspaper, remember to ask questions and be critical of what you see or hear. Read different kinds of sources. Be more aware of what the media selectively reports, distorts, and leaves out. Remember that the media don't represent "the truth," only certain perspectives.

When Standing Up to Experts or Obeying Authority Is *Not* a Good Idea

"I fought the law and the law won . . ."
—Old pop song by the Bobby Fuller Four[9]

I've spent nine chapters advising you how to stand up to experts and authorities. Now I'm going to talk about when *not* to stand up. The idea that you should resist all the time is as foolish as the idea that you should never resist. Sometimes it's in your best interests to accept the opinion of the experts or to obey the authorities—unless you want to be a martyr or a fool.

WHEN THE EXPERT OR AUTHORITY IS RIGHT AND YOU ARE WRONG

Most people hate to admit they are wrong. Some steadfastly refuse to change their minds even when they are shown proof that they have made a mistake. Their own emotions and wishes may be more important to them than the truth. Others may pigheadedly insist on their own way even if they know they are wrong. But, for many people, the process is more subtle. Psychologists know there are lots of reasons that people do or believe dumb things, not because they are necessarily pigheaded but because they make mistakes in thinking. I have already suggested some books that deal with errors in critical thinking, cognitive processing, and other errors in reasoning. A list of recommended readings on this topic is below. Being willing to admit you are wrong doesn't make you less of a person, it makes you someone with integrity.

Experts

Let's say that you have a different opinion than the expert. First, follow the suggestions I've made elsewhere in this book for arriving at reasonable answers. Gather evidence from several sources, including reputable books and Internet sites. Get a second opinion from another reputable professional. Look at the actual evidence—not just at what you *want* it to be but what it really *is*. Don't let wishful thinking or your ego get in the way of coming to a rational decision.

Suppose that your physician has suggested that you stop smoking or get more exercise. It's clear in this example that the advice is reasonable. If you poo-poo the idea because you don't like it, you are going against a mountain of evidence that smoking is bad for you and exercise is good. It's your right to do so but don't kid yourself about the wisdom of the suggestion. But if the advice of your physician is less obvious, it may be tempting to dismiss it as unnecessary. Timothy's physician suggested to him that he should have a test for sleep apnea. Not quite in the same clear-cut league as smoking—so Timothy ignored it for a long time. In this case, Timothy simply didn't like the idea of having to use a breathing mask (a standard treatment for sleep apnea) so he made up excuses for why he couldn't wear a mask even if he did have this problem. The excuses were all bogus. He let his own imagined fear cloud his judgment. Sleep apnea is a serious disease that can shorten your life or even kill you. Wouldn't you rather wear a breathing mask at night than take the risk of dying? I know I would.

So before you reject your physician's advice, do your homework. Have a good reason to say no, not just your irrational fears. The same is true of any issue where your basis for rejecting the advice of authority is based more on emotion than reason. Talk your situation over with a trusted friend. If your friend tells you that you are being irrational, you might want to listen or at least give the advice some serious thought.

Another issue to watch out for is thinking that you know the solution to a problem, so you don't need an expert. Maybe. I've given lots of suggestions for "doing it yourself" and sometimes it's a good choice. But sometimes we think we know what we're doing and we don't! A recent issue of *Prevention* magazine, for example, discussed some examples of bad medical self-diagnosis.[10] A study done at a vaginal disease clinic found that nearly 75% of the women who came there for treatment for what they thought was a recurrent yeast infection actually had a different problem. Many of them simply had irritations from personal products, such as soap or menstrual pads. They had self-treated for years, suffering needlessly because they came to wrong conclusions. Another example that the *Prevention* article gave was people who mistakenly concluded that they had depression because they were lethargic and felt in a down mood. In fact, these are also symptoms of sleep apnea or hypothyroidism. When it comes to medical diagnoses, you're likely to be better off asking the experts first.

People often overestimate their own competence. A study done on "incompetence" found that the people who are the least skilled in an area (critical thinking, grammar, and humor were the ones tested) were the ones most likely to grossly overestimate their ability in that area.[11] They didn't know how much they didn't know! If you are not a medical doctor or a psychologist or a contractor or a lawyer, maybe you shouldn't be doing your own diagnosing or your own work. Be honest about your level of skills. Just because you are competent in one area doesn't mean you will be competent in all. Don't fall victim to the "incompetence" syndrome.

Many of my students (especially freshman), for example, often overestimate their own competence. They think just because they did well in high school without much effort that they get away with this in college. So they don't listen to me when I tell them that they really have to study hard for exams. Letting their eyes merely glaze over a few notes the night before the exam won't cut it. Only when the hard reality of a bad grade they get on the first exam confronts them, do they begin to get a glimmer that maybe I was right. They didn't realize how much they didn't understand. The wiser ones get the picture and come to my office hours and talk to me about how to study more effectively.

Two other "gotchas" that derail people into opposing experts are wishful thinking and false pride. In Chapter Seven, I gave the example of parents who didn't want to believe that their little Timmy was doing poorly in school. Critical thinking teachers call this rationalization; psychologists call it denial. If you stubbornly refuse to believe the teacher even when she or he has reasonable evidence, you do a disservice to your child. You don't help your child by being blind to his or her faults. It should be about your child, not your ego. The same goes for the wishful thinking that my freshman students engage in. They want to believe that somehow they will do OK on the exam by minimal studying (and partying instead), even though I tell them how hard they have to study. Don't reject information because you don't like it or because you're too proud to admit you're wrong.

Or maybe the mechanic says you need new brakes. You don't want to spend that kind of money right now so you try to rationalize your reluctance by wondering if the guy is just trying to con you. Try another mechanic or ask a trusted friend who knows something about cars. If the next mechanic or your friend say the same thing as the first mechanic, it would be foolish to put off something as critical for your safety as brakes just because you don't want to accept the advice.

Perhaps an editor has told you that your writing is not that good. You could whine and try to publish your own book, errors and all, or you could be reasonable and get a good editor. Don't be a self-centered narcissist and assume that "they" are all against you. The experts often do know what they're talking about. If you stubbornly refuse to take good advice, you may end up looking like a dope just because your ego has been damaged a bit.

The way to deal with all these examples and others where there is a conflict between what the expert advises and what you want to believe is the same. Gather reliable evidence, evaluate all the alternatives carefully, ask friends whose judgment you trust, and be honest with yourself about your reasons for opposing the expert. If your reasons are more emotionally based than rationally, you need to be honest with yourself. Ultimately, however, it is you who must make decisions about your life, not others. But if you screw up and realize you've made a mistake, have the integrity to admit it.

Authorities

What if you have broken the law? It's probably OK to try and get off as lightly as possible for minor offenses, but maybe you don't deserve to get off completely. If you were caught driving 100 miles an hour on the freeway weaving in and out because you were drunk, you were acting stupidly and endangering people's lives. Have the integrity to admit that you were wrong and accept your punishment. If you have a conscience, you will live with yourself more easily. If you don't have a conscience or you think that you deserve special privileges, I'd prefer that you weren't reading my book. My book wasn't written for you. Go away, you make the world worse, not better.

WHEN THE COSTS OF STANDING UP OR RESISTING OUTWEIGH THE BENEFITS

Sometimes it really *is* best to cut your losses. Arguing with or resisting a police officer, for example, is just plain foolish, even if you're right. As the old saying goes, being "right" and $1.75 will get you on the bus (at least till the price of bus fare goes up . . .). If being right is more important than getting what you want, then I can't help you. The place to bring up your point of view is in the courtroom or other processes of the legal system (see Chapter Eight for some suggestions). Arguing too vigorously with a police officer can get you into more trouble than you already are. Being rude will only make matters worse.

If the amount of effort and/or money it will cost to deal with the problem is very high, you have to ask yourself: Is it worth it? Only you can answer that question. I have suggested ways to fight back—letters, protests, and campaigns. But if dealing with your issue would take time away from other, more important goals, then maybe you should let it pass. But don't just let it go because you are too timid or scared to fight. Have a good reason.

Here's an example. Lou had a speeding ticket for $400. Because he was unemployed, this would really hurt. I suggested several ways he might beat the ticket, but he wanted to be able to apply for a chauffeur's job. He couldn't take the chance of losing in court and having a speeding ticket on his driving record. He would never get a job that involved driving if that happened. He opted for paying the ticket (ouch!) and attending driving school instead. That way the ticket would not go on his driving record. Frankly, I couldn't argue with his reasoning. He had made the right decision for his situation.

WHEN IT WOULD BE IMMORAL TO DISOBEY

I've talked a lot about disobeying unjust authority but many laws are based on entirely appropriate and decent moral principles. Laws against killing innocent people and stealing are obviously reasonable and desirable. People should clearly obey those just laws if they want to live in a civilized society.

But what about the little ways we sometimes fool ourselves into thinking it's OK to flaunt the authority "this time"? Drive after a "few" drinks, for example, or cheat on the construction project, lie to a consumer rep about the allegedly defective product. We go back to Kant's rule: What if everyone did that? Would you like the world that such actions would produce? No? Then maybe it's not OK. Would your children be proud of you if they knew that you did it? Are you setting a good example for them? Children learn from what you do, not just what you say. Think about the example you're setting.

Wrapping It All Up

If you don't want to be a victim, you must stop acting like a victim. Recognize your rights. Every human being should be treated with dignity and respect. But the world isn't a just place and there will be many times when you will *not* be treated well or fairly. You can continue to let it happen or you can stand up and say "no." The choice is yours.

REFERENCES

BOOKS

I can't guarantee that the books listed below will help you. No book works for everybody. I recommend that you look for reviews on Amazon.com (most books will have them) or other places and see what other reviewers say about these books. Read between the lines and then decide for yourself. That's particularly important with the self-help books on assertiveness and on self-esteem. Some people need gentle books; some need straightforward, no nonsense, "kick in the butt" books. Only you can decide which approach is right for you.

Critical Thinking

Brooke Noel Moore and Richard Parker. *Critical Thinking*. New York: McGraw-Hill. Any edition will do but the latest one is the 9th.

Judith Boss. *Think: Critical Thinking and Logic Skills for Everyday Life*. New York: McGraw-Hill, 2009.

Assertiveness and Self Confidence

Robert E. Alberti and Michael L. Emmons. *Your Perfect Right: Assertiveness in Your Life and Relationships*. Atascadero, CA: Impact Publishers, 2008. Well-regarded by the professional psychology community, it offers many practical techniques for standing up for yourself. It's in its 9th edition but any edition will be helpful.

Duke Robinson. *Too Nice for Your Own Good: How to Stop Making 9 Self-Sabotaging Mistakes.* New York: Warner Book, 1997. Some practical advice based on cognitive therapy ideas that will help you get over the idea that you *must* help others at the cost of your own self-worth and best interests.

Manuel Smith. *When I Say No I Feel Guilty.* New York: Bantam, 1985. Another book on assertiveness that is well-regarded by many professionals.

Self-Esteem

The books below have somewhat different techniques. Read the reviews and pick the one that sounds right for you.

Nathaniel Branden, Ph.D. *Honoring the Self: Self-Esteem and Personal Transformation.* New York: Bantam, 1985.

Nathaniel Branden, Ph.D. *How to Raise Your Self-Esteem: The Proven Action-Oriented Approach to Greater Self-Respect and Self-Confidence.* New York: Bantam, 1988.

Nathaniel Branden, Ph.D. *The Six Pillars of Self-Esteem.* New York: Bantam, 1995.

Nathaniel Branden, Ph.D. *Self-Esteem at Work: How Confident People Make Powerful Companies.* San Francisco: Jossey-Bass, 1998.

Nathaniel Branden, Ph.D. *A Woman's Self-Esteem: Struggles and Triumphs in the Search for Identity.* San Francisco: Jossey-Bass, 1998

David D. Burns, M.D. *Ten Days to Self-Esteem.* New York: Collins Living, 1999.

Matthew McKay and Patrick Fanning. *Self-Esteem: A Proven Program of Cognitive Techniques for Assessing, Improving, and Maintaining Your Self-Esteem.* Oakland, CA: New Harbinger, 2000.

Patrick Fanning, Carole Honeychurch, Catherine Sutker, and Matthew McKay (editor). *The Self-Esteem Companion: Simple Exercises to Help You Challenge Your Inner Critic & Celebrate Your Personal Strengths.* Oakland, CA: New Harbinger, 2005.

Positive Psychology

Martin Seligman, Ph.D. *Authentic Happiness: Using the New Positive Psychology to Realize Your Potential for Lasting Fulfillment.* New York: Free Press, 2004. This book is not another silly pop psych title; it's solidly based on research and written by a well-respected psychologist.

Martin Seligman, Ph.D. *Learned Optimism.* New York: Vintage, 2006. How to have realistic optimism about the things you do and why optimism is healthy for you.

Martin Seligman, Ph.D. *What You Can Change . . . And What You Can't: The Complete Guide to Successful Self-Improvement.* New York: Fawcett, 1994.

Cognitive Therapy

Most books on cognitive therapy have helpful suggestions but the two below are the most highly regarded.

David D. Burns, M.D. *Feeling Good: The New Mood Therapy.* Considered *the* best book on cognitive therapy by the professionals. New York: Harper, 1999.

David D. Burns, M.D. *The Feeling Good Handbook.* New York: Plume, 1999. This companion piece gives many practical techniques for getting over the irrational beliefs that make you feel bad about yourself.

Mistakes in Reasoning

All the books below discuss various kinds of cognitive mistakes that even smart people unknowingly make. There's very little overlap—plenty of human error to go around without saying the same things as other books.

Thomas Gilovich, Ph.D. *How We Know What Isn't So: The Fallibility of Reasoning in Everyday Life.* New York: Free Press, 1993. This was the first book I read on this topic and it's still one of my favorites.

Thomas Kida. *Don't Believe Everything You Think.* Amherst, NY: Prometheus Books, 2006. I assign this to students in my Critical Thinking classes. It's easy to read but solidly based on psychological research.

Carol Tavris, Ph.D. and Eliot Aronson, Ph.D. *Mistakes Were Made (but Not by Me): Why We Justify Foolish Beliefs, Bad Decisions, and Hurtful Acts.* New York: Harcourt, 2007. Solidly based on research but written in an engaging style by two well-known psychologists, it will make you more humble about your own thinking processes.

Michael Shermer, Ph.D. *Why People Believe Weird Things: Pseudoscience, Superstition and Other Confusions of Our Time.* I review this insightful book at www.rit.org (See the Reviews button on the web site), but you can find many other positive reviews on the Web too. Dr. Shermer writes in an engaging style that is substantive but easy to read. If you have ever been tempted to believe that John Edward actually communicates with the dead or that ESP is a reality, this book will give you something to think about.

WEBSITES

Critical Thinking

Critical Thinking on the Web: A Directory of Online Resources

www.austhink.org/critical
A wealth of information at this directory.

Logical Fallacies
www.logicalfallacies.info

Foundation for Critical Thinking
Critical Thinking Community
www.criticalthinking.org
Articles, books, workshops, conferences.

Resources for Independent Thinking
www.rit.org
Articles and other resources that help you think for yourself and encourage you to think critically.

Skeptic Society
www.skeptic.com
Full of resources for thinking critically about many issues, especially the paranormal.

Prometheus Books
www.prometheusbooks.com
A huge array of books raising critical thinking issues, including critical thinking books for children. It's not afraid to tackle controversial issues such as atheism either.

Cognitive Therapy

There are many web sites promoting their brand of cognitive therapy (there are several) and many of them provide helpful resources. I've picked one that is more general in its scope. You can find the rest by an Internet search, if you want tapes or videos to help you. The ones connected with Albert Ellis or Aaron Beck are reputable, though many others may be also. Just watch out for the ones with a hard-sell approach and too high a price.

www.psychologyinfo.com/depression/cognitive.htm
One of the many web sites that discuss cognitive therapy and how it works.

Assertiveness, Self Confidence, Self-Esteem, Self-Efficacy, and Positive Psychology

Nathaniel Branden
www.nathanielbranden.com
Dr. Branden is the leading pioneer in the application of the psychology of self-esteem. His web site has helpful books and products.

Values in Action Institute Authentic Happiness Center
www.authentichappiness.sas.upenn.edu/testcenter.aspx
A variety of surveys here will assess your level of optimism, gratitude, work satisfaction, compassionate love, gratitude, character strengths, and other areas of interest. Dr. Martin Seligman is the driving force behind this organization. The surveys are insightful and fun too. I especially recommend the VIA Signature Strengths survey to gain insight into your values and character strengths.

Speak Up for Yourself
www.speakupforyourself.com/free%20class.htm
A quick mini-course on how to stand up for yourself and be assertive in a nonaggressive way. Straightforward and low key.

Queendom.com
www.queendom.com
This is a web site with many kinds of surveys to assess not only self-esteem but depression, anxiety, assertiveness, and many other individual characteristics. I like the tests here and appreciate the fact that they don't ask you to sign up, let alone pay (at least for the short tests). Low key but very good.

Values Clarification

Resources for Independent Thinking
www.rit.org/valueslist.html
The Values List that I have compiled can be found here, along with an exercise to help you clarify what is most important to you.

Journey Way
www.journeyway.com/download/valuesclarification.pdf
This is a somewhat similar idea to mine but only some of the list overlaps. It also has an exercise.

UPDATES

For updates on books, web sites, web site URLs and links (they sometimes change), articles and other relevant information, check the web site for my book: www.standuptoauthorities.com

Feedback

I want to hear from you. I want to know if my advice helped you—or if it didn't help you. I want to hear your success stories and your failure stories too. I'm always looking for ways to improve my advice. Please do visit the web site and blog for this book (www.standuptoauthorities.com) and leave your comments. I'll also answer questions about your specific situations, if I can.

If you are a woman, I especially want your feedback and questions. The sequel to this book will specifically address women's issues in greater detail than was possible in this book. I'll talk more about assertiveness and being "too nice for your own good." I'll address the subtle ways that women are often treated with condescension and discrimination at work and in the marketplace. I'll suggest techniques for dealing with many still-existing stereotypes about women, for example, that women aren't good leaders. Our society has come a long way but it's far from an even playing field for women, minorities and others with little power. Anyone who thinks the playing field *is* even now has not been paying attention. I guarantee that social science research shows otherwise.

I look forward to your feedback.

Notes

Author's note: When I edited these endnotes for the last time, I checked the Internet sources to make sure that the pages were still there, so the URL listings below are accurate as of the date indicated. I have followed the convention of citing original sources only when I have actually read them myself. When I read about a study or set of statistics in a secondary source, I have cited that source. The secondary sources have the original citations.

INTRODUCTION

1. Brooke Noel Moore and Richard Parker, *Critical Thinking*, 5th Ed. (Mountain View, CA: Mayfield Publishing, 1998), 6.
2. Robert Bierstedt, "The Problem of Authority," in *Freedom and Control in Modern Society*, ed. Morroe Berger, Theodore Abel and Charles H. Page (New York: Van Nostrand, 1954), 67–81.

CHAPTER ONE: THE SEDUCTION OF THE SITUATION

1. Stanley Milgram, *Obedience to Authority: An Experimental View* (New York: Harper & Row), 1974.
2. Douglas T. Kenrick, Steven L. Neuberg and Robert B. Cialdini, "Chapter 6: Social Influence," *Social Psychology: Unraveling the Mystery* (Boston: Allyn & Bacon, 1999), 192–232.
3. Ibid., 204.
4. Ibid., 207.
5. Many books deal with the various factors that influence obedience to authority. In addition to Milgram, there is, for example, Nancy Henley, *Body Politics: Power, Sex and Nonverbal Communication* (New York: Simon & Schuster, 1986) and Philip Zimbardo, *The Lucifer Effect* (New York: Random House, 2007) in addition to the articles cited below in Notes # 13–15.
6. See http://en.wikipedia.org/wiki/Laura_Schlessinger (accessed July 8, 2009).
7. Here is a link to an archived press release about John Gray's credentials directly from the California Department of Consumer Affairs: http://web.archive.org/web/20060528023756/http://www.dca.ca.gov/press_releases/1999/990210.htm (accessed July 2, 2009).
8. Karen Dion, Ellen Berscheid and Elaine Walster, "What is Beautiful Is Good," *Journal of Personality and Social Psychology*, 24, no. 3 (1972):

285–290. There are many references on the Internet to this classic article.

9. Philip G. Zimbardo and Michael Leippe, *The Psychology of Attitude Change and Social Influence* (New York: McGraw-Hill, 1991), 256.

10. Philip Goldberg, "Are Women Prejudiced Against Women?" *Transaction* 5 (1968): 28–30. For a more recent discussion of evaluations of women's work, see Janet Shipley Hyde, *Half the Human Experience*, 7th Ed. (Boston: Houghton-Mifflin, 2007), 253–256. She notes that not all recent studies find discrimination but also points out that the studies mostly use college students in laboratory rather than real-life settings. A whole issue of the *Journal of Social Issues* 57, no. 4 (2001) was devoted to research on women as leaders; most of the research found considerable reluctance to view women as competent leaders, so the problem of discrimination against women in a work setting is far from over. Also see Hilary Lips, *Sex and Gender* (Mountain View, CA: Mayfield, 2001), 13–14.

11. Mary Crawford and Rhoda Unger, *Women and Gender*, 4th Ed. (New York: McGraw-Hill, 2004), 375.

12. Lips, *Sex and Gender*, 13–14. Also see Susan A. Basow, *Gender Stereotypes: Traditions and Alternatives*, 2nd Ed. (Belmont, CA: Brooks/Cole, 1986), 238.

13. Leonard Bickman, "The Social Power of a Uniform," *Journal of Applied Social Psychology*, 4, no.1 (1974): 47–61.

14. Brad Bushman, "Perceived Symbols of Authority and Their Influence on Compliance," *Journal of Applied Social Psychology* 14, no. 6 (1984): 501–508.

15. Brad Bushman, "The Effects of Apparel on Compliance: A Field Experiment with a Female Authority Figure," *Personality and Social Psychology Bulletin* 14 (1988): 459–467.

16. Milgram, *Obedience to Authority*, 16.

17. For comments on Cimino's debacle, see http://en.wikipedia.org/wiki/Heaven%27s_Gate_(film) (accessed July 8, 2009).

18. See my article "Don't Listen to Dr. Laura: Her advice is unsound, hypocritical, and cruel" at http://www.secularhumanism.org/index.php?section=library&page=presley_21_1 (accessed July 10, 2009). My source was her own book: Laura Schlessinger, *Parenting by Proxy: Don't Have Them if You Won't Raise Them* (New York: Cliff Street Books, 2000). Also see http://yle.bloggingbaby.com/2009/05/13/dr-laura-schlessinger-on-working-moms/ (accessed July 2, 2009).

19. See Claire Etaugh, "Effects of Maternal Employment on Children: A Review of Recent Research," *Merrill-Palmer Quarterly* (1974): 71–98. Some recent researchers have found different results, however, most researchers conclude that maternal employment does not harm children; see Claire A. Etaugh and Judith Bridges, *The Psychology of Women: A Lifespan Perspective* (Boston: Allyn & Bacon, 2001), 335–336.

20. For information about research on the ineffectiveness of the DARE program, see http://www.drugpolicy.org/library/factsheets/dare/index.cfm or http://archive.salon.com/mwt/feature/2001/02/16/dare/index.html (accessed July 15, 2009).

21. Henley, *Body Politics*. First published in 1977 by Prentice-Hall, this classic book brings together the research literature on the "politics of touch." The more powerful can engage in certain behaviors more than the less powerful can: touch the less powerful, 4–5; make eye contact while talking, 155–156; interrupt others, 69; and sit in more relaxed positions, 84–85,126.

22. Paul Ekman, "Chapter 5: Facial Clues to Deceit," *Telling Lies: Clues to Deceit in the Marketplace, Politics and Marriage* (New York: W.W. Norton, 2001), 123–161.

23. Jeffrey D. Fisher, Paul A. Bell, and Andrew Baum, *Environmental Psychology*, 2nd Ed., (New York: Holt, Rinehart and Winston, 1984), 274.

24. Ron Jones R. "The Third Wave," 1972 (accessed July 9, 2009) at http://www.vaniercollege.qc.ca/Auxiliary/Psychology/Frank/RJmore.html. Also see www.ronjoneswriter.com/wave.html (accessed July 16, 2009)

25. See, for example, Carole Wade and Carol Tavris, *Psychology*, 9th Ed. (Upper Saddle River, NJ: Pearson Prentice Hall, 2008), 282.

26. Milgram, *Obedience to Authority*,152.

27. See, for example, Saul Kassin, Steven Fein, and Hazel Rose Markus, *Social Psychology*, 7th Ed. (Boston: Houghton-Mifflin, 2008), 238.

CHAPTER TWO: PSYCHOLOGICAL KUNG FU: HOW TO QUESTION EXPERTS AND STAND UP TO AUTHORITIES

1. This is one of the important lessons of the famous Stanford prison experiment. In that study, young men recruited to role play prisoners and guards were randomly assigned to one of the two conditions. The ones who role-played guards became increasingly cruel and overbearing, as if they were in a bad prison movie. The ones who role-played prisoners became increasingly submissive. There were no differences in the men at the beginning of the experiment; the only differences were the roles they played. For the fullest account of this study, as well as the general conclusions drawn, see Philip Zimbardo, *The Lucifer Effect: Understanding How Good People Turn Evil* (New York: Random House, 2007).

2. Many people, both philosophers and psychologists, have made this point. I first read about the distinction in Jean Baker Miller, *Toward a New Psychology of Women* (Boston: Beacon, 1976),116.

3. Though it is a common catchphrase, there is actually research

evidence to support this idea. See, for example, "How You Too Can Be an Optimist," *Prevention,* 2006 at http://www.prevention.com/cda/article/go-ahead-smile/105250d1fa803110VgnVCM10000013281eac____/health/emotional.health/positive.thinking/0/0/4 (accessed July 14, 2009) cites a law school study by Segerstrom. Dr. Suzanne C. Segerstrom is the author of *Breaking Murphy's Law: How Optimists Get What They Want From Life—And Pessimists Can Too* (New York: Guilford Press, 2006).

4. See Note 1/15–16. Also see Henley, *Body Politics,* 87–91.

5. Frances Elaine Donelson, *Women's Experience* (Mountain View, CA: Mayfield, 1999), 54.

6. Paula Caplan, *You're Smarter Than They Make You Feel* (New York: Free Press, 1994), 147.

7. Henley, *Body Politics,* slumping vs. "standing tall," 88; eye contact, 155–156.

8. Ibid,, speaking too softly, 76; weak language, 67–81.

9. Hyde, *Half the Human Experience,* 7th Ed.,154–155. Also see Henley, *Body Politics,* 77.

10. Ibid., Hyde, 156; Henley, 74.

11. Henley, ibid., 4–5, 68.

12. Caplan, *You're Smarter Than They Make You Feel,* 135,151.

13. See for example, http://michaelbluejay.com/misc/women-grandmasters.html for a list of women grand masters. Susan Polgar was the first women to become a grand master in 1986 (see www.susanpolgar.com). Though we don't know when the "expert" wrote the remark Caplan refers to, Polgar's achievement occurred well before Caplan's book was published in 1994.

CHAPTER THREE: DON'T TRUST ME, I'M A DOCTOR

1. Timothy McCall, M.D., *Examining Your Doctor* (Secaucus, NJ: Citadel Press, 1995), 5.

2. Ibid.

3. Ibid., 25.

4. Ibid., 29.

5. Isadore Rosenfeld, M.D. "Patients, Know Your Rights," *Parade* Magazine, February 24, 2002. Also see http://www.ubpn.org/medicalresources/Parade.html (accessed July 6, 2009).

6. SNH, "Choosing Dr. Right," *Prevention,* July 2005, 40.

7. Carol Svec, *After Any Diagnosis* (New York: Three Rivers Press. 2001), 25.

8. Gardiner Harris, "Report Finds a Heavy Toll from Medication Errors," *New York Times,* July 21, 2006. See this article at http://www.medicalnewstoday.com/articles/47931.php (accessed July 6, 2009).

9. "Wrong-side brain surgery for the third time," *San Francisco Chronicle*, November 28, 2007, A6.

10. Katharine Greider, "Dirty Hospitals," *AARP Bulletin*, January 3, 2007. See http://bulletin.aarp.org/yourhealth/articles/dirty_hospitals.html (accessed July 6, 2009).

11. American Pharmacist Association, "Ask Your Pharmacist about All Your Prescription and Nonprescription Medications." See http://www.pharmacist.com/AM/Template.cfm?Section=Patient_Education_Brochures1&Template=/CM/ContentDisplay.cfm&ContentID=16495 (accessed July 6, 2009).

12. Svec, *After Any Diagnosis*, 30.

13. Kent Holtorf, M.D., "Why Doesn't My Doctor Know This?" April 9, 2007 at http://www.prohealth.com/library/showarticle.cfm?id=7891&t=CFIDS_FM (accessed July 6, 2009).

14. Barbara Basler, "Ties That Bind," *AARP Bulletin*, January–February 2008, 24. Also see http://www.prescriptionproject.org/assets/pdfs/Basler_AARP_giftslaw_Jan-2008.pdf (accessed July 6, 2009).

15. Roanne Weisman with Brian Berman, MD., *Own Your Own Health* (Deerfield, FL: Health Communications Inc., 2003), 299–301, 303.

16. Lynne McTaggert, introduction to *What Doctors Don't Tell You: The Truth about the Dangers of Modern Medicine* (New York: Avon, 1998), xv–xvii.

17. "Support groups don't extend survival of metastatic breast cancer patients" at http://www.huliq.com/28024/support-groups-dont-extend-survival-of-metastatic-breast-cancer-patients (accessed July 6, 2009).

18. Sharon S. Brehm, Saul Kassin and Steven Fein, *Social Psychology*, 4th Ed. (Boston, MA: Houghton Mifflin, 1999), 525. The authors point out that the first line of defense against stress is to accumulate resources to draw on as a buffer. This can include "self-complexity" (having many different social roles and self-relevant activities instead of just one or two), social support and friendships, as well as financial resources.

19. Raymond Lloyd Richman, Ph.D. at http://www.guidetopsychology.com/choosing.htm (accessed July 2, 2009).

20. Robin Dawes, *House of Cards: Psychology and Psychotherapy Built on Myth* (New York: Free Press, 1994), 56–57.

21. Ibid., 60.

22. Many web sites comment on John Gray's questionable credentials. For a link to an archived press release directly from the California Department of Consumer Affairs, see Note #1/7.

23. Dr. Ofer Zur's recommendations are found at http://www.zurinstitute.com/choosing.html. Also see http://www.zurinstitute.com/therapy.html for Dr. Zur's "Philosophy of Treatment," a reasonable, respectful and humane approach that can serve as a model for

what kind of attitude to look for in a therapist. Many other articles are also available at this web site (accessed July 9, 2009).

24. See Richmond, http://www.guidetopsychology.com/choosing.htm (accessed July 2, 2009).

25. John W. Santrock, Ann M. Minnett, and Barbara Campbell, *The Authoritative Guide to Self-Help Books* (New York: Guilford, 1994), 161–163. Hereafter referred to as Santrock.

26. See http://www.springerlink.com/content/k44t35003r3807rv/ for an abstract of the research article: Augustus J. Rush, Aaron T. Beck, Maria Kovacs and Steven Hollon, "Comparative Efficacy of Cognitive Therapy and Pharmacotherapy in the Treatment of Depressed Outpatients," *Cognitive Therapy and Research* 1, no. 1 (March 1977). Also see http://psycnet.apa.org/index.cfm?fa=main.doiLanding&uid=1989-30221-001 for abstract of "A Meta-analysis of the Efficacy of Cognitive Therapy for Depression," by Keith S. Dobson, *Journal of Consulting and Clinical Psychology*. 57, no. 3 (June 1989): 414–419 (accessed July 6, 2009).

27. See http://www.counselormagazine.com/component/content/article/79-cultural-trends/903-what-really-killed-anna-nicole-smith or http://www.cnn.com/2007/SHOWBIZ/TV/03/26/smith.autopsy/index.html or http://www.thesmokinggun.com/archive/years/2007/0326071anna1.html (accessed July 6, 2009).

28. See http://www.zap2it.com/movies/news/zap-heathledgertoxicology,0,4867437.story (accessed July 6, 2009). Also see http://www.nytimes.com/2008/02/07/nyregion/07ledger.html (accessed July 6, 2009).

29. See Law Project for Psychiatric Rights, http://psychrights.org/Stories/PsychMedsDroveSonCrazy.htm (accessed July 6, 2009).

30. Santrock, 369–377.

31. For Ringer, see Santrock, 86–87; for De Angelis, see 357–358.

32. Sharon Presley, "Psychological Self-Reliance: Picking Sensible Self-Help Books," *Independent Thinking Review*, Vol.1 (4), 1995, p. 6. Also see http://rit.org.

33. See http://www.quackwatch.com/04ConsumerEducation/News/cpu.html (accessed July 13, 2009. For the original press release, see Note 1/ 7.

34. See http://www.biography.com/articles/Dr.-Laura-Schlessinger-9542197 (accessed July 6, 2009). For some real dirt on Dr. Laura as well as a questioning of her credentials, see http://www.nndb.com/people/427/000022361/ (accessed July 7, 2009). Also see my article "Don't Listen to Dr. Laura" at http://www.secularhumanism.org/library/fi/presley_21_1.html (accessed July 7, 2009).

35. For the Santrock criticism of Westheimer, see 329; for Dyer, see 319; for Brothers, see 251. Ruth Westheimer has a Doctorate of Education (Ed. D.) in the Interdisciplinary Study of the Family from Columbia University Teacher's College. See http://www.drruth.com/content/view/42/27/ (accessed July 7, 2009. Wayne Dyer has a Doctor-

ate in Educational Counseling from Wayne State University. See http://www.drwaynedyer.com/about (accessed July 7, 2009). Joyce Brothers has a Ph.D. in psychology from Columbia University. See http://www.bookrags.com/biography/joyce-brothers/ (accessed July 7, 2009).

36. Santrock, 180–181.

37. See, for example, Martin Seligman, *Learned Optimism* (New York, Vintage, 2006). This book, written by a prominent research psychologist, talks about the psychological and health benefits of *realistic* optimism.

38. This review by S. Winters ("anastasia35") is no longer on the Amazon web site but there are still two commentaries agreeing with the review. One commentary on this review can be found at http://www.amazon.com/gp/community-content-search/results/ref=cm_srch_q_rtr/?query=s.+winters+anastasia35&search-alias=community-reviews&x=8&y=13 (accessed July 6, 2009). There are, however, 564 other 1-star (lowest rating) reviews, many of which basically say either similar things or other criticisms equally as a scathing.

39. See http://books.google.com/books?id=DotifADlTu8C&pg=PA345&lpg=PA345&dq=deborah+tannen+credentials&source=bl&ots=wokzZ8N_9J&sig=a54FnY_OqcUIMvy_zcnI9OHGITI&hl=en&ei=FRJQSuziH4_8sQPmzuWqDQ&sa=X&oi=book_result&ct=result&resnum=1 and http://en.wikipedia.org/wiki/Deborah_Tannen (accessed July 7, 2009).

40. Santrock, 247–248.
41. Santrock, 248–249.
42. Santrock, 374.
43. Santrock, 251.
44. Santrock, 307–308.

45. All of Dr. Breggin's books on psychiatric drugs have extensive bibliographies of original medical journal sources.

CHAPTER FOUR: DON'T TAKE THIS JOB AND SHOVE IT: DEALING WITH BOSSES WITHOUT GETTING FIRED

1. Patricia King, *Never Work for a Jerk* (New York: Barnes and Noble Books, 1987), 174–175.

2. Muriel Solomon, *What Do I Say When . . . A Guidebook for Getting Your Way with People on the Job* (Englewood Cliffs, NJ: Prentice Hall, 1988), 87. Hereafter referred to as *What Do I Say*.

3. Alberti and Emmons's highly recommended book is praised in Santrock,174–175.

4. *What Do I Say*, 87–88.

5. Claire A. Etaugh and Judith Bridges, *The Psychology of Women: A Lifespan Perspective* (Boston: Allyn & Bacon, 2001), 205. Women not only ask for and expect less, they are in fact paid less, see 261.

6. *What Do I Say*, 87.
7. King, *Never Work for a Jerk*, 65–68.
8. *What Do I Say*, 89–90.
9. Interview with ArLyne Diamond, December 26, 2007.
10. King, *Never Work for a Jerk*, 58–59.
12. See discussion in Chapter One.
13. "How Low Can You Go," *San Francisco Chronicle*, August 26, 2001, W1, W5.
14. Workplace Bullying Institute and Zogby International Study, August, 2007, as cited at http://www.workplacebullying.org/research/WBI-Zogby2007Survey.html (accessed July 8, 2009).
15. See, for example, Hilary M. Lips, *Women, Men and Power*, (Mountain View, CA: Mayfield, 1991), 13.
16. For a review of *Your Perfect Right*, see Santrock, 77–78; for *The Assertive Woman*, see 80–81.
17. Gary Namie and Ruth Namie, Ph.D., *The Bully at Work: What You Can Do to Stop the Hurt and Reclaim Your Dignity on the Job* (Napierville, IL: Sourcebooks, Inc., 2000), 3.
18. Namie and Namie, ibid., 41. Also see http://www.workplacebullying.org/targets/problem/who-gets-targeted.html (accessed July 22, 2009).
19. Namie and Namie, ibid., 43.
20. *What Do I Say*, 99–100.
21. This quote is apparently popular since it appears on many Internet sites. Here is where I first read it: http://www.msnbc.msn.com/id/17629928/ (accessed July 22, 2009).
22. See http://www.workplacebullying.org/targets/solution/three-step-method.html (accessed July 22, 2009).
23. For incidence of sexual harassment of work, see http://www.sexualharassmentsupport.org/SHworkplace.html or http://www.nwlc.org/details.cfm?id=459&section=employment. For incidence of reporting it, see http://www.nwlc.org/details.cfm?id=459&section=employment (accessed July 22, 2009).
24. See http://www.eeoc.gov/facts/fs-sex.html (accessed July 13, 2009).
25. Linda Ellerbee, "Dangerous Propositions," a documentary first aired on June 24, 1992 on Lifetime TV.
26. See http://research.lawyers.com/California/Employment-Law-in-California.html (accessed July 13, 2009).
27. See http://www.lawyersandsettlements.com/case/harassment.html (accessed July 22, 2009).
28. Mary Crawford and Rhoda Unger, *Women and Gender*, 4th Ed. (New York: McGraw-Hill, 2004), 467. Blaming the victim can also occur in rape cases.
29. Deborah Erdos Knapp, Robert H. Faley, Steven E. Ekeberg and

Cathy L. Z. Dubois, "Determinants of Target Responses to Sexual Harassment: A Conceptual Framework," *The Academy of Management Review* 22, no. 3 (July, 1997): 687–729.

30. Ellerbee, "Dangerous Propositions."

31. Joan Kennedy Taylor, *What to Do When You Don't Want to Call the Cops: A Non-Adversarial Approach to Sexual Harassment* (New York: New York University Press, 1999), 57.

32. Ibid.

33. Martha J. Langelan, *Back Off! How to Confront and Stop Sexual Harassment and Harassers* (New York: Fireside, 1993), 162–163.

34. Attorneys William Petrocelli and Barbara Kate Repa, *Sexual Harassment on the Job: What It is and How to Stop It* (Berkeley, CA: Nolo Press, 1999), 3/47.

35. See "Sexual Harassment and Your Rights on the Job" at http://74.125.155.132/search?q=cache:TjyeAU69dvEJ:www.women employed.org/docs/Sexual%2520Harassment.pdf+womenemployed .org+%E2%80%A2+State+the+basic+facts+of+what+happened&cd=1 &hl=en&ct=clnk&gl=us (accessed July 8, 2009).

36. Petrocelli and Rapa, *Sexual Harassment on the Job: What It is and How to Stop It*, 3/42.

CHAPTER FIVE: SERVICES FROM HELL: SURVIVING LAWYERS, CONTRACTORS AND OTHER PROFESSIONALS WITHOUT GETTING RIPPED OFF

1. See http://contractorsfromhell.com/blog/2009/07/17/you-can-add-another-contractor-from-hell-to-your-growing-list/ (accessed July 15, 2009).

2. See http://www.sfbar.org/lawyerreferrals/index.aspx (accessed July 15, 2009).

3. Nicholas Carroll, *Dancing with Lawyers* (Lafayette, CA: Royce Baker, 1992), 100.

4. Attorney William Gore, personal communication, May 29, 2009.

5. See "How Do You Pick a Lawyer" by Judge Thomas C. Warren at http://dmcja.org/how_do_you_pick_a_lawyer.htm (accessed July 15, 2009).

6. Carroll, *Dancing with Lawyers*, 33–36.

7. Carroll, ibid., 42.

8. Tanya Stearnes, *Mad At Your Lawyer* (Berkeley, CA: Nolo Press, 1996), 2/11.

9. Carroll, *Dancing with Lawyers*, 80.

10. Stearnes, *Mad At Your Lawyer*, 1/4.

11. See http://www.courtinfo.ca.gov/selfhelp/smallclaims/research .htm (accessed July 16, 2009).

12. Paul Bianchina and the Editors of Consumer Reports, *How to Hire the Right Contractor: Getting the Right Prices, Workmanship, and Scheduling for Home Remodeling* (Yonkers, NY: Consumer Reports Books, 1991), 2.

13. Georg Bueschi, personal communication, March 11, 2009.

14. See "Warning Signs" at http://www.contractorsfromhell.com/?page_id=17#more-17 (accessed July 15, 2009).

15. Steve Gonzalez, C.R.C., *Before You Hire a Contractor: A Construction Guide for Consumers* (Fort Lauderdale, FL: Consumer Press, 1994), 67.

16. See "Tips on Hiring Home Remodeling and Building Contractors," http://www.contractorsfromhell.com/?page_id=5#more-5 (accessed July 16, 2009).

17. Ibid.

18. Bueschi, see Note 13 above.

19. Sean O'Neill, "What You Need to Know About Hiring a Plumber" www.angieslist.com/Angieslist/Visitor/PressDetail.aspx?i=704 (accessed July 15, 2009).

20. See Report # 225226: http://www.ripoffreport.com/reports/0/225/RipOff0225226.htm (accessed July 15, 2009).

21. O'Neill, "What You Need to Know About Hiring a Plumber."

22. See "Warning Signs" at http://www.contractorsfromhell.com/?page_id=17#more-17 (accessed July 15, 2009).

23. Ibid.

24. http://www.fictionfactor.com/self/vanity.html (accessed July 15, 2009).

25. See "Self Service: An Interview with M.J. Rose" by Mike Atherton at http://www.greatwriting.co.uk/content/view/618/74/ (accessed July 15, 2009).

26. For *Atlas Shrugged*, published in 1957, see http://www.amazon.com/Ayn-Rands-Atlas-Shrugged-Philosophical/dp/0754655490. For *The Feminine Mystique*, published in 1963, see http://en.wikipedia.org/wiki/The_Feminine_Mystique (accessed July 15, 2009).

CHAPTER SIX: ALL THE NEWS THAT'S NOT FIT TO PRINT: THINKING CRITICALLY ABOUT THE PRINTED WORD

1. Solzhenitsyn address on June 8, 1978. See http://www.truthout.org/article/a-world-split-apart (accessed July 15, 2009).

2. Caplan, *You're Smarter Than They Make You Feel*, 142.

3. See, for example, http://en.wikipedia.org/wiki/William_Randolph_Hearst (accessed July 15, 2009).

4. "Only One in Five Say They Trust Journalists to Tell The Truth." See http://www.ipsos-mori.com/researchpublications/researcharchive/poll.aspx?oItemId=2358 (accessed July 15, 2009).

5. Stanley Meisler, "Trust in Media High, but Curbs Favored, Poll Finds - News: *Times Mirror* study examines eight nations. Many rate papers, TV more believable than church," *Los Angeles Times*, March 16, 1994. See http://articles.latimes.com/1994-03-16/news/mn-34826_1_tv-news (accessed July 22, 2009).

6. See, for example, http://www.brainyquote.com/quotes/quotes/m/marshallmc385505.html (accessed July 22, 2009).

7. As quoted in Howard Bloom, "Puppets of Pandemonium," in ed. Russell Kick, *You Are Being Lied To* (New York: Disinformation Press, 2001), 32.

8. Martin A. Lee and Norman Solomon, *Unreliable Sources: A Guide to Detecting Bias in the Media* (New York, Lyle Stuart, 1991), 66. Hereafter referred to as *Unreliable Sources*.

9. Ibid., 84–92.

10. Ibid., 89–91.

11. Project Censored, "US/British Forces Continue Use of Depleted Uranium Weapons Despite Negative Health Effects," In Top 25 Censored Stories in 2004. See http://www.projectcensored.org/top-stories/articles/8-us-british-forces-continue-use-of-depleted-uranium-weapons-despite-negati/ (accessed July 15, 2009).

12. Project Censored, "Drug Companies Influence Doctors and Health Organizations to Push Meds" In Top 25 Censored Stories of 2001. See http://www.projectcensored.org/top-stories/articles/8-drug-companies-influence-doctors-and-health-organizations-to-push-meds/. For a description of the dangers of Prozac, see http://www.garynull.com/documents/prozac1.htm or go to Dr. Peter Breggin's site: http://breggin.com/ (accessed July 25, 2009).

13. For documentation of the dangerous side-effects, see Dr. Peter Breggin's books, for example, *Medication Madness: A Psychiatrist Exposes the Dangers of Mood-Altering Medications* (New York: St. Martin's Press, 2008). For the International Center for the Study of Psychiatry and Psychology, see www.icspp.org.

14. Kristina Borjesson, ed., *Into the Buzzsaw: Leading Journalists Expose the Myth of a Free Press* (Amherst, NY: Prometheus Books, 2004).

15. Ibid., 42.

16. Ibid., 46.

17. Ibid., 207–219.

18. Ibid., 137.

19. Don Feder, "*New York Times* Won't Tell Real Story On $700 Billion Bailout," October 2, 2008 at http://boycottnyt.com/new-york-times-wont-tell-real-story-on-700-billion-bailout/ (accessed July 17, 2009).

20. Russell Roberts, "The Price of Everything." YouTube video at http://www.youtube.com/watch?v=AsvCqxV31D4 (accessed July 17, 2009).

21. See http://www.projectcensored.org/articles/story/nominations-for-april-2008/ (accessed July 27, 2009).

22. See http://www.projectcensored.org/articles/story/nominations-for-2003-2004 (accessed July 22, 2009).

23. See http://www.projectcensored.org/top-stories/articles/15-worldwide-slavery (accessed July 22, 2009).

24. Howard Bloom, "The Puppets of Pandemonium" in ed. Russell Kick, *You Are Being Lied To: The Disinformation Guide to Media Distortion, Historical Whitewashes and Cultural Lies* (New York: Disinformation Company, 2001), 37.

25. See http://www.disinfo.com.

26. For Gray, see Note 1/8; for Tannen's credentials, see Note 3/49.

27. See http://www.alfiekohn.org.

28. See http://en.wikipedia.org/wiki/Alfie_Kohn (accessed July 15, 2009).

29. For Singer, see http://en.wikipedia.org/wiki/Margaret_Singer. For *Journal of Cultic Studies*, see http://www.icsahome.com/infoserv_bookreviews/bkrev_cultsinmidst.htm (accessed July 23, 2009).

30. See http://www.frc.org or http://en.wikipedia.org/wiki/Family_Research_CouncilFRC (accessed July 25, 2009).

31. There are many textbooks on the psychology of gender. I have read quite a few of them. Not one would agree with what John Gray says about gender differences (except for what he took from Deborah Tannen's work). The textbooks are based on peer-reviewed research; Gray's is apparently based on his personal notions since he did not include a bibliography. See, for example, Hyde, *Half the Human Experience* or Crawford and Unger, *Women and Gender*, 4th Ed.

32. See, for example, "My worst nightmare is that John Gray is the leading gender expert in America," says Jeanne Marecek, a Swarthmore College professor of psychology. "Nothing he says stands to any literature in the field." As quoted in Karen Heller, *Knight Ridder Tribune*, April 15, 2002. An extensive web site with many criticisms, The Rebuttal from Uranus, can be found at http://web.archive.org/web/20060305091408/http://ourworld.compuserve.com/homepages/women_rebuttal_from_uranus/ (accessed February 22, 2010). There are also 89 1-star and 39 2-star reviews of the paperback at Amazon.com.

33. Julius Fast, *Body Language* (New York: Pocket, 1971), front and back cover.

34. See *Unreliable Sources*, 36–39 for examples of loaded language; see 39–41 for politically charged labels.

35. For a description of this famous ad, see http://en.wikipedia.org/wiki/Daisy_(television_commercial) (accessed July 9, 2009).

36. *Unreliable Sources*, 42.

37. See, for example, Brooke Noel Moore and Richard Parker, *Critical Thinking* (Mountain View, CA: Mayfield Publishing, 1998), 112–113.

38. *Unreliable Sources*, 26–27.

39. John Stossel, ABC News Special, *Boys and Girls Are Different:*

Men, Women and the Sex Difference, Feb. 1, 1995. For a discussion of this TV program, see http://www.fair.org/extra/9505/abc-gender-differences.html (accessed July 2, 2009). I once asked Stossel about this program after a talk he gave at California State University, Hayward (now CSU East Bay) on October 18, 2002. He claimed he didn't really remember the program. When I pressed him, he became even more vague and expressed astonishment that anyone would question the differences between the sexes. He never responded to my point about the lack of balance on his program.

40. For one account, see, for example, http://www.fair.org/index.php?page=1034 (accessed July 26, 2009).

41. *Unreliable Sources,* 35.

42. There is much criticism of so-called "genetic determinism," both on the Internet and in scientific books. For one typical textbook discussion of the complex interaction between genetics and environment that influence human behavior, see, John W. Santrock, *A Topical Approach to Life-Span Development* 2nd Ed. (New York: McGraw-Hill, 2005), 62–65.

43. See http://en.wikipedia.org/wiki/Lies,_damned_lies,_and_statistics (accessed July 26, 2009).

44. *Unreliable Sources,* 52–53.

45. Paul Armentano, "Drug War Mythology," in *You Are Being Lied To,* 235.

46. *Unreliable Sources,* 54–55.

47. Moore and Parker, *Critical Thinking,* 107–108.

48. Any psychology of gender textbook will discuss the considerable cultural and social influences on gender roles. See, for example, Hyde or Crawford and Unger (Note # 31 above), 185–196.

49. See, for example, Wade and Tavris, *Psychology,* 9th Ed., 501–504. For the effect of peer pressure on conformity, also see Santrock (Note # 42 above), 527.

50. See, for example, Wade and Tavris, *Psychology,* 9th Ed, 336–337.

51. There are many criticisms of of Palmer and Thornhill's book. See, for example, http://www.fair.org/index.php?page=1034 or http://www.saidit.org/archives/mar00/mar_article2.html (accessed July 23, 2009). There is, in fact, a whole book dedicated to criticism of this book. See ed. Cheryl Travis *Evolution, Gender and Rape* (Cambridge, MA: MIT Press, 2003).

52. "Today" show, NBC-TV, January 24, 2000. For a discussion of the controversy over Thornhill and Palmer's book, see http://www.fair.org/index.php?page=1034 (accessed July 9, 2009). Says FAIR: "Rather than including biologists who could add scientific counterpoints to the debate, Today (1/24/00) pitted Thornhill against New York sex crimes prosecutor Linda Fairstein. As was the case in every debate where Thornhill was the only scientist in the conversation, he appeared by default to be the defender of natural reality, allowing the

sociobiologist to round off his claims with the assertion, "these are not debatable issues." When Fairstein criticized Thornhill for doing no research on rape victims or rapists, and instead basing much of his theory on his studies of the sexual practices of scorpion flies ("This is not, professor, *A Bug's Life*," Fairstein said), Thornhill huffed, "It's very, very tragic for critics of our approach to try to mislead the public about the nature of science." In a review of the book, Adriene Sere points out that Mary Koss, professor of Public Health, Psychiatry and Psychology at the University of Arizona in Tucson, comments that "Thornhill and Palmer never subjected their deductions to peer review, and did not respond in their book to the peer criticism they have received over the years—a very unorthodox practice, given the cloak of "science" they wrap their argument in. Furthermore, the authors relied on documentation about insects and birds to support their theory about the nature of man, but they made virtually no reference to empirical findings on sexual assault." See http://www.saidit.org/archives/mar00/mar_article2.html (accessed July 25, 2009).

53. See, for example, ed. Mary Roth Walsh, *Women, Men and Gender* (New Haven, CT: Yale University Press, 1996), 272. Dr. Janet Hyde also questions the biological basis, finding no gender differences overall in her meta-analysis of math abilities; see Hyde, *Half the Human Experience*, 228–229.

54. One of the first media uses of this idea was Dennis A. Williams with Patricia King, "Do Males Have a Math Gene?" *Newsweek*, December 15, 1980, 73. There are many criticisms of the conclusions of the Benbow and Stanley study. One excellent criticism about it is made by the Association for Women in Mathematics. They point out that in the original study done in 1980–82, the ratio of males to females scoring above 700 (which is very high) on the math portion of the SAT was 13:1. In 2005, the ratio was 3:1. Genes cannot account for the drastic shift in ratio in such a short time, only culture can. See http://www.awm-math.org/benbow_petition/statement_UNC.html (accessed July 20, 2009). For a look at the social factors that influence female math scores, see J. S. Eccles and J. E. Jacobs, "Social Forces Shape Math Attitudes and Performance," *Signs*, 11 (1986): 367–380.

55. Veronica Fowler, "Male Math Skills Linked to Brain Damage in Womb," *Des Moines Register*, April 4, 1987, 1T.

56. Caplan, *You're Smarter than They Make You Feel*, 143.

57. Carole Wade and Carol Tavris, *Critical and Creative Thinking* (New York: HarperCollins, 1993), 12–14.

58. For the relation between environment and IQ, see, for example, John W. Santrock, *A Topical Approach to Life-Span Development* (New York: McGraw-Hill, 2005), 281–292.

59. See Robert Sapolsky, Ph.D., "The Trouble with Testosterone," in *The Trouble with Testosterone* (New York: Scribner, 1997), 147–173.

60. For two well-done popular books on the research and applications of neuroplasticity, see Sharon Begley, *Train Your Mind, Change Your Brain* (New York: Ballantine Books, 2007) and Norman Doidge, *The Brain That Changes Itself* (New York: Penguin, 2007).

62. See http://www.wisdomquotes.com/003393.html (accessed July 8, 2009).

63. Anonymous reviewer, November 17, 2003. See http://www.amazon.com/Bias-Insider-Exposes-Media-Distort/product-reviews/0060520841/ref=cm_cr_pr_viewpnt_sr_4?ie=UTF8&showViewpoints=0&filterBy=addFourStar (accessed July 8, 2009).

64. Walter Goodman, "Let's Be Frank About Fairness And Accuracy," *New York Times*, June 17, 1990. See http://query.nytimes.com/gst/fullpage.html?res=9C0CE6DA173AF934A25755C0A966958260&sec=&spon=&pagewanted=all (accessed July 8, 2009).

PART III: I AM NOT A NUMBER

1. Lance Winslow, see http://ezinearticles.com/?Criminals-of-Bureaucracy-and-Their-Meaningless-Paperwork&id=590364 (accessed July 2, 2009).

2. Russell L. Ackoff and Sheldon Rovin, *Beating the System: Using Creativity to Outsmart Bureaucrats* (San Francisco: Berrett-Koehler Publishers, 2005), 10.

3. See, for example, ed. Valerian J. Derlega, Barbara A. Winstead and Warren H. Jones, *Personality: Contemporary Theory and Research*, 3rd Ed. (Belmont, CA: Wadsworth, 2005), 311–312.

4. Denise Kersten, "How to Bend the Rules of Corporate Bureaucracy," *USA Today* at http://www.usatoday.com/money/jobcenter/workplace/rules/2002-11-08-corporate-bureaucracy_x.htm (accessed July 26, 2009).

CHAPTER SEVEN: NOT ANOTHER BRICK IN THE WALL

1. See lyrics at http://www.tnellen.com/ted/brick.html (accessed July 2, 2009).

2. See http://health.usnews.com/articles/health/brain-and-behavior/2009/04/21/narcissism-epidemic-why-there-are-so-many-narcissists-now.html (accessed July 11, 2009) for a discussion of the book, *The Narcissism Epidemic (New York: Free Press,* 2009), by research psychologists Jean Twenge and W. Keith Campbell.

3. Lawrence H. Diller, M.D., *Running on Ritalin* (New York, Bantam Books, 1998), 2.

4. Ibid., 36.

5. Peter Breggin. M.D., *Talking Back to Ritalin* (Monroe, ME: Common Courage Press, 1998), 2–37. The rest of this book expands upon the dangers of Ritalin.

6. Ibid., 336–339.

7. Ibid., 338.

8. Santrock, *A Topical Approach to Life-Span Developmental Psychology*, 2nd Ed., 313.

9. Bill Kurtis, *Investigative Reports*, "Generation Rx: Reading, Writing and Ritalin," 2000.

10. Chris Mercogliano, *Teaching the Restless: One School's Remarkable No-Ritalin Approach to Helping Children Learn and Succeed* (Boston: Beacon Press, 2003), 247. Mercogliano writes a narrative with heart about some of the children in the Albany Free School who were helped by its educational and philosophical approach. This is the way schools should be but rarely are.

11. Kathleen Winkler, *Bullying: How to Deal with Taunting, Teasing and Tormenting* (Berkeley Heights, NJ: Enslow Publishers, 2005), 15. Also see James Garbarino, Ph.D. and Ellen deLara, Ph.D., *And Words Can Hurt Forever* (New York: The Free Press, 2002), 1.

12. The study was conducted in 2001 by the Kaiser Foundation, in conjunction with Nickelodeon TV and Children Now, as cited in Barbara Coloroso, *The Bully, the Bullied, and the Bystander* (New York: HarperCollins, 2003), 12.

13. Hyde, *Half the Human Experience,* 7th Ed., 228–230. For the vast majority of children and adults in the middle ranges of math ability, Dr. Hyde's meta-analysis (a way of statistically comparing many different studies) found no gender differences in average ability overall. This was also true overall in other European countries. While small differences are found in certain specialized areas (e.g., problem-solving, high SAT scores), overall, the idea that girls can't do math is archaic, harmful and not supported by present research.

14. SuEllen Fried and Paula Fried, Ph.D., *Bullies, Targets & Witnesses: Helping Children Break the Pain Chain* (New York: M. Evans, 2003), 149.

15. Adam Hibbert, *Why Do People Bully?* (Chicago: Raintree, 2005), 41.

16. Winkler, *Bullying: How to Deal with Taunting, Teasing and Tormenting*, 66.

17. Wendy M. Craig, Debra Pepler and Rona Atlas, "Observations of Bullying in the Playground and in the Classroom," *School Psychology International* 21, no. 1 (2000): 29.

18. See, for example, Wade and Tavris, *Psychology*, 9th Ed., 371–373. They discuss the conditions under which young children may be highly

suggestible in regard to questions about what they have witnessed. They have a section on "How Not to Interview Children" on p. 371. The bottom line: ask neutral questions rather than ones that presuppose a certain answer. Young children want to please you and may sometimes tell you what they think you want to hear rather than what really happened.

19. Fried and Fried, *Bullies, Targets & Witnesses*, 162.

20. Garbarino and de Lara, *And Words Can Hurt Forever*, 50.

21. U.S. Department of Education's Office for Civil Rights, as cited in Debbie Stanley, *Everything You Need to Know about Student-on-Student Sexual Harassment* (New York: Rosen Publishing Group, 2000), 39.

22. Garbarino and de Lara, *And Words Can Hurt Forever*, 125–126.

23. Grace Llewellyn and Amy Silver, *Guerrilla Learning: How to Give Your Kids a Real Education With or Without School*. (New York: John Wiley and Sons, 2001), 43.

24. Traci Truly, Attorney at Law, *Teen Rights (and Responsibilities)*, 2nd Ed. (Napierville, IL: Sphinx Publishing®, 2005).

25. Ibid., 36.

26. Ibid., 37.

27. See http://www.aclu.org/studentsrights/index.html (accessed July 6, 2009).

28. See http://www.aclunc.org/news/press_releases/the_devil_wears_winnie-the-pooh_suit_charges_napa_middle_school_dress_code_goes_too_far.shtml (accessed July 6, 2009).

29. Ackoff and Rovin, *Beating the System*, 111.

30. Ibid.,128.

31. Jeffrey D. Fisher, Paul A. Bell, and Andrew Baum, *Environmental Psychology*, 2nd Ed. (New York: Holt, Rinehart and Winston, 1984), 158. For a nonacademic overview of the research, see the *Salon* article, "Personal-space Invaders" by Jon Bowen at http://www.salon.com/health/feature/1999/09/01/personal_space/print.html (accessed July 11, 2009).

CHAPTER EIGHT: YOUR CALL IS NOT IMPORTANT TO US: GETTING WHAT YOU DESERVE FROM CONSUMER SERVICES

1. Ron Burley, *Unscrewed: The Consumer's Guide to Getting What You Paid For* (Berkeley, CA: Tenspeed Press, 2006), 162–165.

2. John Bear and Mariah Bear, *Complaint Letters for Busy People* (Franklin Lakes, NJ: Career Press, 1999), 45.

3. Many psychology textbooks discuss the research on learned helplessness. See, for example, Saul Kassin, Steven Fein, Hazel Rose Markus, *Social Psychology* (Boston, MA: Houghton–Mifflin, 2008), 522.

4. Burley, *Unscrewed*, 1.

5. Shannon Wirchniansky, personal communication, May 16, 2009.
6. Beka Wildman, personal communication, April 19, 2009.
7. See http://www.aarp.org/money/consumer/articles/seven_things_always_say.html (accessed July 25, 2009).
8. See http://www.aarp.org/money/consumer/articles/seven_things_never_say.html (accessed July 25, 2009).
9. Bear and Bear, *Complaint Letters for Busy People,* 61.
10. John Bear, Ph.D., *Send This Jerk the Bedbug Letter* (Berkeley, CA: Tenspeed Press, 1996),131–138. Bear looks at many studies of the Better Business Bureau.
11. Ibid., 132.
12. For "Town Crier," see Burley, *Unscrewed*, 127–129; For "Spokesman for the Competition," see 35–138.
13. Burley, ibid., 152–55, 157–159.
14. Bear, *Send This Jerk the Bedbug Letter,* 92.
15. Ackoff and Rovin, *Beating the* System, 89
16. Lori Andrews, "Fight for Your Health Care," *Parade* magazine, January 20, 2008, 14–15.
17. Readers Digest, *Fight Back and Win: What to Do When You Feel Cheated or Wronged* (Pleasantville, NY: Reader's Digest Association, Inc., 2001), 301–302.
18. See http://www.hmohelp.ca.gov (accessed July 25, 2009).
19. Reader's Digest, *Fight Back and Win*, 93–94.
20. Paul Bianchina and the Editors of Consumer Reports Books, *How to Hire the Right Contractor* (Yonkers, NY: Consumer Reports Books, 1991), 2.
21. See http://www.elliott.org/help/how-to-fix-your-trip.
22. Ibid.
23. Ibid.
24. Ibid.
25. Ibid.
26. Ibid.

CHAPTER NINE: YOU CAN FIGHT CITY HALL: TACKLING GOVERNMENT BUREAUCRACIES AND DEALING EFFECTIVELY WITH THE POLICE

1. Quoted in Denise Kersten, "How to Bend the Rules of Corporate Bureaucracy," *USA Today*, at http://www.usatoday.com/money/jobcenter/workplace/rules/2002-11-08-corporate-bureaucracy_x.htm (accessed July 26, 2009).
2. See http://news.bbc.co.uk/2/hi/uk_news/2757067.stm (accessed July 26, 2009).
3. See Note 1/15–17.

4. For example, see Wade and Tavris, *Psychology*, 9th Ed., 369. Much has been written about the unreliability of eyewitness testimony by many researchers, including, most prominently, Elizabeth Loftus. See Loftus below, Note 9/6.

5. Attorneys Paul Bergman and Sara J. Bergman-Barrett, *Criminal Law Handbook: Know Your Rights: Survive the System*. Berkeley, CA: Nolo Press, 2007, 18.

6. In the case of Steve Titus, he was never told he was a suspect (even though he was) while he was being questioned. He knew he was innocent so he babbled away. The police used what he said against him. See Dr. Elizabeth Loftus and Katherine Ketcham, *Witness for the Defense: The Accused, the Eyewitness and the Expert Who Puts Memory on Trial* (New York, St. Martin's Press, 1991), 36–60.

7. Ibid.

8. Bergman and Bergman-Barrett, *Criminal Law Handbook*, 13.

9. Ibid., 26.

10. Ibid., 17

11. Ibid., 16

12. See http://www.time.com/time/magazine/article/0,9171, 978105-2,00.html (accessed July 26, 2009).

13. Bergman and Bergman-Barrett, *Criminal Law Handbook*,13.

14. David T. Lykken, *A Tremor in the Blood: Uses and Abuses of the Lie Detector* (New York: Plenum, 1998), 60–61.

15. Ibid., 134.

16. Ibid., 264–265.

17. See Shermer's video at http://www.youtube.com/watch?v=GLL3wtgBiFA.

18. Bergman and Bergman-Barrett, p. 27. In Lawrence S. Wrightsman and Solomon Fulero, *Forensic Psychology* 2nd Ed. (Belmont, CA: Thomson Wadsworth, 2005), 242; the authors point out that the ones most likely to waive their rights are the innocent; they suggest that this is a bad idea. They also point out that the police are legally allowed to lie and manipulate suspects to a far greater degree than most people realize, 244–250.

19. Bergman and Bergman-Barrett, *Criminal Law Handbook*, 29.

20. Wrightsman and Fulero, *Forensic Psychology* 2nd Ed., 238, 240.

21. Attorney David Brown, *Beat Your Ticket: Go to Court and Win* (Berkeley, CA: Nolo Press, 2005), 7/7-7/8. Hereafter referred to as *Beat Your Ticket*.

22. Ibid., 5/2.

23. Mel Leiding, *How to Fight Your Traffic Ticket and Win!!!* (Anaheim, CA: Avenir, 2006), 18.

24. *Beat Your Ticket*, 7/11.

25. *Beat Your Ticket*, 3/7–3/10

26. *Beat Your Ticket*, 3/11.

CHAPTER TEN: WON'T GET FOOLED AGAIN: WRAPPING IT UP AND TAKING IT WITH YOU

1. See lyrics at http://www.metrolyrics.com/we-dont-get-fooled-again-lyrics-who.html (accessed July 2, 2009).

2. See http://www.freemeditations.com/buddhist_meditation.html for a discussion of the Buddhist concept of "mindfulness" (accessed July 2, 2009). Psychologists have also investigated this idea. Not being "mindful" can lead to inappropriate automatic behavior and unthinking responses to silly requests; see, for example, Ellen Langer, Ph.D., *Mindfulness* (Reading, MA: Addison Wesley, 1989).

3. See http://www.authentichappiness.sas.upenn.edu/Default.aspx (accessed July 16, 2009).

4. The reviews start at http://www.amazon.com/Authentic-Happiness-Psychology-Potential-Fulfillment/product-reviews/0743222989/ref=dp_top_cm_cr_acr_txt?ie=UTF8&showViewpoints=1 (accessed July 16, 2009).

5. Kathleen A. Lawler, Rebecca L. Volz, and Martina F. Martin, "Chapter 16: Stress and Illness," in ed. Valerian J. Derlega, Barbara A. Winstead and Warren H. Jones, *Personality: Contemporary Theory and Research*, 3rd Ed. (Belmont, CA: Wadsworth, 2005), 472.

6. See http://en.wikipedia.org/wiki/Self-efficacy (accessed July 16, 2009).

7. See the review at http://www.amazon.com/Your-Perfect-Right-Assertiveness-Relationships/product-reviews/1886230854/ref=dp_top_cm_cr_acr_txt?ie=UTF8&showViewpoints=1 (accessed July 16, 2009).

8. Wade and Carol Tavris, *Psychology*, 9th Ed., 7.

9. See http://artists.letssingit.com/bobby-fuller-four-lyrics-i-fought-the-law-and-the-law-won-fx4r9mq (accessed July 16, 2009).

10. "Are You Your Own Worst Doctor?" *Prevention*, March 2009. See this article online at http://www.prevention.com/cda/article/are-you-your-own-worst-doctor/97f3233cb14ce110VgnVCM10000013281eac____/news.voices/in.the.magazine/march.2009.issue (accessed July 16, 2009).

11. Justin Kruger and David Dunning, "Unskilled and Unaware of It: How Difficulties in Recognizing One's Own Incompetence Leads to Inflated Self-Assessments," *Journal of Personality and Social Psychology*, 77 (1999):1127–1134. See a PDF of the original research at http://www.apa.org/journals/features/psp7761121.pdf (accessed July 16, 2009). See a summary of this research, "Why We Overestimate Our Competence" by Tori DeAngelis at http://www.apa.org/monitor/feb03/overestimate.html (accessed July 16, 2009).

Index

"1001 Ways to Market Your Books," 163
1984, 186
"7 Things You Should Always Say to Customer Service," 250
"7 Things You Should Never Say to Customer Service," 251
9to5National Association for Working Women, 122, 127
AARP, 61, 90, 269, 280, 343, 356
ABC-TV, 75, 188, 350
Abuse Your Illusions, 197
Abzug, Bella, 189
Ackoff, Russell L., x, 204, 206–208, 230, 240, 259, 308, 353, 355–356
Accuracy in Media (AIM), x, 175, 178, 199
ADHD, see Attention Deficit Disorder; drugs for, see drugs
After Any Diagnosis, 60, 88, 342, 343
Age of Propaganda, 22
Albany Free School, 354
Alberti, Robert, 97, 107, 126, 320, 332, 345
allies, bring backup, 43
Alstad, Diana, 21
Amabile, Carmen, 161
Amazon.com, 83, 126, 158, 161, 162, 163, 197, 198, 208, 318, 320, 322, 345, 348, 350, 353, 358
American Bar Association, 63
American Board of Medical Specialties, 57, 89
American Civil Liberties Union (ACLU), x, 266, 227, 240, 355
American Civil Liberties Union Northern California (ACLUNC), x, 227
American Medical Association, 57
American Pharmacists Association, 63, 64, 89
American Society of Travel Agents, 276
And Words Can Hurt Forever, 222, 239, 354, 355
Andrews, Lori, 269, 356
Angie's List, 166, 167, 348
Anti-Depressant Fact Book, The, 88
appearance, 5; beauty and, 10; dress and, 33; gender and, 10, 34; influence and, xv; perception and, 42; power and, 34; seduction of the situation and, physical attractiveness and, 10, 23
Armentano, Paul 351
Aronson, Elliot, 22, 325, 335
Arrogance: Rescuing America from the Media, 197
The Assertive Woman, 107, 125, 346
assertiveness, being assertive, xviii, 35–36, 160, 315–316; books on, 332; boss and, 97, 100; bullying and,107,109,124; building skills and, 319–320; children and, 219–220; complaints and, 252–254; contractors and, 149; customer service and, 245, 247–248; language and, 38; lawyers and, 139; physicians, medical, and 56, 61; politeness and, 40; resources for, 337
Association for Women in Mathematics, 352
Atlas, Rona, 354
Atlas Shrugged, 160
Attention Deficit Disorder (ADD) or Attention Deficit Hyperactive Disorder (ADHD), 214, 215, 321, 332, 333, 337, 338; drugs for, see drugs
Attorneys, see lawyer
Austin, Nancy, 126
author, credentials of, 82, 181, 183, 189; also see journalist
*Authoritative Guide to Self-Help Book*s, 81–87, 89, 334, 344
authority, xv, xviii, 152; authority figures and, 27–29, 40, 96, 219, 294, 319; body language and, 15; books on, 20–21; confront, stand up to, 31–48; credibility of, 8; critical thinking and, 3–5, 50–51, 69, 316; definition of, xviii; influence of,16,17,18, 19, 20; obedience to, motivational factors and, 4–6; obedience to, situational factors and, 12, 16, 339–340; parental teaching and, 17–18; passive reaction

authority (*continued*)
 to, 17; police and, 296, 308; pressures from, 318, 320, 323; situational etiquette and, 19; Stanley Milgram, studies of obedience and, see Stanley Milgram; studies of and clothing, see power of a uniform; symbols of, 16–17; when not to stand up to, 326–328, 331
Authentic Happiness, 318, 334
Avorn, Jerry, 67, 87

Back Off! How to Confront and Stop Sexual Harassment and Harassers, 118, 347
backup, see allies
Bandura, Albert, 319
Basler, Barbara, 343
Bauer, Ann, x, 80
Baum, Andrew 355
BBC, x, 175, 176, 177, 181, 356
Beane, Allan L., 239
Bear, John, 244, 246, 252, 255, 258, 259, 279
Bear, Mariah, 252, 279
Beat Your Ticket: Go to Court & Win, 131, 302, 309, 357
Beating the System, x, 204, 230, 259, 353, 355, 356
Beattie, Melodie, 85
Because I Said So, 125
Beck, Aaron T., 344
Before You Hire a Contractor, 150, 162, 348
Begley, Sharon, 353
Bell, Paul A., 355
Bellaccomo, Josephine, 208
Benbow, Camille, 194, 352
Bergman, Paul and Sara Bergman-Barrett, 160, 161, 297, 299, 300, 301, 309, 357
Berman, Brian, 88, 343
Best of Alternative Medicine, The, 67, 88
Better Business Bureau, 152, 255
Beverly Hills Diet, The , 83
Bianchina, Paul,161, 348, 356
Bias: A CBS Insider Exposes How the Media Distort the News, 197
Bickman, Leonard, 11, 12, 340
Blakeman, M.C., 284
blaming the victim,116, 346
Blass, Thomas, 21, 23, 51

Bloom, Howard, x, 178
body language, 21, 37, 38, 139, 213, 220, 254, 273, articles on, 23, 51; authority and, 7, 15, 37, 38; book about, see *Body Politics*; see also Paul Ekman
Body Language (Fast), 185, 350
Body Politics, 21, 50, 339, 341, 342
Boland, Mary, 126
Borjesson, Kristina, x, 174,197, 349
boss, asking for a raise and; books on dealing with,125; bullying and, see bullying; performance appraisal and, 99–101; prepare your case and, 94, 98–99, 102; questioning policy and, 102–104; unethical behavior and, 104–106; 321–322
Boss, Judith, 196, 324, 332
"Boys and Girls Are Different" (Stossel), 188, 350
Bowerman, Peter, 162
Bramson, Robert M., 125
Branden, Nathaniel, 317, 318, 319, 337; books by, 333
Breggin, Peter, x, 78, 82, 83, 87, 91, 215, 216, 217, 241, 345, 349, 354; books by, 88, 238
Brehm, Sharon S., 343
Breitman, Patti, 49
Bridges, Judith, 340
Brighter Side of Human Nature, The, 182
Brothers, Joyce, 82, 86, 344, 345
Brown, Attorney David W., 302, 303, 305, 306, 308, 311, 357; books by, 309
Brown, David, (*Organization Smarts*), 292
Browne, M. Neil G., 49
Buechi, Georg, 149, 151, 152
Bulletin of the Atomic Scientists, 177
Bully at Work, The, x, 107, 111, 126, 127, 346
Bully, the Bullied, and the Bystander, The, 239, 354
Bully-Free Classroom®, The, 239
Bullies Are a Pain in the Brain, 239
Bullies, Targets & Witnesses, x, 239, 354
bullying, 94, 95, 106, 107, 108, 115; allies and, 110; alternative actions and, 110; books on, 126,

Index

239; characteristics of bullied and, 108; dealing with, 109, 111, 112, 122, 210; gather information and, 112; prepare your case and, 218; resources for, 123, 127, 241, 242; schools and, 218, 219, 221, 222, 223, 224, 234, studies of, 106, 107, 218, 221; women and, 107; work and, 106, 107

Bullying: How to Deal with Taunting, Teasing and Tormenting, x, 221, 354

Bureau of Labor Statistics, 190

bureaucracies, allies and, 206, 231; books on 308, 356; college and, 227; dealing with, 205–207; overview of, 203–207; red tape and, 204, 207, 290–295; resources, 208; school, 213, 224

Burley, Ron, 243, 244, 246, 248, 250, 251, 255, 256, 257, 258, 276, 278, 279, 280, 355, 356

Burns, David D., 76, 85, 89, 319, 333, 334

Buscaglia, Leo, 84

Bushman, Brad, 11, 12, 340

buzzwords, 184, 186

Bykofsky, Sheree, 162

Byrne, Rhonda, 83

California State University, Hayward (now CSU East Bay), 351

Campbell, Barbara, 81, 344

Campbell, W. Keith, 353

Camus, Albert, 322

Caplan, Paula, ix, 29, 35, 45, 50, 169, 195, 342, 348, 352

Carroll, Nicholas, x, 133, 135–138, 141, 145, 161, 347

categorical imperative, 322

CBS-TV, 172, 175, 197

cease and desist, 121–123, 128, 164

Center for Critical Thinking, 24; see also critical thinking

Center for the Study of Psychiatry and Psychology, 78, 91, 174, 349; see also Peter Breggin

chain of command, 48, 101, 206, 222, 229, 245, 249, 285

Christian Science Monitor, 179

Chron Watch, 290

CIA, 174

Cialdini, Robert, 5, 399; book by, 21, 23, 50; influence and, 5; web site for, 51

Cimino, Michael, 13

City Council or Board of Supervisors, 284, 286, 291

City Hall, fighting and, 283–294; prepare your case and, 287, 293; also see community problems

civil liberties, 186; see also ACLU

Coercion: Why We Listen to What "They" Say?, 198

cognitive behavioral therapy, see cognitive therapy

cognitive fallacies, 325, 335

cognitive therapy, 72, 77–78, 82, 85, 318, 334, 336, 344; books on, websites and, 336

cognitive shortcuts, 6, 17

Cohen, David, 88

Cohen, Jeff, 172

Coloroso, Barbara, 239, 354

Columbia Journalism Review, 172

community groups, bring backup and, 254; books on, 309; problems, 283–289; Web resources and, 310

company policy, allies and, 95, 104; list of questions and, 95; questioning, see boss

complaint, letter, alternative options and, 273; documentation and 220; how to write, 251, 279, 281; get it in writing and, 277; prepare your case and, 254

Complaint Letters for Busy People, 252, 279, 355–356

Complete Guide to Book Marketing, The, 163

Complete Idiot's Guide to Getting Published, The, 162

Complete Idiot's Guide to Self-Publishing, The, 162

conservative media, see media

Contra Costa County Public Library, ix

contractors, 129, 147, 148, 211, 347–348; bring backup and, 139, 149; documentation and, 156; gather information and, 148; get it in writing and, 154; licensing and, 150, 152; second opinion and, 157; warning signs and what to look for, 150–157

Contractors from Hell (CFH), x, 129, 147, 165–166, 150–152, 166, 347–348
Contractors State Licensing Board, 46,152
Coping with Difficult Bosses, 125
Coping with Difficult People, 125
Corder, Cheryl, 239
Costello, Jody, x, 147
Coyne, Jerry, 193
Craig, Wendy M., 354
Crawford, Mary, 340, 346
credentials, 8, 11, 46, 130, 160, 189; authors and, 82, 181,183; contractors and, 150; Deborah Tannen and, 84, 345, 350; John Gray and, 8, 182
physicians and, 56, 57, 66; psychologists and, 71–72; Martin Seligman and, 318; writers and, see authors
Crilley, Jeff, 208–209
crime prevention, 284, 310
Criminal Law Handbook, The, 160, 297, 299, 357
critical thinking, xvii, 36, 40, 45, 55, 242, 288, 301, 309, 316, 328–329; articles about, 24–25; authority and experts and, 3, 5–6, 14, 17, 20, 47, 315; books about, 29, 196, 327, 332, 335; media and, 169–201, 348; physicians and, 55, 56, 67; psychologists and, 56, 69–70, 78, 90; self-help books and, 80–87; psychiatric drugs and, see psychiatric drugs; websites and, 22–24, 50, 53, 335–36
Critical Thinking (Moore and Parker), xvii, 196, 324, 332, 339, 350
Critical and Creative Thinking, 195, 352
cults, 19, 21,183
Cults in Our Midst, 183
customer satisfaction, 166, 244, 250, 255
customer service, 207, 211, 243–244, 247, 251, 253, 255, 276; phone support and, 204, 247–250, 265; take notes and, 25–251, 267; tech support and, see tech support

Dale, Nancy, ix

Dan Poynter's Self-Publishing Manual, 16th Edition, 163
Dancing with Lawyers, x, 133, 135, 161, 164, 347
"Dangerous Propositions," 114, 117, 223, 347
DARE program, 14–14, 341
Dawes, Robin, 72, 89, 343
De Angelis, Barbara, 81, 344
De Angelis, Tori, 358
deLara, Ellen, 222–223, 239, 354
Department of Transportation's Aviation Consumer Protection Division, 276
Derlega, Valerian J., 353, 358
Des Moines Register, 352
Deutsche Welle, 176
Dobson, Keith S., 344
Doidge, Norman, 353
Donelson, Frances Elaine, 342
Don't Believe Everything You Think, 325, 335
Don't Believe It: How Lies Become News, 198
Diamond, ArLyne, ix, 102–103, 107–108, 110, 113–114, 117, 127, 346
Diamond Certified, 166
Diller, Lawrence, 214–215, 238, 241, 354
Dilsaver, Evelyn, 105
disinformation, 170–171, 174
Disinformation Company, x, 178, 197–198, 349–350; books by, 197–198
Disraeli, Benjamin, 190
Dr. Atkins' Diet Revolution, 83
dress for success, 33–34, 42, 97, 138, 254
drugs, ADD and, 215; ADHD and, 321; study on anti-depressants and, 173; illegal,14, 190; prescription, 87, 90, 56, 58–60, 63, 65–66, 87, 90, 281; psychiatric, see psychiatric drugs; Ritalin and, 241
Dubois, Cathy L. Z., 347
Dun and Bradstreet Directory, 252
Dunning, David, 358
Dutch Central Planning Bureau of Statistics, 190
Dyer, Wayne, 82, 344–345

Eccles, J. S., 352

Index

education, allies and, 213, 221–222, 231, 238, 266; alternatives, see home schooling; bullying and, see bullying; colleges, 227–237; questioning policies 214–218; Ritalin and, see Ritalin; student rights and, see student rights
Elder, Linda, 198
Ekeberg, Steven E., 346
Ekman, Paul, 15, 21, 341
Ellerbee, Linda, 114, 346–347
Elliott, Christopher, x, 75–78, 274, 281, 356
Emotions Revealed, 21
Equal Employment Opportunity Commission (EEOC), 113, 121–122, 128, 347
Etaugh, Claire, 340, 345
Evaluating Online Resources, 49
evaluation at work, see boss
Every Landlord's Legal Guide, 280
Every Tenant's Legal Guide, 279
Everything You Know is Wrong, 178, 197, 199
Everything You Need to Know about Student-on-Student Sexual Harassment, 239, 355
Examining Your Doctor, x, 56, 88, 342
eye witness testimony, 296–297, 299; articles about, 311; unreliability of, 310, 357; faulty memory and, 311

facework, 117–118
fairness, 44, 103, 193, 237, 322
Fairness and Accuracy in Reporting (FAIR), 172, 178, 199, 353
Fairstein, Linda, 351, 352
"fake it till you make it," 33, 38
Faley, Robert H., 346
false positives, see polygraph
Family Research Council (FRC), 183, 350
Fanning, Patrick, 334
FAQs (Frequently Asked Questions), 263–264
Fast, Julian, 185
Fausto-Sterling, Anne, 189
Fay, Floyd, 301
faxing for dollars, 257, 270, 278
FBI, 190
Feder, Don, x, 349

Federal Citizen Information Center, 280
Federal Trade Commission, 276
feedback, ix, 47, 76, 338
Feeling Good, 76, 85, 89, 334
Feeling Good Handbook, The, 76, 89, 334
Fein, Steven 341, 343, 355
Feminine Mystique, The, 160, 348
Fight Back and Win, 261, 274, 279, 356
Fight Back: How to Take Back Your Neighborhood, Schools, and Families from the Drug Dealers, 309
"Fight for Your Health Care," 269, 356
Fight Your Ticket & Win in California, 302, 309
Fisher, Jeffrey D., 355
"foot-in-door" technique, 19, 20
forensic psychology, 299, 301, 357
Fortunato, Alfred, 162
Forward, Susan, 85
Foundation for Critical Thinking, 198, 336; see also critical thinking
Fowler, Veronica 352
Fox News, 171
Fox TV "Fair and Balanced," 174
Free Publicity (Crilley), 208, 209
Fried, Paula and SuEllen, x, 220, 222, 239, 354–355
Friedan, Betty, 160
Fulero, Solomon, 357

Garbarino, James, 222, 239, 354–355
gender, 21, 41, 50, 181; beauty and, 10; standard for evaluation and, 11, 12
stereotypes and, xvii, 11, 43, 86; impact of on opinions of author's work and, 11
"Generation Rx: Reading, Writing and Ritalin," 217, 354; see also Ritalin
Gilovich, Thomas, 325, 335
GoDaddy, 262
Goldberg, Bernard, 197
Goldberg, Philip, 11, 340
Golden Rule, 322
Goldwater, Barry, 186
Gonzalez, Steve, 150–53, 348
"good cop-bad cop" routine, 302

Goodman, Walter, 353
Gore, William, ix, 134–137, 139, 141–143, 347
Gray, John, 9, 81, 84, 183, 339, 343, 350; questionable credentials of, 9, 72, 82, 182, 339, 343
Green Party, 186
Greenberg, Michael, 309
Greider, Katharine, 61, 343
A Guide for Nonprofits and Activists, 208
Guru Papers: Masks of Authoritarian Power, The, 21

"Hail Mary," 278
HALT, 161, 164–165
Handgun Control Inc., 186
harassment, 93, 95, 111, 114–115, 122, 123, 255, 257; books on, 126, 239; prepare your case and, 235; schools and, 218–220, 222–223; resources for, 123–124,127; sexual, see sexual harassment
Harding, Caroline, 87
Harris, Gardiner, 342
Hatch, Connie, 49
Harvard Medical School study, 58
health insurance complaints, 267–271
Hearst, William Randolph, 169, 348
Heller, Karen, 350
Helm, Adrian, 161
Henley, Nancy, 15, 21, 23, 39, 50–51339, 341–342
Herndon, Felix, ix
Hibbert, Adam, 220, 239, 354
high pressure techniques, 41, 158
Hollon, Steven, 344
Holtorf, Kent, M.D., 343
home schooling, 242
home repair professionals, 129–130; contractors, see contractors
Honeychurch, Carole, 334
Honoring the Self, 317, 333
hostile work environment, 113–114
Hotwire, 275
House of Cards, 72, 89, 317
How to Detect Media Bias & Propaganda,198
How to Fight Your Traffic Ticket and Win!!!, 304, 309, 311, 357
How to Hire a Home Improvement Contractor without Getting Chiseled, 162

How to Hire, Manage, and Fire Your Contractor, 162
How to Hire the Right Contractor, 162, 356
How to Raise Your Self-Esteem, 333
How to Say No Without Feeling Guilty, 49
How to Talk to Your Doctor, 88
How We Know What Isn't So, 325, 335
Howard, Linda Gordon, 126
Hrdy, Sarah Blaffer, 193
Hubbard, L. Ron, 87
Hyde, Janet Shipley, 340, 352
The Hyperactivity Hoax, 338

Imhoff, Carolyn, ix
"incompetence" syndrome, 328, 358
Influence: The Psychology of Persuasion, 21, 23, 50–51
Insider's Guide to HMOs, The 88
Intelligent Patient's Guide to the Doctor Patient Relationship, The, 87
Internet, searching the, 52
interrupting, others and, 341; letting yourself be interrupted and, 39, 109
International Center for the Study of Psychiatry and Psychology, 78, 91, 173–174
Into The Buzzsaw, x, 174,197, 349
Iowa State University, 194

Jackson, Grace E., 89
Jacobs, Eleanor, 105
Jacobs, J. E., 352
Jacobs, Michael B., 59, 87
Jaff, Jennifer C., 269
jargon, 31, 37, 46, 64, 141
Jedi, 293
Johnson, Lyndon, 186
Jones, Ron, 16, 23, 17, 341; also The Wave
Jones, Warren, 353, 358
Journal of Cultic Studies, 183, 350
journalists, 172; evaluate the expertise of, 181; pressure on, 174, 175; skepticism about, 170, 348

Kaiser Family Foundation and Nickelodeon TV study, 218, 354
Kant, Immanuel, 322
Kassin, Saul, 341, 343, 355

Keeley, Stuart M., 49
Kelly, John, 174–175
Kenrick, Douglas T., 5, 339
Kersten, Denise, 353
Ketcham, Katherine, 310, 357
Kick, Russell, x, 197, 349, 350
Kida, Thomas, 325, 335
Kimura, Doreen, 188
King, Patricia (*Never Work for a Jerk*), x, 93, 99, 125, 345, 353
King, Patricia (math genes), 352
Kiplingers, 153, 167
Kitty, Alexandra, 198
Knapp, Deborah Erdos, 346
Knight Ridder Tribune, 350
Kohn, Alfie, 182, 350
Korsch, Barbara M., 87
Koss, Mary, 352
Kovacs, Maria, 344
Kramer, Joel, 21
Kramon, James M., 279
Kremer, John, 163
Kruger, Justin, 358
Kurtis, Bill, 354
Kwitny, Jonathan, 173

Landers, Ann, 9
landlords, 261, 271–274; tenants and, 143, 261, 271–274
Landon, Alf, 190
Langelan, Martha J., 118, 347
Langer, Ellen, 358
language, 38, 138, 141,172, 185, 254, 342, 350; body and, see body language; interruptions and; 39; nonverbal and, see body language power and, 39; rising inflections and, 38; tag questions and, 38
Law Project for Psychiatric Rights, x, 79, 81, 344
Lawler, Kathleen A., 358
Lawsuit Survival Guide, The, 161
lawyer, 260, 272, 329, 346–347; alternatives to, 131, 143, 224, 270, 274, 277, 279; be an active participant and, 139–142; choosing a, 124, 132–134; language and, 138–139; police and, 299–300, 303, 308; resources about, 125, 160–165; second opinion and, 140–142; second opinions and, 141–143; specialty of, 132; take notes and, 140,

142; what to look for at meeting with, 135–138
Learned Optimism, 334, 345
Ledger, Heath, 79, 344
Lee, Martin A., x, 172
Leiding, Mel, 304, 309, 311, 357
Neuberg, Steven L., 5, 339
Levine, Michael, 309
liberal media, see media
libertarian, 326; media and, see media
Libertarian Party, 186
Liberty magazine, 178, 200
Leippe, Michael, 22, 340
lie detector test, see polygraph
lies, watch for, 45
Lifetime TV, 346
Lip Service, 159
Lips, Hilary M., 340, 346
Llewellyn, Grace, 355
loaded language, terms, 184–185, 350
loaded question, 191
Loftus, Elizabeth, 299, 310–311, 357
Looking Out for Number One, 81
Los Angeles Times, 349
Loving Each Other, 84
Lucifer Effect, The, 339; website of, 50
Lyyken, David, 301, 310, 357

Mad At Your Lawyer?, 130, 146, 161, 347
Magedson, Ed, x
Mann, Stephanie, 284, 309
Marecek, Jeanne, 350
Markus, Hazel Rose, 341, 355
Martin, Martina F., 358
Martindale-Hubbell®, 133, 163
Matthews, Joseph L., 161
Maurer, Janet R., 88
Mayo Clinic, 80
McCaffrey, Barry, 190
McCall, Timothy B., x, 56–57, 88, 342
McGoohan, Patrick, 203
McKay, Matthew, 334
McLaughlin Report, 173
McTaggert, Lynne, 88, 343
media, 169–201; books critical of, 197–198; bias in 171, 180–181, 184, 187; conservative and, 171, 173, 175, 178; 180, 183–184, 197, 200, 326; controversial topics and, 174, 192–193;

media (*continued*)
disinformation, 170–171, 173, 174; evaluate source and, 179, -180, 183, libertarian and, 175, 178, 181, 200, 326; liberal and, 173, 175, 178, 180, 181, 200, 326; progressive and, 172, 178, 181, 200–201, 326; reporting of research and, 188–189, 193–194; skepticism about,170; *Times Mirror* study and, 170
medical issues, resources for, 88–89; see also physician
medical self-diagnosis, 68, 328
Medication Madness, 88, 349
Meisler, Stanley, 349
Men Are from Mars, Women Are from Venus, 9, 81, 84–85, 182–183, 185
mental preparation, 33
Mercogliano, Chris, x, 218, 238, 354
messenger, separating from message, 9, 14, 15, 177–178; body language of authority and,15; expert's appearance and, 10; beauty and, 10; gender and, 10; clothing and,11; reputation or ideology and, 13; people we like and, 13; people we don't like and, 14
Microsoft®, 262, 266
Milgram, Stanley, 21, 23; entrapment and, 18; obedience to authority and, 3, 12, 21–22, 339–340; "situational etiquette" and, 19; web site for, 23, 51
Miller, Jean Baker, 341
Minnett, Ann, 81, 89, 344
Mintz, Ann P., 50
Miranda warning, rights, 225, 229–30
Mismeasure of Woman, 86
mistakes in reasoning, thinking, 327, 335
Mistakes Were Made (but Not by Me), 325, 335
modeling others, 48, 49
Moore, Brooke Noel, xviii, 196, 324, 332, 339, 350
moral dilemma, 323
moral values, see values
Mornelle, Pierre, 106
Mother Jones, 178, 181, 200
Move the Message, 209

motivational factors for obedience, 4–6
Murphy, Dave, 105

Namie, Gary and Ruth, x, 111, 126, 107–109, 346
narcissists, xvii, 214, 330, 352
Nation, The, 178, 180
National Geographic Traveler magazine, 274, 281
National Institute of Child Health and Human Development survey, 218
National Lawyers Guild, 133
National Practitioner Data Bank, 178, 181
National Review, 178, 181
National Rifle Association, 186
Natural History of Rape, 189, 193, 352
neighborhood group, 147, 283, 286, 288–289, 310–311; allies and 285–286, 286
neighborhood complaints, a model, 284
neighborhood organizing and improvement, 309 (also see community problems) web sites for, 310; web sites for crime prevention, 310
Never Work for a Jerk, x, 95, 99, 125, 345–346
New 9to5 Office Worker Survival Guide, The, 122
New York Post, 179
New York Times, 171, 175, 177, 179, 342, 349, 353
Newsweek, 177, 352
Nightline, 187
No Asshole Rule, The, 111,126
Nolo Press, 119, 121–122, 130–131, 133, 142–144, 164, 261, 271–272, 306, 310
No Child Left Different, 238
note taking, see taking notes
nonverbal cues, see body language

Obedience to Authority, 21, 339–41; see also Stanley Milgram
Obedience to Authority: Current Perspectives on the Milgram Paradigm, 21
O'Grady, Sharon, 227
Olfman, Sharma, 238

O'Neill, Sean, 167, 153–154, 348
Organization Smarts, 292
Orwell, George, 186
Ostberg, Kay, 161
Own Your Own Health, 67, 88, 343

Palmer, Craig, 193, 351–352
Parker, Richard, see Brooke Noel Moore
Patients are Powerful, 270, 282
Paul, Richard, 198
PBS, 171–173
peers, 10, 110; influence of, 5–6, 18, 192
Pelletier, Kenneth, 67, 88
Pepler, Debra, 354
performance appraisal; responding to, 93–94, 99, 100–101; preparing for, 94– 95; see also boss
Petrocelli, William, x, 126, 347
pharmacists, 63, 64, 89
Phelps, Stanlee, 107, 126
Philbin Tom, 162
Phillips, Ellen, 279
physician, be an active participant and, 63–64; bring backup and, 65; credentials of, 56–57; list of questions and, 30, 36, 59, 63, 64; second opinions and, 47, 56, 65–66, 73; take notes and, 64
Pillsbury Winthrop Shaw Pittman LLP, 227
Polgar, Susan, 342
Pollar, Odette, 106
police, xviii, 41, 43, 119, 156, 330–331, 357; dealing with, 296–308; confrontation and, 297–302, 308; resources and, 309–310; teens and, 225–226
politeness,19, 33, 40, 42, 61, 96; children and, 219, 222; City Hall and, 295; consumer services and, 243, 249, 252–253, 256–259, 267, 275–276, 294; indiscriminately, overly and, 19, 40–41, 109, 248; police and, 297
professors and, 236; sexual harassment and, 106, 110, 118–119; therapist and,171–172
polygraph, 300–302, 312; dangers of, 300, 312; false positives and, 300; how to beat, 301, 312

Portman, Janet, 279–280
positive psychology, 318, 334, 337
power, viii, xix, xv, 7, 17, 27–28, 31, 33, 36, 40–41, 48, 67, 73, 125, 206, 223–224, 250, 252, 274, 291, 338; boss, workplace and, 96–97, 111; children and, 220; documentation and, 27; dress and, 33–34; also see right to question and, 29; sexual harassment and, 118, 121; symbols of, 16; taking notes and, 36–37, 251; titles and, 39–40; written documents and, 95,103
"power of a uniform", xv, 11–12, 16, 296, 340
Power to the Patient, 58–59, 69
Powerful Medicines, 87
Poyter, Dan, 163
Pratkanis, Anthony, 22
prescription drugs, see drugs
Presley, Sharon, 344
press releases, 172, 258; how to write, 207–11, 259
Prevention magazine, 328, 342, 358
Prisoner, The, 203
pro bono, 134
professional services, 129–130, 158; books about, 160–162; web resources, 163–168
professors, allies and, 229; dealing with, 228–229, 232–235; challenging a grade and, 236–237; sexual harassment and, see sexual harassment; unfair grading and, 229
progressive media, see media
Project Censored, x, 173, 177, 199, 349–350
Protect Your Child from Bullying, 239
psychiatric drugs, 70, 73, 77–78, 80, 82, 89, 91, 173–174, 345; Abilify, 80; ADD, 215; ADHD, 321; Geodon, 80; Paxil, 77; Prozac, 70, 73, 77, 88, 173, 349; Ritalin, see Ritalin; Zoloft, 77, 82
psychiatrist, 55, 69, 77–82, 215, 321; choosing a, 70, 78; books and, 88–90
Psychology of Attitude Change and Social Influence, The, 22
psyching yourself up, 32–33, 60

psychologist, psychotherapist, 69–77; alternative options and, 76; be an active participant and, 75; choosing a, 71; books and, 88–90
Public Citizen Health Research Group, 66, 89
public humiliation, authorities and, 225, 231
publicity, 159, 163, 207–209; also see press release
publishing a book, 158–5, 163, 167–168

questions, list of, 31,

Rabiner, Susan, 162
raise, how to get, see boss
Rand, Ayn, 160
rapport, 35, 40; bureaucrats and, 294; complaints and 254; consumer reps and, 247; lawyers and,135; teachers and, 216
Rather, Dan, x, 174
Ratner, Ellen, 208
Readers Digest, 261, 268, 270–272, 275, 277–278, 356
Ready, Set, Talk!, 308
Reagan, Ronald, 189
Reason magazine, 178, 200
red-light runners, 302–303
Red Light Enforcement Bureau (RLEB), 303
Reevy, Gretchen, ix
Reina, Charles, 174
Register, The, 178–179
Represent Yourself in Court, 161
Repa, Barbara Kate, x, 126, 347
Resources for Independent Thinking, 23, 50, 90, 131, 336–337, 344
Restoring America's Neighborhoods, 89
Richmond, Raymond Lloyd, x, 71, 91, 344
Riemann, Dick and Irene, ix
right to question, 29, 58, 71, 75, 80, 94
right to protest, 75, 80, 113, 116, 145, 213–214, 245, 302
Ringer, Robert, 81, 344
Ritalin, 214–217, 321, 354; second opinion and, 215; see also "Generation Rx"

Ritalin Fact Book, The, 238
Ritalin Nation, 238
Richard DeGrandpre, 238
Ripoff Report®, x, 153, 166, 281, 348
Robin, Peggy, 309
Robinson, Duke, 333
Romain, Trevor, 239
Roosevelt, Franklin, 190
Roper Poll, 191
Rose, M.J., 159–160, 348
Rosenfeld, Isadore, 58–59, 69, 342
Rovin, Sheldon, See Russell Ackoff
Running on Ritalin, 238, 241, 354
Rush, Augustus J., 344
Rushkoff, Douglas, 198
Russell, Robert, 175

Safe Homes Safe Neighborhoods, 284, 309
Safeway, 289
Salzman, Jason, 208
Sampson, Brent, 163
San Francisco Bar Association, 132
San Francisco Chronicle, 105, 193, 260, 289, 343, 346
San Francisco Council for the Arts, 133
Sanday, Peggy, 189
Sander, Jennifer Basye, 162–163
Santrock, John, 51–52, 81, 89, 344–346
Sapolsky, Robert, 195, 352
Saving the Neighborhood, 309
Scarrah, Kathie, 208
Schlessinger, Laura, 13–14, 82
Scholastic Achievement Test, Math SAT, 194; SAT, 354
school policies, resolving conflicts with, 214–218
Secret, The, 83
Secrets about Men That Every Woman Should Know, 81
seduction of the situation, xv–xvi, 8, 3, 7, 316
Segerstrom, Suzanne C., 342
self-confidence, build your, 318; how you dress and, see dress for success; mental preparation and, 32, 33
self-efficacy, 319
self-esteem, 6, 106, 125, 242, 317–319, 321, 332
Self-Esteem: A Proven Program of Cognitive Techniques for As-

sessing, Improving, and Maintaining Your Self-Esteem, 334
Self-Esteem at Work, 333
Self-Esteem Companion, The, 334
self-help, psychology books and, 332, 334; children and, 242; cults and, 19; legal and, 134, 143, 164, 261, 281, 309; tech support and, 262–263; thinking critically about books and, 80–87, 185, 192
self-publishing, 159; resources for, 162–163, 167–168
Seligman, Martin, 81, 89, 318, 334, 337, 345
Sell Your Book on Amazon, 163
Send This Jerk the Bedbug Letter, 258, 279
Sere, Adriene, ix, 352
Seven on Your Side, 260
sexual harassment, 94, 113, 114, 117–122; allies and, 121–122, 235; books on, 124; definition of, 113; documentation and, 233; hostile work environment and, 113–114; college professors and, 229, 233, 355; studies of, 113; Web resources and, 127–128, 346–347
Sexual Harassment Handbook, The, 126
Sexual Harassment in the Workplace, 126
Sexual Harassment on the Job, x, 119, 121, 126, 347
Shankle, William, 66
Shebeko, Natasha, ix
Shermer, Michael, 24, 188, 211, 301, 312, 325, 335, 357
Shocked, Appalled, and Dismayed, 279
Shorr, Daniel, 172
Silver, Amy, 355
Singer, Margaret, 183
situational etiquette, 19
situational pressure, 6
Six Pillars of Self-Esteem, The, 317, 333
Skeptic magazine, 188
Skeptic Society, 24, 336
small claims court, 143–144, 164, 259, 261, 270, 277
Smith, Anna Nicole, 79
Smith, Art, ix, 261

Smith, Manuel, 333
Snopes.com, 52, 199
social influence, books on, 20; motivations behind, 4; Kenrick, Neuberg, Cialdini and, 4
social validation, 5
Solomon, Muriel, 95, 101, 110, 125, 345–46
Solomon, Norman, x, 172, 189, 190–191, 197, 394
Solomon, Raymond, ix
Solomon, Sidney, ix
Solzhenitsyn, Alexander, 169, 348
Sonoma State University, 173, 177, 199
Sparks, Anne, 106
speak up, 42, 44, 60–61, 93, 114, 116, 120, 232, 337; right to, 29, 214
speeding and parking tickets, 302–308; gather information and, 305; resources for fighting, 309
spokesperson for the competition, 257
Standard and Poor's Register of Corporations, Directors and Executives, 252
Stanford University, 195
Stanford University School of Medicine, Faculty of, 87
Stanley, Debbie, 238, 355
Stanley, Julian, 194, 352
Stark, Amy, 125
State Department of Managed Health Care, 270
statistics, 106, 112, 184, 351; don't be suckered by, 190
Stauber, John, 198
Stearnes, Tanya, 139–140, 143, 146, 161, 347
Steinberg, Alan J., 88
Steinem, Gloria, 189
Step Forward: Sexual Harassment in the Workplace, 126
Stephens, Duncan, 162
Stewart, Marcia, 279–280
Stossel, John, 188, 350–351
strength in numbers, 104, 122, 231; also see allies
student rights, 240; allies and, 226; violations of, 224–227
support groups, 59, 68, 343
Sutker, Catherine, 334
Sutton, Robert, 111, 126

Svec, Carol, 60, 65, 88, 342–343
Swan, Melanie, ix

taking action, 116, 120, 122–123, 223
Talking 9 to 5, 125
Talking Back to Ritalin, x, 216, 238, 254
take notes, 36, 64, 140, 142, 250–251, 267
Taking Care, 59, 87
Tannen, Deborah, 84, 86, 125, 182, 184, 345, 350
Tavris, Carol, 81, 189, 195, 323, 325, 335, 341, 351–352, 354, 357–358
Taylor, Joan Kennedy, 117, 124, 216, 347
Teaching the Restless, x, 238, 354
tech support, 243, 261–271; see also consumer services
Teen Rights (and Responsibilities), 225, 240, 355
Ten Days to Self-Esteem, 333
tenants, see landlords
Thatcher, Margaret, 189
think things through, 17, 130, 148
Think: Critical Thinking and Logic Skills for Everyday Life, 196, 324, 332
thinking critically, see critical thinking
Thinking Like Your Editor, 162
Thomas Register of American Manufacturers, 252
Thornhill, Randy, 189, 193, 351–352, 374
Times Mirror study of media, 170, 349
Titus, Steve, 219, 357
Too Nice for Your Own Good, 333
Toronto Star, 195
Town Crier, 256, 356
Toxic Parents, 85
Toxic Sludge is Good for You, 198
traffic tickets, see speeding and parking
Travis, Cheryl, 351
Tremor in the Blood, 301, 310, 357
Truly, Traci, 240, 225–226, 355
Turbin, Flora, 269
Twain, Mark, 190, 196
Twenge, Jean, 353

UCLA/Rand Corporation, 56
unethical behavior, see boss

Unger, Rhoda, 340, 346
University of Arizona, 352
Unofficial Guide to Hiring Contractors, The, 162
Unreliable Sources, x, 191,197, 349–351
Unscrewed, 244, 256, 279–280, 355–356
Urquhart-Brown, Susan, 105
Using a Lawyer . . . And What to Do If Things Go Wrong, 161,165
U.S. Department of Education's Office for Civil Rights, 355
U.S. State Department's 2004 Trafficking in Persons Report, 177
USA Today, 356
Utne Reader, 178

values. 19, 31, 74, 105, 171, 320–322; allies and 322–323
values clarification, 337–338
Values In Action Institute, Signature Strengths survey, 321, 337
Values List, 321, 337
vanity publishing, 159, 168
Vantage Press, 159
Volz, Rebecca L., 358

Wade, Carole, 195, 323, 341, 352
Wall Street Journal, 172–173
Walsh, Mary Roth, 352
Warner, Ralph, 280
Washington Post, 171, 179
Wave, the, 16, 23; also see Ron Jones
Web of Deception: Misinformation on the Internet, 50
Web searches, how to do, 52
Webb, Susan, 126
Weisman, Roanne, 167, 188, 343
Well-Fed Self-Publisher, The, 162
Westheimer, Ruth, 82, 344
What Do I Say When . . . , 95, 125, 145–146
What Doctors Don't Tell You, 88, 67, 343
What Every Woman Should Know about Men, 81, 185
What to Do When You Don't Want to Call the Cops, 117, 124, 126, 347
What You Can Change . . . And What You Can't, 81, 89, 334
When I Say No I Feel Guilty, 333

Why Do People Bully?, 220, 240, 354
Why People Believe Weird Things, 24, 188, 211, 325, 335
Wildman, Beka, ix, 247, 248, 258, 356
Williams, Dennis A., 352
Winkler, Kathleen, x, 221, 240, 354
Winslow, Lance, 203
Winstead, Barbara A., 353, 358
Wirchniansky, Shannon, ix, 247–250, 356
Witness for the Defense, 299, 310, 357
Woman's Self-Esteem, A, 333
Workplace Bullying Institute, 111–112, 127, 246
Wrightsman, Lawrence S., 357
writer, see author
written information, ask for, 45, 68

yellow journalism, 169
You Are Being Lied To, x, 179, 197, 199, 349–351
You Are STILL Being Lied To, 197
You Don't Need a Lawyer, 279
You Just Don't Understand, 84, 86, 182, 184
Your Drug May Be Your Problem, 78, 88
Your Perfect Right, 107
You're Smarter than They Make You Feel, ix, 29, 50, 169, 195, 342, 348, 352

Xena, 48

Z magazine, 201
Zimbardo, Philip, 22, 50, 339–341
Zur, Ofer, ix, x, 72–73, 76, 82, 343
Zur Institute, 91, 343